# HISTORY OF SOUTHERN BAPTISTS

Revised Edition

DR. ROGER C. RICHARDS
GRACEVILLE, FLORIDA

© 12/15/2015. All rights reserved. Roger C. Richards

*No part of this book may be reproduced, stored in a retrieval system, or transmitted by any means without the written permission of the author.*

*Printed in the United States of America*

# Table of Contents

Table of Images ............................................................................. viii
Acknowledgements ........................................................................ ix
Introduction .................................................................................... 1
Chapter 1 – From England to America ........................................... 5
   British Antecedents ................................................................... 5
   Baptists in England .................................................................... 7
   The American Haven ............................................................... 12
   Earliest Baptist Churches in the South .................................... 16
Chapter 2 - Early Baptist Expansion ............................................. 19
   Progress by the Older Baptists ................................................. 19
   Whitefield's Chickens Become Ducks ..................................... 25
   Onnaquaggy, Opekon, and Sandy Creek ................................. 27
   An Alarmed Neighborhood ...................................................... 28
   Growth of Separate Baptists .................................................... 32
   Union of Separate and Regular Baptists ................................. 37
Chapter 3 - Liberty: Political and Religious ................................. 39
   Southern Baptists and the American Revolution .................... 40
   Struggle for Religious Liberty ................................................. 44
   Baptists and the Federal Constitution ...................................... 49
Chapter 4 - Post-War Advance ...................................................... 53
   Second Great Awakening in the South .................................... 53
   The Missionary Impulse .......................................................... 55
   Summary .................................................................................. 63
Chapter 5 - Baptists United for Benevolence ............................... 67
   The General Missionary Convention ....................................... 67
      Organization of the Foreign Mission Body ........................ 71
      Struggle for Direction .......................................................... 72
      Work of General Missionary Convention .......................... 77
   The Baptist General Tract Society ........................................... 78
   American Baptist Home Mission Society ............................... 80
Chapter 6 - Divisive Controversies ............................................... 87
   Campbellism ............................................................................ 87
   Antimissionism ........................................................................ 89
   Sectionalism ............................................................................ 93

Chapter 7 - The Southern Baptist Convention .................................................. 103
    An Old Dilemma ........................................................................................ 103
    A Proposed Structure ................................................................................ 107
    The Consultative Convention ................................................................... 109
    The Address to the Public ......................................................................... 113
    Why This Kind of Structure Was Chosen ............................................... 117
    Benevolences Outside the Convention .................................................... 122
        Southern Baptist Publication Society .................................................. 123
        Southern Baptist Sunday School Union. ............................................ 126
        Southern Baptist Theological Seminary ............................................. 127
Chapter 8 - The Antebellum Years ................................................................... 131
    Increasing Activity Through State Bodies ............................................... 134
        New State Organizations. ..................................................................... 134
    The First Years of the Southern Baptist Convention ............................. 143
        The Foreign Mission Board ................................................................. 147
        The Domestic and Indian Mission Board ........................................... 148
        The Bible Board. .................................................................................. 149
    The Convention's Greatest Internal Crisis .............................................. 150
        The Beginning of the Landmark Movement ...................................... 150
        The Principal Emphases of Landmarkism ......................................... 152
        The Sources of Graves' Views. ........................................................... 155
        The Rapid Spread of Landmarkism .................................................... 157
        The Development of Controversy. ..................................................... 158
Chapter 9 - From the Civil War Through the Reconstruction Years .... 167
    The Civil War (1861-65) ......................................................................... 168
        Foreign Mission Board ......................................................................... 169
        Domestic and Indian Mission Board ................................................... 170
        Bible Board ........................................................................................... 172
        First Sunday School Board. .................................................................. 172
    The Reconstruction Period (1868-77) ..................................................... 173
        Progress in Several States ..................................................................... 173
        The Southern Baptist Convention. ...................................................... 178
        The Domestic and Indian Mission Board ........................................... 180
        The Death of the First Sunday School Board. .................................... 187
        The Foreign Mission Board ................................................................. 189
        Theological Education. ........................................................................ 190
        The Women's Work. ............................................................................ 190

The Fortunes of Landmarksim .......................................................... 191
Chapter 10 - The Struggle to Live ..................................................... 193
　Establishing a Geographical Base ................................................. 196
　　Rivalry by Southern States. ...................................................... 196
　　Confrontation by the Home Mission Society ............................. 197
　　A New Location and Secretary................................................... 198
　　The Beginning of Comity Agreements........................................ 203
　Sustaining a Multibenevolence Ministry......................................... 208
　　The Home Mission Board ......................................................... 209
　　The Sunday School Committee. ................................................ 212
　　The Rebirth of the Sunday School Board................................... 214
　　Rivalry with the American Baptist Publication Society ............... 217
　Eliciting, Combining, and Directing the Denomination ................... 219
　　The Gospel Mission Movement ................................................. 220
Chapter 11 - The Convention Claiming Its Birthright........................... 227
　The Ministry of the Three Boards ................................................. 227
　　Foreign Mission Board.............................................................. 227
　　Home Mission Board................................................................ 229
　　Sunday School Board. .............................................................. 235
　Expanding Horizons ..................................................................... 238
　　The Enlistment and Organization of Lay Constituency. .............. 238
　Theological Education .................................................................. 245
　　Southern Baptist Theological Seminary..................................... 245
　　Southwestern Baptist Theological Seminary.............................. 247
　Relations with Other Christian Groups .......................................... 248
　　Baptist World Alliance............................................................... 248
　Structural Tensions in the Convention ........................................... 249
　　Making the Convention More Responsive and Representative.... 250
　　Deepening a Denominational Consciousness............................. 254
Chapter 12 - Denominational Changes................................................ 257
　Committee on Co-operation ......................................................... 258
　Improving the Convention's Effectiveness ..................................... 260
　Formation of the Executive Committee.......................................... 262
　An Improved Basis of Representation............................................ 264
　A Supplementary Structure for Decision-Making........................... 266
Chapter 13 - The Beginning of the Modern Era to World War II ........ 271
　The Seventy-five Million Campaign .............................................. 271

Struggle for Financial Integrity ................................................. 273
The Cooperative Program............................................................ 275
A Confession of Faith.................................................................. 280
The Commissions ........................................................................ 282
    Education Commission............................................................ 282
    Southern Baptist Commission on the American Baptist Theological Seminary.................................................................................. 283
    The Brotherhood Commission ................................................ 285
    The Social Service Commission.............................................. 285
Relief and Annuity Board............................................................ 286
The Great Depression .................................................................. 287

Chapter 14 - The Influence of Liberalism: From World War II to 1960 ............................................................................................ 293
    Sociological Changes .............................................................. 295
        Women's Issues.................................................................. 295
    Ecclesiological Struggles......................................................... 299
    Enlarged Geographical Base ................................................... 307
    Structural Refinements ............................................................ 309
    The Liberal-Fundamentalist Encounter .................................. 313

Chapter 15 – The Conservative Resurgence................................ 319
    Growing Revolutions............................................................... 319
    The Elliot Controversy ............................................................ 320
    *Broadman Bible Commentary* ................................................ 323
    Women's Ordination ............................................................... 325
    Inerrancy.................................................................................. 326
    Missions in the Middle ........................................................... 328
    Other Changes in Leadership ................................................. 329
    Battle for the Gavel................................................................. 330

Chapter 16 – Since the Conservative Resurgence ..................... 339
    The Cooperative Baptist Fellowship ...................................... 339
    Battles in the States ................................................................. 339
    Under the Executive Committee............................................. 342
    Domestic Missions .................................................................. 344
    Foreign Missions ..................................................................... 347
    Baptist Faith and Message....................................................... 347
    Changes in the Seminaries....................................................... 350
    Calvinistic Resurgence ............................................................ 357

Great Commission Resurgence ......................................................... 359
　　A New Era ................................................................................. 361
　　What Does the Future Hold? ........................................................ 364
Bibliography ................................................................................. 365
Index ........................................................................................... 375

# Table of Images

William Bullein Johnson ................................................................. 107

James P. Boyce ............................................................................... 129

John A. Broadus ............................................................................. 129

Basil Manly, Jr. ............................................................................... 129

James Robinson Graves ................................................................. 151

I. T. Tichenor ................................................................................. 199

J. B. Gambrell ................................................................................ 213

William H. Whitsitt ....................................................................... 224

Charlotte "Lottie" Moon ................................................................ 228

Annie Armstrong ............................................................................ 239

Crawford H. Toy ............................................................................ 246

Edgar Young Mullins ..................................................................... 246

Benjamin H. Carroll ....................................................................... 247

George W. Truett ........................................................................... 273

M. E. Dodd .................................................................................... 278

Arthur Flake .................................................................................. 290

I. J. Van Ness ................................................................................. 291

K. Owen White .............................................................................. 321

Herschell H. Hobbs ........................................................................ 322

R. G. Lee ........................................................................................ 329

## Acknowledgements

I would be remiss if I did not thank several people for their assistance in the production of this manuscript. First, is my Prime Rib, Sandra, who has always encouraged me to do things I did not believe I could do. Second is my father, Dr. Wiley Richards, who introduced me to the Lord, who instilled in me a love for my denomination, and who also assisted with editorial comments. Geraldine (Deannie) DeFelix also provided invaluable editorial assistance. Additionally, Rosie Strickland assisted with the typing over many long hours. Rosie's husband, Olan, spent many late nights proofreading. John (JJ) Lain did the cover design, using a photo of one of the restored churches located on the campus of The Baptist College of Florida. I appreciate the president, Dr. Thomas A. Kinchen, giving me permission to use the photo on the cover of the book. The photo is actually of Cypress Baptist Church, an historic church building that was moved to the campus of The Baptist College of Florida. I am very grateful to Mrs. Fredona Baker who graciously agreed for me to use her late husband's book extensively in the writing of this work. Also, Dr. Jesse Fletcher has been a very gracious encouragement in the completion of this opus, even to the point of allowing me to draw liberally from his history of our denomination. Finally, I would like to thank those who answered the call to endure so much in bringing this denomination back to its conservative roots. *Soli Dei Gloria.*

# Introduction

One thing that I teach in all of my classes is, "Context determines the meaning." It carries the idea that the facts should be interpreted in the context of the events in which they occurred. This is true of Southern Baptist history, as well. When writing a history of Southern Baptists, one starting point could be the formation of the Convention in May of 1845. The problem with this is, it is also important to study the events which lead to the division between Baptists in the North and in the South. That being said, we could begin with the establishment of the Triennial Convention in 1814, but there are some things in early Baptist history in North America that influenced how Southern Baptists felt about such things as religious liberty. However, some of these issues are related to why Baptists migrated to North America to begin with. But we must start somewhere. I made the decision to begin with the English Separatists. The reason for this is the fact that, while there have been some of the ideas and principles that are held to by Baptists since the time of Christ, the name *Baptist* was not used until around 1600. For this reason, I chose to begin briefly with the origin of those who called themselves Baptists. They did so because of their belief that baptism is reserved for believers alone, after they have confessed faith in the atonement of Christ. Only a very brief sketch is given to the early Baptist beginnings and to the beginning of Baptists in America. For the purposes of this book, the background material is simply to establish the religious and historical context that caused Baptists to meet in Augusta, Georgia, on May 8, 1845, and to adopt their constitution on May 10.

There are several reasons for this book. First, I believe it is a story that is worth telling and needs to be told. When the people of Israel crossed the Jordan River to take possession of the Promised Land, Joshua and the people were commanded to take twelve stones from the center of the riverbed where the priests had stood with the Ark. They were to erect a monument and use it as a teaching tool to remind future generations of the work God has done in the past with the promise that He will continue to work among His people in the future. It is important to remind ourselves of who we are as Southern Baptists, to learn from the past, and to follow God as He leads us into the future.

Second, I teach a course called, History of Southern Baptists. I have struggled to find an adequate textbook over the years. One of the more recent books I have used Jesse Fletcher's work *The Southern Baptist Convention: A Sesquicentennial History*. Unfortunately, the book is out of print and becoming increasingly difficult to make available to students each year. Dr. Fletcher did an excellent job in describing the events leading up to the Conservative Resurgence, as well as the decade-long struggle in the Convention itself. He devotes several chapters to the events, but I have chosen to condense them into a single chapter, not because of their unimportance, but simply because space does not allow everything to be covered adequately. I strongly encourage anyone who is interested in studying that period of the denomination's history to consult his work, among the others listed in the bibliography. Dr. Fletcher has encouraged me and has offered for me to draw freely from his work, which I have done. The great disadvantage the book has is that it ended in 1995, just as the convention was about to undergo a major reorganization, enter a new millennium, and enter into what has come to be known as The Great Commission Resurgence.

The book prior to his in the line of outstanding histories of this denomination was Robert A. Baker's book, *The Southern Baptist Convention and Its People, 1607-1972*. Dr. Baker passed away several years ago, but his wife, Fredona Baker, graciously allowed me to draw heavily from her husband's work, just as he had done with W. W. Barnes' work, *The Southern Baptist Convention, 1845-1953*. One thing that I did with Baker's work was to redact much of the statistical data. One reason was simply because of the lack of space. This work is already just under five hundred pages. Also, most of the data that Baker used is not readily available online. The staff of the Southern Baptist Historical Library and Archives have labored long hours to make all of the minutes of the Southern Baptist Convention meetings beginning with the first one in 1845 available online. Another change I made to Baker's book was to amplify the information concerning the establishment of the Executive Committee and the establishment of the Cooperative Program. The Executive Committee needed greater treatment because this is when Southern Baptists went from being an association of Baptist churches to actually becoming a denomination. The Cooperative Program is the means by which that great work is funded.

One last thing important for the reader to understand is the bias of the author. I make no attempt to hide the fact that I am firmly entrenched in the Conservative and Denominational camps. I love this denomination and believe in it. I also see the Conservative Resurgence as a positive, though painful, period in the life of the Convention.

I have divided this work into three major periods. The first period begins with the time at which Baptists were first identified by that name and runs until the formation of the Southern Baptist Convention. It includes the migration of Baptists to North America, the development of Baptists throughout the colonies, and the role of Baptists in the struggle for independence and the early formation of the young nation. It deals briefly with the first attempt to form a Baptist denomination, as well as the difficulties faced by Baptists in those early years. It also summarizes the three major controversies which contributed to the formation of the Southern Baptist Convention.

The second major era covers the formation of the Southern Baptist Convention until what I prefer to call the modern era. This section deals with the formation of the denomination prior to the Civil War, as well as the recovery of the denomination after the war's end. It also addresses the struggles Southern Baptists experienced in the continuing development of educational institutions and in the two mission boards. It ends at the end of the nineteenth century.

The last section of the book, the Modern Era, picks up with the events which led to the establishment of the Executive Committee. This is a crucial point in the formation of the convention, as this is when Southern Baptists actually moved from a voluntary, but loose association of churches to a Convention made up of cooperating churches, funded by a systematic method. It deals with the struggle of the convention over the span of several wars, theological controversies, and the Conservative Resurgence. Ending with the period since the Conservative Resurgence, it touches on recent trends and developments in the Convention. I have preserved the original spelling in all written quotes, even when the original work has a misspelling, or when the spelling has changed to a more modern spelling.

This work could easily be expanded into several volumes, each dealing with one of the major eras in the Convention's history. For now, this will have to be sufficient. It is my sincere hope that at the end of this book, the reader will feel the same sense of respect for this great denomination and will prayerfully consider assisting it as the Southern Baptist Convention strives to advance the Kingdom of God.

Roger C. Richards
Graceville, Florida, 2012

# PERIOD ONE: BAPTIST BEGINNINGS IN AMERICA: 1607-1845

*From the First Permanent Settlement in the South to the Formation of the Southern Baptist Convention*

## Chapter 1 – From England to America

The first Baptists in America originated principally with the emigration of General and Particular Baptists from Great Britain in the seventeenth and eighteenth centuries. Such a statement, of course, needs amplifying. Why did these Baptists come from Britain? Why were some called General and some called Particular Baptists, and what distinguished one group from another? Why did they leave their comfortable homes to make the perilous trip to crude hamlets in the American wilderness?

### British Antecedents

To understand Baptist beginnings in America, one must plant his feet firmly on the soil of Great Britain. It is true that the stage for this drama was the American wilderness, yet the script was written in Britain; the players were British; their thoughts, attitudes, and reactions were British; all of the stagehands were British; and the theater belonged to a British proprietor. The British background explains the presence of Baptists in America, the doctrinal differences that existed among them, and the kind of people they were.

Great Britain created the world for early American Baptists. What a world it was! A millennium of history focused on seventeenth-century Britain, the very century that brought British Baptist people to American shores. The Council of Whitby in A.D. 664 had introduced Roman Catholic domination into England. Open dissent followed. From these dissenters at Whitby runs a direct road through Hastings, Wycliffe, Lollardy, Mortmain, Premunire, Provisors, and Reformation that finally led to complete alienation between Canterbury and Rome. Under Henry VIII (1509-47) England severed her relationship with Rome, and Henry was declared to be both secular sovereign of England and head of the church in England. The monarch now became both the political head of a nation and the religious leader of all his people. The two medieval swords, symbols of secular and spiritual sovereignty once shared by emperor and pope, now belonged to the king of England in his realm. He demanded loyalty and conformity in religious matters as well as secular. To differ with him religiously was more than heresy; it was treason.

It is not difficult to understand why this state of affairs would create religious dissent. Many Englishmen who would gladly bow the knee to their secular sovereign were unwilling to shackle their consciences to submit to his religious convictions. This was especially true when religious convictions might change radically from sovereign to sovereign. Henry himself wavered in his doctrinal ideas between a strict Roman Catholicism and a tendency toward reform; his daughter Mary (1553-58), a devout Roman Catholic, forced legislation through Parliament that returned the English church to the control of the pope; her half-sister Elizabeth (1558-1603) wrenched the English church back into Protestantism (which took place when Elizabeth gained control) demanded that the consciences of all the people of England promptly oscillate in this same fashion. This was a monstrous dilemma for any person who really believed something, for he could not discard true doctrinal convictions simply because a new occupant had come to the palace. Orthodoxy and heresy exchanged places so rapidly at times and so often that conformity was more important than conviction. It was more needful to please the king or queen than it was to please God.

Dissent from this unfortunate situation was already taking place before the death of Queen Elizabeth I in 1603. The tension was increased when a distant cousin of Elizabeth, James VI of Scotland, came to England as James I. He brusquely bellowed that anyone who did not agree with him religiously would be harried out of the land. To compound the problem, his subjects did now know at first what his religious convictions would be. He was the son of a pious Roman Catholic mother and for many years had been king in Scotland where Presbyterianism dominated. Before long he developed anti-Catholic and anti-Presbyterian feelings, and demanded that the Church of England, which was halfway between Roman Catholicism and Protestantism, become the religious standard for every one of his subjects. Dissenters of many kinds were severely persecuted during the remainder of his rule. His son, Charles, succeeded him in 1625 and continued persecution of dissenters. Civil war sparked by religious differences broke out early in the 1640s, and Charles was defeated and beheaded in 1649. From then until 1660, Protestant dissent was permitted under Oliver Cromwell.

The most severe persecution of dissenters took place during the reign of Charles II from 1660 to 1685. Five acts known as the Clarendon Code were passed. The Corporation Act of 1661 excluded all dissenters from taking part in local government in England. The Act of Uniformity in 1662 banished all pastors from the pulpits and all teachers from public or private schools who did not conform doctrinally to the Church of England. The Conventile Act of 1664 forbade dissenters from meeting for religious purposes. The Five Mile Act of 1665 prohibited dissenting ministers from coming within five miles of any city or town or of any parish in which they had ministered. The Test Act of 1673 excluded dissenters from all civil and military positions. On his deathbed in 1685, Charles was received into the Roman Catholic Church and was succeeded by his brother James, an active Roman Catholic. This situation gave rise to fears by non-Catholics that additional persecution was in the offing.

## Baptists in England

The demand that the consciences of the English people coincide with the religious position taken by the crown and the attempt to enforce conformity by physical persecution brought several types of response from the people in the sixteenth and seventeenth centuries in England. Some followers of John Calvin determined to remain within the established Church of England to attempt to purify it from its corruptions, particularly those copied from the Roman Catholic system. By 1564 these were known as Puritans, and they played an important part in the controversies of the next century.

Inevitably, some dissenters were unwilling to remain within the church system which they regarded as unscriptural and unjust. As early as 1567 the authorities apprehended a group in London who had withdrawn from the Church of England and organized a church whose authority was conceived to be in the congregation itself. Several of these Separate or Independent churches can be identified in the early seventeenth century.

It was in this context that English Baptists emerged. The full story of these worthy forebears cannot be told here, but their courageous stand for religious liberty is a matter of record. They were the first Englishmen to reject totally the episcopal government of the established church, its ordinances (baptism and the Supper), and the authority of the secular sovereign to coerce the people in matters of conscience.

Two types of Baptists developed in England: General Baptists and Particular Baptists. The early history of the two is quite dissimilar. General Baptists originated historically from the Smyth-Helwys-Murton [1] separation that formed what is regarded as the first Baptist church on English soil in 1611 or 1612 at Spitalfield, just outside of London. Thomas Helwys, the actual founder of this church, boldly published the doctrine of full religious liberty about 1612, the first time this principle had been advocated in writing in England. A presentation copy addressed to King James I bluntly said that the king was a man, not God, and thus had no authority to bind the souls of men to follow the religious convictions of the crown. For writing this, Helwys died in prison, but the church lived.

These Baptists were called General Baptists because they believed in the doctrine of the general atonement of Christ. Their confession of 1678 clearly enunciated this view in the following words:

> God the father, our of his royal bounty, and foundation of love, when all mankind was fallen by sin, in breaking of the first covenant of works made with them in Adam, did chuse [sic] Jesus Christ, and sent him into the world to die for Adam, or fallen man. And God's love is manifest to all mankind, in that he is not willing, as himself hath sworn, and abundantly declared in his word, that mankind should perish eternally, but would have all to be saved, and come to the knowledge of the truth. And Christ died for all men, and there is a sufficiency in his death and merits for the sins of the whole world, and hath appointed the gospel to be preached unto all, and hath sent forth his spirit to accompany the

---

[1] For a full discussion of this period, see H. Leon McBeth's work, *The Baptist Heritage: Four Centuries of Baptist Witness*.

word in order to beget repentance and faith: so that if any perish, it's not for want of the means of grace manifested by Christ to them, but for the non-improvement of the grace of God, offered freely to them through Christ in the gospel.[2]

General Baptists were probably influenced toward these views by their sojourn in the Amsterdam area to which John Smyth and company had fled from English persecution in 1609. In that very section of the Low Countries, the Mennonite adherents were dominant and were strongly pressing this distinct view of the work of Christ.

By 1626 there were five General Baptist churches in England with about 150 members. They numbered about forty churches by 1644. In 1654 they formed the General Assembly of General Baptists and in 1678 adopted a strong confession of faith a part of which was quoted above. Many of these General Baptists, holding the distinctive doctrine set out heretofore, emigrated to Carolina and Virginia in the colonial period.

Another distinctive characteristic of the General Baptists was their centralized ecclesiology. While Particular Baptists magnified the autonomy of their local congregations almost to the point of fault, General Baptists delegated considerable authority to the general body which they organized in 1654. This general body disciplined church members, handled churches rather high-handedly, and in general overwhelmed the authority of the churches in its structure. Article XXXIX of their 1678 confession of faith made the following assertions:

> General councils, or assemblies, consisting of Bishops, Elders, and Brethren, of the several churches of Christ, and being legally convened, and met together out of all the churches, and the churches appearing there by their representatives, make but one church, and have lawful right, and suffrage in this general meeting, or assembly, to act in the name of Christ; it being of divine authority, and is the best means under heaven to preserve unity, to prevent heresy, and superintendency among, or in any congregation whatsoever within its own limits, or jurisdiction. And to such a meeting or assembly, appeals ought to be made, in

---

[2] W. J. McGlothlin, *Baptist Confessions of Faith* (Philadelphia: American Baptist Publication Society, 1911), 137-38.

> case any injustice be done, or heresy, and schism countenanced, in any particular congregation of Christ, and the decisive voice in such general assemblies is the major part, and such general assemblies have lawful power to hear, and determine, as also to excommunicate.[3]

This centralizing tendency of General Baptists appeared among Baptists of this type after they moved to American shores.

Particular Baptists, on the other hand, developed historically from the Jacob-Lathrop-Jessey separation. Probably about 1638 the first Particular Baptist church was organized in England, and this movement grew under the leadership of men like John Spilsbury, Henry Jessey, and William Kiffen.

The name Particular Baptist was applied to them because they believed in a limited or particular atonement; that is, that Christ died only for the elect. Their confession of faith of 1689 was quite specific at this point, as follows:

> 3. By the *decree* of God, for the manifestation of his glory some men and Angels are predestined, or fore-ordained to Eternal Life, through Jesus Christ, to the praise of his glorious grace; others being left to act in their sin to their just condemnation, to the praise of his glorious justice.
>
> 4. These Angels and Men thus predestinated, and fore-ordained, are particularly, and unchangeably designed, and their number so certain, and definite, that it cannot be either increased, or diminished.
>
> 5. Those of mankind that are predestinated to life, God, before the foundation of the world was laid, according to his eternal and immutable purpose, and the secret Council and good pleasure of his will, hath chosen in Christ unto everlasting glory, out of his mere free grace and love; without any other thing in the creature as a condition or cause moving him thereunto.
>
> 6. As God hath appointed the Elect unto glory, so he hath by the eternal and most free purpose of his will, fore-ordained all the means thereunto, wherefore they who are elected, being fallen in

---

[3] Ibid., 154.

Adam, are redeemed by Christ, are effectually called unto faith in Christ, by his spirit working in due season, are justified, adopted, sanctified, and kept by his power through faith unto salvation; neither are any other redeemed by Christ, or effectually called, justified, adopted, sanctified, and saved, but the Elect only.[4]

Some of the early Baptist people in Carolina and Virginia came from the ranks of these Particular Baptists, as will be described hereafter.

Although these two groups of Baptists did not see eye to eye on all doctrines, they agreed on some basic interpretations of the Christian faith. In the Particular Baptist confession of faith of 1644, for example, it was made plain that Baptists expected to suffer for their convictions concerning religious liberty:

> But if God with-hold the Magistrates allowance and furtherance herein; yet we must notwithstanding proceed together in Christian communion, not daring to give place to suspend our practice, but to walk in obedience to Christ in the profession and holding forth this faith before mentioned, even in the midst of all trials and afflictions, not accounting our goods, lands, wives, children, fathers, mothers, brethren, sisters, yea, and our own lives dear unto us, so we may finish our course with joy: remembering always we ought to obey God rather than men.[5]

The Particular Baptist' view of baptism of the believer is expressed in this same confession.

> That Baptism is an Ordinance of the New Testament, given by Christ, to be dispensed only upon persons professing faith, or that are Disciples, or taught, who upon a profession of faith, ought to be baptized. The way and manner of the dispensing of this Ordinance the Scripture holds out to be dipping or plunging the whole body under water: it being a sign, must answer the thing signified, which are these: first, the washing the whole soul in the blood of Christ: Secondly, that interest the Saints have in the death, burial, and resurrection; thirdly, together with a confirmation of our faith, that as certainly shall the bodies of the

---

[4] Ibid., 233-34.
[5] Ibid., 185, 188.

Saints be raised by the power of Christ, in the day of resurrection, to reign with Christ.[6]

Because of their view and particularly their insistence upon religious freedom, Baptists felt the heavy hand of persecution, not only from the Anglicans but from other groups as well during this entire period in English history. It is not surprising, then, that they turned their eyes toward the new world in colonial America.

## The American Haven

Many dissenters fled their British homes fearing persecution. Among them were Baptists. The members who constituted the first Baptist church on English soil, referred to previously as being founded about 1611-12, had first gone to Amsterdam in 1607 to escape their persecutors, but being desirous of bearing witness in their own land, they returned to form the church near London. Other dissenters also sought refuge in the Low Countries.

The principal haven of dissenters, however, was America. There is evidence that there were Baptist people among some of the earliest settlements that were located in Massachusetts under John Myles and Thomas Gould, in Maine under William Screven, and in Pennsylvania at Pennepek under the pastorate of Elias Keach. Baptist growth in these northern areas was slow. One Baptist historian estimated that by 1740 there were less than a dozen small churches with not more than three hundred total members, most of them by emigration from Britain.

It is curious that with the rather extensive migration to the new world taking place between 1607 and 1660, there is no record of Baptists appearing in the South until after the restoration of Charles II to the throne in 1660. What had deterred Baptists from fleeing in larger numbers to America, and in particular why had some of them not appeared in the southern colonies before 1660?

For one thing, the expense of the journey itself was not inconsiderable. The very poorest accommodations generally cost approximately the equivalent of two years' income of the average worker. Baptists in general were of the lower economic class, and although some may have bound themselves to indentured servitude in America in return

---

[6] Ibid.

for the price of the voyage, the economic factor itself was vital in preventing extensive migration of British Baptists.

Another very basic deterrent was the peril involved in making the long trip in relatively small vessels on the stormy Atlantic Ocean. In his *History of the Welsh Baptists*, J. Davis described the trials of Abel Morgan, an early American Baptist preacher who left Wales to immigrate to America. Morgan took his family to the seaport of Bristol, and they embarked for the new world on September 28, 1710. Davis continued:

> The next day the wind being contrary, and the ship exceedingly tossed with tempest, they turned in to Milford Haven, where they were detained three weeks. And when they sailed from that place, they were driven by tempestuous winds to Cork, in Ireland, where they were obliged to stay five weeks, in very uncomfortable circumstances, as most of the passengers were unwell. From there, however, they all sailed on the 19th of November. On the 14th of December, Abel Morgan's little boy died, and on the 17th of the same month, his dearly loved wife breathed her last, and both of them were committed to the deep. This was to him a severe trial, indeed.... He arrived in America on the 14th of February, 1711.[7]

Added to these perils were many dangers of the American environment, including unfriendly Indians and unfavorable climate, illustrated vividly by the loss of lives and suffering during the early years at Jamestown and at Plymouth.[8]

Another factor that may have given English Baptists pause was the recognition that dissenters might be jumping from the frying pan into the fire by going to the colonies. The perilous journey to America not only failed to take them beyond the strong arm of England, as will be noted shortly, but reports from the several colonies themselves showed that the rude settlements on the virgin continent of America were already well familiar with persecution. Baptists in England were quite familiar with the tragic situation through the publication there of Roger Williams' *The*

---

[7] J. Davis, *History of the Welsh Baptists* (Pittsburg: D. M. Hogan, 1835), 69.
[8] See Marcus W. Jernegan, *The American Colonies 1492-1750* (New York: F. Unger Pub. Co., 1959), *passim.*

*Bloody Tenet of Persecution* and John Clarke's *Ill News from New England*. These writings described the principles and practice of Congregational intolerance in Massachusetts Bay Colony. Maryland, settled in 1634, tolerated some types of dissent in order to attract needed settlers, but the limited type of toleration and the Roman Catholic character of the colony caused considerable distrust. Providence Plantations[9] was the only northern colony in 1660 that offered complete liberty of conscience, and this colony was under constant attack from its neighbors to eliminate that feature. In the South, Governor William Berkeley of Virginia had been totally intolerant of dissent of any kind from the Church of England after he took office in 1642.

As indicated, it was evident also that the English government was keeping a careful watch on the colonies across the Atlantic. Three types of colonies were developed during this period: corporate colonies, organized under charters granted by the crown to an incorporated body; proprietary colonies, developed under a grant by the crown to individuals, as in the case of Maryland; royal colonies which were under the direct supervision of the crown. The first two types of colonies were encouraged early as a means of exploiting potentially profitable colonies without the risk to the crown of loss if the colonizing efforts were not successful. Theoretically, under corporate and proprietary colonies, dissenters might be welcome to assist in the arduous task of carving cities out of wilderness. However, the crown began taking over control of the colonies as soon as they were successful. Virginia, begun as a corporate colony in 1607, became a royal colony in 1624. Both Maryland, a proprietary colony, and Massachusetts Bay, a corporate colony, were brought under royal control before the end of the seventeenth century, although Maryland was later returned to obedient proprietors. Thoughtful dissenters pondered the question of whether or not their situation would be improved in a colony that had local repression and still felt the strength of the English crown.

In addition, it is likely that many who contemplated the journey to America, and particularly to the South, for example, were stocked with many marginal workers who entered into indentured servitude to pay for

---

[9] Providence Plantations, now known as Rhode Island, was established by Roger Williams and was the first place in the history of mankind to guarantee absolute religious liberty.

their journey; and at the same time, at the opposite extreme, a large group of Cavaliers fled to that colony after the beheading of Charles I in 1649. The specter of black slavery, introduced in 1619 in Virginia, also raised many moral and economic questions for marginal economic workers like Baptists and was a melancholy harbinger of evil through the centuries to come. Perhaps the hesitating Englishmen remembered that the Virginia House of Burgesses endeavored to eliminate slavery from Virginia but were overruled by the English government on economic grounds.

On the other hand, there were some factors that were encouraging to an Englishman considering emigration. The economic situation in England at the opening of the seventeenth century was deplorable. Peace with Spain in 1604 found many soldiers and sailors without any means of livelihood. American gold and silver had greatly inflated English currency, but an oversupply of labor reduced the average wage to the very minimum amount that would sustain life. The profitable trading enterprises, some large and some small, beckoned for emigrants at every seaport.

In addition, the basic ingredient of success, the land itself, was extremely plentiful and rich in the new world, while in England this was next to impossible for the lower class to secure. Word had also filtered back that the geography of the great coastal plains, which were partitioned from the hinterlands by the Appalachian mountain barrier, along with the numerous sheltered bays and laborsaving rivers and creeks, provided a providential preparation awaiting those that would come.

Added to these favorable ingredients, there were other factors that beckoned British Baptists to the American shores after the middle of the seventeenth century. Some Baptists and other dissenters in the colonies were well satisfied with the risks they had taken and were experiencing relative prosperity in the new world, and they wrote these tidings back to their friends in England. In their desire to secure settlers, several of the colonies were moderating their persecuting tactics and developing a measure of regional stability and local tolerance. Most of all, however, so far as Baptists in the South were concerned, the advertisement of a new colony where complete religious liberty would prevail in a section of the country with rich and abundant land environed by friendly natives proved irresistible to many British Baptists and other dissenters being rigorously persecuted for their religious beliefs. The story of Baptists in the South was begun.

## Earliest Baptist Churches in the South

The earliest Baptist churches of record in the South were planted in South Carolina (1696 or before), Virginia (1715), and North Carolina (1727). By the time the first of these churches was founded, the character of the southern colonies had undergone considerable change. In the first century of English colonization the colonies were closely related to England, and the Baptist churches in America were quite similar to those at home except for their remote location. The Baptist preachers and people in America for the most part came from England. Very few indigenous Baptist preachers were found in the southern colonies before 1740. English Baptist doctrinal divisions were reproduced in the American colonies, including such groups as the Particular Baptists, the General Baptists, the Seventh-Day Baptists, the Six-Principle Baptists, and Seekers. The colonial environment contained a strong Church of England influence, particularly in the southern colonies. Leaders in the American Anglican church reproduced the attitude of their English counterparts toward dissenters. Practically all dissenters themselves were copies of their English prototypes. Fortunately, the Act of Toleration of 1689 in England worked a considerable improvement in relations between the government and dissenters, although it must be admitted that it required time before the benefits of this Act were widely enjoyed in America.

However, this situation began to change early in the eighteenth century. There is a curious parallel between political developments in England and those in the colonies. Extensive and rapid development of the English parliamentary system began with the coming of the first Hanover, George I, in 1714. In the American colonies, this same period marked the growing encroachment of the colonial assemblies on the powers of the several governors and royal councils. By gradually obtaining control of provincial funds and by contesting practically all of the administrative prerogatives of the governor, most of the provincial assemblies, aided by the dilatory and ineffective support of the governors by Parliament in England, practically wrested control from the hands of the royal officials. The efforts of the Lords Commissioners for trade and Plantations, brought into existence in 1696 by William II to supervise the colonies, were directed the first half of the eighteenth century toward reducing the colonies to a uniform type through establishing royal control. They were indeed successful in asserting royal control over most of the colonies by 1740, but absentee government, combined at times with poor governors and the aggressive demands of the several assemblies, greatly diminished the effectiveness of their policies.

From an economic viewpoint, the American colonies moved toward a new destiny. The efforts by the Lords Commissioners of England to heighten the efficiency of the First Navigation Act of 1660 and its subsequent revisions by increasing restrictions upon colonial enterprises ultimately resulted in diversification of agriculture and even brought industry to the colonies and thus helped make them more self-sustaining. As will be noted, some of the colonies were helped by the English mercantile policies, while others were hurt.

Another factor of change was the increasing immigration of settlers from elsewhere than England, many of whom felt no loyalty toward the English government and would be inclined to resent its authority.

Writers have often noted that from a religious standpoint both the background and the environment of the colonists on the American shores began to develop a different sort of religious climate than had been found in England or on the continent. The several reformations had worked their purifying effects so that even Roman Catholic Christianity, transplanted primarily from England, was of a different character than that developed in pre-Reformation days. Most American colonists knew of the conflict between Parliament and Charles I and gloried in the rights of Englishmen even in opposition to the crown. The avalanche of English tracts and books in the seventeenth century advocating religious toleration and even religious liberty was familiar to colonial America. With this background and the comparative isolation of the American colonies, a new sort of Christianity began to develop in America. It magnified religious individualism, the development of separate denominations, religion by conviction rather than coercion, competition in religion, a sharpened sense of lay obligation, and similar distinctive features that are seen in American Christianity. By the close of this period in 1740, there were probably over 350,000 white people in the southern colonies. From 1725 on, an increasing number of non-English immigrants arrived. By 1750 perhaps nine tenths of the people of New England were still of English descent, probably due to scarcity of land and to religious intolerance. Nearly two-thirds of the population in the middle colonies was made up of Dutch, Irish, Germans, Scots, Swedes, and French. In the southern colonies by this time, the English primarily occupied the coast, while the western areas were principally settled by Irish and German immigrants.

During this period the social and economic aspects of southern society began to polarize. Large planters emerged and became a favored class. The use of indentured servants declined through the extension of black slavery, which had spread rather rapidly in the South due to what amounted to a climatic and geographical determinism. Already questions were being raised about the status of the black person, his rights, if any, and his treatment. A curious item has been recently discovered involving the Baptist church at Charleston. In 1711 a problem arose in the Charleston church concerning the treatment of a black slave who had been severely punished by his master, a church member, for running away. Some in the church wanted to withdraw fellowship from this slaveholder for the severity of his treatment of the slave. William Fry and William Sadler wrote to the Baptist church at South Moulton, Devon, in England asking their judgment in the matter. The reply urged that peace be restored in the church and essentially supported the member in his severity. The South Moulton church took the matter to the Western Baptist Association in England, which subsequently echoed the position of the South Moulton church.[10]

During the period before 1740 in the southern colonies, in addition, relative prosperity had made life much more attractive for the people. The colonies were exporting rice, indigo, tobacco, lumber products, cotton, and tar from Navy purposes. A few semipublic schools and a number of private schools provided education, particularly for the higher social classes. Fox hunts, dinners, dances, and music brought recreation. Even postal service was enjoyed by Virginia in 1732, and newspapers helped keep the colonists abreast of the times.

---

[10] Original of the letter in Backus Collection, Newton, Massachusetts. Reprinted in the *Journal of Southern History*, November, 1963, Vol. 29, No. 4, 495-97.

## Chapter 2 - Early Baptist Expansion

### Progress by the Earlier Baptists

Between 1710 and the American Revolution, despite the developing political crisis in the American colonies, the older Baptist groups in South Carolina, Virginia, and North Carolina made good progress.

The Charleston church, which had been greatly weakened by controversy in the 1730s and 1740s, was revived when George Whitefield visited that city in 1745. The coming of Oliver Hart, a minister from the Philadelphia Association, to be pastor of the Charleston church in 1749 gave new impetus to the work. He remained as a successful pastor until driven north by the Revolutionary War in 1780.

In 1740 the General Baptists meeting at Stono, bolstered by a new pastor from England, Henry Heywood, entered suit to secure the property of the old undivided church and were successful in securing this property on Lot No. 62, while the Particular Baptists were awarded the parsonage. The General Baptist congregation dwindled away until the time of the Revolution, and subsequently the Particular Baptists were able to secure the old meetinghouse on Lot No. 62 again.

Important low-country churches organized before the Revolution included Coosawhatchie in 1759 and Pipe Creek in 1775. Other churches were establishing branches which would ultimately become separate churches. In the Peedee section of South Carolina, the Welsh Neck church expanded into the Catfish area, where a church was organized in 1752. The Beauty Spot church was organized from Catfish in 1768, and a number of smaller churches developed in the Catfish area thereafter. Another branch of the Welsh Neck church formed a separate congregation at Cashaway in 1756, and from this area thereafter a number of branches and private-home churches were established before the Revolution. These included Muddy Creek, Black Creek, two churches on Lynches Creek, Flat Creek, and others. Important ministers during the period were Philip James, Nicholas Bedgegood, Evan Pugh, and others.

The first Baptist association in the South was organized at Charleston, South Carolina, on October 27, 1751, and took the name Charleston Baptist Association.[11] Its minutes before 1775 have been lost or destroyed, but they were used by Wood Furman in his history of the association published in 1811. These minutes declared that the object of the association was

> the promotion of the Redeemer's kingdom, by the maintenance of love and fellowship, and by mutual consultations for the peace and welfare of the churches. The independency of the churches was asserted, and the powers of the Association restricted to those of a Council of Advice.[12]

This association was formed primarily from the initiative of Oliver Hart, who had become pastor of the Charleston church in 1749. He had been an active member of the Philadelphia Association prior to his southern ministry and was familiar with "the happy consequences of union and stated intercourse among Churches maintaining the same faith and order." The original organization was approved by "delegates" from the Charleston, Ashley River, and Welsh Neck churches. In the early years the association met annually, usually at Charleston. This association contributed greatly to the unity and edification of Baptists in South Carolina. It kept the churches current with respect to contemporary religious issues, not only in South Carolina but with happenings in all Baptist life in the colonies. Among other things, in 1775 it secured John Gano, a distinguished minister of the Philadelphia Association, to preach the gospel in the back country, which he did for a year very effectively.[13]

The older Baptists in Virginia made good progress during the period between 1740 and the Revolution. A General Baptist church was organized at Opekon on Mill Creek, now Berkeley County, West Virginia, by immigrants from Maryland in 1743. After their minister had been excluded for licentiousness, they applied to the Philadelphia Association for assistance. Benjamin Miller, Isaac Sutton, John Thomas, and John

---

[11] Robert A. Baker. *A Baptist Source Book*. (Nashville: Broadman Press, 1966), 16.
[12] Wood Furman, *A History of the Charleston Association of Baptist Churches in the State of South Carolina* (Charleston: Press of J. Hoff, 1811), 8-9.
[13] Baker, *Source Book*, 16.

Gano (all Particular Baptists) met at the Opekon church, in 1752, and finding that the church had General Baptist doctrines, proceeded to sift out the chaff, "retaining the supposed good grain." John Gano reported to the Association:

> We examined them, and found that they were not a regular church. We then examined those who offered themselves for the purpose, and those who gave us satisfaction we received, and constituted a new church. Out of the whole who offered themselves, there only three received. Some openly declared they knew they could not give an account of experiencing a work of grace, and therefore need not offer themselves. Others stood ready to offer if the church was formed. The three before mentioned were constituted, and six more were baptized and joined with them. After the meeting ended, a number of old members went aside and sent for me. They expressed their deplorable state, and asked me if I would meet with them that evening, and try to instruct them. They were afraid the ministers blamed them. They had been misled, but it was not their fault, and they hoped I would pity them. I told them I would with all my heart, and endeavored to remove their suspicion of the ministers. They met, and I spoke to them from these words; *"They being ignorant of God's righteousness, and going about to establish their own righteousness, have not submitted themselves unto the righteousness of God."* I hope I was assisted to speak to them in an impressive manner, and they to hear, at least some of them, so as to live. They afterwards professed and became zealous members, and remained so, I believe, until their death.[14]

The church was received into the Philadelphia Association in 1754. It was to this church that Daniel Marshall, the outstanding Separate Baptist, came in 1754 where he was baptized and licensed. That story will be told in connection with the Separate Baptist movement.

In 1751 John Thomas organized a church of eleven members at Ketocton, Virginia, and in the following year the church appealed to the Philadelphia Association for assistance in administering the ordinances.

---

[14] Ibid., 12.

John Gano was sent by the Association, and both on this occasion and intermittently during the next several years assisted them in their services. In 1754 this church was received into the fellowship of the Philadelphia Association.[15]

Probably as early as 1754 a group of Pennsylvania Baptists settled on Smith's Creek in Frederick County, Virginia, and in 1756, John Alderson organized the Smith's Creek Baptist Church there and remained as its pastor until the Revolutionary War.[16] After 1756, the three churches at Opekin (Mill Creek), Ketocton, and Smith's Creek arranged to have a fellowship and communion meeting together each year, and this was done when circumstances permitted. In 1762, Smith's Creek church was admitted to the Philadelphia Association, reporting thirty members at that time. Two significant names in this church were Silas Hart and Nicholas Fain.

One of the outstanding early leaders of Virginia Baptists was David Thomas, who came to Opekon from Pennsylvania in 1760. His zeal resulted in the organization of the Broad Run church in 1762 with twelve members. Thomas was an educated and talented preacher, and Broad Run, through his leadership and the assistance of half a dozen young ministers whom he had influenced, took the gospel throughout the entire area. These ministers included Nathaniel Saunders, who became pastor of the Mountain Run church in 1768; Richard Major, who became pastor of the Little River church in 1768 and subsequently served at Bull Run church; Daniel Fristoe , who became co-pastor with David Thomas at Chappawamsic in 1771; William Fristoe, ordained in 1769 and served extensively in the churches among which was Broad Run after 1787; John Creel, who became pastor of the Birch Creek church in 1771; and Jeremiah Moore, who was ordained about 1771 and served many churches, the one in Alexandria in particular being significant. The sweep of the work of David Thomas and these men included the organization of the church at Chappawamsic (1776) with several arms, Mountain Run, in 1768, Little River in 1768, Birch Creek in 1769, and Thumb Run in 1771.

Other Baptist preachers helped found several other churches of this period, including Joseph Thomas, who helped constitute New Valley

---

[15] Ibid.
[16] Ibid., 13.

in 1767; Isaac Sutton, who organized Great Bethel in 1770; and John Marks and John Garrard, who planted the church at Buck Marsh in 1771.[17]

On August 19, 1766, messengers from the three churches that belonged to the Philadelphia Association (Opekon, Ketocton, and Smith's Creek), along with David Thomas and Joseph Metcalf from Broad Run, met Ketocton and organized the Ketocton Baptist Association, the first in Virginia, comprised of four churches with 142 members. By 1772 the minutes of the association showed 13 churches with approximately 1,150 members. Although the association adopted no confession of faith for many years, its leaders were of the Particular Baptist persuasion.

Before the Revolution the General Baptists in North Carolina had advanced under the leadership of Joseph Parker, William Sojourner, and Josiah Hart, assisted by many faithful General Baptist preachers associated with them. Parker continued his service to the Meherrin church, and doubtless had a large part in the founding of churches at Bertie (Sandy Run), Lower Fishing Creek, and the Swift Creek church in 1742 with a number of the members of that church, due to an epidemic of some sort which had taken the lives of many of the people in that area. Sojourner and his flock promptly organized the Kehukee church near the present town of Scotland Neck. This became one of the influential centers of Baptist life in the area. Josiah Hart, evidently a long-time resident of the province, probably founded the Pungo Church in Beaufort County and the Fishing Creek church in Warren County. Hart is best known for the large number of preachers whom he had either baptized or ordained, including such influential pastors as William Walker, Henry Ledbetter, James Smart, John Thomas and his two sons Jonathan and John, Charles Daniel, John Moore, Sam Davis, and probably others.

Through the efforts of these men there were sixteen General Baptist churches in North Carolina by 1755.[18] These churches were located as far west as Granville and as far south as the Great Cohara, and the records intimate that their influence far outweighed any other religious group in eastern North Carolina during this period.

---

[17] Ibid., 12-13.
[18] George W. Paschal, *History of North Carolina Baptists*. (Raleigh: General Board, North Carolina Baptist State Convention), I, 176.

To a greater extent than either South Carolina or Virginia, Baptists in North Carolina underwent a radical doctrinal revolution between 1750 and 1760 in the transformation of practically all of the General Baptist churches into Particular Baptist churches.[19] George W. Paschal followed Morgan Edwards in crediting the initiation of this Calvinizing process to a Welsh Neck pastor, Robert Williams.[20] A native North Carolinian, Williams had gone to the Welsh Neck church in South Carolina in 1745, and upon his return in 1750, he exercised remarkable influence in turning the minds of the preachers from the General Baptist doctrines to those of the Particular Baptists. Some of the stalwarts whom William won to these views were James Smart, Henry Ledbetter, William Walker, John Moore, Thomas Pope, Edward Brown, and later on, Charles Daniel. It is difficult to understand how such fundamental theological shifts could take place with such seeming ease, but doubtless the movement was accelerated because most of these General Baptist preachers were untrained theologically, were aware of the lack of discipline in their churches, and were conscious of the absence of assurance on the part of parishioners.

Williams was not satisfied to make individual conquests but notified the Philadelphia Association of the situation and urged that preachers be sent from that Calvinistic center to help the North Carolina General Baptists to find the true faith. John Gano came in response to this plea and in May, 1755, visited Fishing Creek in Warren County and preached with great power. After his report to the Association, they voted to send further assistance to North Carolina, and on October 28, 1755, Peter Van Horn and Benjamin Miller left Philadelphia for this purpose.[21] They visited the Kehukee church first where Thomas Pope, the pastor, had already accepted Calvinistic views. The church was reorganized on a Calvinistic basis. It is significant, however, that in the reorganization of these churches, an average of less than ten members began each of the reorganized churches. Paschal estimated that only about 5 percent of the older General Baptist members were in the new churches.

This Calvinizing movement was significant in that it brought new emphasis upon regeneration, church discipline, and a church covenant, all

---

[19] Baker, *Source Book*, 13-14.
[20] Ibid.
[21] Ibid.

of which had been minimized under the old order.[22] W.L. Lumpkin is doubtless correct in suggesting that many of the General Baptists became a part of the Separate Baptist movement which was beginning about this time.

Just after the opening of this new period in 1740, Baptist work was begun in the Roman Catholic colony in Maryland. In the interest of securing settlers, the proprietors of this colony granted religious toleration to most Trinitarian Christians. However, there is no record of Baptists in the colony until a General Baptist from England, Henry Sater, invited visiting Baptist ministers to preach in his house on Chestnut Ridge, not far from Baltimore. As a result, in 1742, a church was organized in Sater's home, known at first as Chestnut Ridge church, then at Sater's Baptist Church. The first pastor was Henry Loveall. A second church was organized in 1754 by Benjamin Griffith and P.P. Van Horn at Winter Run, which was later called the Hartford church, but was admitted to the Philadelphia Association in 1755 as the Baltimore church. These were the only Baptist churches in Maryland before the Revolution.

Without minimizing the importance of these events in the story of the older Baptists in the South between 1740 and the American Revolution, it should be reiterated that the most significant and far-reaching event of this period in the Baptist story was the Separate Baptist movement that developed from the First Great Awakening.

## Whitefield's Chickens Become Ducks

The First Great Awakening in America, probably begun through the work of Jacob Frelinghuysen, Gilbert Tennant, and Jonathan Edwards in the second and third decades of the eighteenth century, affected Baptists in the South secondhand. George Whitefield, the Calvinistic associate of the Arminians John and Charles Wesley, brought to a climax in New England the earlier controversy stirred up by Jonathan Edwards concerning the need for a personal experience of grace through the power of the Holy Spirit. The New England Congregationalists had been at odds over this question since the Cambridge Platform of 1648 and the Half-Way Covenant of 1662. New England Congregationalism divided between the "New Lights," who affirmed that God brought new light into the hearts of

---

[22] Ibid., 14-16.

men by a conversion experience, and the "Old Lights," who said that baptized babies, as children of the covenant, needed no such new light. The intensification of this conflict by 1744 closed the open doors that Whitefield had found when he first came to New England in 1740. In spite of this he toured New England and preached to large crowds. Some of the New Lights, unable to form new churches without the permission of the older ones and being unable to get that permission, separated themselves form the established Congregational church and were known as Separates. Two of these Congregational Separatists who became Baptists were used of God to transmit the fire of the revival to Baptist in the South.

The first of these was Shubal Stearns, a member of the Congregational church in Tolland, Connecticut, who became a New Light under the preaching of Whitefield in 1745.[23] Stearns led a small group of the New Lights to meet apart, and shortly they became a Separate church. After studying the Scriptures, Stearns declared that he had become a Baptist by conviction, and in 1751 he was immersed by Wait Palmer, the New Light pastor of a Baptist church nearby. Stearns became pastor of a new Baptist church in Tollan on May 20, 1751, where he remained as pastor for about three years.

His companion, Daniel Marshall, also born in 1706, was a prosperous farmer in Windsor, Connecticut, not far from Tolland. He had been a deacon in the First Congregational Church there for about twenty years. Marshall, however, had questions about the Old Lights as early as 1744. When George Whitefield toured Connecticut in 1745, Marshall listened avidly and the fires of revival were kindled within his heart. By 1747, when he married Stearns' sister, Martha, he was a confirmed Separatist and after 1750 became a Baptist.[24]

Of the two, Stearns was the natural leader. He was small in stature, possessed a musical and strong voice that he used very effectively in reaching the convictions and emotions of his hearers. Although not formally well educated, he was an avid reader of books and was a man of sound judgment, according to Morgan Edwards.[25] Daniel Marshall, while

---

[23] Ibid., 17-18.
[24] Ibid., 19.
[25] Ibid., 17-18.

not as gifted as Stearns, was a man of overpowering earnestness and zeal, which made his plain exhortations most effective in presenting the gospel.

These two men, each almost fifty years of age when they came to North Carolina, were used of God to make fundamental changes in the character and development of Southern Baptists. No wonder George Whitefield, a Church of England Methodist who disdained the use of much water in baptizing infants or adults, as he pondered how he had helped produce many Baptists who immersed their candidates fully into the baptismal pool, ruefully said, "All my chickens have become ducks."

## Onnaquaggy, Opekon, and Sandy Creek

Although Stearns became the leader, it was Daniel Marshall that acted first upon his inner convictions of a special Christian mission. In 1751 or 1752, with his wife and three children, Marshall traveled northeastward in a wagon to witness to the Mohawk Indians in east-central New York. The friendly Indians permitted them to settle at Onnaquaggy, where the Marshalls and perhaps one other couple witnessed for eighteen months. The English-French rivalry among the Indians disrupted the work, and after a brief stop in Pennsylvania, the Marshalls drove southward to Virginia, arriving at Opekon in 1754. Here Marshall became acquainted with the Baptist church and its pastor, Samuel Heaton. He and his wife were baptized by Heaton in that year, and Joseph Breed and his wife, who may have been at Onnaquaggy with the Marshalls, were also baptized. Marshall was soon licensed by this church to exercise his gifts. He must have exercised them zealously, for some of the church complained to the Philadelphia Association about this display of enthusiasm. However, Benjamin Miller from that body was delighted with the warmhearted Christians that he found when he visited the church there.[26]

Meanwhile, Shubal Stearns in Tolland, Connecticut, felt God's call to a missionary service. In August, 1754, he and five or six couples from his church, most of them related to him, loaded their possessions into a wagon and before the close of the year joined the company of Daniel Marshall in Opekon, Virginia. Together the party moved to Cacapon Creek and constructed homes for a new settlement. The response to their witnessing in this neighborhood, however, was not good. For the first time,

---

[26] Ibid., 19.

the differences between the new Separate Baptists, as they were called, and the older Baptists, brought a strained relationship between Stearns' group and the older Baptists of the community. The zeal and emotional preaching of the Separates, the use of uneducated ministers, the "noisy" meetings, and even the extensive ministry of women in the services alienated the more formal older Baptists, who became known as Regular Baptists. This confrontation, along with the impending Indian hostility, caused Stearns and his party to consider another location. The decisive factor probably was a letter which Stearns received from North Carolina describing the need of the people there. In the summer of 1755, unnoticed by contemporary historians, Stearns and company traveled to Sandy Creek in what is now Randolph County in central North Carolina, arriving, according to Morgan Edwards, in the late fall, to begin a revolution in Southern Baptist life. Here the eight men and their wives promptly formed themselves into a church of sixteen members and built a meetinghouse.

## An Alarmed Neighborhood

North Carolina, indeed the South, was never the same after this group settled at Sandy Creek. The immediate impact was obvious. Morgan Edwards remarked that "the neighborhood was alarmed," and so it was. In an area of the back country where the population was growing rapidly, particularly with settlers uncommitted to Christianity, the impact of these sixteen people was remarkable. Three of the busiest roads of the entire South converged at Sandy Creek: the Settlers Road running from north to south along the edge of the Alleghenies, the Boone Trail from Wilmington west to the Yadkin settlements, and the Trading path from southeastern Virginia to Waxhaw country.[27]

This little church promptly sounded the alarm in the immediate neighborhood. Not only the preachers, but the entire congregation was conscious of standing under the judgment of God. All of the church looked to the leadership of the Holy Spirit. No less than 125 ministers were called into service during the next seventeen years from this church and her daughters. Preaching tours promptly began to characterize the ministry of the minister. A strong organizational structure was developed as each was

---

[27] William L. Lumpkin, *Baptist Foundations in the South* (Nashville: Broadman Press, 1961), 38.

planted, perhaps a result of the Congregational background of Stearns and Marshall. Every sermon was preached with compassion and zeal in an effort to win the hearts of those not yet committed to the service of Christ. The preachers themselves in the early years steadfastly refused to receive any remuneration for their services, which helped to win the confidence of the masses about them, but at the same time perpetuated an untrained, part-time ministry of zealous men who earned their own livings as they preached.

It is difficult to describe in a few words what Paschal devoted almost a hundred pages to outlining—the expansion of this Sandy Creek church in every direction. Stearns and Marshall made repeated tours into almost every part of the province. Large throngs gathered, and many conversions resulted wherever they went. Many years later in describing some of these results, Morgan Edwards said:

> Sandy Creek is the mother of all the Separate Baptists. From this Zion went forth the word, and great was the company of them who published it; it, in 17 years, has spread branches westward as far as the great river Mississippi; southward as far as Georgia; eastward to the sea and Chesapeake Bay; and northward to the waters of the Potomac; it, in 17 years, is become the mother, grandmother, and great-grandmother to 42 churches, from which sprang 125 ministers.... I believe a preternatural and invisible hand works in the assemblies of the Separate Baptists bearing down the human mind, as was the case in the primitive churches, I Cor. xiv: 25.[28]

Before 1760, a large band of stalwarts had been called out of God to become preachers in the Separate movement. Among these were James Younger, John Newton, Ezekiel Hunter, James Reed, John Dillahunty, Philip Mulkey, Joseph and William Murphy, Dutton Lane. Charles Markland, Nathanel Powell, James Turner, Jeremiah Walker, Elnathan Davis, and perhaps the most influential of all the converts, Samuel Harris, who became the "Apostle of Virginia."

William L. Lumpkin summarized the early rapid progress of the Separates in North Carolina:

---

[28] Baker, *Source Book*, 20.

Within three years of the Separates' settlement at Sandy Creek there were three fully constituted churches with a combined membership of over nine hundred. Vigorous branches thrived in the region of Sandy Creek at Little River in Montgomery County and Grassy Creek in Granville County, and other branches were located well to the eastward at Southwest in Lenoir County, Black River in Duplin, New River in Onslow, and as far away as Lockwood's Folly in Brunswick. Preaching had been carried on from the Moravian settlements to the Cape Fear and northward into Virginia.[29]

The Separate Baptist movement was also set forward by the organization of the first separate association in 1758.[30] Shubal Stearns felt that an association would "impart stability, regularity and uniformity to the whole." So he visited each Separate congregation and urged them to meet at Sandy Creek for the purpose of organizing such a general body. As many as nine or ten congregations may have been represented in the meeting, probably held on the second Monday of June, 1758. The utmost democracy prevailed at this meeting, even the election of a moderator not being attempted lest the free work of the Holy Spirit might be counteracted. This was the second association to be organized in the South, the first being Charleston seven years earlier. The inspiration from these annual meetings of the association gave great impetus to the zeal of the preachers. Lumpkin judged that a definite missionary strategy was planned by the leadership. Shubal Stearns worked primarily in eastern North Carolina and to the west of Sandy Creek, Daniel Marshall itinerated to the norths Philip Mulkey preached primarily in the east and southeast.

However, in 1770 a new direction was taken at the meeting of the Sandy Creek Association. Usually no action was taken at the meeting of this association without unanimous approval, but such was the division among the representatives in 1770 that they could not agree even on a moderator. The only unanimity came when they agreed to divide into three bodies, one for North Carolina (the Sandy Creek Association), one for Virginia (the General Association of Separate Baptists in Virginia), and

---

[29] Lumpkin, *Baptist Foundations*, 44.
[30] Baker, *Source Book*, 20-21.

one for South Carolina (the Congaree Association). Morgan Edwards described the cause for this division in the following words:

> The cause was partly convenience, but chiefly a mistake which this association fell into relative to their power and jurisdiction; they had carried matters so high as to leave hardly any power in particular churches, unfellowshipping ordinations, ministers and churches that acted independent of them; and pleading "That though complete power be in every church yet every church can transfer it to an Association"; which is as much to say that a man may take out his eyes, ears, etc., and give them to another to see, hear, etc. for him; for if power be fixed by Christ in a particular church they can not transfer it; nay, should they formally give it away yet it is not gone away.[31]

In addition, David Benedict noted that a part of the reason for this division was the somewhat autocratic attitude of Shubal Stearns himself.

> The good old Mr. Stearns, who was not wholly divested of those maxims which he had imbibed from the traditions of his fathers, is said to have been the principal promoter of this improper stretch of associational power, which, however, was soon abandoned by those who, for a time, tampered with it, to their embarrassment and injury.[32]

Through the withdrawal of churches in Virginia and South Carolina and the heavy migration of Separate Baptists to Kentucky and Tennessee, as will be described in the following chapter, the strength of Separate Baptists in North Carolina greatly diminished. In 1771 only nine churches were represented in the Sandy Creek Association, and some of these were quite small in membership, including the parent church itself. The story, then, must turn toward Virginia, South Carolina, and Georgia, if the trail and influence of the Separate Baptists is to be followed.

---

[31] Ibid., 21.
[32] Ibid.

## Growth of Separate Baptists

The story of Separate Baptists in Virginia has political, economic, social, and religious antecedents. The early center of the Virginia commonwealth was the tidewater section of the state, where the older settlements had stopped some sixty or seventy miles from the coast line. Wesley M. Gewehr drew the line separating the Old Dominion from the Piedmont area as running south through Fredericksburg, Richmond, and Petersburg. West of this line the political, social, economic, and religious atmosphere was completely different from that of the tidewater. In the older section, life centered on large estates operated by tobacco planters who constituted the aristocracy. Williamsburg was the capital and center of their activities, and most of them were engaged in political scuffles that influenced the entire state. Democracy and equality were not popular words with this group, and religion was generally not taken seriously.

West of the tidewater, however, the land had been settled by numerous marginal farmers, some from the tidewater and some newcomers, for attractive terms had been offered to the poorer class who would move to the frontier in the Piedmont and the Valley, mainly Scotch-Irish and Germans. These counties in central and western Virginia west of the Blue Ridge were settled by sturdy men who opposed almost everything the planters in the tidewater section espoused. Equality in the state, absolute liberty in religion, and freedom of choice in all matters social or political characterized these new settlers. The non-English background of many of them helped intensify the tension with England.

Between 1742 and 1758 the Presbyterians under William Robinson and Samuel Davies worked strenuously with considerable success among these settlers, not without ecclesiastical opposition. As mentioned earlier in this chapter, Regular Baptists also began work in this area as early as 1743 and gathered several churches.

The Separate Baptists initiated their work in Virginia in 1760 and by the time of the Revolution had spread phenomenally. Their expansion into Virginia can be glimpsed in four rather distinct phases.

The first phase began in August, 1760, when Daniel Marshall and Philip Mulkey from the Sandy Creek Association in North Carolina established the Dan River church in Pittsylvania County, just across the line from North Carolina. The church consisted of sixty-three white and eleven black members originally. The most distinguished of them was

Samuel Harris, a leading citizen of the area who had been honored with almost every public office in the county. He had experienced a remarkable conversion under the preaching of Joseph Murphy and had been baptized by Marshall in 1758. Other Separate churches were at Staunton River and Black Water, both organized in 1761, and both just across the line from North Carolina.

The second phase of their expansion occurred in 1765. In January of that year a convert of David Thomas in Culpeper County, about a hundred miles north of the border, came to Harris and urged him to come far up into central Virginia and preach at Culpeper. Harris promptly responded to this call. This was the beginning of a new center of Separate Baptist work. Although driven from Culpeper by armed men, Harris preached extensively in Orange County and later, with James Read, evangelized the entire surrounding area. On November 20, 1767, with Dutton Lane, Harris and Read organized the first Separate Baptist church north of the James. It was called Upper Spotsylvania, and became the mother of churches in the entire section. Continued preaching by Harris and Read led to the organization on December 2, 1769, of the Lower Spotsylvania church and, two days later, the Blue Run church. Lewis Craig, Elijah his brother, and John Waller were ordained in the following year. Lewis became pastor of the Upper Spotsylvania church, Elijah became pastor of the Blue Run church, and Waller became pastor of the Lower Spotsylvania church.

A third distinct period of advance by Separate Baptists in Virginia took place in 1769, when the movement began to spread quite rapidly there. Samuel Harris was ordained in that year, and with Jeremiah Walker established the Amelia church in southern Virginia, where Walker remained as pastor. In November, 1769, James Ireland and Harris established Carter's Run church in Fauquier County, the first Separate church in northern Virginia, and it grew rapidly. A number of other churches were established in the next two years. One rather interesting situation developed at Ebenezer in what is now Amherst County where a church was constituted in 1771. Ordinarily the Separate Baptist pastors received no salary at all, which pleased the churches, of course. However, this church bound itself to pay its minister fifty shillings a year. Perhaps this was one reason for its rapid growth.

It will be recalled that the Sandy Creek Association decided to divide into 3 bodies in 1770.[33] In May, 1771, 12 of the Separate churches in Virginia met in Orange to organize the General Association of the Separate Baptists in Virginia. Representatives to this organizational meeting came from 12 churches located in 11 counties with a total of 1,335 members. No representative attended this meeting from 3 other Separate Baptist churches in Virginia. Some of the ministers who formed this body and were quite influential in this period of Virginia Baptist life were Allen Wyley, William Marshall, Thomas Hargate, Christopher Clarke, Rane Chastain, John Williams, John Burrus, William Webber, John Young, Reuben Pickett, William Lovell, James Shelbourne, Elijah Baker, John King, Reuben Ford, and John Koontz.

The Virginia Association had grown so large by 1773 that it was divided into the Southern and Northern districts, the James River being the dividing line. At the general meetings in 1774, the Northern District had grown to include at least 24 churches with a total membership of 1,921, while the Southern District included 30 churches with 2,083 members.[34]

The fourth phase of the Separate work in Virginia began about 1775. In that year both districts met at the Dover meetinghouse near Richmond, where letters from 60 churches were received: 29 from the Northern District and 31 from the Southern. It was reported that only about 300 had been baptized altogether and that this proved "that cold times were now not only appearing but actually arrived." This decline was probably caused by the outbreak of the Revolutionary War, the Arminian incursion as seen in the defection of strong leaders like John Waller and Jeremiah Walker, and the beginning of the Methodist revival about this time. Although the growth of the Separates was slowed and several problems appeared, they were an important influence during the American Revolution and in the struggle thereafter for liberty of conscience. Gewehr said that the Separate Baptists "were the greatest factor in destroying the Establishment and securing religious liberty."[35]

---

[33] Ibid.
[34] Robert B. Semple, *A History of the Rise and Progress of the Baptists in Virginia* (rev. by G. W. Beale, Philadelphia: American Baptist Publication Society, 1894), 79-80
[35] Wesley Gewehr, *The Great Awakening in Virginia, 1740-1790* ( Durham: Duke University Press, 1930), 109.

The Separate Baptist movement flowed into South Carolina like a vast refreshing stream pointed toward the center of the state, approaching within a hundred miles of the first Regular Baptist church at Charleston, then swerving to the west to fill up the Carolina back country and crossing into Georgia. Regular Baptists had been growing slowly in the low-country and the Peedee sections, but had done little in the back country of the state. It was in this area that the Separates made rapid growth, and in less than two decades, they had surpassed the number of Regular Baptists in the entire state.

The Separate Baptists thrust into South Carolina were led by Philip Mulkey and Daniel Marshall. Mulkey was a North Carolinian, reared as an Anglican, experienced a remarkable conversion, was baptized by Shubal Stearns at Sandy Creek in 1756 at the age of twenty-four, and was ordained in the following year. After several years as pastor of the Deep River church in North Carolina, he led twelve other members of the church in 1759 or 1760 to South Carolina and established a church at Broad River. Two years later, the church prospering meanwhile, the same thirteen members who had come from Deep River moved south about a hundred miles to constitute a Separate Baptist church at Fairforest, the oldest Baptist church in the back country. As was usually the case in connection with Separate Baptist churches, this church became a center from which a large area was evangelized. Growing out of the ministry of the church, additional congregations were gathered at Lawsons Fork, Thickety, and Enoree. Also probably related to the Fairforest ministry were churches constituted at Tyger River, Little River of Broad, Little River of Saluda, and Buffalo. Mulkey's preaching in the Congaree section, followed by Daniel Marshall and Joseph Murphy, led to the constitution in 1766 of the Congaree church. Other churched developing from the influence of this center probably were Watertree Creek, Mine Creek, Red Bank, Twenty0Five Mile Creek, Amelia, Four Holes, and, perhaps most important of these, High Hills of Santee. Joseph Reese was instrumental in constituting the High Hills church, and among his principal converts was Richard Furman. Furman became pastor of this church in 1774 at the age of twenty, and distinguished himself for the next half century in South Carolina Baptist life. The High Hills church in turn became a center for additional Baptist churches of the Separate type, and within a few years the churches at Bethel, Swift Creek, Ebenezer, Second Lynches Creek, and Upper Fork of Lynches were constituted.

Another whole set of Separate Baptist centers developed from the preaching of Daniel Marshall, who had been pastor of Abbotts Creek in North Carolina. In 1760 Marshall moved to South Carolina and organized a church at Beaver Creek near Broad River. Two years later he and his family traveled south to Stevens Creek, about ten miles from Augusta, Georgia, where a church was constituted in 1766. The leadership of Marshall is seen in the organization of the churches at Horns Creek, Bush River, and Raeburns Creek.

It will be recalled that the Sandy Creek Association divided in 1770 to permit the organization of bodies for Virginia and South Carolina. Separate Baptists in South Carolina formed the Congaree Association on December 26, 1771, with seven or eight constituent churches. Benedict described how this association began correspondence with the Philadelphia Association after Morgan Edwards from that body visited the churches in 1772. Probably the statement in the 1774 minutes of the Philadelphia Association referred to this correspondence.

> A letter from the Association at Little River and Broad River, South Carolina, was read, by which it appears that sixty-six joined them by baptism the year past; their number of members six hundred and ninety-two. Good news from a far country.[36]

Although the name *Congaree* does not appear in this reference, later on in the minutes for the same year the Association approved letters of fellowship to be written to a number of associations including the Congaree in South Carolina.[37] The Congaree Association dissolved about the time of the Revolution, partly because of internal dissension and partly because of the war.

It will be recalled that beginnings in Georgia Baptist life probably sprang from the older Regular Baptists, but that no church of that type was organized before 1773. It is probable that the Separate Baptist from South Carolina established the first organized church in Georgia. Daniel Marshall had been preaching extensively in the southwestern section of

---

[36] A. D. Gillette, ed., *Century Minutes of the Philadelphia Baptist Association: 1707-1807* (Philadelphia: American Baptist Historical Society, 1851), 135.
[37] Ibid., 143.

South Carolina and moved to Georgia in January, 1771. In the spring of the following year he led in the organization of the Baptist church at Kiokee, a few miles from the South Carolina border. From this Separate Baptist center a number of outstanding Georgia Baptist leaders developed, including Silas Mercer, father of Jesse Mercer.

## Union of Separate and Regular Baptists

The early distrust between the Separate and Regular Baptists was quite marked. Instances of open antagonism are found in the histories of North Carolina, Virginia, and South Carolina. As Lumpkin points out, the principal story of the uniting of these two groups took place in Virginia, where all Baptists joined together to fight for liberty and a common revival was sweeping both groups. As a result, a formal union of Separates and Regulars took place in Virginia in 1787.[38] A formal union in North Carolina took place in 1788, when two Separate churches were received into the reformed Kehukee Baptist Association.[39] In South Carolina and Georgia there came the gradual elimination of distinctions between the two types of Baptists without formal action.

William L. Lumpkin evaluated the significance of the Separate Baptist movement at the close of his study of this group. After describing some of their weaknesses, including their strong appeal to the emotions, their neglect of the ministerial education, their tendency to alarm people more than to feed them, their non-support of ministers, and their anti-confessionalism, he outlined some of their major contributions, as follows: (1) They revived the Great Awakening in the South in a unique way. (2) They helped establish the character of American evangelical Christianity. (3) They provided religious leadership for the American frontier. (4) They made moral and spiritual preparation for American political liberty. (5) They played a large part in the triumph of Free Church principles in America. (6) They contributed largely to the evangelization of the blacks in the South. (7) They greatly advanced the cause of religion in America and shaped the character of Protestantism in the South. (8) They brought great numerical gains to Baptists in the South. (9) They provided the antecedents for the Southern Baptist Convention in such things as their

---

[38] Baker, *Source Book*, 22.
[39] Ibid., 23.

aggressiveness and evangelical outlook, their centralized ecclesiology that was influential in 1845 when Southern Baptists chose their type of organizational structure, and many other aspects, such as their self-conscious attitudes, their hymnody, their lay leadership, many ecclesiastical practices, and their strong Biblicism.[40]

There seems to be a providential element in the mingling of the Separate Baptist distinctive from those of the older General and Particular Baptists in the South. Taken alone, any one of these three large Baptist movements possessed many weaknesses. In the uniting of the three movements, Southern Baptists were prepared fundamentally for the remarkable development that came in the next two centuries. The General Baptists provided emphasis on the necessity for human agency in reaching men with the gospel; the Regular Baptists added doctrinal stability and a consciousness of the divine initiative; while the Separates united some of the best features of both and in addition to magnifying structural responsibility, emphasized the necessity of the presence and power of the Holy Spirit. Thus, Baptists in the South were fundamentally equipped to begin the surge in numbers and influence during the following centuries.

---

[40] Lumpkin, *Baptist Foundations*, 147.

# Chapter 3 - Liberty: Political and Religious

The participation of Southern Baptists in the Revolutionary War and the victory of efforts to include the principle of religious liberty in the new American Constitution of 1789 will be discussed in this chapter. Both political independence from England and religious liberty had their roots in the First Great Awakening. The spiritual unifying of colonies, that in many other respects were isolated from one another, was an important factor in the preparation for American independence, and the extensive strengthening of minority denominational groups laid the foundations for achieving religious liberty in the new nation.

Baptists shared in the events leading to the Revolution and in the war itself. The whole drama of war and independence had such radical effects in every area of American life that anyone living in the colonies was involved. The many economic policies, for example, that bound the colonies tightly to English interests—mercantilism, the several Navigation Acts, the Sugar Act, the paper money regulations, the Stamp Act, etc.—were elements that made up the world for the colonists, giving direction to their day-by-day activities. The disruption of the economic structure alone, apart from the many other substantial factors that made up the complex story of the American colonial revolt against England, was bound to have radical effects upon every colonist.

The sequence of events conspired to lead the American colonies more fully toward revolutionary action after 1750. In the three earlier wars between France and England (King William's War, 1689-97; Queen Anne's War, 1701-13; and King George's War, 1744-48), the American colonies actually were on the periphery, and none of these wars determined which European nation should control the American continent. Bu the French and Indian War (1756-63) was significant. Its complex effects, both immediate and remote, were decisive: it gave England the controlling hand in America; it involved a closer cooperation among the American colonies than they had heretofore known; and, most immediately, it caused England to determine to make radical reforms in colonial administration. British officials now saw firsthand the inept customs service in the colonies; they recognized the need to revise the obsolete Navigation Acts in the interest of mercantilism and the balance of trade; they reported numerous loopholes in the laws and widespread efforts to evade British trade restrictions; and they expressed their dismay at the refusal of the colonies to submerge individual interests in order to defend the interests of England. It was the effort of the British government to correct these deficiencies, brought to their attention by the French and Indian War, that led directly to repressive taxation and rigid enforcement; and, finally, to revolt.

## Southern Baptists and the American Revolution

Baptists in each of the four southern states (Virginia, North Carolina, South Carolina, and Georgia) faced a somewhat different situation before and during Revolutionary War, although their basic interest was liberty, political and religious. As was true with Baptists in the North, Southern Baptists did not hesitate to identify political liberty with religious liberty. For this reason, most Southern Baptists took the patriot side during the war. This can be glimpsed more clearly by reviewing developments in the four southern states named.

The direct link between the French and Indian War and the American Revolution can be taken back one more step. The French and Indian War was probably triggered by the efforts of Virginia to colonize the western areas which she claimed by virtue of her original charter. One can imagine the bitterness of Virginia in 1763, after the war was won, when the crown issued a proclamation forbidding settlements west of the Allegheny watershed. This, along with "taxation without consent," brought Virginia into conflict with England.

While Baptists in Virginia were more or less remotely related to these political developments, their principal issue with England was at the point of religious liberty. The vigorous prosecution and persecution of dissenters from 1767 on, sometimes by legal authorities and sometimes by an aroused Tory populace, led Baptists almost to a man to believe that the only possibility of securing religious liberty was bound up with the achievement of political liberty. The climax for them came in August, 1775, when, after deliberate reflection and discussion, the combined northern and southern district associations of Separate Baptists, representing the great majority of Baptists in Virginia, submitted to the Virginia Convention (assembled to chart Virginia's course for freedom) a memorial proposing complete political independence of Virginia from England and the inauguration of total religious liberty in the colony, and pledging Baptist support.[1] This memorial produced a profound effect on the Virginia Convention and identified Virginia Baptists as strong patriots in the forthcoming struggle with England. They were active both on the field of battle and through political agitation in behalf of civil and religious liberty.[2] England recognized this, and Baptist churches were regularly burned by their troops during was as "nests of rebellion."

What has been called the first battle of the American Revolution took place on May 11, 1771, at Great Alamance Creek between the state militia sent by Governor William Tyron and about 2,000 unorganized farmers from the back country, who had become known as Regulators. The causes of this conflict between the common people and the state authority included

> Unlawful exaction of taxes under color of legislative authority, unlawful exaction of fees by clerks and county registers of deed, unequal distribution of the burdens and benefits of government, unequal incidence of taxation, the land policy of Lord Granville's district, and the scarcity of money.[3]

There had been protests against official corruption and taxation without representation before Tryon became governor in May, 1765, but his spirited defense of those in authority, corrupt or not, and his active efforts to strengthen the hold of the Church of England in the province exasperated the victims of the system in the central and western sections. As early as 1758 a spontaneous meeting of about 700 farmers took place near Salisbury in a protest against political and religious injustices. The flames of the movement were fanned in 1767 and 1768 when Edmund Fanning in Orange County began to heap up unjust demands upon the

---

[1] Lumpkin, *Baptist Foundations*, 113-15, and Garnett Ryland, *The Baptists of Virginia 1699-1926* (Richmond: The Virginia Baptist Board of Missions and Education, 1955), 95.
[2] See summary in Gewehr, *Great Awakening in Virginia*, 188-218.
[3] Lumpkin, *Baptist Foundations*, 73.

people. Fanning was convicted of extortion in 1768, but retained his office through gerrymandering by governor Tryon. The people began to react violently against Fanning by 1768. Despite continued efforts to petition the government to settle the matter peaceably, things went from bad to worse. Tryon launched a vendetta against the Baptists, whom he considered to be ringleaders in the Regulator movement. After Alamance, Tryon terrorized the countryside in the very areas where Baptists had their strength. He camped for a week at Sandy Creek after laying waste to plantations, burning homes, and arresting many men. Tryon then moved against the Baptist settlements near the Jersey church, followed by the intimidation of another principal Baptist area in the neighborhood of Shallow Fords.

Although Shubal Stearns had counseled his followers against violence, and the Sandy Creek church was divided over the issue, it is likely that many Baptists took part in the exciting events of this period. It cannot be determined whether it was Baptist involvement or despair in the failure of their efforts to secure justice that caused wholesale Baptist emigration from North Carolina after Alamance.

> Morgan Edwards reported in 1772 that fifteen hundred families departed straightaway and that "a great many more are only waiting to dispose of their plantations in order to follow them." The Alamance region was almost emptied of Baptists and did not recover a considerable Baptist population for a hundred years. Sandy Creek Church in a few years was reduced from six hundred and six members to fourteen by 1772. Little River Church dropped form five hundred members to scarcely a dozen. Tidence Lane and some others from Abbott's Creek went northward into Virginia, but most went south and west. It was as though the Battle of Alamance, but most went south and west. It was as though the Battle of Alamance and the death of Shubal Stearns six months later had been twin signals for most of the Baptist people of central North Carolina to disperse.[4]

When the Revolutionary War broke out, North Carolina Baptists supported it wholeheartedly with only a few exceptions.

---

[4] Ibid., 85.

As was true in both North Carolina and Georgia, South Carolina had experienced little religious persecution at the hands of the royal governor and council, but had been engaged actively for many years prior to the Revolution in the struggle to enlarge the prerogatives of the local government against royal control. Similar to the activities of the other colonies, South Carolina resisted the economic and political legislation following the French and Indian War, set up a provincial government in 1774, and drove out the royal governor in 1776. There were many Tories in South Carolina. Baptists were numbered among the colonial supporters, although in the back country many Separate Baptists were strongly pacifistic and refused to join in any type of military conflict. Leaders like Oliver Hart and Richard Furman strongly supported the Revolution and, in addition, were used extensively in persuading their fellow countrymen to become engaged in the struggle. So effective was Furman in this task that the British put a price on his head, and he was forced to flee from his church. In May, 1780, General Cornwallis captured Charleston, and for the next year British armies dominated South Carolina.

American leaders never forgot the part that Furman had in the struggle. Harvey T. Cook described how Furman happened to be passing through Washington some years later and met an acquaintance in company with Colonel James Monroe (later President) who introduced him to Monroe.

> Col. Monroe, in taking his hand, remarked thoughtfully, as if trying to recall something, Furman, Furman of Charleston! The name and the countenance seemed familiar. "May I inquire if you were once of the High Hills of Santee?" said Col. Monroe. He was answered affirmatively. "And were you the young preacher who fled for protection to the American camp, on account of the reward which Lord Cornwallis had offered for his head?" "I am the same," said Mr. Furman. Their meeting was now deeply affecting and Col. M. could hardly let him go, and did not until he related to the distinguished by-stander the circumstances to which he alluded. "It seems young Furman was not only an enthusiastic Baptist preacher, but an ardent advocate of rebellion, and everywhere, on stumps, in barns, as well as in the pulpit, prayed and preached resistance to Britain and alarm to the Tories. Urged

by the latter, Lord Cornwallis, who had been made aware of his influence and daring, offered a thousand pounds for his head. Ascertaining that the Tories were on his track, young Furman fled to the American camp, which, by his prayers and eloquent appeals he reassured, insomuch that it was reported Cornwallis made the remark that he feared the prayers of that godly youth more than the armies of Sumter and Marion." Col. Monroe related these particulars with much feeling and enthusiasm. Dr. Furman was not so much a lion in the national capitol that he prepared to leave immediately, but Monroe would not let him go- but made an appointment for him to preach in the Congressional Hall. In vain did the quiet minister disclaim his ability as a court preacher. All the elite, the honorable, the notable of the metropolis were there, including the president, Cabinet, Ministers, Foreign Ambassadors, etc., for his early adventures and eloquence had been noised abroad.[5]

Baptists as a group emerged from the war with the reputation of being strong supporters of the colonial cause, and many Baptists served with distinction in the colonial side.

Georgia was late in joining the revolutionary movement, but did send delegates to the Second Continental Congress in 1775. There were few Baptists in Georgia at this time. Evidently most of them took the colonial side.

## Struggle for Religious Liberty

Without question the battle for political liberty was a large factor in the South, as it was in New England, in advancing the struggle of Baptists to attain religious liberty. There had been little religious persecution in South Carolina during this period. One isolated instance of this kind was so frowned on by the community that there is no record of another such occurrence. In Georgia the only case of record was the arrest of Daniel Marshall in 1771, and the stout words of Martha Marshall and faithful testimony of Daniel brought the conversion of most of those involved in his trial. In North Carolina Morgan Edwards mentioned a

---

[5] Harvey T. Cook, ed., *A Biography of Richard Furman* (Greenville: Baptist Courier, 1913), 72-73

persecution occurring about 1767, in which Baptists were charged with blasphemy, riots, and heresy, but he gave no particulars, and George W. Paschal, the North Carolina historian, could no further record of this. It is true that in 1740 at New Berne, when several Baptists petitioned to register a house for Baptist preaching they were harassed and put under bond to keep peace. There is a tradition that even though charges against them were later dismissed, James Brinson, Nicholas Purefoy, and William Fulsher were publicly whipped or imprisoned.[6] Paschal also described similar harassment in Beaufort and Pamlico counties in 1742.

However, the story was different in Virginia. Persecution there was of two kinds, popular and legal. Popular violence against the Baptists was aroused pertly by their fidelity to their own convictions and partly by "frivolous" charges that "ignorance or malice" mustered against them. They were unpopular for dissenting from the Church of England, for refusing to baptize infants, for immersion in baptism, and for making divisions. There were also reports that they continually condemned others in their preaching, that they had little human learning, and that they held noisy meetings; and it was even whispered that when they became strong enough they would massacre the inhabitants and take possession of the country. The earlier Regular Baptists were no more exempt from persecution than were the Separate Baptists. Of the former, David Thomas in 1763 was driven from Culpeper County by a mob, and in Stafford, a gang armed with firearms attacked the people at worship and a violent battle ensued. Even legal harassment took place. In December, 1762, Thomas and seventeen of his members were indicted for absenting themselves from the parish church. Ministers had difficulty obtaining licenses to preach. Many other legal methods of intimidation were attempted.

A similar story can be told of the Separate Baptists. When Samuel Harris preached at Culpeper in 1765, he was driven out by a mob of armed men. Similar savage action was taken in Pittsylvania, Amherst, Louisa, Fauquier, Chesterfield, Middlesex, Orange, Caroline, and elsewhere.

Garnett Ryland, the Virginia Baptist historian, judged that the first legal attempts to suppress Separate Baptist preachers came before 1767 when Lewis Craig was fined in Spotsylvania County for preaching. The

---

[6] Paschal, *History of North Carolina Baptists,* 186 ff.

occasion proved to be dramatic and fruitful. Craig said to the grand jury that indicted him:

> I thank you, gentlemen, for the honor you did me. While I was wicked and injurious, you took no note of me, but now having altered my course of life and endeavoring to reform my neighbors, you concern yourself much about me.[7]

One of the jury, John Waller, known for his gambling and profanity as "Swearing Jack" Waller and the "Devil's Adjutant," was brought to Christian conviction by his testimony, was baptized and began preaching, and was himself presented to a grand jury the next year for his preaching.

The principal period of persecution of Virginia Baptists occurred between 1768 and 1774 with the exception of one isolated instance occurring in 1778. This legal persecution probably ended when it did because of the new phase of Baptist activity in 1775, which will be described hereafter.

Two instances of legal persecution occurred in 1768. The first was on June 4, 1768, when John Waller, Lewis Craig, James Chiles, James Read, and William Marsh were arrested in Spotsylvania. After forty-three day in jail, Chiles, Craig, and Waller were released, and promptly returned to their vigorous preaching. In July, 1768, in the adjoining county of Orange, Allen Wyley, John Corbley, Elijah Craig, and Thomas Chambers were arrested and committed to jail. It is known that Craig and Wyley spent a considerable time in prison in 1768 under very difficult circumstances.

In November, 1769, James Ireland, then a youth of twenty-two, was arrested in Culpeper County for his "vile, pernicious, abhorrible, detestable, abominable, diabolical doctrines." From November until April, Ireland lay in the Culpeper one-room jail. Ryland described the conditions of imprisonment as being shocking, his keeper the most avaricious and heartless, and his persecutors, most outrageous. Attempts were made to suffocate him through burning sulphur and pepper, to kill him by exploding gun powder under the jail, and a plot was hatched to poison him. He was released without trial when a competent attorney threatened the magistrates with prosecution for illegal action. Promptly Ireland began a

---

[7] Ryland, *Baptists of Virginia*, 60.

missionary journey as far west as Ohio, preaching day and night despite opposition.

Two examples of persecution occurred in 1770. In Fauquier County in February, John Pickett was jailed for three months. In Chesterfield County in December, William Webber and Joseph Anthony were arrested for "itinerate preaching" and lodged in jail, where they remained for several months.

Between June and August, 1771, in Caroline County, John Young, Bartholomew Choning, James Goolrich, Edward Herndon, John Burrus, and Lewis Craig were arrested for preaching the gospel. It is not certain how long they remained in custody. In Middlesex County in the same year the authorities indicted several members of a new congregation for absenting themselves from the parish church. A petition for a place of public worship was denied. On August 10, John Waller, William Webber, and Thomas Wafford came to the community and promptly felt the hand of the law. John Waller described the experience in a letter from Urbanna Prison on August 12, as follows:

> At a meeting which was held at brother McCain's, in this county, last Saturday, whilst brother William Webber was addressing the congregation from James III; 18, there came a running towards him, in a furious rage, Captain James Montague, a magistrate of the county, followed by the parson of the parish, and several others, who seemed greatly exasperated. The magistrate, and another, took hold of brother Webber, and dragging him from the stage, delivered him, with brethren Wafford, Robert Ware, Richard Falkner, James Greenwood and myself, into custody, and commanded that we should be brought before him for trial. Brother Wafford was severely scourged, and brother Henry Street received one lash, from one of the persecutors, who was prevented from proceeding to farther [sic] violence by his companions; to be short, I may inform you that we were carried before the above magistrate, who, with the parson and some others, carried us, one by one, into a room, and examined our pockets and wallets for fire-arms, &c., charging us with carrying on a mutiny against the authority of the land. Finding none, we were asked if we had license to preach in that county; learning we had not , it was

required of us to give bond and security not to preach any more in the county, which we modestly refused to do, whereupon, after dismissing brother Wafford, with a charge to make his escape out of the county by twelve o'clock the next day on pain of imprisonment, and dismissing brother Falkner, the rest of us were delivered to the sheriff, and sent to close jail, with a charge not to allow us to walk in the air until court day.[8]

Waller, Ware, Greenwood, and Webber preached from the windows and carried on a fruitful ministry. They were released on September 26 of that year; it is possible that Patrick Henry, the great advocate of liberty, assisted in their release.

In 1772 three cases of imprisonment were recorded. In May in Chesterfield County, Augustine Eastin was arrested for preaching without license. In August in King and Queen County, James Greenwood and William Lovell were imprisoned for sixteen days. In August in Caroline County, two laymen, James Ware and James Pitman, were imprisoned for sixteen days for preaching in their homes, and a month later John Waller was placed in jail for the same offense. How long Waller remained confined is unknown.

The officers were busy in 1773. In Chesterfield County John Tanner, John Weatherford, and Jeremiah Walker were imprisoned. Patrick Henry paid the jail fees for Weatherford, but did not reveal this for many years. Jeremiah Moore was arrested in the same year in Fairfax County. In Culpeper County on August 21 of this year Nathaniel Saunders and William McClannahan were arrested and placed in jail. In Orange County on October 23, 1773, Joseph Spencer was imprisoned for "teaching and preaching the Gospel as a Baptist, not having license." It is perhaps this case that led James Madison who lived nearby to write a friend in Philadelphia and remark:

> I have nothing to brag of as to the state and liberty of my country. Poverty and luxury prevail among all sorts; pride, ignorance and knavery among the priesthood, and vice and wickedness among the laity. This is bad enough; but it is not the worst I have to tell you. That diabolical, hell-conceived principle of persecution rages

---

[8] Baker, *Source Book*, 33 f.

among some, and, to their eternal infamy, the clergy furnish their quota of imps for such business. There are at this time in the adjacent country not less than five or six well-meaning men in close jail for publishing their religious sentiments, which, in the main, are very orthodox. I have neither patience to hear, talk, or think of anything relative to this matter; for I have squabbled and scolded, abused and ridiculed, so long about it, to little purpose, that I am without common patience. So I must beg you to pity me, and pray for liberty of conscience to all. [9]

The year 1774 marked almost the end of this kind of legal harassment. In Chesterfield County David Tinsley was imprisoned for over four months and suffered many indignities. In Essex, John Waller, John Shackelford, Robert Ware, and Ivison Lewis were arrested for preaching the gospel. They were released on bond after a few weeks.

In addition to these specific instances, Semple recorded arrests in Culpeper County and imprisonment without dates of John Corbley, Thomas Ammon, Elijah Craig, Thomas Maxfield, Adam Banks, and John Delaney. Ryland added the name of Anderson Moffett as being a prisoner in Culpeper, according to oral tradition.

With the exception of the imprisonment of Elijah Baker in Accomack in 1778, these are the definite records of imprisonment. Ryland remarked in summary:

> These imprisonments of more than thirty individuals in the jails of nine counties so far from arresting the Baptist movement had accelerated it by arousing sympathy for the prisoners, by kindling interest in their message and by awakening understanding and appreciation of their insistence on unrestrained exercise of freedom of belief in religion and liberty to preach the Gospel to every creature.[10]

## Baptists and the Federal Constitution

This struggle for religious liberty occurred at a very auspicious time in the formative years of the American Republic. The Continental

---

[9] Ryland, *Baptists of Virginia,* 81-82 quoting from Hunt, *Writings of James Madison,* I, p. 21.
[10] Ibid, 84.

Congress had anticipated the need for some type of confederation after the close of the war for independence. On November 15, 1777, that body sent the Articles of Confederation to the states for approval. They were not ratified until March 1, 1781, and were not satisfactory thereafter. On May 25, 1787, a Constitutional Convention was assembled, purportedly for amending the Articles to correct some of their principle deficiencies. However, this Convention prepared an entirely new instrument of government produced in secret sessions. On September 17, 1787, the new Constitution was adopted by most of the Convention and submitted to the Continental Congress, who in turn sent it to the stated for ratification. In Virginia, the General Committee of Baptists studied the proposed Constitution and unanimously agreed that it did not make proper provision for religious liberty, although it was recognized that any powers not specifically granted to the central government were reserved to the states. As a result, John Leland, popular Baptist pastor in Orange County, entered the campaign as a candidate for the Virginia Convention that would vote on ratification of the Constitution. His opponent was James Madison, who favored ratifying the document. After consultation with Madison relative to providing additional safeguards to religious liberty, Leland announced his support of Madison, who was elected. The Constitution was ratified, and Baptists supported Madison to the first Congress of the United States. In June, 1789, Madison introduced the amendments he had promised to make to the Constitution, the first of which said, "Congress shall make no law respecting an establishment of religion, or prohibiting the free exercise thereof."

    An interesting exchange of correspondence took place between the Committee and the new President of the United States. The General Committee wrote a letter to George Washington in August, 1789, voicing their concern for liberty of conscience in the new Constitution, and expressing the confidence that "if religious liberty is rather insecure in the Constitution 'the administration will certainly prevent all oppression, for a *Washington* will preside.'" Washington replied in a letter of appreciation and assured then that "no one would be more zealous than myself to establish effectual barriers against the horrors of spiritual tyranny, and every species of religious persecution."[11]

---

[11] Baker, *Source Book*, 43-45.

While the principal struggle for religious liberty necessarily took place in the area of most persecution (that is, in Virginia), it is clear from various sources that Baptists in Virginia took counsel with Baptists in other states, both North and South, in this struggle. As early as 1776, North Carolina specifically granted all ministers of every denomination the right to celebrate matrimony and in a Bill of Rights asserted that all men have a natural and inalienable right to worship God according to the dictates of their own consciences. The North Carolina Constitution, adopted in 1776, contained the following religious liberty clause adopted partly as the result of Baptist influence:

> There shall be no establishment of any one religious church or Denomination in this State in Preference to any other, neither shall any person, on any pretense whatsoever, be compelled to attend any place of worship contrary to his own Faith or Judgment, or be obliged to pay for the purchase of any Glebe, or the building of any House of Worship, or for the maintenance of any Minister or Ministry, contrary to what he believes right, or has voluntarily and personally engaged to perform, but all persons shall be at liberty to exercise their own mode of worship.[12]

At the very time this struggle for religious liberty was taking place, Southern Baptists were multiplying in numbers, expanding into new areas, and finding new ways to share the gospel.

---

[12] Ibid., 42.

# Chapter 4 - Post-War Advance

At the same time the political and religious struggles described in the previous chapter were taking place, Southern Baptists experienced solid growth in the older southern states; expanded rapidly westward; participated in a widespread revival that began west of the Alleghenies in the opening years of the nineteenth century; and shared the missionary impulse generated by William Carey, which was implemented by the Second Great Awakening in New England and emphasized by the spiritual needs of the immigrants on the receding frontier.

## Second Great Awakening in the South

During the American Revolution and immediately thereafter, the vitality of Christianity in America fell to low ebb. Part of the reason was the bitterness and cynicism that war always brings. In addition, English deism and French infidelity greatly influenced the colonies. The anti-Christian writings of Voltaire (1694-1778) in France and Thomas Paine (1737-1809) in America were widely circulated. The 1790 census reported only 275,000 out of 3,929,214 inhabitants in the new nation to be Christians. Remarkable religious awakenings, however, took place both in New England and in the South. There was considerable difference between the Second Great Awakening in New England around the turn of the eighteenth century and the earlier First Awakening stirred up by Whitefield. The Second Awakening in New England had less emotional excitement, little immediate controversy over methods of revival, and fewer outstanding leaders. Most of the power of the Second Awakening consisted not simply in large numbers of additions to the churches, but as well in the initiation of extensive benevolent Christian ministries, such as home and foreign missions, Bible distribution, Sunday School extension, the printing and circulation of Christian tracts, and the organization of many societies for carrying on these Christian benevolences.

Although occurring about the same time that the second New England revival took place, a revival of a different sort was begun west of the Alleghenies in Tennessee and Kentucky. Many descriptions have been written of the rough and violent society that had gathered on this southwestern frontier in the closing years of the eighteenth century. Revival for these multitudes began through the agency of James McGready, a Presbyterian minister, who assumed the charge of Presbyterian churches in Logan County, Kentucky, in 1796. As he traveled from one church to another under his supervision, he found responsive hearts and evidences of revival. In 1799 two brothers, William and John Magee, one a Presbyterian and one a Methodist, stirred the fires of revival in both Kentucky and Tennessee as they preached. In July, 1800, the first American camp meeting occurred in Logan County, Kentucky, and great crowds of people from miles around drove to the preaching services. The climax to these meeting came at Cane Ridge, Tennessee, in August, 1801, when between twenty and thirty thousand persons assembled on the camp ground. These meetings in general were characterized by excessive emotional display, including jerks, the barks, dancing, rolling, shouting, fainting, and similar exercises.

Baptists, while engaging in many of these services, for the most part refused to be involved in the emotional manifestations taking place. As has been mentioned already, this revival spread into the older states among the Baptists and spurred revivals there. Benedict described the effect of this awakening upon Kentucky Baptists as follows:

> This great revival in Kentucky began in Boone county on the Ohio River, and in its progress extended up the Ohio, Licking, and Kentucky Rivers, branching out into the settlements adjoining them. It spread fast in different directions, and in a short time almost every part of the State was affected by its influence. It was computed that about ten thousand were baptized and added to the Baptist churches in the course of two or three years. This great work progressed among the Baptists in a much more regular manner than people abroad have generally supposed. They were indeed zealously affected, and much engaged. Many of their ministers baptized in a number of neighboring churches from two to four hundred each. And two of them baptized about five hundred a-piece in the course of the work. But throughout the whole, they preserved a good degree of decorum and order. Those

camp-meetings, those great parades, and sacramental seasons, those extraordinary exercises of falling down, rolling, shouting, jerking, dancing, barking, &c. were but little known among the Baptists in Kentucky, nor encouraged by them.[1]

Part of the increase in Baptist statistics in Kentucky and Tennessee, mentioned heretofore, came from the Baptist participation in the revival in these states.

## The Missionary Impulse

Baptists in America had no organizational structure beyond the local churches from 1639 to 1707 when the Philadelphia Association was formed. The second association (Charleston, South Carolina) was not formed until 1751 and was a direct offshoot from the Philadelphia body. It was promoted by one of her ministers who had accepted the pastorate in South Carolina. It took more than a full century after the first association was organized to develop a general denominational body for missionary purposes, and the first state convention was not formed until 1821.

This rather long period of time before bodies beyond the local congregation were formed suggests that American Baptists were true followers of the principle of congregational authority. Other denominational bodies beyond the local congregations were important for the *bene esse* (well being) but not the *esse* (being) of Baptist life. This point of view reflected explicit statements by English Baptists of the seventeenth century. John Smyth, for example, in an answer to Henry Ainsworth in his *Paralleles* said that "Christ's ruling power is originally and fundamentally in the body of the Church, the multitude." He voiced the belief that "the last definitive determining sentence is in the body of the Church." Both the General and the Particular Baptists in England followed this view. In the Confession of Faith of 1611, Thomas Helwys reflected the language of Smyth as in Article XI he defined the church as consisting of particular congregations, with each congregation a whole church and authoritative. The Particular Baptist confession of 1644 said in Article XXXVI that every individual church has power given them from Christ for their better well-being

---

[1] David Benedict. *A General History of the Baptist Denomination in America and Other Parts of the World* (Boston: Lincoln and Edwards), II, 251-52.

to choose to themselves meet persons into the office of Pastors, Teachers, Elders, Deacons, being qualified according to the Word, as those which Christ has appointed in his Testament, for the feeding, governing, serving, and building up of his Church, and that none other have power to impose them, either these or any other.[2]

It was the departure of General Baptists from this earlier principle of the autonomy of the local body that caused the downfall of the General Assembly of General Baptists. Conversely, the extreme efforts of the Particular Baptists to maintain the total autonomy of the local congregations left their general body without effective powers.

American Baptists maintained this view of the authority of local bodies. The first association in the colonies was organized in 1707 at Philadelphia. In 1749 this body adopted an essay on the power of an association and specifically said that

> each particular church hath a complete power and authority from Jesus Christ, to administer all gospel ordinances, provided they have a sufficiency of officers duly qualified, or that they be supplied by the officers of another sister church or churches, as baptism, and the Lord's supper, &c.; and to receive in and cast out, and also to try and ordain their own officers, and to exercise every part of gospel discipline and church government, independent of any other church or assembly whatever.[3]

In the correspondence of the Philadelphia Association during the eighteenth century, it is clear that the Association was quite sensitive to the authority of the churches at every point. In 1768, for example, it was reiterated that "the Association claims no jurisdiction, nor a power to repeal any thing settled by any church; but if, before settlement, parties agree to refer matters to the Association, then to give their advice."[4]

In the South, it will be recalled that one reason for the division of the Sandy Creek Association in 1770 was the "improper stretch of associational power." It will also be recalled that in Virginia as late as 1778

---

[2] McGlothlin, *Baptist Confessions of Faith*, 184.
[3] Baker, *Source Book*, 17.
[4] Ibid., 18

there was a serious debate as to whether any extra-church body like the association was necessary. It was finally agreed that so long as an association did not threaten the authority of the churches, it was helpful for advice and counsel.

However, American Baptists in the South as in the North saw the necessity of organization beyond the local level for inspiration, fellowship, and the achievement of tasks too large for a single church. Committees of correspondence were established in Virginia, the Carolinas, and Georgia, and were influential in assisting Baptists in the struggle for religious liberty. In the case of Virginia, their General Committee of Correspondence had fraternal relations with Baptist bodies in the North, as well.

Baptists in the North, perhaps as a reflection from the political developments in that area, were quite sensitive to the need for more cooperation on the part of Baptists. As early as 1767, when the Warren Association was formed, the Philadelphia Association wrote to the leaders of the new body and said:

> For, as particular members are collected together and united in one body, which we call a particular Church, to answer those ends and purposes which could not be accomplished by any single member, so a collection and union of churches into one associational body may easily be conceived capable of answering those still greater purposes which any particular Church could not be equal to. And, by the same reason, a union of associations will still increase the body in weight and strength, and make it good that a three-fold cord is not easily broken.[5]

Four years later Morgan Edwards suggested a plan by which the Philadelphia Association might be incorporated and delegates from other associations be admitted to the corporation to form a type of national body. In 1775 the Warren Association (Rhode Island) urged that a meeting be called of delegates from Baptist bodies in every colony to forward religious liberty. A "Continental Association" was called to meet in 1776, perhaps a reflection of the Continental Congress which was then in

---

[5] Quoted by W. W. Barnes, *The Southern Baptist Convention* (Nashville: Broadman Press, 1954), 2, from R. A. Guild, "The Denominational Work of President Manning," *Baptist Review*, II (1880), 559.

session, but the religious meeting was not held. In 1799 the Philadelphia Association called for a national meeting of all Baptist bodies to form a General Conference "composed of one member, or more, from each Association, to be held every *one, two,* or *three* years, as might seem most subservient to the general interests of Christ's kingdom."[6] At the turn of the century Richard Furman of Charleston was in correspondence with northern leaders concerning a possible national union of all Baptists.

Despite all of this agitation for a general body, Baptists were not willing to organize such a structure unless they saw a real necessity for it. That real necessity occurred in the great missionary impulse. The desire to win others beyond the local church field can be called either evangelism or missions. At any rate, warmhearted pastors quite early in American Baptist history began itinerating for the purpose of winning others to Christ. An example was John Clarke, a pastor at Newport, who traveled to various sections of New England for gospel preaching. The nest step, as Albert L. Vail pointed out, was the missionary church. The outstanding example of this was the Sandy Creek church in North Carolina with Shubal Stearns and Daniel Marshall as its leaders. Other examples were the church at Middletown, New Jersey, under the leadership of Abel Morgan; Cazenovia, New York, under John Mason Peck; and Brentwood, New Hampshire, under Samuel Shepherd.

Not unexpectedly, the Philadelphia Association, the first in America, became a missionary body, although tardy in this movement. Vail remarked:

> The year 1755 is the fountain-head year of Baptist mission work in America beyond the individual and the church. In this year the Philadelphia Association first reached the realization of itself as a missionary organization.[7]

In that year two ministers were appointed to visit North Carolina, their expenses to be borne by the several churches making up the associational structure. In 1766 another large step was taken by the Philadelphia Association, when a permanent missionary fund was provided "the interest whereof to be by them laid out every year in support

---

[6] John Rippon, ed., *The Baptist Annual Register* (London, 1790-1802), II.,262.
[7] Albert L. Vail, *The Morning Hour of American Baptist Missions* (Philadelphia: American Baptist Publication Society, 1911), 309.

of ministers traveling on the errand of the churches, or otherwise, as the necessities of said churches shall require." This fund was developed through quarterly collections by the churches to be handled by trustees of the Association. By 1773 the fund had grown to over five hundred dollars. Other associations, as they were formed, followed the example of the Philadelphia. In 1751 the Charleston, in 1758, the Sandy Creek, and in 1767, the Warren Association of Rhode Island became involved in associational missionary programs. The climax to the associational method of missionary work came in 1802 when the Shaftsbury Association of Vermont adopted a plan that resembled on a small scale the type of structure subsequently adopted by the Southern Baptist Convention; namely, a committee of the association was appointed to handle mission contributions, examine the candidates, recommend the time and place of appointments, and pay salaries of missionaries.[8] Two years later, a plan was developed to make pledges in advance for missionary contributions. Other associations followed suit, and it appeared that missions, both domestic and foreign (as some associations sent missionaries into Canada) were firmly entrenched in the hands of associational bodies.

However, this kind of organizational mission structure was challenged by another method. William Carey in England had made impassioned appeals to the association in 1792. In America, this missionary society method was eagerly adopted, at first including members of various denominations who were endeavoring to minister to the Indians and others in their immediate vicinity. Vail listed five of these societies, beginning in 1796, with which Baptists were connected. The very simplicity of the pattern made it appealing, for weak and unorganized denominations who could not afford to carry on extensive missionary operations even if they had been organized to do so, could have members in this type of society base strictly upon what each person felt that he could do. In addition, without authorization from any denomination, without previous experience, without a complex pattern, a small group of individuals could meet in a home, take a small offering, and use the funds as seemed best to them.

---

[8] Baker, *Source Book*, 24-26.

The climax to the society type of structure came on May 26, 1802, when the Massachusetts Baptist Missionary Society was organized. Three missionaries were appointed, not for full-time service but for taking certain missionary tours. One of these, Joseph Connell, traveled northward through New York beginning on December 2 and in a sixteen-week tour preached in many areas of Canada.[9]

Thus, by 1802 there were two types of missionary structure among American Baptists. As fully developed, the two methods presented different philosophies, one of which (the society) was used by Baptists in the North until 1907, while the other (the associational) was used by Southern Baptists from the beginning to the present.

Some of the differences between these two methods are quite evident. The associational method was *geographically* based, while the society method was *financially* based. That is, as associations became more completely geographically oriented, the support of the missionary projects of an association included those who were geographically a part of the area covered by a particular association. The society method, on the other hand, could never be limited by geography. Those individuals interested in giving to missions, regardless of geography or structural form, were related immediately to the enterprise by the giving of their money to society.

Another difference between the two methods of operation was that the associational method usually involved a denominational structure fostering many benevolences, while the society became involved with only one benevolence. In the former, a denominational body (the association) already in existence simply took up another aspect of denominational life, which was added to other benevolent activities such as the education of the ministry, the publication of circular letters on doctrine and program, etc. The missionary society, on the other hand, had no other interest than missions, foreign missions, or publication and tract work. If additional benevolences were to be undertaken, a new society for each one would be organized.

A third difference between the two methods was the relationship sustained to the churches. Under the associational plan, as developed, no one could engage in the missionary program unless he was a member of a

---

[9] Ibid., 26, has the constitution of the new society.

church related to the association. That is to say, relationship to the program was channeled through the agency of the churches as they in turn were a part of the associational ministry. On the other hand, although it was expected that a member of a missionary society would be a member of a Baptist church, the relationship of the individual to the society was in no way connected with the relationship of the church to the society. The churches were entirely bypassed in this type of mission program, as pointed out by President Francis Wayland of Brown University during the abolitionist controversy.[10]

A fourth difference between the two methods was the fact that the associational method was denominationally centered, while the society plan was benevolence centered. Under the associational plan all of the interests of the denomination were fostered through the association, and the missionary program, as one part of the entire denominational thrust, had its place. The interests of the entire denominational program were always considered in setting up the mission program of an association. On the other hand, a missionary society was totally autonomous and utilized its entire efforts in one direction only; viz., for the promotion of the particular benevolence represented by that society. Thus, the focus of the individual in the missionary society was not primarily on the balanced objectives of the whole denomination, but rather upon the immediate work and finances of the particular society to which he belonged. Ultimately, this was the principle that brought the change from the missionary society plan in the North in 1907 and the development of the Northern Baptist Convention.

Finally, there was an interdependent and connectional relationship in all the benevolent work through the association that was not evident in the independent and voluntary societies for a particular benevolence.

Before 1814, then, American Baptists had developed two rather distinct methods of carrying on benevolent work. One looked toward a denominational body with churches as its base; the other emphasized a society entirely separate from the churches and consisting solely of individuals interested in missions. Vail remarked that it was the "collision

---

[10] See also Vail, *American Baptist Missions*, 150-55; and Robert A. Baker, *Relations Between Northern and Southern Baptists*, 2nd ed., (Fort Worth: 1954), 15. Note also Wayland's earlier essays that set forth this view, which can be found in Baker, *Source Book*, 70-71.

of these two currents" of thought that produced a "revolution" in Baptist organizational life.[11] The victory was quickly, although temporarily, won by the society method. Although the associations had been conducting missionary work for over half a century, within a decade the society plan was almost universally adopted in American Baptist life. In the opening decade of the nineteenth century, Vail estimated that at least sixty-five societies were organized north of Philadelphia alone to raise money for missions. He felt that the principal reason for this revolutionary change to the society method took place because of the extreme sensitiveness of the Baptist churches and leaders toward the development of ecclesiastical bodies that might usurp the autonomy of the local congregations. He wrote:

> The excessive sensitiveness in behalf of church independency then characteristic of Baptists probably had influence. In those times even the Association must protest its innocency on this score very distinctly. The churches were exceedingly jealous for their authority. We have seen how long the Philadelphia Association fumbled over this point, and when the Warren came into being it was under keen suspicion, so that at first some of the best pastors stood aloof. This state of mind prevailed more or less everywhere, and although necessity had pushed the Associations into mission work, it had been done gingerly and from hand to mouth in the main. In this situation the society opened the way out of some of the perplexity. The Associations were based in the churches, having some organic or semi-organic relation with them; therefore they were specially and inevitably watched with reference to centralization. But start a society without any direct connection with the churches, and this free from the suspicion of usurpation in that measure of authority essential to effectiveness, and there would be plainer sailing. Mission-minded brethren might tolerate in the society what they would not in the Association, and omission-minded brethren would keep out of the way by keeping out of the society. This might have constituted to judicious and

---

[11] Albert L. Vail, *Baptists Mobilized for Missions* (Philadelphia: American Baptist Publication Society, 1911), 309.

irenic leaders a reason for the society, and probably it was the chief reason with those who thought thoroughly.[12]

## Summary

Between 1740 and 1814, Southern Baptists made substantial advances in many areas. At the opening of the period they had only one organizational structure- the local congregation (although some of the churches of the South were affiliated with the Philadelphia Association, the only one in America until 1751). In the seventy-five years of this period, their churches increased from fewer than 10 to more than 1,282. (The figures from Benedict do not include churches in Louisiana and Missouri, but his Mississippi statistics perhaps include what became the early Alabama churches). The first association in the South was organized in 1751 in South Carolina, and by 1814, there were at least 60 in the South. The total number of Baptists in the South increased from several hundred in 1740 to over 110,514 in 1814.

Revival and migration accounted for growth in the several areas. The First Great Awakening sparked the rise of the Separate Baptists, whose remarkable expansion was responsible for much of the growth. The westward trek accelerated after the Revolution, and by 1810 the South Central states had 708,590 inhabitants, including 166,256 slaves. It is hard to overestimate the effect of this migration on Baptists. Large numbers were transported to the very areas where a democratic people's church movement like that of the Baptists was very popular. The invention of the cotton gin in 1793 rescued and spread the institution of slavery.

The Baptist image was almost totally reversed during this period. They had been vilified and scorned in the pre-Revolutionary period, particularly in Virginia, but their rapid growth, support of the patriot cause, and successful leadership in securing religious liberty enhanced their status. Gewehr judged that the social status of Baptists, even in Virginia, was equal to any other religious group by 1790. Life on the frontier maintained primitive social and economic patterns, and church and revival meetings became a social as well as religious exercise, as neighbors would make long trips from isolated farms to meet for fellowship and worship.

---

[12] Vail, *The Morning Hour of American Baptist Missions*, 150-51.

As many historians have noted, church life provided moral discipline and order on the frontier. Both black and white Baptist members were subjected to rigid surveillance by the corporate religious judicature at the church business session. There are many extant church minutes which paint this picture clearly.[13] The early Baptist associational structure provided a responsible body which had gone beyond the control of the churches.[14] They also engendered a wider fellowship by the exchange of correspondence and by swapping ministerial assistance of various sorts.

Southern Baptists were groping toward a wider unity. The committees of correspondence in the principal southern states presaged the development of the state bodies in the next period. It is likely that the struggle for religious liberty accelerated greatly the uniting of the newer Separate Baptists and the old Regulars. The General Baptists, with their Arminian doctrines, were greatly reduced by the "Calvinizing" activities of the Philadelphia Association and the work of strong individual ministers. Paschal pointed out that only a small percentage of the older General Baptists joined the reconstituted Calvinistic churches. It is likely that the remainder were either swallowed up in the Separate Baptist movement or continued in a local fellowship as a separate group. The integration of the General Baptists, the Regulars, and the Separates laid the doctrinal foundation for the religious activism of Baptists in the South: a mild Calvinism that involved active human agency in spreading the gospel. This stance brought rejection of antimission and anti-effort groups.

The achievement of religious liberty released the Baptists to new opportunities. Their thrust in this period was primarily missionary or evangelistic, but other benevolences were beginning to develop. Before the South had a denominational college, many of the states supported Rhode Island College, later named Brown University.[15] Ministerial education was promoted by societies and associations in several of the

---

[13] See, for example, John Taylor, *A History of Ten Baptist Churches* (Frankfurt, KY: J. H. Holeman, 1823), 75 f.
[14] See Lemuel Burkitt and Jesse Read, *A Concise History of the Kehukee Baptist Association* (Halifax, N. C.: A. Hodge, 1803), 40 ff.
[15] See Reuben A. Guild, *Chaplain Smith and the Baptists* (Philadelphia: American Baptist Publication Society, 1885), 133-34.

southern states. Southern Baptists were ready for the larger challenges of the nineteenth century.

The first half of the nineteenth century was one of the most significant periods in American Baptist history. Most important, chronologically, was the organization of the first Baptist general bodies in America for benevolent purposes. Baptists in the North and South cooperated in these enterprises. The story will be told in this chapter. Contemporaneously, Baptists in the southern states advanced rapidly in many ways, coming to a climax with the sectional division between northern and southern Baptists in 1845.

The thirty-one years between 1814 and 1845 marked an era of organized benevolent activity by northern and southern Baptists on a national scale. Structural and methodological patterns were developed that still influence Baptist thinking. In the midst of an exciting and revolutionary era, American Baptists united to meet the challenge of missions abroad and at home.

# Chapter 5 - Baptists United for Benevolence

The first half of the nineteenth century was one of the most significant periods in American Baptist history. Most important, chronologically, was the organization of the first Baptist general bodies in America for benevolent purposes. Baptists in the North and South cooperated in these enterprises. The story will be told in this chapter. Contemporaneously, Baptists in the southern states advanced rapidly in many ways, coming to a climax with the sectional division between northern and southern Baptists in 1845.

The thirty-one years between 1814 and 1845 marked an era of organized benevolent activity by northern and southern Baptists on a national scale. Structural and methodological patterns were developed that still influence Baptist thinking. In the midst of an exciting and revolutionary era, American Baptists united to meet the challenge of missions abroad and at home.

Three principal benevolent societies were formed jointly by northern and southern Baptists: one for foreign missions (the General Missionary Convention of the Baptist Denomination in the United States for Foreign Missions) in 1814; one for the publication and distribution of religious tracts (the Baptist General Tract Society) in 1824; and one for home missions (the American Baptist Home Mission Society) in 1832. The organization of these three societies and the work that they did during the united period will be the burden of this chapter.

## The General Missionary Convention

The initial factor that led to the organization of a foreign mission society among American Baptists was the beginning of the modern foreign missionary movement in England by William Carey in 1792. American societies were formed to support Carey, and the several denominations in England and America were challenged to become active in this new and blessed ministry. In the midst of this milieu, and perhaps encouraged by it, the Second Great Awakening in New England occurred with the coming of the nineteenth century. This Awakening was different in character from the First Great Awakening of about 1740. There was less emotional excitement and mass evangelism, and much of the power of the revival was channeled into benevolent activity for advancing the Christian cause, similar to the work of Carey. Increased efforts were made to evangelize the American Indians, and the Christianizing of the American frontier was vigorously attempted. American Congregationalists formed their American Board of Commissioners in 1810 to begin foreign mission work. Baptists developed their foreign mission body in 1814. An interdenominational society for Bible printing and distribution was begun in 1816, along with the American Sunday School Union in 1824 and the American Home Mission Society in 1826. Baptists formed their Tract Society in 1824, just one year before the interdenominational American Tract Society. Baptists organized their Home Mission Society in 1832.

In addition to bringing into existence these various benevolent organizations for Christian activity, the Second Great Awakening undoubtedly played a substantial role through Charles G. Finney and Theodore D. Weld in laying the foundations for the abolitionist movement of the fourth decade.

Two men were involved in this flurry of missionary organization and activity after the turn of the century. Both of them were initially related to the American Board of Commissioners of the Congregationalists, and both of them played large roles in the organization of the first foreign mission general body by American Baptists in 1814. These two men were Adoniram Judson and Luther Rice.

Judson was born at Malden, Massachusetts, on August 9, 1788. His father was a Congregational minister. Graduating from brown University in 1808, young Judson entered Andover Seminary, and, caught up in the desire to take the gospel around the world to every creature, he along with other Andover student petitioned the Congregational Association of Massachusetts for advice and assistance. In 1810, the Congregationalists organized the American Board of Commissioners for Foreign Missions. On February 5, 1812, Judson marries Ann Hasseltine, and two weeks later the couple sailed for India as missionaries of the Congregational Board. On February 14, 1813, Ann Hasseltine wrote her parents and sisters to say that en route to India, "Knowing he [Judson] should meet the Baptists at Serampore, he felt it important to attend to it [the Baptist position] more closely, to be able to defend his sentiments."[1] That is to say, he knew that William Carey, Joshua Marshman, and William Ward had been on the field for about two decades and that he would be expected to be able to give an accounting for the faith that was in him. Thus, simply the presence of Carey and others in India turned Judson toward serious consideration of his denominational views. After several weeks of intensive study in Serampore, Judson addressed a letter to Carey, Marshman, and Ward, in Calcutta on August 27, 1812, advising them of his entire conviction "that the immersion of a professing believer is the only Christian baptism." He then asked for Mrs. Judson and himself the opportunity to "profess our faith in Christ by being baptized in obedience to his sacred commands." On September 1, 1812, Judson sent his letter of resignation to the Congregational Board, and on the same day wrote Lucius Bolles, a prominent American Baptist, appealing to Baptists in American for support in his mission work.[2]

At the very time these things were taking place, one of Judson's companions was undergoing a similar experience. Luther Rice was born at Northborough, Massachusetts, on March 25, 1783. When almost nineteen, he joined a Congregationalist church. Two years later he entered Leicester Academy and in October, 1807, enrolled at Williams College as a sophomore. He was a member of the famous Haystack Prayer Meeting group, and in 1810 was one of several, including Judson, who urged the Congregationalists to form a foreign mission body. Rice was appointed to go to India on the condition that he should raise the necessary money for expenses to reach the field. On a ship separate from that of Judson, Rice sailed on February 18, 1812, for Calcutta. He also became convinced by independent study of the correctness of the Baptist position. On November 1, 1812, he was baptized by William Ward, who had also baptized Judson and Ann Hasseltine. On October 23, 1812, he wrote Thomas Baldwin, prominent Boston pastor, concerning his change of views and soliciting Baptist support.[3]

Baptists in America received several letters from the English missionaries in India urging them to form a missionary society to support

---

[1] Baker, *Source Book*, 53.
[2] Ibid.
[3] Ibid., 55-56.

these new missionaries. When some influential American Baptist leaders suggested that English Baptists assume the care of the Judsons and Rice, the English missionaries in India urgently replied that this was the time for American Baptists to begin this important enterprise. The gracious nature of William Carey is suggested in one of his letters, probably about December 20, 1812. Despite the fact that at this very time America was at war with England, Carey, after urging American Baptists to begin this important enterprise. The gracious nature of William Carey is suggested in one of his letters, probably about December 20, 1812. Despite the fact that at this very time America was at war with England, Carey, after urging American Baptists to "take these two brethren under their protection," ended up by saying, "We shall not desert them, nor their companions, should they be in want."[4]

In an earlier letter William Carey said to Thomas Baldwin, "Do stir in this business; this is a providence which gives a new turn to American relations to Oriental Missions."[5] There is evidence of a peculiar providence that shaped the events of these days. For one thing, there had been an extensive amount of missionary correspondence between Carey and his companions in India and American Baptist leaders, particularly William Rogers and William Staughton of Philadelphia, and Thomas Baldwin of Boston.

Not only so, but what was considered a harsh blow turned out to be the forwarding of the gospel. In the opening years of the nineteenth century the British East India Company resented the English Baptist missionaries working in India, feeling that it would hurt their business if the masses were Christianized. After many threats, the blow finally fell: no more missionaries would be allowed to sail from England to India. Through their control of shipping between England and India, the British East India Company felt that they could stop any missionary from making the journey. However, providentially the missionaries were routed by way of America. In America these dedicated men would sometimes have to wait many weeks before a ship could be found to take them from America to India. While they waited, they stayed in the homes of American Baptists leaders, sharing their zeal for foreign missions with American

---

[4] Ibid., 59.
[5] Ibid., 58.

Baptists. For about ten years American Baptists were conditioned in this way to begin their own foreign mission program.

Furthermore, Baptists leaders knew that it would be possible to raise funds for foreign missions among the Baptist people in America. Out of the contributions made to send Rice and the Judsons to India, more than $3,000 was given by American Baptists. Not only so, but American Baptists contributed over $20,000 for foreign missions during the years 1806 through 1814.

It is no wonder, then that in Octobers, 1812, upon learning about the Judsons and Rice, Boston Baptists promptly organized a society by the name of The Baptist Society for Propagating the Gospel in India and Other Foreign Parts."[6] Other societies were organized elsewhere, including one at Savannah, Georgia. Meanwhile, it was agreed by the three missionaries in India that one must return to raise funds to support that others and the logical one was Luther Rice. He returned to Boston in September, 1813, and at the suggestion of the New England leaders, made an extensive tour through the seaboard states as far south as Georgia.

In December, 1813, edition of *The Massachusetts Baptist Missionary Magazine,* the editor reported that Luther Rice had been received in every part of the country with utmost cordiality, and had suggested that delegates promptly be appointed to meet in Philadelphia to organize a national body for missionary work.

**Organization of the Foreign Mission Body.** On May 18, 1814, at the First Baptist Church in Philadelphia, thirty-three representatives (of whom more than half were from the Philadelphia Association) organized the General Missionary Convention of the Baptist Denomination in the United States of America for Foreign Missions. Difficulty in preparing an agreeable constitution was experienced, and the convention was in session, forenoon and afternoon of each day except Sunday, from Wednesday, May 18, until Tuesday, May 24. Albert L. Vail paid tribute to these pioneers and the work of their hands in eloquent words.

> The modifying of this constitution will soon begin, indeed; the responses of the denomination will be comparatively sluggish, fluctuating, and inadequate: sources then inspected of disruption

---

[6] Ibid., 56.

will arise, waves of protest and assault will surge against the craft there launched, the ambitions of men, the defections of friends, the deficiencies of missionaries and administrators, will follow each other and combine with each other to wreck the enterprise almost; but that was begun there on which God will lay his hand to steady it when men stumble, and crown it when human laurels fail! For that was in some appreciable sense the inauguration of one of the great forces for the salvation of the world. And it may be deliberately questioned whether any Baptist vote ever meant more for the denomination or for mankind.[7]

**Struggle for Direction.** At the very time this convention met in 1814, there had been two points of view concerning the proper type of denominational structure for a general body carrying on missionary work among Baptists. The associational method of organization stressed denominationalism, while the society type magnified church independency and benevolences. These two divergent types of thought unquestionably met in the Philadelphia meeting, and part of the extended length of the meeting probably stemmed from warm discussion at this point. A compromise resulted. The new organization had elements of both views. Two things suggested the influence of the associational stream of thought. (1) The organization was given a denominational name – the General Missionary Convention of the Baptist Denomination in though United States of America for Foreign Missions. Because the constitution arranged that the body should meet every three years, this organization was popularly known as the Triennial Convention. (2) It constituency, according to Vail, included only Baptist organizations – societies, churches, and other groups, but no individuals. It should be said, however, that Francis Wayland interpreted the constitution to mean that individuals formed the base.[8] On the other hand, there were elements suggesting the society idea in the constitution, for its specifically named one benevolence only (foreign missions) as its object. Furthermore, membership was fixed upon a modified money basis, thus reproducing to some extent the *modus operandi*. Of the society plan of operation, rather

---

[7] Vail, *The Morning Hour of American Baptist Missions*, 384-85.
[8] Francis Wayland, *Notes on the Principles and Practices of Baptist Churches* (Boston: Gould and Lincoln, 1856), 184.

than the associational idea which permitted *all* churches to associate themselves together regardless of financial contributions.

The body had hardly been organized before evidences of the struggle for direction were apparent. Luther Rice himself favored a strong denominational body. In his diary he noted:

> While passing from Richmond to Petersburg in the stage, an enlarged view of the business opened upon my contemplations. The plan which suggested itself to my mind, that of forming one principal society in each state, bearing the name of the state, and others in the same state, auxiliary to that: and by these large, or state societies, delegates be appointed to form one general society.[9]

It is hardly coincidental that Rice received this impression while traveling in the South, for Southern Baptists in general held more centralized views organizationally than did Baptists in the North. In fact, Rice probably received a suggestion from W. B. Johnson at this point.[10]

It appeared that the denominational proponents would achieve a quick victory. At the first triennial meeting in 1817, in a carefully worded statement the convention voted "That the powers of this Convention be extended so as to embrace home missions and plans for the encouragement of education."[11] Perhaps the influence of Richard Furman of South Carolina was involved in this move. In his presidential address in 1817, Furman had said, "The same gracious direction which it becomes all Missionary Societies earnestly to solicit, and conscientiously to obey, is opening other spheres on our own continent." Furman continued by observing the need for home mission in New Orleans and in the West, as well as the great opportunities in the field of education. Relative to the latter, he mentioned that a scheme for carrying out this benevolence had been suggested to the board, and added, "It is hoped that something on this point will be speedily and vigorously attempted."

As a result, the General Missionary Convention modified its original plan to promote only foreign missions, and, a mentioned, voted to include home missions and the sponsorship of a Baptist college. John M.

---

[9] Baker, *Source Book*, 67.
[10] See *The Christian Index* (Georgia), January 27, 1835.
[11] Baker, *Source Book*, 67.

Peck and James E. Welch were appointed as missionaries in Missouri Territory. They were set apart in a moving service of dedication for home mission work.[12] Columbian College was chartered in 1821, and opened in Washington, D.C., in that year under the auspices of the General Convention.

The adoption of these additional benevolences was a definite move toward the associational emphasis, for if this body were to assume control of all benevolent interests of all of its constituent members, it would become a general denominational body according to the associational pattern. The flow of favorable public opinion evidently when the additional functions of the convention were recognized and perhaps the avenues were opened for additional enlargement in various directions by the adoption of an addendum to the title showing the object of the body, which said, "for foreign missions and other important objects relating to the Redeemer's kingdom."

Still another factor moving American Baptists toward the organization of a denominational-type structure was the development of the first Baptist state convention in America in 1821 by South Carolina Baptists. Its original constitution described the state convention as a "coalition of Associations," and its membership consisted of delegates from the associations in the state, along with representatives from other religious bodies of the Baptist faith. Richard Furman was the first president of this state body, which has another characteristic of the associational or denominational type of structure; namely, it looked toward the promotion of many benevolences, not just one. Interestingly enough, the editors of the *American Baptist Magazine* in Boston, Massachusetts, taking note with favor of the action of the South Carolina group, urged that a state body be established in Massachusetts, remarking, "Our Associations united our churches, why should not a Convention unite our associations?"[13] Other signs hinted that at the 1826 meeting there would surely come a strong movement to develop a national body for Baptists based upon delegates from various state bodies that were rapidly organizing.

---

[12] Ibid.
[13] Ibid., 76-77.

One important factor looked in this direction was a series of articles written by Francis Wayland, at that time the associate editor to Thomas Baldwin of the *American Baptist Magazine* in Boston. Baldwin's centralizing ideas were well known, and doubtless he influenced his associate at this point. Under the pseudonym "Backus," Wayland wrote six letters between November, 1823, and May, 1824, in which he made observations about contemporary Baptist organizational forms and suggested ways of improvement. The first four letters described the defects of the contemporary system: the most striking defect was that the plan was unfinished, in that there was no national body that represented Baptists in the various parts of the nation; the associations should send delegates to a general convention, this bringing the whole denomination into concentrated and unified action; the General Missionary Convention

> at present is composed of delegates from missionary societies, and of course must, in its very nature, be mostly composed of persons elected from the vicinity of its place of meeting. And besides, were the meeting ever so universally attended, its foundation is radically defective. A missionary society is not a representative body, nor can any number of them speak the language of a whole denomination.... Every one sees at a glance the difference between the representative of a state convention, which comprised two or three hundred churches within its limits, and thus the bearer of their opinions, and him who is only the delegate from a missionary society which contributes fifty or one hundred dollars to the treasury.[14]

In fact, Wayland went so far as to suggest a Baptist world alliance whereby "Baptists on both sides of the Atlantic, would be united together in a solid phalanx."[15]

Just prior to the 1826 meeting, Luther Rice reflected these statements of Wayland in his suggestion that the missionary body be changed into a structured denominational body through state convention representation.

---

[14] Ibid., 68-71.
[15] Ibid., 71.

However, as Winthrop Hudson has pointed out, the very man who had spoken so clearly in the *American Baptist Magazine* (Francis Wayland) became the leader of the movement which reversed all centralizing trends that looked toward a more rigid denominational structure. With the aid of the Massachusetts and New York delegates, who constituted almost two thirds of the entire General Convention of 1826, three major goals were accomplished—Columbian College was separated from the convention, Boston was able to retain control of the foreign mission program, and the proposal to centralize the convention by causing it to be composed of delegates from state conventions was defeated.[16] The *American Baptist Magazine* for June, 1826, and July, 1826, reported the removal of the seat of foreign missions from Washington to Boston and the elimination of the educational program, and gave reasons for this action.[17] Later on Francis Wayland, without describing his own radical reversal in thinking, made reference to the struggle in these words:

> An attempt was made, pretty early in the history of this organization, to give it the control over all our benevolent efforts. It was proposed to merge in it our Education Societies, tract Societies, Home Mission Societies, and our Foreign Mission Societies, so that one central Board should have the management of all our churches, so far as their efforts to extend the kingdom of Christ were concerned. After a protracted debate, this measure was negative by so decided a majority that the attempt was never repeated, and this danger was averted. We look back, at the present day, with astonishment that such an idea was ever entertained.[18]

As the result of this internal struggle, American Baptists in 1826 chose to decentralize their denominational operations and utilize only the society plan, previously described, for all general benevolent work. As will be seen shortly, new societies, each autonomous in itself, were organized for additional benevolences. This remained the principal denominational

---

[16] See Winthrop Hudson, "Stumbling Into Disorder," in *Foundations*, April, 1958, 55-71.
[17] Baker, *Source Book*, 71-73.
[18] Wayland, *Principles and Practices,* 185.

structure, with some variations in representation in the societies, until 1907 in Northern Baptist life.

**Work of General Missionary Convention.** The activity of the convention during thirty-one years between 1814 and 1845 falls naturally into two sections, separated by the years 1832. From 1814 to 1832 the principal fields were Burma and Africa, although between 1820 and 1822 India was briefly entered, and in 1832 a beginning was made in Siam.

From the early center at Rangoon, the work was expanded into other sections of Burma. Particularly in 1826, when George Dana Boardman began a new mission in eastern Burma, this expansion accelerated. Although Boardman died in 1831, he had enlarged the vision and work in India, including extension into Tavoy and, after his death, the opening of a center in Siam. The work of Judson in Burma struck a responsive chord in the hearts of American Baptists. The imprisonment of Judson during the first Burman war between 1823 and 1826 brought to him great suffering, followed shortly by the death of his beloved Ann Hasseltine. It is likely that these sacrifices inspired the expansion of Baptist work after the war. By 1832 there were 14 missionaries in Burma, 5 more under appointment, and another 5 awaiting appointment.

Missionary work in Africa was begun at the initiative of the African Baptist Mission Society formed in Richmond by blacks in 1814. In 1819 the General Convention assisted financially in the sending of Lott Carey and Collin Teague to what became Liberia. Calvin Holton was the first white missionary to be sent to Africa by Baptists in 1824. However, due to the diseases and fevers that attacked white missionaries in Liberia, it became necessary to withdraw the white missionaries from the field for a season.

The second period of activity brought a considerable enlargement of the program of this body. France was entered in 1833; the incomparable John G. Oncken began work in Germany in 1834, which soon spread under his influence to Denmark to the north and Switzerland to the south; J. Lewis Shuck and his wife were sent to China in 1835; and in 1836, South India and Assam were entered.

By 1845 the reports of the General Missionary Convention revealed an impressive achievement in foreign mission work. Curiously enough, until 1865 work among Indians in North America was included in the foreign mission program. By 1845 the convention had work among the Ojibwas, Ottawas, Tonamondas, Tuscaroras, Shawanos, Cherokees, Creeks, and Choctaws. In the European field, which included France, Germany, Denmark, and Greece, the report in 1844 showed 3 missions, 21 stations and 34 outstations, 4 preachers, and 5 female assistants, 28 native preachers and assistants, 28 churches with 900 members and 123 baptized the previous year, and 1 school with 50 pupils. In the African field, the report showed 1 missionary, 2 stations and 1 outstation, 2 preachers with 1 assistant and 2 female assistants, 2 native assistants, 1 church with 24 members, and 2 schools. In the Asiatic field, which included Burma, Siam, China, Assam, and India, the report showed 7 missions with 51 stations and outstations, 66 missionaries and assistants and 84 native assistants, 34 churches reporting 2,360 baptisms in 1844 along with 2,257 members, and 42 schools with about 1,000 students.

In a recapitulation of this significant work, the 1845 report named 17 distinct missions, 130 stations and outstations, 109 missionaries and assistant missionaries of whom 42 were preachers, 123 native preachers and assistants, 79 churches, 2,593 baptisms, more than 5,000 church members, and 1,350 students in 56 schools.

## The Baptist General Tract Society

The second of the important societies organized by American Baptists in the united period between 1814 and 1845 was body to publish Baptist tracts and distribute them. Impetus was given to this movement by the beginning of the foreign mission program in 1814. As early as 1819 or 1820 such leaders as Luther Rice, William Staughton, and Irah Chase, among others, were discussing the need for establishing a Baptist tract society.

A dramatic scene may have provided the inspiration for the organization of the body. At Washington, particularly among the leaders who had moved the seminary from Philadelphia to the nation's capital in 1820, repeated calls came to establish a tract society for Baptists. Luther Rice, George Wood, James D. Knowles (editor of the *Columbian Star*) along with preachers like O. B. Brown and William Staughton, often met to discuss this project. At one of these meetings a newly-ordained young minister, Noah Davis, was listening to the discussion, when Samuel Cornelius came into the room. He wore a bell-crowned hat, and as he removed it upon coming into the room, out of the tall top of it fell a number of tracts. Cornelius was a walking depository, and this scene so fired the emotions of Davis that he wrote to Editor Knowles proposing a tract society be organized immediately.

As a result, on February 25, 1824, the Baptist General Tract Society was organized and a constitution was adopted.[19] George Wood was named the first General Secretary and served two years. Within ten months 86,500 copies of nineteen tracts were printed. It was soon obvious that a printing center like Philadelphia was needed for this work, and despite the opposition of Luther Rice, who wanted to make Washington a Baptist center of influence, on November 14, 1826, the society moved to Philadelphia. Before 1845 the society had moved five times to different locations in rented quarters in Philadelphia. Financial problems beset them severely during these early years. Between 1824 and 1840 the society issued over 3,500,000 copies of 162 different titles of tracts. Its ministry reached to Burma to help Adoniram Judson and to Germany to assist J. G. Oncken; and by 1838, had provided tracts for Africa, Nova Scotia, Canada, Texas, Mexico, and South America.

A radical reorganization took place in 1840. The constitution of the society was amended to enable it "to publish such books as are needed by the Baptist denomination, and to promote Sunday schools by such measures as experience may prove expedient." The term "books" included tracts, Sunday school books, and biographical, doctrinal, historical, and other religious works, chiefly of a denominational character. A new name was adopted which in 1845 became its permanent title: the American Baptist Publication Society. In the years between 1840 and 1844, the society published 34,750 bound volumes, 5,000 pamphlets, and 266,573 copies of tracts. In addition it circulated over 100,000 bound volumes, of which about one fourth were its own publications.

It should be said that Baptists in the South enthusiastically supported this society. At the close of its second year of history, it had 26 persons enrolled as life-members, of whom 21 were living in the South. Of the $1,010.33 received during the first two years, all but $133.73 came from the South. Noah Davis succeeded Wood as General Secretary and remained until 1830; Ira M. Allen served until 1838; J. Rhees Morgan, from 1840 to 1842; and John M. Peck, from 1843 to 1845.

---

[19] Baker, *Source Book*, 73-74.

## American Baptist Home Mission Society

American Baptists recognized the need for home mission work from their earliest years. Antedating Eliot, Brainerd, and Jonathan Edwards in their ministry with the Indians was Roger Williams, who began preaching to them as early as 1631. Before there was any organized work, warmhearted pastors like John Clarke, at considerable risks to themselves, preached the gospel in a wide area surrounding what is now Rhode Island. As previously pointed out, the Philadelphia Association began a home mission program as early as 1754, which was quickly imitated by other associations as they were organized thereafter. Before 1832 when the American Baptist Home Mission Society was formed, there were Baptist bodies in fourteen stated carrying on home mission work. In the story of the General Missionary Convention it was mentioned that in 1817. Peck was then a young man of twenty-eight years, with a wife and three small children. Peck had met Luther Rice in 1815, and a fire was kindled in his heart to work on the western frontier. Promptly after his appointment, Peck and his family braved the wilderness in a small one-horse wagon for 128 days. He united and inspired the small group of Baptists in the area of St. Louis, and in the following year the Missouri Association was formed. In 1819 his plan for a society to spread the gospel was approved by this association and one in Illinois, and its achievements in missionary work, education, and Indian work were remarkable.

However, in 1820, as has been noted, the General Missionary Convention voted to eliminate home missions form its support, due primarily to the lack of funds and internal opposition. For two years Peck supported himself, and then he was accepted as a missionary by the Massachusetts Baptist Missionary Society. His labors were prodigious. In 1826, while on a visit to the East, Peck met Jonathan Going, pastor of the church at Worcester, Massachusetts. So impressed was the board of the Massachusetts Baptist Missionary Society by the message of Peck that the board requested Going to study the conditions of the western mission fields and report his findings. He arrived at Peck's home on June 20, 1831, five years after their first meeting in Worcester. For three months Going and Peck traveled in Missouri, Illinois, Indiana, and Kentucky, Peck wrote in his journal: "Here we agreed on the plan of The American Baptist Home Mission Society." When Going returned to Massachusetts and reported what he had seen and felt in his journey to the Massachusetts Baptist Missionary Society in November,

> the Board without a dissenting vote solemnly declared its conviction that a general home mission society should be formed, and in a resolution recorded their belief that Jonathan Going himself should give his full time and strength to the promotion of its work.[20]

A committee consisting of Daniel Sharp, Lucius Bolles, and Going went from state to state discussing the need for the general home mission society. As a result a Provisional Committee was formed wand a circular issued to meet on April 27, 1832. This date coincided with the meeting of the General Missionary Convention, and consequently the representation was gratifying, Fourteen out of the twenty-three states and one of the five territories were represented. Careful consideration was given to the kind of organization to be formed. Two distinct plans were debated.

> The first contemplated "an independent society" with officers separate from the General Convention (for foreign missions) and with headquarters at New York City. The second plan proposed that the General Convention be changed from a foreign mission society into a general denominational body with power to appoint a board for foreign missions and one for home missions, "each with their Treasurers and Secretaries, the first to be located at Boston, and the last in this city." The first plan (the *society* method) prevailed, and the constitution provided for the organization of a separate society for domestic missions. The idea of converting the General Convention into a general denominational body was rejected.[21]

On April 27, 1832, the American Baptist Home Mission Society was formed.[22] Its first secretary was Jonathan Going (1832-37), followed

---

[20] Charles L. White, *A Century of Faith* (Philadelphia: American Baptist Publication Society, 1932), 36.
[21] Robert A. Baker, *Relations Between Northern and Southern Baptists* (Fort Worth: Marvin D. Evans Printing Co., 1954), 28.
[22] See Baker, *Source Book*, 74, for its constitution.

by Luther Crawford (1837-39), and Benjamin M. Hill (1839-62) during this united period. Between 1832 and 1845 its contributions and legacies totaled $165,586.71; its missionaries, 1,116; baptisms reported, 14,426; churches organized, 531; and missionary years of labor, 829.[23]

The interest shown in this aspect of mission work is emphasized by the fact that during the first year 50 missionaries served the society in 10 states, 2 territories, and Lower Canada. The western stated included Ohio, Indiana, Michigan, Illinois, Missouri, and Arkansas. In the following year, 80 missionaries were appointed, and work was begun in Louisiana and Upper Canada. By 1835-36 there were 150 missionaries and agents at work in 14 states, 2 territories, and 2 provinces. They supplied 300 churches or congregations, to which 1,040 were admitted by baptism and 736 by letter. These missionaries reached 1,676 people for Christ, helped ordain 33 ministers, constituted 96 churches, and organized 7 associations. Wisconsin and Iowa were entered in 1837, Texas in 1840, and Oregon in 1845.

The work was most difficult. White described some of the problems that constantly faced the missionary in these words:

> Fancy to yourself a man obliged, through a rough country and over rough roads, to travel from thirty to fifty miles a day, without where to lay his head; to preach, to ten or a dozen members in open houses, and be exposed to all kinds of weather, dangers and difficulties; to be opposed and maligned by those calling themselves the children of God, and accused of preaching for lucre's sake- and you have some idea of a missionary.[24]

Some idea as to the rapid development of the ministry of this society can be glimpsed from the reports of the first decade which show that 804 missionaries had been appointed for 31 states and territories, and that a total of $99,368.00 had been expended in this task. In the states of Kentucky, Missouri, Indiana, and Michigan in 1832 there were but 955 Baptist churches, with 484 ministers, only 10 of whom were regular pastors; in contrast in 1842 in the same states there were 1,689 churches with 772 ministers.

---

[23] Henry L. Morehouse, *Baptist Home Missions in North America* (New York: American Baptist Home Mission Society, 1883), 551.
[24] White, *Century of Faith*, 51.

This brief resume of the cooperative work carried on by both Northern and Southern Baptists in the three benevolent societies does not describe the growth and expansion of Baptists in the southern states during this period, nor does it recount the several controversies of the period, one of which caused Northern and Southern Baptists to adopt separate bodies for home and foreign mission in 1845.

In the thirty-one years from 1814 to 1845, Southern Baptists increased form no state bodies to 9, from 60 associations to 213, from 1,282 churched to 4,395, and from a membership of 110,514 to 365,346. This represented an average annual increase in membership of 7.20%, compared with the average annual population growth in the same area of 3.63%, about half the Baptist rate.

The substantial growth of Baptists during this period did not result from sweeping revivals, involving some dominant central figure (like George Whitfield in the previous period) or some single event (like the First Great Awakening). Rather, growth came from active evangelism by warmhearted ministers; more structured missionary work by associations, state bodies, and missionary societies; more structured missionary work by associations, state bodies, and missionary societies; more zeal accelerated by increasing unity in state bodies and the challenge of great benevolent societies on a national scale; the popularity and appeal of the "grass roots" denominations (like Baptists and Methodists) on the western frontier; the improved communication and enlightenment afforded by the publication of Baptist papers in many of the southern states; and the contributions of missionaries appointed by the American Baptist Home Mission Society after 1832. Still an important factor was the nature of Baptist ecclesiology. Where some other denominations had great difficulties relative to securing and supporting proper ministers, Baptist views provided accessible avenues for zealous, self-supporting men to be ordained on the basis of a divine call to preach. Such a situation neglected ministerial education and ecclesiastical support, but under the circumstances it solved knotty problems of ministerial personnel and support and blended well with the democratic ideas of the frontier.

Yet Southern Baptists were already busy during this period in providing educational opportunities for their ministry. The state bodies sprang forth partly as an answer to educational and missionary needs. Four of the seven principal schools founded during this period were advocated fervently in corporate meetings and initiated by the action of the state bodies. This included Furman (South Carolina), whose founding in 1827 followed the action of their convention two years before; Mercer (Georgia), which had opened its doors in 1833 as the result of a resolution at the Georgia Baptist Convention two years before; Wake Forest (North Carolina), begun in 1834 from the initiative of their convention; and Howard (Alabama), whose founding in 1842 followed the action of the state body. Georgetown (Kentucky) in 1829 developed from community action; University of Richmond (Virginia) in 1832 was sponsored by the Virginia Baptist Education Society organized two years before; and Judson (Alabama), opened in 1839 as a school for girls, was initiated by private gifts (including the sponsorship of E. D. King), but was accepted by the state body in 1843. King also had a part in the founding of Howard, now known as Samford University.

E. C. Dargan remarked that the "hireling: ministry under the Virginia establishment and the difficulty of securing an education, particularly for a dissenting clergyman, had initially caused Southern Baptist ministers to pass up "book learning" as not being a significant part of their preparation for ministry; but that during this period the denomination gave more emphasis to "scholarly and accomplished men." The patterns of leaders like Richard Furman, Henry Holcombe, Jesse Mercer, and Richard Fuller, to name a few, commended the use of educational preparation for an effective service. In addition, in one of those curious turns that history occasionally takes, the Campbell controversy distinctly forwarded theological education by showing the need for training to serve apologetic and polemical purposes. Furthermore, Baptist newspapers began to spring up rapidly in this period, providing both stimulation to education and opportunity for its use by Baptist writers. In a little more than a decade, six of the principal Southern Baptist state papers were born: *The Christian Index* (Georgia), 1832; the *Western Recorder* (Kentucky), 1826; the *Religious Herald* (Virginia), 1828; the *Biblical Recorder* (North Carolina), 1833; the *Alabama Baptist* (Alabama), 1835; and the *Baptist and Reflector* (Tennessee), 1835. Other states published less permanent periodicals of various sorts.

Without question, many important contributions to Southern Baptists life flowed from their relationship with the national benevolent societies organized in 1814, 1824, and 1832. Every southern state cooperated with these benevolent societies, inculcating a larger sense of unity than Baptists had ever known. The Bible translation controversy, begun in this period, flowered in Southern Baptist life in the next period. The Campbell and anti-effort excisions from Southern Baptist life were not unmixed evils: by the end of this period most of the dissidents had been expelled or had withdrawn from the large missionary-minded majority of Southern Baptists, and the improved fellowship and cooperative spirit in the ranks of the missionary churches and associations gave impetus to their advance. It should be said, however, that Baptists in some southern states were still involved in the struggle with these alien groups at the end of this period.

Southern Baptists were bound up with the culture of their region. This does not mean that they were substantially involved in slavery, but the one-crop system, predicated upon the use of slave labor, brought almost total collateral economic dependence upon King Cotton. All of society, religion, and economics were affected by this system, and when sectional prejudices and political rivalry over a relatively long period were added to the mixture, an explosion occurred. For American Baptists, this explosion included a rupture of cooperative relations between Baptists North and South.

# Chapter 6 - Divisive Controversies

At the very time Baptists in Philadelphia formed a foreign mission society to support the Judsons and Rice in 1814 and endeavored to find the proper method of structuring their national benevolent bodies, three divisive movements were developing that would either wrench large numbers from Southern Baptist ranks, or, as in the case of the last one, bring a structural separation between Baptists in the North and those in the South in home and foreign missions. These were Campbellism, antimissionism, and sectionalism deepened by the slavery-abolitionist controversy.

Another less significant conflict began during this period, but it had more impact among Southern Baptists during the following one. In 1835 many American Baptists belonged to the American Bible Society, founded in 1816 on an interdenominational basis. Some of them requested that the society aid in printing a Bengali version of the Bible in which Baptist missionaries had translated *baptizein* by the native word for *immerse*. The society refused to aid in a translation of this sort because it would not be used by denominations that did not immerse for baptism. Whereupon, a relatively large number of Baptists organized the American and Foreign Bible Society in 1837 at Philadelphia. When this body in 1850 also declined to print a version of the Bible with the Baptist interpretation of *baptizein*, another Baptist society was formed for this express purpose, called the American Baptist Union. Southern Baptists were in somewhat of a dilemma as to which society to support, as will be noted in the events of the next period.

## Campbellism

Thomas Campbell and his son Alexander were Scotch-Irish Presbyterians, greatly influenced in their Biblicism by men like Greville Ewing, John Glas, and Robert Sandeman in the Glasgow community. In America, after a careful study of the Scriptures, both Campbells and their families were immersed by a Baptist preacher in 1812, and remained loosely affiliated with American Baptist life from then until the 1820's.

However, the theological and practical orientation of Alexander Campbell made him uncomfortable in Baptist life. Even his view of baptism, which had originally turned him toward the Baptists, differed from the Baptist position. Campbell looked upon baptism as the formal washing away of the sins of penitent believers, while Baptists viewed it simply as a symbol of cleansing from sins already forgiven. In 1823 Campbell began publishing *The Christian Baptist* (replaced by *The Millennial Harbinger* in 1829), and this soon became an organ for attacking practically all Baptist beliefs. He opposed missionary societies, Bible societies, Sunday School, and tract societies, ministerial education, salaries to ministers, and similar practices of Baptists.

In 1825 Campbell preached at the Baptist church in Virginia where Robert Semple was pastor, and in December, 1825, Semple wrote Campbell as follows:

> Your opinions on some other points are, I think, dangerous, unless you are misunderstood, such as casting off the Old Testament, exploding experimental religion in its common acceptation, denying the existence of gifts in the present day commonly believed to exist among all spiritual Christians, such as preaching, &c. Your views of ministerial support, directed against abuses on that head, would be useful, but leveled against all support to ministers (unless by way of alms) is so palpably contrary to scripture and common justice, that I persuade myself that there must be some misunderstanding. In short your views are generally so contrary to those of the Baptists in general, that if a part was to go fully into the practice of your principles I should say a new sect had sprung up, radically different from the Baptists, as they are now.[1]

By 1830 the Appomattox Association of Virginia, following the lead of several western associations, condemned the teachings of Campbell and officially advocated disfellowshipping him. The Virginia association specifically condemned Campbell's assertions that there was no promise of salvation without baptism; that baptism should be administered to all who say they believe that Jesus Christ is the Son of

---

[1] Baker, *Source Book*, 77-78.

God without examination on any other point; that there was no direct operation of the Holy Spirit on the mind prior to baptism; that baptism brought the remission of sins and the gifts of the Holy Spirit; that the scriptures were the only evidence of interest in Christ; that obedience placed it in God's power to elect to salvation; that no creed was necessary for the church, but simply the scriptures literally interpreted; and that all baptized persons had a right to administer the ordinance of baptism.[2] About 1832, with Barton W. Stone and others, Alexander Campbell founded the Disciples of Christ.

The movement of Campbell did not make a great impact on the Atlantic seaboard Baptist churches from Pennsylvania and Jersey southward, partly because his Arminian theology could not counter the vigorous Calvinism of that section. West of the Alleghenies, however, the strict Biblicism which he asserted, along with a latent Arminianism that had moved westward after the American Revolution, attracted large number of Baptists. Many Baptist ministers were won to his views and brought their entire churches into his movement. As far west as Texas in 1841, Campbell's followers split Baptist churches.[3] No definite figures are available, but there can be little doubt that hundreds of Baptist churches left the denomination to follow Campbell. State bodies felt the influence of the movement long after the beginning of the next period in 1845.[4]

## Antimissionism

The antimission movement among Southern Baptists has complex roots. Robert G. Torbet is correct in assigning many contributing factors, including theological differences, the development of organizations for carrying on the work, hostility toward the Indians when missions were directed toward them, the fear that eastern leaders might get financial and political control of Baptist church polity through administering the missionary funds, misunderstanding and misinterpretation of the work being done, jealousy toward the better trained clergy of the East who came as missionaries, the low state of vitality in many churches that opposed

---

[2] Ibid., 78.
[3] Robert A. Baker, *The Blossoming Dessert: A Concise History of Texas Baptists* (Waco: Word Books, 1970), 78-81.
[4] See Errett Gates, *The Early Relation and Separation of Baptists and Disciples* (Chicago: R. R Donnelly & Sons, 1904), 67 ff.

anything demanding effort or finances, and the opposition of charismatic leaders. In addition to these, one can glimpse the appeal made by antimission leaders (some of whom tried to leave the impression that they were of the prophetic order), and various other sectional and local factors.[5]

It cannot be determined exactly who began the southern phase of the antimission movement. Daniel Parker claimed to be the first one "to draw the sword against the error," but B. H. Carroll, Jr., doubted the truth of this. Carroll felt that John Taylor of Kentucky, a pioneer in the settlement of Kentucky and Tennessee, antedated Parker in advocating antimissionism. In many ways Taylor was the most admirable of all the antimission leaders, although even his language sometimes was unkind and incorrect. His principal polemic was a pamphlet entitled *Thoughts on Missions*, written on October 27, 1819, when Taylor was sixty-seven years old. In this document Taylor charged that missionaries were simply involved in the movement because of their love for money, and that the missionary system was hierarchical in its tendencies and contrary to Baptist church government.[6]

Daniel Parker first wrote on antimissionism a year after Taylor had published his pamphlet. Parker was born in Culpeper County, Virginia, in 1781, reared in Georgia, and was described by John Mason Peck, who apparently was not impressed by him, as "without education, uncouth in manner, slovenly in dress, diminutive in person, unprepossessing in appearance, with shriveled features and a small, piercing eye."[7]

Parker's doctrine of the *Two Seeds in the Spirit* divided the human race into the predestined children of God and the predestined children of the devil. God will save his own; the devil will claim his own. There was no place for missions in his theology. Most of his ministry was carried on in Tennessee and Illinois. In 1833 he led a church from Illinois into the Mexican province of Texas, probably the first Baptist church there. He

---

[5] Robert G. Torbet, *A History of the Baptists* (Valley Forge: the Judson Press, Fifth Printing, 1953), 268-69.
[6] See Baker, *Source Book*, 79-81, for copious extracts from this pamphlets.
[7] B. H. Carroll, Jr., *The Genesis of American Anti-Missionism* (Louisville: The Baptist Book Concern, 1902), 91.

died in 1844 after organizing a number of churches in east Texas.[8] He greatly influenced Wilson Thompson, another well-known antimissionist.

As has been mentioned previously, Alexander Campbell was also a strong opposer of missions. Most of the other antimission leaders were strong Calvinists or hyper-Calvinists, claiming that it was blasphemy for men to attempt to win people to salvation whom God had not elected, or to try to win people who God had elected, because these efforts amounted to taking the work of God out of God's hands. Campbell, on the other hand, was an Arminian. He claimed that his opposition was primarily to the methods rather than the principle of missions, but as one reads his vitriolic and sarcastic arguments against missions and missionaries, many of which were manifestly untrue as well as unfair, it seems likely that his views concerning the church and the ministry were more dominant than his view of the atonement.[9]

Another influential antimission leader in the South was Joshua Lawrence, veteran pastor in Edgecomb County, North Carolina, who had many followers in Georgia, Alabama, and Mississippi. The Kehukee Association, to which he belonged, had been missionary from almost the time it was founded in 1769. About the year 1820 Lawrence published a pamphlet opposing missions. By 1826 the antimission party in this association became organized and vocal. In 1827 the association adopted a resolution to "discard all Missionary Societies, Bible Societies, and Theological Seminaries..." The exact action that was taken at this time was disputed from the beginning.[10] At any rate, the year 1827 marked the beginning of the antimission schism in North Carolina. The Kehukee Association became the rallying point for antimissionism in a large area surrounding it. "Kehukeeism" became synonymous with "Hardshellism," "Primitivism," and the anti-effort movement.

Still another center of antimissionism developed in the old Baltimore Association. This association was formed in 1793 and was an

---

[8] J. M. Carroll, *A History of Texas Baptists* (Dallas: Baptist Standard Publishing Co., 1923), 45 ff.
[9] B. H. Carroll, Jr., *American Anti-Missionism*, 124-55.
[10] C. B. Hassell, *History of the Church of God From the Creation to A. D. 1885*, revised and completed by Sylvester Hassell (Middletown, New York: Gilbert Beebe's Sons, 1886), 763 ff. See also Henry Sheets, *Who Are Primitive Baptists?* (Raleigh, N. C.: Edwards and Broughton Printing Co., c1908).

active missionary body in its early years. After the adjournment of the 1832 meeting at the Warren church, however, the anti-effort party called for a meeting to "oppose all these inventions of men"–missionary, Bible, and tract societies; Sunday Schools; etc.–declaring they were the "progeny of Arminianism." A call was then made for "all Old School Baptist Churches" to send delegates to a convention. On September 28-30, 1832, this convention met at the Black Rock church, Baltimore County, Maryland. The nonlocal leadership of this meeting was shown by the fact that William Gilmore of Virginia was elected moderator, while Gabriel Conkling of New Jersey became clerk. The principal voice in the meeting was that of Gilbert Beebe, pastor in New York, who edited *The Signs of the Times* for forty-nine years proclaiming the anti-effort position. His language may be glimpsed in the address published by this group.

> Upholding the principles of genuine Christianity, and denouncing the Arminian men-made societies that had so rapidly increased in number and influence within a few years, and which seems designed to supplant the church of God itself, and scatter to the winds the faith and practice and all the ancient landmarks of God's chosen people.[11]

This address, prepared by a committee of seven (including Beebe), was totally anti-effort. Missions, Christian tract distributions, Sunday Schools, theological education, and Bible Societies were pungently anathematized.[12]

Four years later, on May 12, 1836, the Baltimore Association's regular meeting was held at the Black Rock church, "attended by only 28 persons, seven of whom were not properly authorized messengers, and the one elected as moderator was not a member of the body."[13] By a vote of sixteen to nine, a resolution expelling all "uniting with and encouraging others to unite in worldly societies" was passed. The missionary-minded churches formed another association with the same name as the old one, but this body was greatly weakened when several of the stronger churches

---

[11] Hassell, *Church of God,* 900.
[12] See Baker, *Source Book* for excerpts from the *Address*, 82-84.
[13] Norman Cox, ed., *Encyclopedia of Southern Baptists* (Nashville: Broadman Press), II. p. 830.

affiliated with the Maryland Baptist Union Association, organized in 1836.

The effect of the antimission movements (including Campbell) on Southern Baptists was devastating. Many churches and sometimes whole associations declared themselves antimissionary. The western frontier, in particular, felt their blighting effect.[14]

> From 1820 to 1840, they wrecked the missionary cause on the frontier and created confusion in the older states, throughout the South and beyond. They reached their zenith about 1840. From that time they began to decline, but not before causing untold harm to the cause of missions in the South.
>
> Baptists lost a large percentage of their total strength to the antimission movement. A large number left the denomination with Campbell, though the exact figure cannot be accurately estimated, as no sources on this point are available. Others refused to join the Baptists because of the controversy. Schools and colleges were not founded in the West during this time, further delaying the growth and progress of Baptists for lack of trained leadership.[15]

## Sectionalism

Nowhere can the overwhelming effects of social, economic, and political factors upon religious life be glimpsed more clearly than in the story of the separation between Northern and Southern Baptists in 1845. The settlement of the West, for example, was likely the principal factor that brought the formation of the American Baptist Home Mission Society in 1832; it was this settled West that within a few years became the greatest political threat to eastern suzerainty, particularly in the Senate, and fanned the flames of sectionalism to the consuming point.[16] As Marcus Lee Hansen pointed out, the problem of slaveholding was not in itself divisive, but translated into political control through the support of a common institution of this sort, it multiplied sectionalism to its highest component.

---

[14] W. W. Sweet, *Religion on the American Frontier* (New York: Henry Holt & Co.) I, 62 and 67-68.
[15] Cox, ed., *Encyclopedia*, I. 54.
[16] Baker, *Relations*, 16-26.

Simply stated, sectionalism is the advocacy of any particular interest by a community, whether local or widespread, that shares in that interest. Sectionalism has played a large part in American history. Perhaps the classic treatment is that of Frederick Jackson Turner, *The Significance of Sections in American History*. Sectionalism may be glimpsed in the Constitutional Convention, for example, when Gouverneur Morris of Pennsylvania, asserting the sectional interests of the Atlantic states, wanted to arrange the ratio of representation in the national government so that the number of representatives from the Atlantic states would always be larger than the number from the western states. As A. L. Burt pointed out, the early West was strongly conscious of its peculiar needs and struggled vigorously for its sectional interests. New England displayed sectionalism in the Hartford Convention; so did Georgia in the litigation with the Creek and Cherokee Indians. The Nullification Ordinance of 1832 by South Carolina almost brought civil war over sectionalism without reference to slaveholding or abolitionism.[17]

The literature had many instances of sectional differences between Northern and Southern Baptists during this period. The Annuals of the Home Mission Society printed complaints from different parts of the West (the South Central region) and the South to the effect that their sections were being neglected in the appointment of missionaries and asserting that a mission society in the remote northeast could not understand the needs of other sections. The Kentucky Baptist paper, for example, in 1837 alleged that the southern states were being neglected in the appointment of missionaries, and urged the formation of a southern home mission society.[18] The Georgia Baptist paper in 1840 advocated the formation of a "Southern society" to transmit funds for the "Texan mission" in the event the Home Mission Society did not heed the call.[19] Both papers alleged that the southern states were sending more money to the society than was being expended on sending missionaries to the South.[20]

Relative to the claims that the South was furnishing more money to the society than was being expended for missionaries to work in the South, it is difficult to untangle the true facts. C. B. Goodykoontz insisted

---

[17] Ibid., 16-19.
[18] Baker, *Source Book*, 84.
[19] Baker, *Relations*, 33, 36 ff.
[20] Baker, *Source Book*, 84-85.

that Kentucky, Tennessee, and Missouri were *western*, not *southern* states at this time; if this be so, southern states gave $28,149 for missions between 1832 and 1841 through the society, while the society expended only $13,646.50 in the South during that time. However, if these are counted southern states during that period, the society expended about the same amount as was contributed by the South. It is true that the Southwest (Kentucky, Tennessee, Louisiana, Mississippi, Arkansas, and Missouri) was greatly neglected in comparison with amount of missionary work done by the society in the Northwest (Illinois, Indiana, Michigan, and Ohio).[21] The greatest problem faced by the society at this point was to find missionaries willing to work in the South because, according to Goodykoontz, the missionaries were principally northern people who preferred not to live in the midst of slavery, they felt that they would not be welcomed by the people in the South, and many feared the enervating climate. Another element was the fact that the North, especially from New England, and northern missionaries preferred to work among their own people in that area.[22]

It was likely this sectional wrangle over home missions that caused Robert T. Daniel to organize a Southern Baptist society for home missions, with headquarters in Columbus, Mississippi, asserting that the mission needs of the region were the only motivation for forming the body.[23] Similarly, the attempt to form "a general organization for home missionary operations throughout the western valley" in 1839 at Louisville, Kentucky, was motivated only by home mission needs in the Mississippi Valley, and not by abolition-slavery considerations.[24]

However, the greatest sectional issue ever to confront the American nation was black slavery. It had been introduced into Virginia in 1619, and at first was vigorously resisted by the southern colonies. Against the wishes of the colonists and nullifying repeated acts by some of the colonial legislatures, Great Britain forced a profitable slave trade to be continued.[25] In the Declaration of Independence, as originally drawn by Thomas Jefferson, it was stated that among the grievances which produced

---

[21] Baker, *Relations*, 34-37.
[22] Ibid., 38-39, and note the documentation.
[23] Baker, *Source Book*, 84 ff.
[24] Ibid., 86-87.
[25] Ibid., 88-89.

the Revolution was that the King of England had steadfastly resisted the efforts of the colonies to prevent the introduction of slaves.

W. W. Barnes pointed out that slavery was not a divisive issue until the 1830's.

> The principle and practice of slavery were not divisive issues when the national government was established on the basis of the federal Constitution. There was opposition to slavery in the South and in the North. It had not become a sectional issue. In the 1787 convention that framed the constitution, it was proposed to give Congress the authority to limit the trade in slaves. A committee, the majority of which were from the free states, reported adversely, denying Congress the power at any period to prohibit the African slave trade. Later, another committee, the majority of which were from the slave states, reported a new section giving Congress the authority to prohibit the trade after 1800. The commercial interests of New England especially hindered leaders in the Southern and Middle states from including provisions in the federal Constitution that would curtail the traffic both in time and extent. A manumission society was formed in Tennessee in the second decade of the century, and in 1817 it presented a memorial on slavery to the legislature. The leader of the society, Elihu Embree, published in Jonesborough, Tennessee, in 1820, *The Emancipator*, the first antislavery paper in the United States.
>
> Baptists in the Southern states contributed their part of the opposition to slavery. They gained their first supporters among the population within the lower economic brackets. Hence, most of their members were found among the nonslaveholding majority of the population of the South. In the upper South, where plantation life was not on a scale so extensive, this was especially true. In Virginia, Kentucky, and other states, associations passed resolutions against slavery. In 1828, the Cherokee church sent a remonstrance to the Holston Association, Tennessee, against the traffic of slaves. The association unanimously approved the remonstrance. In Kentucky, Baptist churches and associations, known as the "Friends of Humanity," passed resolutions of nonfellowship with slaveowners. Many of these Baptists left

Kentucky for Missouri, thus strengthening the antislavery sentiment in that state. Many Baptist families, among them that of Thomas Lincoln, father of Abraham Lincoln, left Kentucky for Indiana and Illinois, because of opposition to slavery south of the Ohio.

Of all the divisive issues in American life in the second quarter of the nineteenth century, slavery cut the deepest because it was at once a political, economic, social, moral, and religious issue. But not until the opposition took the form of abolitionism in the 1830's did the issue begin to portend those divisions in the religious and political spheres realized in the following decades.[26]

As late as 1832, when the American Baptist Home Mission Society was formed, the issue was not yet divisive. Two men who later became active leaders of Baptist abolitionism (Elon Galusha and Duncan Dunbar) were on the Board of Directors for the society; and in a resolution offered by Galusha, he made it plain that at that time he saw no objection to cooperating with the South in home missions.

The documents reveal almost exactly the time the issue became divisive among American Baptists. Baptists in England had been in the forefront of the agitation in that country to eliminate slavery in the West Indies. In 1833 the English Parliament passed legislation designed to eliminate all slavery in the Empire by 1838. Rejoicing in this victory, English Baptists on December 31, 1833, addressed American Baptists in a lengthy treatise and described the victory of the English emancipation movement. The letter concluded by asking:

> Is it [slavery] not an awful breach of the Divine law, a manifest infraction of that social compact which is always and everywhere binding? And if it be so, are you not, as Christians, and especially as Christian ministers, bound to protest against it, and to seek, by all legitimate means, its speedy and entire destruction?[27]

This letter promptly divided American Baptists, although the division was not yet clearly between the North and the South. On September 1, 1834,

---

[26] Barnes, *The Southern Baptist Convention*, 18-19. See also Baker, *Relations*, 18-21.
[27] Baker, *Source Book*, 87-88

Corresponding Secretary Lucius Bolles replied for the General Board. The gist of these resolutions was that the constitution of the General Convention precluded any discussion on this subject.

> We have the best evidence that our slaveholding brethren are Christians, sincere followers of the Lord Jesus. In every other part of their conduct, they adorn the doctrine of God our Savior. We cannot, therefore, feel that it is right to use language or adopt measures which might tend to break the ties that unite them to us in our General Convention, and in numerous other benevolent societies; and to array brother against brother, church against church, and association against association in a contest about slavery.[28]

However, as soon as this correspondence was published, about fifty Baptist ministers met at Boston on May 26-27, 1835, and voted their approval of another reply, which was subsequently signed by about 130 Baptist ministers before it was mailed. This letter acknowledged the guilt of slaveholding and pledged all efforts "to labor in the use of weapons not carnal but mighty through God to the overthrow of this as well as every other work of wickedness."[29]

The supporters of abolitionism increased rapidly in numbers in American Baptist ranks. Agitation from abroad continued. During 1835 two distinguished Baptist abolitionists from England toured America in behalf of their views, although they said very little about the slavery issue.[30] In 1836 a flood of strong abolitionist resolutions were published from English Baptist associations. Meanwhile, the slave uprising in the South, which endangered the lives of the whites there, and the increasing political emphasis in abolitionism tended to polarize the antagonists North and South. Baron Stow, one of the leaders in the General Convention, is an example of the shift toward dominant abolitionist sympathies. In 1837, answering for the General Convention another letter from the English abolitionists, Stow said that since "the constitution of the Board limits them to the business of Foreign Missions, they will not, under existing circumstances, intermeddle in any way the question of slavery." However,

---

[28] Ibid., 89-90.
[29] Ibid., 90.
[30] Baker, *Relations*, 42.

in the following year Stow replied to still another letter from the English Baptists, and this time he urged the English brethren to be patient "and not think us tardy in accomplishing an object which we as well as they, are anxious to see immediately effected." By this time he had become an avowed abolitionist proponent.[31]

Baptist abolitionism was accelerated by the organization of the American Baptist Anti-Slavery Convention. The initial meeting took place in New York on April 28-30, 1840, with about 100 in attendance. At this meeting two addresses were prepared, one to Northern and one to Southern Baptists. The address to the South was vigorously written and widely circulated throughout the South. Recognizing that most of the states had passed laws, because of slave uprisings, which legally forbade southerners to free their slaves, the address urged the Baptists to "forsake, like Abraham, your father-land, and carry your children and your households to the vast asylum of our prairies and our wilderness."[32] Partly as a result of this agitation and the bitterness it engendered among Baptists in the South, the several societies felt it necessary to issue circulars affirming their neutrality. Both the General Convention for Foreign Missions and the Home Mission Society based their neutrality upon their constitutions. The foreign mission body took this action in December, 1840, while the Home Mission Society published their disclaimer on February 16, 1841.[33] The editor of the *Christian Watchmen* of New York frowned upon the agitation taking place in 1840, remarking that the fellowship of the churches should not be "a matter of convenience, a matter of retaliation, nor a tool of political philanthropy."

When the General Convention met in Baltimore in 1841 for its triennial session, a determined effort was made by northern and southern leaders to maintain the unity of the body. At a caucus in mid-April just before the opening of the convention, a group of northern and southern leaders prepared a Compromise Article which in effect condemned abolitionists as introducing new tests for Christian fellowship in benevolent work. This was signed by seventy-four of the principal

---

[31] Baker, *Source Book*, 90-91.
[32] Ibid., 92-94.
[33] Ibid., 55 ff.

northern and southern leaders.[34] It probably delayed the separation of the two sections for a few years.

The newspaper controversies over slavery-abolitionism, however, intensified during 1842 and 1843. A literary battle of particular vehemence and bitterness erupted just before the meeting of the three societies in 1844. This set the stage for the critical anniversaries of 1844. Controversy began on December 27, 1843, when an anonymous inquiry in the Baptist paper of New Hampshire asked whether or not it was true that James Huckins and William Tryon, missionaries of the Home Mission Society in Texas, were slaveholders. Baptist papers in North Carolina, Boston, Maine, Georgia, and other areas quickly joined a lively discussion. It developed that James Huckins of Vermont had purchased a slave after beginning his work in Texas, while William Tryon had married a Georgia woman who owned slaves. This confrontation continued to the very week of the benevolent anniversaries. The minutes of the societies made explicit reference to this last extensive newspaper fuss. The Home Mission Society in 1844 appointed a committee to work out plans for the amicable dissolution of the society,[35] while the General Convention revealed that it was overwhelmingly abolitionist in its spirit.

An exception to the abusive language of the time was provided by the literary debate in Baptist papers between President Francis Wayland of Brown University and Richard Fuller, pastor in South Carolina at this time. Although they advocated opposite sides of the issue, the two men were courteous, logical, and explicit, qualities which most of the literature of this period did not exhibit.[36]

Meanwhile, on May 4, 1843, Baptist abolitionists met in separate convention and organized a mission society which subsequently supported foreign and home missions.[37] Some of the prominent abolitionists preferred not to join this society but to remain within the constituted bodies and make strong efforts to separate Southern Baptists from these bodies.[38]

---

[34] Ibid., 100.
[35] See Baker, *Relations*, 67-68 for the detailed story.
[36] Richard Fuller and Francis Wayland, *Domestic Slavery Considered As a Scriptural Institution* (New York: Lewis Colby, 1845), 101-4.
[37] Baker, *Source Book*, 94-95.
[38] See J. A. Smith, *Memoir of Nathaniel Colver* (Boston: George A. Foxcroft, Jr., 1875), 199; also *The Emancipator* (New York), May 25, 1843.

The crisis came in 1844. In what has become known as the Georgia Test Case, Georgia Baptists were not satisfied with the neutrality assurances of the Home Mission Society, since many of the leaders of the society were busy in abolitionist activities. On August 2, 1844, the Georgia Baptist Executive Committee submitted to the Home Mission Society the name of James E. Reeve for appointment, openly volunteering the information to the society that Reeve was a slaveholder.[39] After many discussions about Reeve, the Executive Board refused to consider the application for the appointment of Reeve because this application constituted a test, and as such, violated the purposes and letter of the constitution, compromised the principles of the neutrality circular issued by the society in 1841, ignored a resolution introduced in 1841 by Richard Fuller which denied the right of anyone to introduce the subject of slavery or anti-slavery into the society, and, because of all of this threatened to destroy the harmony of the society. Georgia Baptists were furious.[40]

The final event that led to separation was initiated in Alabama. The Baptist state convention met in November, 1844, and on November 25, addressed a resolution to the General Convention demanding the distinct avowal that slaveholders were equally eligible to all the privileges enjoyed by nonslaveholders, especially with reference to the appointment of agents and missionaries. Under date of December 17, 1844, although not released for publication until much later, the Acting Board replied to the Alabama Resolutions to the effect that if anyone having slaves should offer himself as a missionary "and should insist on retaining them as his property, we could not appoint him. One thing is certain; we can never be a party to any arrangement which would imply approbation of slavery."[41]

When this correspondence came to the attention of the Virginia Baptist Foreign Mission society, they issued an official call for a consultative meeting of Baptists of the South "to confer on the best means of promoting the Foreign Mission cause, and other interests of the Baptist denomination in the South." Augusta, Georgia, was suggested as a meeting place, and the first part of May was named as a possible date.[42]

---

[39] Baker, *Source Book*, 105-6.
[40] Baker, *Relations*, 74-75.
[41] Baker, *Source Book*, pp. 106-8 has the Alabama Resolutions and the reply.
[42] Ibid.. 109-113.

In 1845, when the anniversaries of the three principal societies were held at Providence, Rhode Island, there were few Baptists from the South in attendance. They had turned their eyes toward Augusta.

# PERIOD TWO: FROM THE FORMATION OF THE SOUTHERN BAPTIST CONVENTION TO THE MODERN ERA: 1845-1917

*From the Formation of the Southern Baptist Convention to the First Executive Committee of the Convention*

## Chapter 7 - The Southern Baptist Convention

When Baptists from various parts of the South met at Augusta, Georgia, on May 8, 1845, in response to the call issued by the Virginia Baptist Foreign Mission Society, some of them had been giving considerable thought to the kind of denominational body or bodies that Baptists in the South should organize. The kind of structure finally adopted was, in fact, somewhat of a departure from the former practice of carrying on benevolent work through separate, autonomous societies. The ancient dilemma that they faced, the kind of organization that they formed, and their new relationship to the older societies in the North will be considered briefly in this chapter.

### An Old Dilemma

Southern Baptists in 1845 faced the same basic problem that has confronted all Baptist groups who have attempted to establish denominational bodies, namely, how to unite independent churches into an effective denominational structure without overwhelming the autonomy of the local congregations. It should be noted that this was a relatively new problem in the history of Christianity. This does not mean that the principle of congregational autonomy was new. In intensive linguistic and theological research, non-Baptists like F. J. A. Hort, as well as non-Landmark Baptists like John L. Dagg, John A. Broadus, John R. Sampey, and H. E. Dana have described the autonomous nature of the primitive churches. *Clement of Rome*, one of the earliest noncanonical writings, provides evidence that at the close of the first century this autonomy still existed among the churches. This letter, addressed by the church at Rome to the church at Corinth about A.D. 96, was written because the latter church had dismissed some of their elders who had been put into office by the apostles themselves. The Corinthian church had taken this action without asking the permission of anyone, and the letter from Rome was an appeal for reconsideration. The Roman letter gives no indication that any other church or individual could require the Corinthian church to reinstate these leaders.

However, even though congregational autonomy was practiced in primitive Christianity, the problem of the best way to structure independent churches for benevolent work was not faced because no such general bodies were organized during the period of congregational autonomy. There were no associations, state conventions, missionary societies, or national bodies for benevolent work in the first century. One could hardly confuse Paul's concept of the church as the Body of Christ with a geographic and organizational structure.

The assumption of church government by the bishops interrupted further development in this area. There were probably monarchial bishops in Asia Minor by A.D. 165 and in Rome not long thereafter. The Council of Nicaea in A.D. 325 made reference to large areas of control by strong bishops, and a papal structure was evident by the time of Chalcedon in A.D. 451. The independence of the local congregations was swept away with the rise of territorial bishops, so there was no particular problem in structuring a strong hierarchical body under an authoritative judicature which ultimately was headed by the pope at Rome. After Constantine, the Roman Empire provided both the pattern and the assistance for developing a Catholic church which held sway almost universally until the Reformation. In sixteenth-century England the *imperium* and *sacerdotium* were united in the person of the sovereign, bringing to its ultimate form in this country the concept of Constantine that the sovereign was the bishop of the bishops. In this same country and in the same century, the rise of congregationalism, in which the authority of the local body was enunciated, set the stage for a new type of polity.

Thus, all groups in the sixteenth century holding to congregational autonomy were forced to pioneer in the development of denominational structures beyond the local level. English independency developed on theological and historical grounds, and serious consideration was not given initially to the question of how that type of ecclesiology could be utilized in forming effective denominational structures. As a matter of fact, both English and American Congregationalists have wavered at the point of denominational structure. A "semi-Presbyterian conception of the internal government of the church," says Williston Walker, "instead of a democracy of Browne, dominated all early English and American Congregationalism."[1]

English Baptists, emphasizing extensively and precisely the authority of the congregation, were faced with the problem of devising denominational structures beyond the local church in such fashion that congregational autonomy would be maintained. In the 1650's English Baptists developed associations, and General Baptists structured their General Assembly of General Baptist Churches. However, in their struggle to prevent heresy and maintain unity through their General Assembly, General Baptists compromised the autonomy of the congregations related to this general body, as mentioned in an earlier chapter. They gave so much authority to general bodies that the local congregations lost their autonomy. It is no wonder that the historian of General Baptists in Suffolk remarked that their church order was more Presbyterian than Baptist.

English Particular Baptists, on the other hand, were reluctant to organize beyond the associational level. A loose type of union was created in 1689 called the General Assembly of particular Baptists. Their point of view with reference to polity was seen in a Confession of 1677, reprinted by order of the new body in 1689, which said:

> These messengers assembled are not intrusted [sic] with any church-power properly so-called; or with any jurisdiction over the churches, themselves, to exercise any censures either over any churches or persons; or to impose their determination on the churches or officers.[2]

---

[1] Williston Walker, *A History of the Congregational Churches in the United States* (New York: The Christian Literature Co., 1894), 46.

[2] McGlothlin, *Baptist Confessions of Faith,* 268.

General Baptists in England, therefore, dealt with the problem of local church autonomy versus denominationalism by making the denominational structure inhibitive, while Particular Baptists attacked the same problem by limiting the effectiveness of the general body as a means of safeguarding the autonomy of the churches.

American Baptists also faced the question of church independency as they began to organize beyond the local level. The first association in America organized in Philadelphia in 1707 carefully refrained from usurping the autonomy of the churches. In 1749 it adopted an Essay which plainly said that an association

> is not a superior judicature, having such superior power over the churches concerned; but that each particular church hath a complete power and authority from Jesus Christ, to administer all gospel ordinances, provided they have a sufficiency of officers duly qualified, or that they be supplied by the officers of another sister church or churches, as baptism, and the Lord's supper, &c.; and to receive in and cast out, and also to try and ordain their own officers, and to exercise every part of gospel discipline and church government, independent of any other church or assembly whatever.[3]

As pointed out previously, it is likely that the rapid swing from the associational program for carrying on missions to the society plan for carrying on these activities was caused by the extreme sensitiveness toward developing ecclesiastical bodies that might usurp the autonomy of the local churches.

The struggle of the founding fathers of the General Missionary Convention in 1814 to find the proper direction between 1814 and 1832 has already been described. Through the influence of Francis Wayland, the autonomy of the churches was safeguarded by the organization of independent societies for carrying on the several benevolences of American Baptists between 1814 and 1845. Wayland, in fact, was so opposed to denominational structures that might inhibit the local

---

[3] Baker, *Source Book*, 10.

congregations that he even urged the elimination of state conventions and their replacement with missionary societies in each state.[4]

Thus, in 1845 when Southern Baptists met at Augusta, Georgia, the old dilemma of how to unite independent churches for effective denominational functions without violating their autonomy was one of their basic problems and a very live issue.

## A Proposed Structure

One of the ablest minds among Southern Baptists in 1845 was that of William B. Johnson, president of the South Carolina Baptist Convention. He was the only person at the meeting in 1845 who had been in the organizational sessions of the General Missionary Convention in 1814 and had served as president of that body. He also had been a member of the committee to prepare the constitution of the General Convention. His genius had been displayed on many occasions in his defense of missionary societies and the organization of state bodies when they were very much opposed by some of his brethren.

Johnson, as president of the state body, called a special meeting of the South Carolina Baptist Convention on May 3, 1845, one week before the meeting to take place at Augusta, Georgia. In a lengthy address he confessed that despite his personal involvement in the organization of the General Missionary Convention, he had now reluctantly come to the conclusion that there must be separation. He compared the situation to that when Paul and Barnabas had sharp contention and separated one from the other on the second missionary journey, and as a result, "two lines of service were opened for the benefit of the churches."

**William Bullein Johnson, architect of the Triennial Convention and the Southern Baptist Convention**
(Courtesy Southern Baptist Historical Library and Archives)

Such, I trust, will be the result of the separation between the Baptists of these United States in their general benevolent

---

[4] Wayland, *Principles and Practices,* 181 ff.

Institutions. When we embarked in the cause of Foreign Missions, the union of the whole denomination was necessary, for it was then comparatively small. But now, such state of things, that we may part asunder and open two lines of service to the heathen and the destitute, instead of one only, and the vast increase in our numbers, and the wide extent of territory, over which we are spread, seem to indicate the hope, that our separation will be attended with no sharpness of contention, with no bitterness of spirit. We are all the servants of the same Master, "desirous of doing the will of God from the heart." Let us, then, in generous rivalry, "provoke each other to love and good works."[5]

Johnson went on to say in this message that in view of the need for a new organization, he wished to offer a suggestion. He called their attention to the fact that they had been functioning for years past through the use of a separate and autonomous society for each benevolence. He then proposed the formation of

one Convention, embodying the whole Denomination, together with separate and distinct Boards, for each object of benevolent enterprise, located at different places, and all amenable to the Convention.[6]

This kind of organization, Johnson said, would provide judicious concentration, which he termed "of the first moment in all combinations of men for important enterprises."

In its successful operation, the whole Denomination will be united in one body for the purpose of well-doing, with perfect liberty secured to each contributor of specifying the object or objects, to which his amount shall be applied, as he please, whilst he or his Delegation may share in the deliberations and control of all the objects, promoted by the Convention.[7]

It is evident from this that Johnson was suggesting a different kind of denominational organization than the one utilizing the three

---

[5] See the *Edgefield Advertiser* (Edgefield, South Carolina), May 7, 1845.
[6] Baker, *Source Book*, 114.
[7] Ibid.

autonomous benevolent societies as had been done heretofore. Disdaining the possibility of overwhelming the authority of local congregations, Johnson was suggesting a more centralized body that would have control over all the benevolent objects projected by Southern Baptists.

## The Consultative Convention

In his study of the enrollment of the messengers at the meeting in Augusta, Georgia, on May 8, 1845, W. W. Barnes concluded that there were 293 separate accredited messengers attending the meeting. All but twenty of these were from Georgia, South Carolina, and Virginia. The others were from Alabama, District of Columbia, Kentucky, Louisiana, Maryland, and North Carolina. In addition, one corresponding messenger from Pennsylvania and the American Baptist Publications Society attended. The messenger from Kentucky was Isaac McCoy, the renowned Indian missionary.

Most of the leaders in Kentucky, as well as Tennessee and Mississippi, questioned the wisdom of separation at this time. Editor W. C. Buck of Kentucky pointed out that the Acting Board (which served for the full board between its triennial meetings and had made the reply to the Alabama Resolutions) could not finally speak for the full Board nor for the General Convention, and that Southern Baptists should wait until the next full meeting of the convention in 1847 before taking precipitate action. The editor of the *Biblical Recorder* of North Carolina, Thomas Meredith, agreed with this, as did the Board of the Tennessee Baptist Foreign Mission Society. R. B. C. Howell of Nashville sent a letter to Augusta asking for a delay in the meeting, remarking that Tennessee, Mississippi, Arkansas, Missouri, and Kentucky did not have time to appoint representatives, and also suggested that the General Convention probably would not sustain the Board at its meeting in 1847. The call issued by the Virginia Baptist Foreign Mission Society was not published until April 10, and there was hardly time for many of the southern societies and state bodies to meet, elect messengers, and discuss the issues, even if there had been good communication and transportation. That almost three hundred messengers appeared at Augusta was remarkable. At the first meeting it was announced that Mississippi, Tennessee, Arkansas, and Florida had sent letters, due to the fact that the short notice of the meeting prevented further representation.

On the opening day, William B. Johnson of South Carolina was named president; Wilson Lumpkin of Georgia and J. B. Taylor of Virginia were vice-presidents; and Jesse Hartwell of Alabama and J. C. Crane of Virginia were secretaries. A committee of one from each state represented, along with seven others, was appointed to prepare a preamble and resolution. In the afternoon Richard Fuller, the chairman, submitted the report, which was discussed during the remainder of the day.

The entire second day (Friday, May 9) was spent reviewing and making verbal amendments to the preamble and resolution presented by the committee on the previous day. The preamble specifically named the action of the Boston board, in their answers to the Alabama resolutions, as evidence that the board "most clearly and unnecessarily exceeded their power and violated their trust." The preamble continued:

> It is a question admitting no debate, that the Triennial Convention was formed on the principle of a perfect equality of members, from the South and North. And what is all important, the very qualifications of missionaries are prescribed by the original constitution of that Convention, - the fifth article providing that "such persons as are in full communion with some regular church of our denomination, and who furnish satisfactory evidence of genuine piety, good talents and fervent zeal for the Redeemer's cause, are to be employed as missionaries."
>
> Besides this, too, the declaration of the Board, that if "any one should offer himself as a missionary, having slaves, and should insist on retaining them as his property, we could not appoint him," is an innovation and a departure from the course hitherto pursued by the Triennial Convention, (such persons having been appointed). And lastly, the decision of the Board is an infraction of the resolution passed the last spring, in Philadelphia; and the General Board at their late meeting in Providence, have failed to reverse this decision.[8]

The resolution that accompanied this preamble read:

---

[8] *Annual*, Southern Baptist Convention, 1845, 12-13. The title *Proceedings* is sometimes used, but this reference hereafter will show *Annual*.

> *Resolved*, That for peace and harmony, and in order to accomplish the greatest amount of good, and for the maintenance of those scriptural principles on which the General Missionary Convention of the Baptist denomination of the United States, was originally formed, it is proper that this Convention at once proceed to organize a Society for the propagation of the Gospel.[9]

The preamble and the resolution were adopted separately after extensive discussion. Then, upon motion, eight additional names were added to this same committee, including William B. Johnson to act as its chairman, "who should prepare and report a Constitution for a Southern Association."

On the third day (Saturday, May 10) the body met at 8:00 A.M. and the day was spent receiving and approving a preamble and constitution for the new organization. In the preamble the purpose of the new body was named as "carrying into effect the benevolent intentions of our constituents, by organizing a plan for eliciting, combining and directing the energies of the whole denomination in one sacred effort, for the propagation of the Gospel." The constitution finally adopted was almost precisely, in many instances word for word, the one suggested by William B. Johnson during the previous week at the meeting of the South Carolina convention. The critical section of the new constitution was Article V, by which the denomination departed radically from the society principle that each organization should deal with only one benevolence. The new article provided:

> The Convention shall elect at each triennial meeting as many Boards of Managers, as in its judgment will be necessary for carrying out the benevolent objects it may determine to promote, all which Boards shall continue in office until a new election.... To each Board shall be committed, during the recess of the Convention, the entire management of all the affairs relating to the object with whose interest it shall be charged.[10]

The constitution was discussed seriatim and adopted unanimously. One change was discussed carefully. The committee had

---

[9] *Annual*, 12-13..
[10] Baker, *Source Book*, 117.

suggested that the body should be called the Southern and Southwestern Baptist Convention. When the motion came to strike out "Southwestern," many expressed their fears that "Southern" was such sectional name that their constituents might take exception to it.

This completed, the convention upon motion appointed William B. Johnson, Thomas Curtis, Richard Fuller, and C. D. Mallary as a committee to prepare an Address to the Public setting forth the reasons which led to the formation of this body.

J. B. Jeter of Virginia then submitted a resolution raising a question that had been in the minds of all during the first two days of the meeting. His resolution proposed:

> That the individuals, churches and other bodies, approving the constitution of the Southern Baptist Convention, adopted by this body, be recommended to meet, according to its provisions, for organization, by members or delegates, on the Wednesday after the first Lord's day in June, 1846, in Richmond, Va. and that this Convention now proceed to the election of its Officers and Boards of Managers, to continue in office until said meeting.[11]

This resolution brought an extended discussion about whether this consultative convention had the power to take this action. Some messengers said that they had come without instructions from their constituency and for that reason were loath to take part in initiating any organizational action. The presiding officer, W. B. Johnson, expressed a doubt that this body had the power to organize even a provisional government. However, after a long break for lunch the resolution was adopted in the afternoon session, and a provisional structure organized. W. B. Johnson of South Carolina was elected president, while Wilson Lumpkin of Georgia, James B. Taylor of Virginia, A. Dockery of North Carolina, and R. B. C. Howell of Tennessee were named vice-presidents. M. T. Mendenhall, a medical doctor form South Carolina, was elected treasurer, while Jesse Hartwell of Alabama and James C. Crane of Virginia were named secretaries. A Board of Managers for Foreign Missions, to be located at Richmond, Virginia, was named, with J. B. Jeter of Virginia as president and C. D. Mallary as corresponding secretary. A Board of

---

[11] *Annual*, 1845, 14.

Managers for Domestic Missions was located at Marion, Alabama, and Basil Manly of Alabama was named president. J. L. Reynolds was elected corresponding secretary of this body.

On Monday the convention met for its closing session, only about a hundred members being present. Several resolutions were passed, as follows: (1) an invitation for auxiliary societies to affiliate with this new body; (2) a request that state conventions and other bodies who might have funds for foreign or domestic missions to forward such funds to the treasurer of the proper board; (3) an appeal for the support of the Indian Mission Association; (4) an instruction to the Board of Domestic Missions to take all prudent measures for the religious instruction of the black population; (5) an instruction to the Foreign Mission Board to communicate with the proper board of the General Missionary Convention relative to any claims each may have upon the other; (6) an authorization to the Foreign Missionary Convention "to take a portion of its Missions under the patronage of this Convention"; (7) a committee to apply for a charter of incorporation from the state of Georgia; and (8) a recommendation to the Board of Domestic Missions to give attention to the needs of the city of New Orleans. The convention then adjourned to meet the following year in Richmond to perfect a permanent organization.

Meanwhile, however, a charter was secured on December 27, 1845, from the state of Georgia, incorporating the convention "for the purpose of eliciting, combining, and directing the energies of the Baptist Denomination of Christians, for the propagation of the gospel." The two boards also began to function. However, the numbering of the sessions of the Southern Baptist Convention was reckoned from 1846 from the very beginning.

## The Address to the Public

There is no evidence that the convention in 1845 saw or approved the Address to the Public which was prepared by its authorization. The document is dated May 12, 1845, and perhaps the committee named to prepare the address simply remained at Augusta after the adjournment of the body.

The address began with a statement that a painful division had taken place in the missionary operations of American Baptists, but remarked that the extent of this disunion should not be exaggerated.

At the present time it involves only the Foreign and Domestic Missions of the denomination. Northern and Southern Baptists are still brethren. They differ in no article of the faith. They are guided by the same principles of gospel order.[12]

Three main emphases were made by this address. In the first division, it endeavored to show that the cause of the separation was constitutional. It noted that in the early years of the history of the General Missionary Convention "there was no breath of discord between them." It affirmed the resolution passed in the 1841 convention that "in co-operating together, as members of this Convention, in the work of foreign missions, we disclaim all sanction, either expressed or implied, whether of slavery or anti-slavery." The reply to the Alabama Resolutions was described as "a new qualification for missionaries" and a "usurpation of ecclesiastical power." By this decision, continued the address, the Boston board had placed itself in direct opposition to the constitution of the convention. It was noted that at the full meeting of the Board of Managers at Providence in April, 1845, they were entreated to revise and reverse the obnoxious interdict, but instead a resolution expressed sympathy with the Acting Board and sustained them.

The address asserted secondly that the new Southern Baptist Convention would carry on under the principles of the General Missionary Convention.

>The constitution we adopt is precisely that of the original union; that in connection with which, through his missionary life, Adoniram Judson has lived, and under which Ann Judson and Boardman have died. We recede from it no single step. We have constructed for our basis no new creed; acting in this matter upon a Baptist aversion for all creeds but the Bible. We use the very terms, as we uphold the true spirit and great object of the late "General Convention of the Baptist denomination of the United States." It is they who wrong us that have receded. We have receded neither from the Constitution nor from any part of the original ground on which we met them in this work.[13]

---

[12] Baker, *Source Book*, 118.
[13] Ibid., 120.

The third emphasis of the address affirmed that the object of the new body was to extend the Messiah's kingdom and the glory of God.

The reason given for separation was basically constitutional. This had been asserted in the call for the consultative convention by Virginia Baptists, had been the burden of the address by William B. Johnson at the called meeting of the South Carolina Baptist Convention just one week before the meeting of the consultative body, and, of course, was the principal thrust of the Address to the Public. It is likely that Francis Wayland had this aspect in mind when he wrote William B. Johnson at the time of the consultative convention and said:

> You will separate of course. I could not ask otherwise. Your rights have been infringed. I will take the liberty of offering one or two suggestions. We have shown how Christians ought not to act, it remains for you to show us how they ought to act. Put away all violence, act with dignity and firmness and the world will approve your course.[14]

It is likely also that it was this constitutional aspect that caused a northern Baptist historian like H. C. Vedder to speak favorably of the southern withdrawal.

Another of the reasons alleged by the South for withdrawal could be called the missionary imperative. Southern leaders were saying, in essence, that the General Missionary Convention and the Home Mission Society would not appoint slaveholders to serve as missionaries; therefore, under the present situation they were cut off from carrying out the Great Commission. This is what Johnson meant in the address when he asserted that the northern brethren were "forbidding us to speak unto the Gentiles." The argument was that if the South wanted to have any part in sending missionaries, it must form its own organization to do so.

A third argument for separation was based upon ecclesiology. The abolitionists, said the southerners, claim that the missionary societies have the right to judge the moral character and Christian integrity of the slaveholders when, as a matter of fact, it was asserted, these prerogatives belong only to a local church. Discipline, it was asserted, is the privilege and responsibility only of the local body of which the person in question

---

[14] Ibid.,116.

is a member. Thus, as Johnson said in his message to the South Carolina convention on May 3, 1845, the prerogatives of the autonomous local body were being taken over by some portions of the missionary societies, which was a breach of Baptist ecclesiology.

Underlying all three of these arguments for separation, of course, was the involvement of the South with the "peculiar institution," and the ordinary prejudices of sectionalism fanned into flames by the political consequences of the spread of this institution into the West.

Another southern argument for separation, however, had nothing to do with slavery. Before this matter ever became seriously controversial, there had been cries from all parts of the South to the effect that a separate body was needed for this section because their missionary needs were not being met by the Home Mission Society. As early as 1837 the editor of the Kentucky Baptist paper wrote:

> It appears from the "last report of the Executive Committee of the American Baptist Home Mission Society" that they have not a single missionary in all Kentucky, Alabama, Louisiana, and Florida, and that they partially or entirely sustain one missionary in Mississippi, three in Tennessee and three in Arkansas, making in all seven missionaries for these six states and one Territory... only one missionary to every 428,581 souls, while in the state of Michigan,...they have sixteen missionaries...one missionary to every 4,000 souls.... Why are these states (Illinois and Indiana) so liberally supplied? Are they more needy? Are they more destitute? They are more liberally supplied because of Northern contributions, and because Northern preachers refuse to come to the south.... It is, therefore, apparent, that the only way to produce effort in the south must be brought about by the formation of a Southern Baptist Home Mission Society.[15]

Similar editorials came from other southern states.

Almost simultaneously in 1839, as has been mentioned already, there had been two efforts to establish missionary bodies in the South. On May 11, 1839, William C. Buck of Kentucky was chairman of a meeting to organize a separate body to have "the general supervision of home

---

[15] Ibid., 84-85.

missions in this field." It was planned that the organization would be formed

> by delegates from State conventions and associations, and other Baptist bodies, in each State where such general organizations have been formed, and by delegates from Baptist associations, churches, and missionary societies under Baptist management, where such State organizations do not exist.[16]

The skillful maneuvering of John Mason Peck prevented the organization of this body.

However, on May 16, 1839, Robert T. Daniel led in the organization of the Southern Baptist Home Mission Society, with headquarters at Columbus, Mississippi.[17] In the circular calling for this organization, published on March 21, 1839, there is no mention at all made of abolitionism or slavery, which had not yet become critical issues. The mission needs of the Southwest were the only motivation for the formation of this body. When Daniel died in 1842, the society died with him.

These two movements, however, show clearly that in addition to slavery-abolitionism, there were other strong considerations for a separate southern body.

## Why This Kind of Structure Was Chosen

The adoption by Southern Baptist of this kind of denominational structure poses some questions. Manifestly, the organization of one convention to oversee multiple benevolences differed from the former method of utilizing three separate and autonomous societies for benevolent work.[18] What was there in the background of W. B. Johnson, who proposed this shift, and the consultative convention of representative Southern Baptists who adopted the new plan with remarkable unanimity, that would provide antecedents for such action?

---

[16] Ibid., 86-87.
[17] Ibid., 85-86.
[18] It should be observed, however, that even as recently as 1843, the Free Mission Society (first called the American and Foreign Baptist Missionary Society), organized by Baptist abolitionists when they withdrew from the General Convention and the Home Mission Society, contemplated both home and foreign missions through the single body. See Baker, *Relations*, 62-64.

W. W. Barnes has suggested that Southern Baptists were generally more centralized in their thinking than were Baptists in the North because of three rather basic factors: first, the widespread popularity in the South of the Philadelphia Confession of Faith with its general, invisible church view; second, the predominance of centralizing English General Baptists among the original settlers in the South; and third, the influence of the Separate Baptist movement, which was just one step removed from New England Presbyterian ecclesiological thinking.[19] Also, the centralizing patterns of the southern culture, as seen in the system of large plantations and in the top-heavy state political structures, provided their influence upon Southern Baptists.[20]

Other factors were involved. One was the development of state conventions in the South after 1821. The South Carolina Baptist Convention organized the first state body in America in 1821; it was built on associations, looked toward sponsoring multiple benevolences, and had other centralizing features. Many southern states had adopted similar state structures in the succeeding years. The experience of Southern Baptists with these bodies led them to feel that there was little to fear that any of them might ever become oppressive.

Another influence in the direction of centralization in the South was what could be called the Furman-Johnson tradition. Richard Furman, pastor of the First Baptist Church, Charleston, from 1787 until his death in 1825, was well-known for his centralized ecclesiological views. Johnson had been trained by Furman and shared his ecclesiological ideas. In fact, the local church ideas of Francis Wayland in the North and, later on, of J. R. Graves in the South, did not represent the ecclesiological views of Southern Baptists in 1845. Rather, Furman and Johnson were in the tradition of the centralizing ideas of the separate Baptists, as were their contemporaries such as A. M. Poindexter of Virginia and J. L. Dagg of Georgia. Dagg's work, *A Treatise on Church Order*, published in 1858 at Charleston, South Carolina, was actually an anti-Landmark polemic, particularly with respect to the High Church ecclesiology of J. R. Graves.[21]

---

[19] Barnes, *The Southern Baptist Convention*, 6-8.
[20] Baker, *Relations*, 147-49.
[21] J. L. Dagg, *A Treatise on Church Order* (Charleston: Southern Baptist Publication Society, 1858), 292, and *passim*.

That this centralizing tendency in 1845 in favor of a single denominational body structure overseeing all benevolences was not a novel concept to Southern Baptist ecclesiology, finds support in the events of almost half a century earlier. The new convention of 1845 favored the old associational pattern of the days before 1802 when all benevolences in a given geographical area were fostered by a single denominational body, the association. It will be recalled that the structure of the General Missionary Convention of 1814 limited it to foreign missions alone, but that in 1817, undoubtedly through the influence of Richard Furman, its president, the convention widened its scope to include other benevolences than foreign missions. The Southern Baptist Convention of 1845 resembled most closely this 1817-20 General Missionary Convention which in those years concerned itself with foreign missions, home missions, and Christian education. Whether W. B. Johnson, who was present and active in the organization of the 1814 body and subsequently served as its president, deliberately fashioned his proposal to the South Carolina convention in 1845 along the lines of the 1817-20 General Missionary Convention's structure can only be conjectured; but the parallel is there and the Address to the Public by the 1845 body asserted that the new convention was fashioned after the structure of the General Missionary Convention.

It is quite evident from the literature and the choice of denominational structure in 1845 that Southern Baptists were not uneasy that the new convention might threaten the autonomy of the churches. It has been mentioned already that there had developed considerable concentration on the state level without any diminution of the independence of the churches related to these bodies. Another protective factor was the nature of the constituency. The members who made up the new convention were also members of the local churches. The abolitionist controversy with the two missionary societies had been widely interpreted as an infringement upon the authority of the churches, and church authority was viewed as primary.

Another strong control for keeping such a new body from usurping the authority of the churches was the democratic nature of the convention. The vote of the floor at the annual meeting was the final authority in the body, and this inhibited usurpation. The constituents of 1845 felt that should there be any evidence of misplaced authority the matter could be firmly and quickly settled through free discussion and decisive vote. It is true that the boards had authority to act in behalf of their own benevolence on matters arising between the meetings of the convention, but review by committees and discussion from the floor were the regular pattern in each case. This public review of decisions made and activity carried on opened the way for public discussion of any item in the work of the boards or of the convention itself. The relatively small numbers attending the conventions before the opening of the twentieth century made it possible for the convention to act almost as a committee of the whole in the supervision of its work.

The location of the headquarters of the two benevolent boards (for foreign and home missions) in different cities may have had some protective overtones to inhibit over-centralization, but this feature may simply have copied the former practice of the united period.

Undoubtedly, however, the principal reason that Southern Baptists were not unduly sensitive about church independence as they organized in 1845 was that a fundamental safeguard, authenticated by many years of experience, was retained in the structure which they adopted. The fact is that with all of the centralization implicit in the adoption of one organization for all benevolences, the continued use of the society plan of financial representation totally isolated the centralized convention from any interference whatsoever with the autonomy of the churches. Article III of the constitution asserted that the convention would "consist of members who contribute funds, or are delegated by religious bodies contributing funds," exactly after the pattern of the society method. In his preconvention address, William B. Johnson specifically mentioned that the interests of the constituency would be safeguarded by the power of financial designation. If the constituency were to see tendencies toward usurping the authority of the congregations, it would be a simple matter for finances to be withheld, quickly undermining the general body. Indeed, this was the weapon that the South had used during the abolitionist controversy in the decade preceding separation. Doubtless one of the reasons that almost three hundred Southern Baptists were willing to change from the society type organization to the more centralized associational plan in the concentration of benevolences was the fact that the financial basis of representation provided an effective method of control.

It is also quite possible that the radical structural potentialities of the new body were not generally recognized. For several decades the body was referred to as the "missionary organization," not conceding that every type of denominational activity was contemplated in the structure. At any rate, by subjecting the activity of the new body to popular support financially by designated gifts, the founding fathers built in safeguards of the society method as well as the centralization of the associational method of fostering many benevolences through a single denominational body. This was not a convention of churches, but a gathering of money-giving Baptists organized to do their benevolent work through a centralized structure.

In the new structure, however, there were two tensions that would surface repeatedly during the next eighty years. Both of them stemmed from the attempt to put new wine into old wineskins: the new type of convention structure could not be contained in the old society type of financing, and representation. The founding fathers of the Southern Baptist Convention recognized no ambivalence in retaining the financial basis of representation, which both provided funds for operations and determined the voting constituency in a society. They sensed no limitation in the potential thrust of the new body through the retention of the older financial basis. This had been the accepted and effective method followed by the several societies during the lifetime of most of those present in 1845. The minutes of the new body, the denominational newspaper accounts, and the several reminiscences by actors in the drama give no hint that any of the messengers to the consultative meeting in 1845 desired to change this basis of representation. As a matter of fact, except for relatively minor adjustments designed to improve the choice of constituency, the constitutional pattern set in 1845 for financing the work of the convention remained rather constant until 1925. Actually, there was nothing inherently wrong in the financial basis of representation, for it followed the equitable principle that those who give the money should be allowed to spend it.

However, the adoption of this financial base provided a limitation that was not intended. The potential thrust of the convention was limited by the popular support accorded to any benevolence, since all finances were provided by designated giving. The convention as such had no funds of its own; even money to print the minutes had to be taken from designated home and foreign mission gifts. Since there were no convention headquarters, who should keep the minute book of the convention? The body voted that it should be kept at the foreign mission office in Richmond. For many decades the convention was looked upon simply as a missionary body, not a structure for implementing all of the varied benevolences of Baptist people in the South as the constitution originally envisioned. This is the reason that additional benevolences during this period like the Southern Baptist Publication Society in 1847 and Southern Baptist Theological Seminary in 1859, unable to share financial support within the framework of the convention, were developed outside of the body and given individual support under the old society plan.

The second point of tension within the structure of 1845 was the method of determining the constituency. For almost a century this strictly financial plan of representation was severely criticized as not being representative and equitable. Many alternatives were offered, but this basis of representation survived chronic tampering until the coming of a new century. Thus came the separation of 1845 between Northern and Southern Baptists. At the time it took place, there was almost complete agreement North and South that this was the best course. J. B. Jeter was assured by northern leaders that this action prevented division within churches and associations throughout the North.[22] John Mason Peck felt that separation would bring more zeal by each group. Many expressed the feeling that with the separate organization and immediate responsibility for the task, Southern Baptists would become more involved in the whole enterprise— management, agencies, appointments, finances, etc.—and would correspondingly enlist more of their people to take part in these tasks.

## Benevolences Outside the Convention

Although the official minutes and newspaper accounts at the time of the 1845 meeting of Southern Baptists at Augusta make no reference to it, it is evident that there was some ambivalence relative to the nature of the convention to be organized by Southern Baptists. The plan adopted at Augusta provided that the new body could carry on as many benevolences as it desired, and contemplated an all-inclusive denominational structure

---

[22] J. B. Jeter, *The Recollections of a Long Life (Richmond*: The Religious Herald Co., 1891), 233.

through which Southern Baptists might carry on every type of work. This was reflected in the call issued by the Virginia Baptist Foreign Mission Society, the address of William B. Johnson to the South Carolina Baptists State Convention on May 3, 1845, and in the constitution that was adopted.

However, although many additional benevolences were being discussed by Southern Baptists in 1845, such as a new Bible society or board, a new publication society, and an education society to provide a school for theological training, none of these was included in the 1845 structure of the Southern Baptist Convention. Instead, during this period Southern Baptist developed a publication society, a Sunday School union, and a seminary outside the structure of the Convention.

**Southern Baptist Publication Society.** Although there is no explanation of the fact in the records, it is evident that the principal target of protest as the consultative meeting in 1845 and in the Address to the public was the foreign mission society. The Home Mission Society of New York and the American Baptist Publication Society of Philadelphia received little attention, if any, although the action of the consultative body brought separation from the home mission body but not from the publication body. The silence of the records on the latter is noticeable, since the call of Virginia Baptists for a consultative convention specifically suggested that Southern Baptists might organize a separate publication society. At the 1844 meeting of the Georgia Baptist Convention, James Davis had introduced a motion calling for the formation of a southern publication society, but is was defeated. At the 1845 consultative meeting in Augusta, J.S. Baker, the aggressive editor of *The Christian Index* of Georgia introduced a resolution concerning a publication society, although not recorded at the time, which was also voted down.[23] Perhaps one of the reasons for the silence concerning the American Baptist Publication Society was that J. L. Burrows came as a corresponding delegate from the publication body of Philadelphia and was invited to participate in the discussions. In fact, on the second afternoon of the meeting Burrows addressed the body in behalf of the American Baptist Publication Society. The address to the Public emphasized that the extent of the disunion between North and South should not be exaggerated, since it involved "only the Foreign and Domestic Missions of the

---

[23] See the *Southern Baptist* (Charleston, S.C.), August 29, 1855, 3.

denomination." When it is recalled that there were only three principal Baptist benevolent societies, the General Missionary Convention for Foreign Missions organized in 1814, the American Baptist Publication Society organized in 1824, and the American Baptist Home Mission Society organized in 1832, the southern separation from the two missionary societies but not the publication body in 1845 is noteworthy. The abolitionist literature said that the publication body had not given any cause to the southerners for separating from them.

At any rate, after the 1845 consultative meeting, there came continued appeals for the organization of a publication society for Southern Baptists from almost every part of the South. Editor J. S. Baker published many of these in *The Christian Index* of Georgia. However, the various newspapers of the South were divided on this matter. When Secretary J. M. Peck of the American Baptist Publication Society suggested to Georgia Baptists in the summer of 1845 that an agent be permitted to collect funds in Georgia for the society, the Executive Committee of the Georgia Baptist Convention replied that it was their hope that a southern board for publication and Bible distribution would be organized. After this reply was published, Editor John L. Waller of the *Western Baptist Review* of Kentucky promptly protested that there should be no more divisions.

> We wish to see no further alienation of feelings between the North and South. Discord has already done enough.... Being wholly unapprized [sic] of the existence of any necessity for further division, we solemnly enter our protest against withdrawing from the Bible and Publication societies, merely because their Boards are located north of Mason and Dixon's line.[24]

There was another important factor that caused many Southern Baptist leaders to refuse or delay the publication enterprise. This was the financial stringency of the period. The Panic of 1837 had brought a depression that lasted until the consultative convention of 1845 at Augusta. Even the American Baptist Publication Society, with twenty-five years of financial roots and expertise, was severely shaken by this financial crisis,

---

[24] John L. Waller, ed., *Western Baptist Review* (Frankfort, Kentucky: 1845), I, 57 ff.

and southern members of that society, acquainted with the details of that fierce financial struggle, shrank from venturing into a competitive enterprise with such related perils.

The division of opinion manifested in the discussions between the Georgia and Kentucky editors in 1845 came to the floor of the Southern Baptist Convention when it met at Richmond, Virginia, in 1846. Thomas Stocks of Georgia introduced a resolution calling for the appointment of a committee of two from each state to consider organizing a Board of Managers for Bible and publication work. An extensive discussion followed the report of the committee, and there were numerous amendments. Finally, however, relative to the question of organizing a Southern Publication Board within the Convention structure, the Convention approved the statement that it "does not deem it advisable to embarrass itself with any enterprise for the publication and sale of books," This victory for the Kentucky position provided an attitude toward the publication of books by the Convention that was often repeated during the remainder of the century.

The issue was not settled, however. The Central Baptist Association of Georgia in its 1846 session issued a call to all Southern Baptists for a convention to meet at Savannah on May 13, 1847, just prior to the gathering of the state body, to consider the organization of a separate society for carrying on publication work in the South. Approximately 100 well-known leaders of Southern Baptists gathered at that time and formed the Southern Baptist Publication Society.[25] A constitution was adopted providing membership on a financial basis for individual, Baptist churches, and Baptist societies. The object of the body was to "publish and distribute such books as are needed to the Baptist denomination in the South". An appeal was made to all Baptists in the southern states to affiliate with this society.[26]

This action, of course, was not novel in the sense that Southern Baptists had never organized independent societies of this kind. They had done so both on the state level and on an interstate level, as seen, for example, in the home mission society of R. T. Daniel in 1839. However,

---

[25] Jesse H. Campbell of Georgia claimed credit for its initiation. See Jesse H. Campbell, *Georgia Baptists: Historical and Biographical* (Macon: J. W. Burke & Co., rev. ed., 1874), 81.

[26] See Baker, *Source Book*, 126-28 for the constitution.

this was significant in that it magnified an optional way for benevolent work after the Convention as such had refused to carry on the particular benevolence. It simply meant that a minority of Southern Baptists could organize for benevolences without reference to the action of the Southern Baptist Convention. It provided another safeguard, if one were needed, against the centralization of the Convention, and still constitutes a live option that has been repeated in various spheres of activity, as will be noted.

Many southern organizations which had been auxiliary to the American Baptist Publication Society of Philadelphia changed their affiliation to this new Southern Baptist body. As a matter of fact, the American Baptist Publication Society refrained voluntarily from working in the South from this time until after the Civil War. The question of bringing this southern publication body into the structure of the Convention was agitated regularly after 1858, but nothing came of it. Sometime during the Civil War, perhaps in late 1863, this southern publication society ceased operations, a casualty of the war. During the 16 years of its existence it printed more than 80 different books and booklets, totaling almost 250,000 copies. Southern Baptists gave more than $100,000 for the work during these years showing the interest in this type of ministry by many.[27]

**Southern Baptist Sunday School Union.** In all denominations the Sunday School was becoming recognized as an excellent teaching and enlistment opportunity. In 1840 the Baptist Tract Society changed its name to the American Baptist Publication and Sunday School Society to emphasize its entrance into the area of Sunday School work.

In 1857, R. B. C. Howell, president of the Southern Baptist Convention, introduced a resolution at the Concord Association of Tennessee urging the formation of a Sunday School union. Delegates from eight states met at Nashville on October 13, 1857, and organized the Southern Baptist Sunday School Union. The body became suspect, however, when the Landmark leader, A. C. Dayton, was elected its president. Despite some opposition, the union continued until it was killed by the Civil War.

---

[27] For a summary of this story in larger perspective, see Baker *The Story of the Sunday School Board* (Nashville: Convention Press, 1966), 6-11.

**Southern Baptist Theological Seminary.** Practically all of the southern states recognized quite early the need for ministerial education and endeavored to meet these needs. At least ten southern states provided Baptist colleges which were founded for the specific purpose of providing literary and theological training for ministers. However, in 1835 Basil Manly, Jr., pastor of the First Baptist Church, Charleston, South Carolina, wrote that these efforts in various states were not enough. He suggested a coalition of several states to cooperate in founding a southwide theological school. Nothing came of this suggestion. In 1841 North and South Carolina Baptists pondered a plan for all collegiate students from each state to go to Wake Forest in North Carolina, while all theological students from both states would go to Furman in South Carolina. This also fell through. J. L. Dagg of Mercer in Georgia wrote to Robert Ryland of Virginia stirring the question, and in response the Virginia Baptist Education Society appointed a committee in 1844, which reported in the following year that despite the importance of the enterprise, nothing could be done for the present.

> The difficulty lies in selecting a site for such a School. Our Brethren, in South Carolina, Georgia, and Alabama, have, each of those states, an Institution, partly endowed, which they would gladly have adopted as the common Theological School of the Southern and South-western Baptists.[28]

At the consultative meeting of Southern Baptists in 1845 at Augusta, leaders from the seaboard states discussed the need for such an institution, but all recognized that the Baptist colleges in the South which had theological departments felt they did not need such a southwide body and provided formidable opposition.

Baptists in the West made the first beginning of a cooperative enterprise for theological education. Campaigning had begun as early as 1833, and a Western Baptist Education Society was formed. Under their auspices the Western Baptist Theological Institute opened in Covington, Kentucky, in 1845, but unfortunately for the enterprise, at the very height of northern-southern tension over slavery, the faculties were all northern

---

[28] See *Proceedings of the Baptist General Association of Virginia* (Richmond, 1845), 21.

men of antislavery sentiments in a school located in a slave state. After legal controversy, the school was closed and its property divided.[29]

For almost a decade the pros and cons of a southwide theological institution were discussed in editorials from various states in the South, some opposing and some supporting it. Significant action came in 1855 when an Education Conference, meeting between sessions of the Southern Baptist Convention at Montgomery, called an Education Convention to meet in Augusta, Georgia, in April, 1856. At that meeting there were sixty-eight delegates from Maryland, District of Columbia, Virginia, North Carolina, South Carolina, Georgia, Alabama, Florida, Mississippi, Tennessee, and Louisiana. All but twenty of these were from South Carolina and Georgia. The group recognized that the location of the school and funds for its founding and operation were basic in considering the establishment of a southwide school, and named a special committee to study these matters and report at a meeting in the following year. Two months later, the South Carolina Baptist Convention proposed that the theological funds of Furman University would be turned over to the trustees of a general theological school, and that South Carolina would increase these funds to $100,000 on the conditions that that the proposed seminary would be located in Greenville and that the other states would raise an equal amount. When the education Convention met in 1857 at Louisville between sessions of the Southern Baptist Convention, there were eighty-eight delegates from twelve states. After earnest discussion, the South Carolina offer was unanimously accepted, despite sharp disagreement on the part of advocates of other schools.

The Education Convention met in Greenville, South Carolina, May 1, 1858 but plans to organize the new institution were delayed because a faculty had not been completed. An Abstract of Principles was prepared and adopted by the Education Convention.[30]

The seminary opened in Greenville, South Carolina, in the fall of 1859 with James P. Boyce as chairman of the faculty, along with John A. Broadus, Basil Manly, Jr., and William Williams as professors. There

---

[29] W. C. James, *A History of the Western Baptist Theological Institute* (Louisville: Baptist World Publishing Co., 1910), Kentucky Baptist Historical Society Papers, No. 1, 31-100. See also Cox, eds. *Encyclopedia*, II, 1486.

[30] See Baker, *Source Book*, 137 ff for this document and the discussion of it by James P. Boyce.

were twenty-six students in the first session, representing six southern states. The work of the Seminary was soon suspended by Civil War.

**James P. Boyce, first president of the Southern Baptist Theological Seminary**

**John A. Broadus**

**Basil Manly, Jr.** (Photos courtesy of the Southern Baptist Historical Library and Archives)

# Chapter 8 - The Antebellum Years

Southern Baptists, of course, were a part of the economic, social, and political patterns of the 1840's and 1850's. Economically, cotton had become the king of the crops. Because of the rapid expansion into the south central and southwest portions of the country, the growing of cotton increased geometrically. In 1830 over 500,000 bales were exported; in 1850, this had increased to nearly 2,000,000 bales; while in 1860, exports had reached the amazing total of about 4,000,000 bales. Despite this huge increase in production, the demand was such that the price of cotton itself even began to increase slowly. The price reached an all-time low of below six cents a pound in 1845, but slowly increased until the average in 1857 was nearly fourteen cents a pound. By 1860 the cotton crop reached the enormous total of 5,300,000 bales, seven-eighths of the world's supply. Meanwhile, particularly in Virginia and Kentucky, the tobacco crop was also bringing prosperity. In 1849 this crop had amounted to less than 200,000,000 pounds, but by 1860 it exceeded 430,000,000 pounds.

It should not be overlooked that Baptists in the South were mainly of the lower economic class. Very few, if any of them, were among the 8,000 planters who owned over 50 slaves each and used them on huge plantations in a commercial enterprise. Two thirds of the white families in Virginia owned no slaves; three fourths of the white families in North Carolina owned no slaves; half of the white families in South Carolina owned no slaves; about two thirds of the white families in Georgia held no slaves. Frederick Jackson Turner noted that in about 1845 two thirds of the white families in all the South Central states (which included Kentucky, Tennessee, Alabama, Mississippi, and Louisiana, the repository of most of the slaves in America) were not slaveholders. This meant that while there was general prosperity in the raising of cotton, in particular, Baptists as a group rarely participated directly in such profits. However, the entire culture was built upon King Cotton, and the general prosperity engendered in the whole society by the raising of cotton also affected the Baptists.

Even the panic of 1857 did not greatly affect the South, where cotton crops were good, prices were high, and banks were sound.

Distinguished black Baptist preachers also served in the South during this period. There were some churches of wholly black membership, especially in larger cities. Typical of this class was the church in Savannah, Georgia, organized in 1788, founded under the preaching of Andrew Bryan, who served as its pastor for twenty-four years until his death in 1812. Sometimes these independent black churches were under the pastoral care of a white minister. Robert Ryland, first president of Richmond College, was a pastor of the black church in Richmond for twenty-five years beginning in 1841, and baptized over 3,800 persons into its membership. Sometimes the whites and blacks, in a single church had separate organizations, each with its own pastor, deacons, business session, preaching, and so forth. The First Baptist Church, Montgomery, Alabama, was an example of this. Two thirds of its 900 members about 1860 were blacks.

Most black Baptists before 1860 were members of white churches and occupied separate sections reserved for them. It was not uncommon to find a church with three rather distinct sections: the white men in one area, white women in another and the blacks still in another. Sometimes the rigorous state laws, which set specific rules for allowing manumission, were by-passed in a rather interesting fashion. The Alabama Association, for example, recognized the great ability of Caesar McLemore as a preacher and desired to employ him to win the blacks to Christ in the area of the association. State laws, however, would not permit this; so the association purchased him and appointed a committee to direct his work as a missionary of the association. He was very effective, despite the fact that a Baptist association had to become a slaveholder to secure his services.[1]

Accurate statistics as to the number of black Baptists in 1860 are almost impossible to secure. A scholarly guess of 400,000 has been made, and this may be as accurate as can be secured.[2]

However, there were three factors that combined to destroy the antebellum culture. These were the deepened sectionalism in the 1840's

---

[1] Baker, *Source Book*,. 163 ff.
[2] Ibid., 165.

and 1850's, the rapid development of slavery into a political issue, and the humanitarian reforms of the same decades which centered their attacks on slavery.

The three areas, Northeast, South, and West, it will be recalled, had given evidence before the 1840's of their sectional loyalties. The severe struggles of the 1830's over a protective tariff, the Bank of the United States, and the nature of the constitution had brought wounds that never quite healed. With the rapid economic prosperity based upon cotton which, in turn, used black slavery, the South united as a section. The Northeast with her new manufacturing interests and the West with her agrarian interests vied with the South for political and economic control.

It was to be expected that such sectionalism would fall into the political realm. The war with Mexico over the annexation of Texas brought strong antislavery repercussions because of the fear that this would open the door to further introduction of slavery to the West. The antislavery Wilmot Proviso of 1846 was the reply of the abolitionists. This argument brought a congeries of sectional antislavery legislation and struggle. The North was rapidly drawing away from the South in population and in senatorial voting. New political parties favoring abolitionism, such as the Free Soil party, arose. In 1849-50, tension deepened when California, New Mexico, and Utah applied for admission as free states. The Compromise of 1850, supported by President Millard Fillmore, doubtless delayed actual military conflict between the sections. However, the Kansas-Nebraska Bill debate in 1854, and the Dred Scott Decision in 1857 led to the organization of the new Republican Party and the election of Abraham Lincoln.

Along with this sectional and political antagonism, the 1840's and 1850's were decades of strong humanitarian reforms. Almost every type of reform agitation occurred in these years over labor, education, women's rights, temperance, prisons, peace, and so on. It was unthinkable that the vulnerable slavery system in the South should not be involved in these humanitarian reforms.

In the midst of these critical and exciting events Southern Baptists moved in new directions during the years between the provisional formation of their convention in 1845 and the close of the period in 1860.

## Increasing Activity Through State Bodies

The formation of Baptist state bodies in the southern states, accentuated by the organization of the new southwide body in 1845, brought an increased unity among Baptists in the South during this period. This does not mean that all Baptists in each state promptly joined with the new state body in a common cause. There were still large pockets of antimission Baptists of various sorts, such as the Primitives, Hardshells, followers of Campbell, and Daniel Parker's Two-Seeders. Some of these remained within the missionary churches. In addition, some missionary Baptists were not yet ready for an additional organizational structure like a state body. But large impetus was given in the several states to a new Baptist unity in both structure and function through the formation of these state organizations.

**New State Organizations.** Nine Baptist state bodies were in operation in southern states before the organization of the Southern Baptist Convention in 1845. These were formed in South Carolina, 1821; Georgia, 1822; Alabama and Virginia, 1823; North Carolina, 1830; Missouri, 1834; Maryland and Mississippi, 1836; and Kentucky, 1837.

Baptists in Alabama played a large part in the confrontation of 1845 that brought the organization of the Southern Baptist Convention. Fourteen messengers were appointed to attend the Augusta meeting, and during the summer and fall of 1845, churches, associations, and the state convention approved the new southwide convention structure. The Domestic Mission Board was located at Marion, Alabama, a strategic and significant choice.

During this period the state body "became well established and was accepted as the unifying agency among Alabama Baptists as a whole." The antimissionary forces had withdrawn to form a separate body, although there continued to be antimission and anti-convention sentiment in northern Alabama. The agitation over slavery distracted Baptists. Despite this, as will be noted, Alabama Baptists had phenomenal growth. State missions were aggressively promoted; after 1850 (when a southwide emphasis was placed upon Sunday Schools) the strength of the Sunday School movement grew rapidly; and the state body was moving toward assistance for aged or disabled ministers and their widows. J. R. Graves visited Alabama often, and many Baptists there read his paper with its strong Landmark views after about 1850. He sowed distrust of the denominational boards and the Southern Baptist Convention itself.

Judson Female Institute, at Marion, which had been chartered in 1841, was given to the state body in 1843, and flourished during this period. Howard College (for men), which had been chartered in 1841, was razed by fire in 1844 and again in 1854. It had barely been rebuilt and occupied before war came. In addition to Judson and Howard, almost a dozen Baptist local schools were scattered across the state.

A state paper, *The Alabama Baptist*, began publication in 1843. Evidently the scholarly M. P. Jewett was the chief editor and manager of the paper in the beginning. In 1850 the paper changed its title to *The South Western Baptist*, which it retained until the close of the civil war. Another short-lived paper was edited by W. C. Buck in 1859.

In Missouri, the general body, organized in 1835, became auxiliary to the Southern Baptist Convention in 1845. State missions were vigorously promoted, including the organization of a German Mission Society in 1853 to carry the gospel to the large numbers of Germans entering Missouri.[3] There was considerable strife after 1847 over the question of employing paid agents in missionary promotion.

After disappointing delays William Jewell College was chartered in 1849 and, except for a two-year closure in 1855-57, flourished until it was closed by the war in 1861.

Despite several vigorous efforts to establish a state denominational paper, a satisfactory publication was not developed during this period. *The Western Watchman* was published intermittently after 1848, but its disfavor was indicated by the beginning of a rival paper in 1860, *The Missouri Baptist*. Both died with the coming of the war.

Mississippi Baptists wholeheartedly approved of the new southwide body and cooperated in its work.[4] Despite transportation and communication difficulties, missionary activity by both the state body and through the missionary associations was effective. Sunday Schools were promoted and a Bible and colportage society was organized in 1859. Several papers were begun during this period. The *Tennessee Baptist*,

---

[3] W. Pope Yeaman, *A History of the Missouri Baptist General Association* (Columbia: E. W. Stephens Press, 1899), 90.
[4] See R. A. McLemore, *A History of Mississippi Baptists, 1780-1970* (Jackson, Miss.: Mississippi Baptist Convention Board, 1971), 142 ff.

published by J. R. Graves, was often recommended to the people (and Graves was often in the state during the 1850's). At the very close of the period, Mississippi Baptists experienced a serious controversy over Graves and his Landmark views. The 1860 convention appointed a committee to help mediate between Graves and the First Baptist Church, Nashville, Tennessee, which allayed some of the pro-Graves feelings in the state.[5] Intermittently the *Mississippi Baptist* was published between 1846 and 1862. Many private Baptist schools flourished, but in 1850 Mississippi College at Clinton was accepted by the Mississippi Baptist Convention, and it quickly became the largest such institution in the state. Mississippi Baptist Female College was established in 1851 under the leadership of William Carey Crane. A state education society promoted the raising of funds during this period.

In Kentucky, this period was characterized "by increased organization of the friends of missions for the spread of the gospel in all the world."[6] This statement was alluding particularly to the elimination of antimissions from Kentucky churches and associations, and the consequent new unity provided among the mission-minded Baptists.

At the 1845 meeting in Georgetown, the new Southern Baptist Convention was the chief topic of discussion. Kentucky Baptists heartily endorsed the organization of the new body, and welcomed J. B. Jeter of Virginia, the president of the new Foreign Mission Board of the southwide body. Plans were made to forward the "union among the various societies and associations of Baptists in the south." The China Missionary Society of Kentucky was placed under the operation of the southwide convention.

A unifying reorganization took place beginning in 1850 in which all separate benevolent societies were united under one board with one agent, and by 1852 it was reported that this movement was already bearing fruit. Refinements in structure were continued, almost annually, until 1857. At the 1857 meeting, many Southern Baptist Convention leaders arrived early for the southwide gathering which met the day following the adjournment of the Kentucky convention, and a long list of distinguished

---

[5] Baker, *Source Book*,150 ff; and see also Lynn E. May, Jr., *The First Baptist Church of Nashville, Tennessee, 1820-1970* (Nashville: First Baptist Church, 1970), 90.
[6] Frank M. Masters, *A History of Baptists in Kentucky*, (Louisville: Kentucky Baptist Historical Society, 1953), 283.

Baptists from the South were present at the Kentucky meeting, including, of course, J. R. Graves of Tennessee.

Year by year the mission program in the state advanced. In 1853, for example, the Board of Managers reported: "Perhaps in no year since the organization of the General Association had more missionary labor been performed than the present."[7] In 1857, unusual because it antedated a general movement of the kind, the body adopted a resolution urging all pastors to endeavor to form "Female Missionary Societies" in their respective churches.

Educational activity among Kentucky Baptists continued during this period. Georgetown College was regularly promoted by the state body; in 1855, in particular, reports showed that Bethel College at Russellville had been developed; eight "Female Schools" of various grades were flourishing; and some Baptist high schools for both male and female were being well patronized.[8] The Ministerial Education Society was active. The new Western Baptist Theological Institute at Covington, Kentucky "ought not, under present circumstances, to receive support of the Baptists of Kentucky," said the General Association in 1845. A committee of the state body was appointed to confer with trustees of the Institute in 1847, and in 1851, the school was commended for young ministers. The minutes of 1853 report the dissolution of the school.[9]

The name of the Baptist paper in Kentucky was changed to the *Western Recorder* in 1851 when John L. Waller again became editor, and the people were urged to patronize the paper. The state body also recommended the *Western Baptist Review*, which was published from 1845 through 1851, principally by Waller; it was renamed the *Christian Repository* and continued during the remainder of the period under the same editorship.

The minutes of the General Association reflect that the Mexican war (1846-48) took many of their young men into service, while occasional epidemics in 1848-49 retarded the work. The Sunday School was urged after 1854 as an aid to evangelism and religious education, and a Kentucky Baptist Ministers' body was promoted during the 1850's.

---

[7] Ibid., 301.
[8] Ibid., 304.
[9] Ibid., 290, 291, 299, 300.

Two rather divisive matters during this period in Kentucky involved abolitionism and Landmarkism. Baptists were divided on the question of slavery in this state, some being fervent on each side. A strong anti-slavery paper was established in Lexington in 1845, and the constitutional convention of 1849 showed the divided opinion of the people. J. M. Pendleton, who wrote the Landmark tract, "An Old Landmark Re-Set," in 1854, was pastor at Bowling Green, Kentucky, but in 1857 moved to Tennessee, thence, when war came, to Pennsylvania. Pendleton's Landmark views brought a literary controversy in 1854-55.[10]

Between 1845 and 1860, four additional states organized new general bodies. The first chronologically was Texas. On September 8, 1848, the Texas Baptist Convention was organized by fifty-five delegates from twenty-one churches gathered at Anderson. The financial basis of representation was initially adopted, but in 1860 the constitution was altered to provide numerical representation from churches and associations. Reflecting the increasing areas of activity of state bodies, from the first this organization manifested its interest in education, publication of a Baptist newspaper, foreign missions, home missions, distribution of the Bible, and the religious condition of the black population. A second state body was organized on May 24, 1855, and in 1868 its name was changed to the Baptist General Association of Texas.

Much of the rapid progress of Texas Baptists in this early period was due to strong leaders like Z. N. Morrell and R. E. B. Baylor, and the two great missionaries, James Huckins and William M. Tryon, both of whom were first sent by the Domestic Mission Board of the South thereafter.

In 1840 the first association (Union) was formed, and in 1848 the Texas Baptist State Convention came into being. Unfortunately, in a sectional disagreement, a second state body was organized in 1853, which was re-formed two years later under the name Eastern Texas Baptist Convention. Both bodies promoted missionary and Sunday School work actively during the remainder of the period. Sunday School interest was kindled quite early with the coming of Thomas J. Pilgrim in 1828, who spent a long life promoting this movement. Blacks, Germans, and Mexicans were the targets of missionary activity.

---

[10]See Masters, *Baptists in Kentucky*, 308-311 for a good review.

A newspaper, *The Texas Baptist*, published from 1855 to 1860, when it became an early casualty of the war. J. R. Graves was quiet influential in Texas, his Tennessee paper being widely circulated and his Landmark publications finding numerous sympathetic readers.

At the second meeting of the Union Association in 1841, two important bodies were organized: the Texas Baptist Home Mission Society and the Texas Baptist Education Society. Working through the latter body, William M. Tryon fathered Baylor University, chartered in 1845 by the Republic of Texas. Over a dozen institutes and female colleges were organized during this period, including Waco Classical School in 1855 and two colleges at Tyler in east Texas.[11]

In 1848, thirty years after the organization of the first church in Arkansas, Baptists there formed a state body. J. S. Rogers, their historian, remarked that in 1848 the "80 to 100 Baptist fathers… found they had no State-wide organization, no newspaper, no schools of college grade, in fact no State-wide institution of any kind." There was still the opposition of antimission groups, preachers needed training, and a Baptist paper was needed.[12] The new state body brought zeal and growth. Before the close of the period the number of associations had doubled, a state paper had been established, and two Baptist academies had opened.[13]

On September 21, 1848, the Arkansas Baptist State convention was organized by seventy-two representatives at Tulip, Arkansas. Membership was composed of "delegates from Baptist Associations, Churches, and individual contributors who are members of Baptist Churches in good standing. Associations shall be entitled to five and churches to three delegates to the Convention." Because this body was located in the southern part of the state, Baptists in the north organized the White River Baptist Convention on September 14, 1850, with messengers from about twenty churches. After 1850, Baptists in eastern Arkansas organized the General Association of Eastern Arkansas.

In 1858 the convention authorized the publication of the *Arkansas Baptist* under the editorship of P. S. G. Watson. The promising beginning in January, 1859, was soon destroyed by civil war.

---

[11] See Baker, *The Blossoming Dessert*, for this story.
[12] J. S. Rogers, *History of Arkansas Baptists* (Little Rock: Executive Board of Arkansas Baptist State Convention, 1948), p. 445.
[13] Ibid., 451.

The Landmark movement, which would become severely divisive in a later generation, was introduced into Arkansas as early as 1851 when J. R. Graves held a sweeping revival meeting at Elena and organized a strong church there. The church was a liberal and loyal supporter of the state body, but Graves had a commanding and enthusiastic following among Arkansas Baptists from about 1850 to 1870 or later.[14]

After several futile efforts to form a state body, Louisiana Baptists on December 2, 1848, at Mount Lebanon, organized the Baptist State Convention of North Louisiana. The word "North" was dropped in 1853. Representation was on a financial basis until well after the close of this period.

In his story of Louisiana Baptists, John T. Christian judged that in the period between about 1835 and 1850, Louisiana Baptists had no common rallying point. They were few in number, new in the land, opposed and despised by many enemies, and had not one minister of commanding influence.[15] During these years the antimission forces of Hardshellism or Primitivism and of Campbellism brought dissension and lethargy.[16] The turning point in Louisiana Baptist history was the organization in 1848 of the Baptist State Convention of Louisiana. At first some associations withheld cooperation, but within a relatively few years the new state body provided the nucleus for the unity needed by Louisiana Baptists.

New Orleans was one of the first recipients of assistance from the new Domestic Mission Board of the Southern Baptists Convention. Russell Holman and I. T. Hinton of New Orleans had assisted in the organization of the southwide body in 1845 at Augusta. The most severe yellow fever epidemic New Orleans had yet known occurred in 1847 and took the life of Hinton along with many others. The discovery of gold in California in 1849 caused New Orleans Baptists to emigrate to the west. The organization of the new state body came at a very critical time in these early years.

In 1852 the state body founded Mt. Lebanon University, which had a promising beginning that was interrupted by civil war. A female

---

[14] Ibid., 588.
[15] John T. Christian, *A History of the Baptists of Louisiana* (Shreveport: The Executive Board of the Louisiana Baptist Convention, 1923), 98.
[16] Christian, *Baptists of Louisiana,* 102-107.

college was also organized at Mt. Lebanon but also died with the war. Keachie Female College was charted in 1857 and flourished, but its operations were suspended during the war.

Before the formation of a state body in 1854, Florida Baptists were led by outstanding pioneer missionaries (several from the Southern Baptist Convention after 1845) like John Tucker, William B. Cooper, Richard J. Mays, Joshua Mercer (brother of Georgia's Jesse Mercer), James MacDonald, and J. M. Hayman, in particular. The antimission struggle affected Baptists here, but when Suwannee Association became antimissionary in 1845, it began an excision of those who opposed missions from Florida churches and associations. This was a healthy development for the inner structure of early Florida Baptists.[17]

Even before a state body was formed, Florida Baptists seriously discussed the founding of a college. Several academies were formed after 1851. E. E. Joiner judged that problems of sectionalism and race played little part in early Florida Baptist history. There was no state paper during this period, but good books distributed by colporteurs, and active interest was expressed in increasing Sunday School work.

The state body was organized in 1854, and their constitution was probably modeled after that of Georgia Baptists.[18] It is rather interesting to note that the ever-present J. R. Graves of Tennessee showed up at this organizational meeting.[19] Florida Baptists organized their state body on November 20, 1854, near the Concord Baptist Church, Madison County. During the remainder of this period the great distances to travel and the financial condition of the people greatly hindered the work of the convention.

Thus, by the close of this period in 1860, Baptists in thirteen of the fifteen states cooperating in the work of the Southern Baptist Convention had developed state bodies. Tennessee remained divided into three sectional conventions despite efforts at unification, while the District of Columbia was still charting its direction. There is considerable evidence that the states organizing new bodies took counsel with the leaders in the states already so structured in an effort to provide the very best kind of

---

[17] See E. E. Joiner, *A History of Florida Baptists* (Jacksonville: Florida Baptist Convention, 1972), 30.
[18] Ibid., 38.
[19] Ibid.. 39 n.

organization. In fact, it is quite characteristic of the minutes of the several state bodies to name distinguished visitors from many other states at each of their annual sessions. These visitors were both teachers and pupils in states not their own, which helped to create a new atmosphere of unity and cooperation that had heretofore been limited to associational or church meetings. Common patterns of state activity clearly began to emerge under these new conditions. State structures were often quite similar; independent state benevolent societies soon began to merge with the state body to bring more unity of action; and the functions of the state bodies began to polarize around common objectives – growth, missions (state, southwide, and foreign), education, state papers, and specialized benevolences (hospitals, orphanages, widows' relief, old ministers' assistance, etc.).

There is also evidence of a new unity among Baptists in the South because of the organization of the Southern Baptist Convention in 1845. This would be expected, of course, as an immediate sectional reaction to withdrawal from cooperation with the General Missionary Convention and the American Baptist Home Mission Society, but signs occasionally appear in the literature that reveal distinct efforts to forward this unity. For example, it is likely that the appearance of W. B. Johnson at the North Carolina state meeting in 1845 and of J. B. Jeter at the Kentucky meeting in the same year marked a planned purpose by leaders of the new Southern Baptist Convention to strengthen the ties of the general body with the several states.

There was no single state body in Tennessee during this period. Instead, after the disintegration of the Tennessee Baptist convention in 1842, three sectional bodies developed: the General Association of Baptists of East Tennessee; the Baptist General Association of Tennessee, which in 1849 took the name Baptist General Association of Middle Tennessee and North Alabama; and the West Tennessee Baptist Convention. Unification into a single body was delayed because of differences involved in geographical location, lack of communication, localized historical background, and diverse reactions to the various controversies sweeping Tennessee during this and the previous period.

The East Tennessee body organized Carson College in 1850 and carried on missionary work in its section during the period. It split in 1859 over the Graves-Howell controversy.

The Middle Tennessee body established Union University at Murfreesboro in 1848 under the aegis of the Tennessee Baptist Education Society. The school closed with the outbreak of the civil war. R. B. C. Howell dominated this Middle Tennessee body until he accepted a pastorate in Virginia in 1850, after which J. R. Graves assumed this function. The controversy between these two men after Howell returned to Nashville in 1857 almost wrecked this Baptist General Association, but Graves retained control of it.

The West Tennessee Baptist Convention carried on an active missionary program in its section during this period. It established a male institute in Madison County which took the name Madison College in 1859.

The denominational paper, *The Baptist*, owned and published by R. B. C. Howell at the opening of the period, was given by him to the Middle Tennessee body in 1846, after which it came under the control of J. R. Graves and had wide circulation, even beyond the borders of Tennessee.

## The First Years of the Southern Baptist Convention

Although the convention was structured as a triennial body (after the pattern of the General Missionary Convention), it actually convened eight times from the 1845 consultative meeting at Augusta to the May, 1861, meeting in Savannah, Georgia, after civil war had begun. The more frequent gatherings were inaugurated by an unfortunate experience in 1849. The convention was scheduled to meet at Nashville, but a cholera epidemic in that city caused a sparsely attended meeting that was convened there by Vice-President R. B. C. Howell to be shifted to Charleston, South Carolina, for the completion of the session. By a vote of forty-two to seventeen, the Convention adopted a resolution to amend the constitution to arrange for biennial rather than triennial meetings, but this suggestion was not supported by the body. The presiding officers during these eight meetings, William B. Johnson (1845-49), R. B. C. Howell (1851-87), and Richard Fuller (1859-61), were gifted and wise leaders.

The general attendance at these meetings of the Convention was somewhat discouraging. Except for the session at Richmond in 1859 (where Virginia alone reported 241 delegates), the average attendance was around 160. The finances, although shaky at first, were bolstered by the use of agents in the various states to appeal for funds. In a review by the *Religious Herald of Virginia*, it was pointed out that during the thirty-three years previous to separation, while all American Baptists were united in missionary work, the South had contributed $250,656 to home and foreign missions: while by 1859, during the thirteen years the Southern Baptists Convention had been in existence, the southern states had contributed $266,359 for domestic and Indian missions and $384,339.07 for foreign missions, or a total of $650,698.07. This amounted to an average annual contribution seven times greater than that given by the South before the organization of the new body.[20]

During these first fifteen years of its existence, the new Southern Baptist Convention was confronted with several severe threats to its life.

One of these was the problem of communication and transportation. Long distances, mountain ranges, and wide rivers were formidable enemies of unity, understanding, and fellowship. To send a package of books from Richmond, Virginia, to Charleston, South Carolina, for example, it was necessary to send them to Baltimore, Maryland, first; and to send a bookcase from Tuscaloosa, Alabama, to Penfield, Georgia, it must be sent to Mobile, Alabama, to New York City, back to Savannah, Georgia, thence to Penfield by way of Augusta or Atlanta, Georgia.[21] Small attendance at conventions, expensive and slow gathering of funds and provincial prejudices were faced.

Another virulent foe was the antimission movement. As pointed out in the résumé of the state activities, most antimission followers had withdrawn or been expelled from missionary churches, associations, and state bodies by 1845, but enough of them remained to provide vigorous opposition to the new southwide body.

Still another threat to the Convention may be called localism. A vital factor in assuring the continuance of the Convention was the ability to secure funds from the constituents to promote the benevolent work. Most Southern Baptists recognized the need for giving funds for foreign missions, but missionary work on the home field was another matter. There was widespread spiritual destitution in every state of the South, and there was reluctance to give funds for home mission work somewhere else

---

[20] *Religious Herald* (Virginia), May 11, 1876, 2, col. 2.
[21] *Religious Herald,* August 13, 1847.

when the needs were so great within a local area. The Convention's first corresponding secretary for home missions resigned after less than six months of service and said that he was convinced that the people preferred to work through their associations and state bodies rather than provide funds for the Domestic Mission Board of the southwide body.

> Throughout the period from 1845 to 1894, there was friction between the Home Mission Board of the Convention and those states which desired to keep their funds and do their own work. Some of the Southern leaders gently chided these states by reminding them that they had clamored for aid from a general organization before 1845, but now that an agency had been organized to render such aid they were unwilling to give their support. For many years the funds collected and expended by the various Southern States for domestic missions greatly exceeded the amount provided for the Southern Convention's Domestic or Home Board.[22]

Some structural changes were made in the body during this period. The Indian Mission Association had been organized as an independent society in 1842, and its work was principally supported by Southern Baptists. In 1855 the association proposed union with the Convention, who instructed its Domestic Mission Board to take over the work of the association.[23] For a short time the name of the board was the Domestic and Indian Mission Board.

Also, a new board was created. From 1846 to 1851 the Convention authorized it mission boards to act as agents for the distribution of the Bible. Year by year, however, there was agitation to create a separate board for this work, and in 1851 a Bible Board, to be located at Nashville, was authorized.[24] The controversy between the American Bible Society and Baptists desiring a literal translation of the scriptures had brought a schism in 1850 with the formation of the American Bible Union. It was evident that Southern Baptists, rather than choosing officially one way or another, preferred to organize their own Bible Board. From that time until the close of the period, the board made reports to the Convention

---

[22] Baker, *Relations*, 151.
[23] Baker, *Source Book*, 129, has the document.
[24] Ibid., 128-29.

concerning funds raised for the Bible distribution and the work that was done.

Functionally, the Southern Baptist Convention had not as yet departed substantially from the old society plan followed before separation in 1845. Representation in the body still depended upon designated gifts, and agents for each benevolence in the field continued the sense of rivalry that had existed under the old society plan. The potential thrust of the Convention that was implicit in providing Boards of Managers for multiple benevolences, as set out in Article V of the constitution, was limited by the method of financing under which designated giving provided support for only two benevolences foreign and home missions.

In addition, there was no authoritative *ad interim* body or committee to represent the Convention between the regular meetings of the body. This made it necessary to continue allowing boards to be totally autonomous between sessions of the Convention. The designated giving to two benevolences (foreign and home missions) and then three (the Bible Board) eliminated any financing for the Convention body itself.

However, there were signs that the new character of the body was beginning to emerge. This was not yet recognized by those involved in it, but from a later point of vantage it can be seen. At the 1846 meeting, out of the total 135 who were present, 91 of them were from missionary societies, churches, and individuals making gifts to the convention, while state bodies and local associations had 42 representatives. By 1861, however, missionary societies, churches, and individuals sent only 8 representatives, while state bodies and local associations accounted for 169 of the 177 delegates. This is exactly the reverse of the development between 1802 and 1814 when the missionary program was rapidly taken from the hands of the associations and put into autonomous missionary societies. Now in Southern Baptist life, missionary societies were giving way to structured bodies like the associations and the state bodies as agencies to raise money for missions. Perhaps Southern Baptists were beginning to recognize the truth of what Francis Wayland had said in 1823 when criticizing the make-up of the General Missionary Convention that "missionary societies are not representative bodies," so that many were advocating that representation for a body such as the Southern Baptist Convention must be sought in structured organizations like associations and state conventions, rather than in missionary societies.

Although rather minor, another straw in the wind in developing multi-benevolence function of the Convention may be glimpsed in the fact that at first the Convention sermon was concerned only with foreign missions. Belatedly, it was recognized that the Domestic Mission Board also had an interest in the matter, so a second sermon was arranged for the purpose of forwarding domestic missions. Then, after a brief period, the Convention sermon was separated from the functions of the board, and the subject of it was left to the initiative of the preacher.

**The Foreign Mission Board.** At the 1846 session in Richmond, it was reported that C. D. Mallary, who had been elected Corresponding Secretary for the Board of Foreign Missions, had been unable to take the post because of failing health. James B. Taylor, pastor at Richmond, had temporarily assumed leadership, and the Convention enthusiastically named him as permanent corresponding secretary. He served with distinction until his death in 1871.[25] Taylor reported that by agreement with the General Missionary Convention, the northern body would retain the property that had been accumulated but would also assume responsibility for the substantial debts involved therewith. Relative to the transfer of any fields to the new body, the Boston board notified the Foreign Mission Board late in 1846 that if any of the missionaries should prefer to change their relations from Boston board to the southern board, they should "in the spirit of fraternal regard" be allowed every facility for doing so.

The board at Richmond corresponded with J. Lewis Shuck and I. H. Roberts, southerners in China, who indicated their desire to serve under the southern board. The first appointee however was Samuel C. Clopton, named on September 1, 1845, while George Pearcy was appointed in November. Shuck became a missionary of the board in March, 1846, and Roberts was accepted at the same meeting.[26] Other able missionaries were sent to the East Asia field including two giants—R.H. Graves to Canton and Matthew T. Yates.

The other field of service of the southern Foreign Mission Board during this period was Africa. John Day, a black American missionary in

---

[25] Baker J. Cauthen, ed., *Advance: A History of Southern Baptist Foreign Missions* (Nashville: Broadman Press, 1970), 28.
[26] Ibid., 78-79.

Liberia, decided to leave the service of the northern board and work under the new Convention, and he was appointed in 1846. The first missionary sent from this country by the new board was B.J. Drayton, a member of the First African Baptist Church in Richmond, who sailed in January, 1848. Thomas, J. Bowen was appointed for Central Africa in 1849. Many other missionary couples and individuals were appointed to Africa but were felled there by death or broken health. Bowen himself had to return to America, and although he worked briefly in 1859 among Yoruba slaves in Rio de Janeiro, his health prevented further service. In 1856 the northern Baptist board transferred its Liberian work to the southern board.

The board began the publication of the *Southern Baptist Missionary Journal* during the first year as a means of communicating with the constituency through the reports of the missionaries.

**The Domestic and Indian Mission Board.** The first year brought many dismal hours to the new Domestic Board, located at Marion, Alabama. Both the President and the corresponding secretary of the board resigned shortly after their appointment at Augusta. Still another corresponding secretary reluctantly accepted the post, and then resigned with the comment that "our brethren prefer carrying on their domestic missionary operations, through their Associations and state Conventions." Russell Holman then served from 1846 to 1851. T. F. Curtis retained the office for two years, and was succeeded by Joseph Walker from 1853 to 1856. Holman again took the post an 1856 and served throughout the remainder of this period.

The board outlined its field as the fourteen states of the south, covering nearly 1,000,000 square miles and a population of about 8,000,000.[27] During this period work was begun among the white population, the blacks, the Indians, the Chinese in California, and the Germans in Missouri and Maryland. It will be recalled that in 1855 the board took over the work of the American Indian Mission Association.

Meanwhile, the Home Mission Society was withdrawing its missionaries from the South in implicit recognition of the territorial field of the southern convention. In 1846 they supported two in Arkansas, one

---

[27] *Annual*, Southern Baptist Convention, 1846, 17, 34. See also W. W. Barnes, "The Dimensions of the Home Mission Task," in *Southwestern Journal of Theology* (Fort Worth), II, 2, 49 ff.

in Florida, three in Kentucky, five in Missouri, one in North Carolina, one in Texas, and one in Virginia; in 1847, there were two In Arkansas, one in Florida, two in Kentucky, four in Missouri, one in Texas, and one in Virginia; in 1848 there were two in Arkansas, one in two in Kentucky, one in Missouri, and one in Texas; In 1849 there was one in Texas, and one in New Mexico. Therefore, only Missouri generally had a missionary until the outbreak of the war.[28]

In 1847, When the Home Mission Society appointed a missionary to Texas, having previously withdrawn from this field, Secretary Russell Holman of the southern board wrote:

> Texas was abandoned by them previous to the division: after the Southern organization it was occupied by this Board. This, together with its geographical position, will furnish an apology for calling it "our field". Yet, if the Northern Board have sufficient funds to "preach the gospel to every creature" in the Northern and Western States, and Territories, and can occasionally send a Missionary to Texas, we will find no fault.[29]

The northern society left the field after a few months.

That the society might reenter the South did not seem to occur to either the society or the southern convention during this period. Since the appointment of missionaries was so closely linked to the area of receipts, and since it was not contemplated that the southern states would voluntarily leave their own Convention to provide receipts for the northern Home Mission Society, the possibility of rivalry on the home filed seemed rather remote. Yet, this remote possibility became a reality during the next period as a result of a reappraisal of its mission by the Home Mission Society of New York.

**The Bible Board.** The third board added to the structure of the Convention in 1851, as mentioned previously, was the Bible Board, located at Nashville, Tennessee, which had several secretaries during its brief life. Southern Baptists were beginning to glimpse the potentialities of Article V of their constitution, which allowed additional benevolences to be promoted by the body. They were somewhat divided over the proper

---

[28] Baker, *Relations*, 86 ff.
[29] *The Christian Index* (Georgia), April 8, 1847, 4, col. 2.

Bible society to support because of the conflict over the translation of the word *baptizein*. Since both the American and Foreign Bible Society and even the older American Bible Society were receiving rather generous gifts from Southern Baptist contributors, the leaders of the Convention thought that the formation of a Bible Board within the Convention structure would promptly guarantee that funds would be diverted from the older societies to the new board. They were mistaken. The Bible Boards' report at each biennial meeting mentioned the large sums still being sent to the other Bible societies by Southern Baptists.

## The Convention's Greatest Internal Crisis

Campbellism and Primitivism, which had been so divisive in the previous period, had now been identified and for the most part had separated from the ranks of missionary Baptists. Daniel Parker, the outstanding leader of the hyper-Calvinists, died in Texas in 1844, and there was no one of his stature to replace him. This does not mean that the antimission movement had disappeared, but its strength within Southern Baptist life had dissipated. A new and potentially divisive movement was articulated during this period, however, the effects of which are still evident in Southern Baptists life.

**The Beginning of the Landmark Movement.**[30] The principle figure in this developing conflict was J. R. Graves, who was born in Vermont in 1820. At fifteen he left Congregationalism and united with the North Springfield Baptist Church in Vermont. His family moved to Ohio in 1839, where young Graves taught school. During his two years here he was ordained as a Baptist minister, and along with his pastor entered fiercely into the struggle with Campbellism. Moving in 1841 to Kentucky, he spent four years teaching school, at the same time carrying on an intensive program of self study to compensate for his meager formal education.

---

[30] The best account of the Landmark movement is James E. Tull, *A Study of Southern Baptist Landmarkism in the Light of Historical Baptist Ecclesiology* (privately circulated Ph.D. dissertation at Columbia University, 1960), 790 pages.

In 1845 he went to Nashville, Tennessee, to take a teaching position, and for a brief season was a pastor of the Second Baptist Church. In 1846, however, he returned to membership in the First Baptist Church were R. B. C. Howell was pastor and editor of *The Baptist (The Tennessee Baptist* after 1847). In November, 1846, he became assistant editor to Howell, and in June 1848, succeeded Howell as editor. Howell moved to Virginia in 1850 to accept a pastorate there, but returned to Nashville in 1857 to serve his old church. While he was away, Graves launched the Landmark movement, and as soon as Howell returned, conflict began between the two former associates. Before describing the tumultuous events of the next several years, it would be well to describe the nature of the Landmark movement which Graves constructed piecemeal. The background of Landmarkism includes a great deal of Graves's Vermont ecclesiology, his unusual skill in integrating various elements into a single theological system, his personal aggressive nature and love for conflict, and his ability to attract strong and able lieutenants for his cause. These personal factors were matched by the immediate context of his ministry. He had learned in earlier years the art of confronting Campbellism and had breathed the heady air of victory in debate. Now in Nashville Graves found himself in a stronghold of Methodist and Disciples leadership that had the temerity to challenge the truth of the Baptist position. As editor of the Baptist paper in Nashville he had the opportunity to strike a blow as a champion for Baptist principles.

**James Robinson Graves, leader of the Landmark movement**
(Courtesy Southern Baptist Historical Library and Archives)

Literary controversies between Baptists and pedobaptists were quiet common both in England and in America. The foreign mission enthusiasm at the turn of the nineteenth century slowed somewhat the doctrinal assaults by Baptists against pedobaptists and the reverse, but the Bible controversy beginning in 1835 and continuing for many decades thereafter renewed the warfare. As described previously, in that year the American Bible Society declined to print a revised edition of Carey's Bengali Bible because pedobaptists did not want the word *baptizein* translated by a word in the language for *immerse*. The society insisted that the translation of this work must "comport with the known views of other Christian denominations." Many Baptists withdrew in 1836 from this society and formed the American and Foreign Bible Society. They were incensed when the American Bible Society used political influence to prevent the issuance of a charter to the new body by the New York legislature. After six years of struggle, the charter was finally secured in 1848, but not before the whole bitter conflict had been widely publicized in Baptist papers everywhere. The Bible translation controversy proved to be a springboard into discussions of other doctrinal differences that separated Baptists and other denominations.

In the very year the Bible translation controversy was touched off, Graves left Congregationalism to become a Baptist in Vermont. Evidently he followed the course of the controversy avidly during the next several years. In his debates later with the pedobaptists, Graves showed an intimate knowledge of this baptismal controversy that marked the days when he chose the Baptist way.

Graves seemed to thrive on controversy. As soon as he became the assistant to Howell in 1846, the paper immediately took a more aggressive stance. In an editorial in 1849 he admitted that he deliberately gave attention to controversial topics, asserting that as long as there was conviction about truth, there must be conflict. Confrontations with pedobaptists, he remarked, had won many of them to Baptist views, and such conflict was the best way to make progress. Before Landmarkism had taken form, Graves already had the temperament, the means for propagation, and the basic views that entered into the movement.

**The Principal Emphases of Landmarkism.** When matured, the system of Graves had three principal emphases, each of which was spun out into various applications in doctrine and polity. The first was the authoritative nature of the local and visible New Testament congregation. Of course he identified a New Testament congregation as a Baptist church only, since Baptists alone were admittedly reproducing the total primitive pattern described in the Scriptures. From this emphasis Graves adopted an antagonistic attitude toward any doctrine or organization that would wrest the primacy from the local churches. General bodies were suspect. Their basis of membership must not be financial, associational, or denominational: they should draw their authority from the local body.

They must not exercise authority over the local body, directly or indirectly. Their programs should not usurp the work of the local churches. Although Graves had formerly been of another mind, he came to the position that only members of a local church could participate in the Supper in that church. No person "of like faith and order" could be allowed, since these persons were not amenable to the discipline of the church observing the Supper unless they were members of it.

The second principal emphasis of Graves asserted that the kingdom of Christ was made up of the aggregate of local congregations that were true churches of Christ. Since he recognized only Baptist churches as true churches, this sounded suspiciously as though he meant that only Baptists could be saved, and he was forced many times to protest that he did not mean this. The kingdom of Christ (that is, the true churches) has had an unbroken continuity from the days of the New Testament to the present, since Christ said that the gates of death would not prevail against it. Graves wrote:

> Landmark Baptists very generally believe that for the word of the Living God to stand, and for the veracity of Jesus Christ to vindicate itself, the kingdom which he set up "in the days of John the Baptist," has had an unbroken continuity until now. I say kingdom, instead of succession of churches, for the sake of perspicacity. Those who oppose "church succession" confuse the unthinking by representing our position to be, that the identical organization which Christ established—the First Church of Judea—had had a continued existence until to-day; or, that the identical churches, planted by the apostles, or, at least, *some one* of them, has continued until now, and that Baptist ministers are successors of the apostles; in a word, that our position is the old Romish and Episcopal doctrine of apostolic succession. I have, for full a quarter of a century, by pen and voice, vehemently protested against *these* misrepresentations, as Baptists have, for twice as many more, against the charge of teaching that no one can be saved without immersion, and quiet as vainly; for those who oppose us seem determined to misrepresent, and will not be corrected. We repudiate the doctrine of apostolic succession; we do not believe *they* ever had a successor, and therefore, no one to-

> day is preaching under the apostolic commission any more than under that which Christ first gave to John the Baptist. They are our opposers who, in fact, hold to apostolic succession; for the majority does believe that, if ministers, they are preaching by the authority contained in that commission! So much for this charge.
>
> Nor have I, or any Landmarker known to me, ever advocated the succession of any particular church or churches; but my position is that Christ, in the very "days of John the Baptist," did establish a visible kingdom on earth, and that his *kingdom* has never yet been "broken in pieces," or given to another class of subjects—has never for a day "been moved," or ceased form the earth, and never will until Christ returns personally to reign over it; that the organization he first set up, which John called " the Bride," and which Christ called his Church, constitute it; and, therefore, if his *kingdom* has stood unchanged, and will to the end, he must always have had, true and uncorrupted churches, since his kingdom can not exist without true churches.[31]

Graves denied that it was necessary for him to prove by incontestable historical facts that this kingdom had stood from the day it was set up by Christ, for to question this continuous succession would be to doubt Christ's promise when he said that the gates of death would not prevail against it.

> We believe that his kingdom has stood unchanged, as firmly as we believe in the divinity of the son of God, and when we are forced to surrender the one faith, we can easily give up the other. If Christ has not kept his promise concerning his *Church* to keep it, how can I trust him concerning *my salvation?* If he has not the power to save his *church,* he certainly has not the power to save me. For Christians to admit that Christ has not preserved his kingdom unbroken, unmoved, unchanged, and uncorrupted, is to surrender the whole ground to infidelity. I deny that a man is a believer in the Bible who denies this.[32]

---

[31] Baker, *Source Book*, 142-43.
[32] Ibid.

Despite his claim that he did not need to prove historical succession, Grave early (about 1855) republished in America a book by C. H. Orchard of England, which attempted to trace Baptists from New Testament days to the present.

The third corollary of Graves's system was the assertion that true churches must possess all the doctrinal and ecclesiastical characteristics of the primitive churches in order to be a part of this unbroken and unmoved Kingdom. This meant that all pedobaptist bodies were unscriptural. Methodist, Presbyterians, Roman Catholics, and other pedobaptist groups, said Graves, were not *churches* at all because they did not follow the scriptural pattern of the New Testament. He called them *societies.* They, therefore, could not authorize or practice scriptural baptism, and could not conduct the Supper. Their ministers were not New Testament ministers and should not be invited into Baptist pulpits, even to pray. Their ordinations were not valid and their activities were without scriptural authority. This is the rationale of "close communion." This aspect of Graves's system, it should not be said, was the initial thrust of the movement.[33]

It is no wonder, in view of these strong assertions, that Graves was difficult to interpret. Baptist historian W. H. Whitsitt accused Graves of saying that salvation was impossible outside of a Baptist church. But in reply, Graves said explicitly that "Old Landmarkism did not deny the spiritual regeneration of those with whom they declined to associate ministerially or ecclesiastically; was not the denial of the honesty and conscientiousness of pedobaptist and Campbellites; that Landmarkism was not a proof of the uncharitable nature of Baptists, since they were simply following the scriptures; that Landmarkism was not a denial of the right of others to exist as professed churches or their ministers to preach their views.[34]

**The Sources of Graves' Views.** A number of complex factors unquestionably provided materials for the system of Graves. He was self-educated, choosing his own reading and areas of study, and as a consequence his theology showed the lack of a complete and systematic

---

[33] See J. M. Pendleton's statement in the *Western Recorder* (Kentucky), February 22, 1877, 1.
[34] Baker, *Source Book*, 144.

understanding of Christian doctrine.[35] James E. Tull has demonstrated that Graves was quiet at loss in trying to handle some of the basic Christian doctrines. His early training in Vermont shaped his ecclesiology, particularly the several historical factors that called for the New Hampshire Confession of Faith, which was developed during his formative years, to magnify only the local congregation. His immediate associates furnished some of the grist for his system. The strong article on pulpit affiliation by J. M. Pendleton implemented his own ideas. The integrative ability of Graves is evident as one notes how he took ideas from these associates and wove them into his thinking. For example, he published an excerpt from *Theodosia Ernest*, a novel by A. C. Dayton, in a periodical he was publishing in 1856, in which Dayton asserted that the word *church* was never used in an "invisible universal" sense in the New Testament. Graves put a footnote to the article and said: "The view is original and against the 'received authorities,' but is it not correct?"[36] Thereafter Graves incorporated this idea more completely into his writing. He could have noted the idea of historical succession in John L. Walker, R. B. C Howell, or Jessie Mercer and others. His church-kingdom emphasis he could have found in Howell or J. Newton Brown. Long before the aggressive assertion of the view by Graves in 1851, there were many references in Baptists papers to the Baptist belief that pedobaptists were unscriptural. In fact there was a startling letter in *The Christian Index* (Georgia) for April 21, 1843, in which a writer asked Editor Joseph S. Baker almost precisely the questions raised by Graves at Cotton Grove in 1851. In his reply Baker remarked that there were many who viewed pedobaptist churches merely as religious societies. Jesse Mercer of Georgia held many views that were reflected in the Landmark movement; Graves called him an "Old Landmarker."[37] When Graves tried to call James P. Boyce a Landmarker, however, Boyce protested.[38] Other portions of Graves' system can be glimpsed in various parts of Southern

---

[35] Tull, *Southern Baptist Landmarkism*, 519 ff.
[36] J. R. Graves, A. C. Dayton, and N. M. Crawford, eds., *The Southern Baptist Review and Eclectic* (Nashville: Southwestern Publishing House, 1855), Vol. II, September-October, 1856, 544.
[37] See J. R. Graves, *Old Landmarkism-What is it?* (Memphis: Baptist Book House, Graves, Mahaffy and Co., 1880), 262.
[38] See letter of Boyce in *Religious Herald* (Virginia), May 11, 1899.

Baptist life before he appeared.[39] The system of Graves, when it matured, took these and many generally received Baptist doctrines and projected them to the extreme at every point.

**The Rapid Spread of Landmarkism.** The synthesis of Graves became popular in many sections of the South, particularly in the Southwest, in a remarkably short time. He was an eloquent and persuasive platform speaker and was widely sought for general meetings. He and his lieutenants were vigorous and skilled writers, Dayton, in particular, entering many homes through his novel, *Theodosia Ernest.* Graves controlled many media for propagation of his views. His newspaper, *The Tennessee Baptist,* was the most influential Baptist paper in all the Southwest, reaching about 12,000 subscribers by 1860. He also edited several regular periodicals, such as *The Southern Baptist Review and Eclectic.* He was a frequent visitor to many southern states and usually, "swept the deck," when called upon to speak.

Graves had a reputation of being a champion of Baptist views in the struggle against Campbellism. Even J. B. Jeter, later to become his principal antagonist, admired Graves in the earlier years for their mutual efforts against Campbell. Not only so, Graves was widely known for his active participation in denominational affairs. He had a significant role in forming societies for education and for Indian missions, assisted in raising funds for Union University, organized a woman's college in Kentucky, and through his newspaper and publishing firm wielded vast influence in supporting many Baptist causes. He had a finger in forming the Bible Board and the Southern Baptist Sunday School Union, and by his opposition, sowed distrust for the Southern Baptist Publication Society, Charleston South Carolina, probably in the hope that he would become the "orthodox" publisher for Southern Baptists.

One considerable factor was the plain fact that his tenets pleased many Baptists as they were identified with true New Testament doctrines, and practices to the discredit of other denominations. In a day when doctrinal debates were common, Graves provided much new grist for the mill, and in the midst of some very trying and disheartening experiences, gave Southern Baptists a sense of "divine right" in their work.

---

[39] See, for example, J. H. Grime, *History of Middle Tennessee Baptists* (Nashville: Baptist and Reflector, 1902), 22 ff.

It is no wonder, then, Graves' system evoked a mixed response. Some viewed him as the champion of orthodoxy against the forces that would dilute the pure Baptist position; others, like John L. Waller, Kentucky editor, denied that Graves and his group held views that were Baptist at all.[40] Apart from the dubious authority and logic in his doctrines, Graves alienated many by his lack of Christian charity, his belligerent attitude, his pejorative stance, his spiritual arrogance, and his personal ambition.

**The Development of Controversy.** Just how long Graves had been formulating his system in his mind is not clear, but evidently his interest in asserting a radically sectarian and integrated system of Baptist beliefs was sparked by a letter from a Baptist association in Alabama to the *Western Baptist Review,* Louisville, Kentucky, on February 25, 1848, asking if immersion on profession of faith by a pedobaptist minister was a valid baptism. John L. Waller, editor of the paper, discussed the question at some length. He noted that it was impossible to trace a succession of "valid" baptisms back to New Testament times, so that no one could be certain whether even a Baptist administrator had an unbroken line of "valid" baptisms leading up to his own. He closed by saying:

> Let all those who can furnish clear and indubitable evidence of the validity of their baptism, according to the terms of the affirmative of the question, vote non-fellowship for those churches and ministers who believe it right to receive a member who has been immersed on profession of faith by a Pedo-Baptist minister, and let all the rest keep silence.... What can be more fair? Surely no bother in all Alabama would wish to condemn in another what he allows in himself.[41]

In direct response to Waller's letter, Graves under a pseudonym in his paper denounced the reply, saying that "the unbroken practice of the Baptist Church, from deep antiquity till now or within a few years, is higher authority than scores of Reviews."

W. W. Barnes felt that it was this discussion that "precipitated the several elements of succession that had been held in solution in Baptist

---

[40] See *Western Recorder* (Kentucky), September 20, 1854.
[41] *Western Baptist Review* (Kentucky), III, March, 1848, 276 ff.

life." He identified four aspects of this succession: church succession (each congregation must be formed by the authority of another true New Testament congregation in historical succession back to the New Testament days); apostolic succession (each ordination must be conducted by an orthodox [Baptist] and properly constituted presbytery which had historical succession from the New Testament); baptismal succession (each baptism must be performed by a "validly" baptized and authorized minister); and spiritual succession (through the centuries "there are traces of our principles and of adherents to our principles").[42] Graves, said Barnes, conjoined the first three views (churches, apostolic, and baptismal succession) into a "logical rigid system" after about 1850. James E. Tull felt that the view of Graves was basically church succession.

The first evidences of the developing synthesis appeared when Graves issued a call for interested Baptists to meet at Cotton Grove, Tennessee, on June 24, 1851, and he submitted the following questions for discussion:

> 1st. Can Baptists consistently, with their principles or the scriptures, recognize those societies, not organized according to the pattern of the Jerusalem Church, but possessing a *government*, different officers, a different *class of membership*, different *ordinances, doctrines* and *practices*, as the Church of Christ?
>
> 2d. Ought they to be called Gospel Churches or Churches in a religious sense?
>
> 3d. Can we consistently recognize the ministers of such irregular and unscriptural bodies, as gospel ministers in their official capacity?
>
> 4th. Is it not virtually recognizing them as official ministers to invite them into our pulpits, or by any other act that would or could be construed into such a recognition?
>
> 5th. Can we consistently address as brethren those *professing* Christianity, who not only have not the doctrines of Christ, and walk not according to his commandments, but are arrayed in direct and bitter opposition to them?[43]

---

[42] Barnes, *The Southern Baptist Convention*, 100-101.
[43] Baker, *Source Book*, 142.

In the following month at the annual meeting of the Big Hatchie Association at Bolivar, Tennessee, these questions were discussed. Question 4 was unanimously answered yes while the others were unanimously answered no as expressing Baptist view.

In the following year (1852), Graves was joined by J. M. Pendleton, at that time pastor of the First Baptist Church, Bowling Green, Kentucky. Pendleton had invited Graves to come to the church for a revival, and in addition to holding an evangelistic meeting, Graves enlisted Pendleton in support of his views. He asked Pendleton to write a tract on the question of whether Baptists ought to recognize pedobaptist preachers as gospel ministers, Graves published this tract in 1854 under the title, "An Old Landmark Re-set," referring to Proverbs 22:28, which said, "Remove not the ancient landmark, which thy fathers have set." From this the movement got its name. The publication of this tract brought immediate controversy.[44]

About this time Graves met A. C. Dayton, who had recently left the Presbyterians to join the Baptists. Graves was impressed with Dayton's writing ability, and soon made him associate editor of the Tennessee Baptist paper. One of Dayton's principal contributions to the movement was his novel, *Theodosia Ernest* (in two volumes), published in 1857, which told the story, complete with romance, of a lovely girl who became a Landmark Baptist by conviction. As James E. Tull has demonstrated, however, these three, acknowledged as the "triumvirate" of the Landmark movement, never completely agreed on the doctrines and emphases of the movement.

The Southern Baptist Convention felt the impact of Graves's views in their 1855 meeting, the year after Pendleton's tract on nonpulpit affiliations and about the time Graves republished Orchard's history of Baptists (tracing Baptist succession from the days of the New Testament to the nineteenth century). After the Convention had completed its initial organization, the usual resolution was offered inviting ministers of other denominations to join the deliberations of the body. This resolution was sharply challenged and the debate that followed lasted the whole day. Writing almost forty years later, John A. Broadus described the surprise

---

[44] See, among other accounts, Masters, *Baptists in Kentucky,* 308-311.

of many at the views and strength of the Landmark followers. He closed by saying;

> After the day's discussion, it was proposed to end the matter by letting the resolution be withdrawn, upon the understanding that those who saw no objection to its passage would concede thus much to the views of their brethren who objected so strongly. Some present thought already that there was no such extreme difference of opinion among us as appeared to exist. The controversy in the next few years rose high, and in some quarters threatened division. But it has now long been felt by most brethren that we could agree to disagree upon the matters involved, and that the great bulk of us were really not very far apart.[45]

When R. B. C. Howell returned to become pastor again of the First Baptist Church, Nashville, in 1857, he found a minority of his church to be avid followers of Graves. Graves was unawed by the return of his mentor, and when Howell refused to cooperate in Landmark objectives, Graves unleashed a scurrilous attack against him. The church brought charges against Graves on September 8, 1858. He was found guilty on five counts and excluded on October 18, 1858. Meanwhile, Graves and a minority had withdrawn from the First Baptist Church and claimed that their schismatic group was the true church.[46] Landmarkers were in control of the General Association of Tennessee and North Alabama and the Concord Association of Tennessee, and each of these bodies recognized Graves and a handful of followers as the true First Baptist Church of Nashville and unseated the pastor, R. B. C. Howell, and the majority of the members, although Howell had been president of the Southern Baptist Convention since 1851. Graves had some difficulty in his ecclesiology explaining how an autonomous New Testament church (such as the First Baptist Church of Nashville) could be rejected in favor of a small, schismatic minority.[47]

---

[45] John A. Broadus, *Memoir of James P. Boyce* (New York: A. C. Armstrong and Son, 1893), 98-99.
[46] See May, *First Baptist Church of Nashville,* 87-88.
[47] See Robert A. Baker, "The North Rocky Mount Baptist Church Decision," *Review and Expositor* (Louisville, Ky.), January, 1955, 59-60.

At the same time he was jousting with Howell, Graves launched severe attacks against the boards of the Convention, particularly the Foreign Mission Board. When a colleague, President N. M. Crawford of Mercer University, Georgia, published an article in 1858 in *The Tennessee Baptist,* in which he denied that Foreign Mission Board had authority over autonomous Baptism churches on the mission field, Graves volunteered his agreement in a footnote:

> No man has lower views of the authority of a Missionary Board to dictate to Missionaries or churches that we have.... We, no more than Brother C., believe that our missionary machinery is scriptural or expedient. The scriptural plan is clearly exemplified in the New Testament and it is simple and effectual, and the sooner we return to it as a denomination, the better for us and for the world...
>
> We do not believe that the Foreign Mission Board has any right to call upon the missionaries that the churches send to China or Africa, to take a journey to Richmond to be examined touching their experience, call to the ministry, and soundness in the faith. It is a high-handed act, and degrades both the judgment and authority of the Church and presbytery that ordained him, thus practically declaring itself above both.[48]

What better method, a correspondent wrote him, could be followed than the present system of entrusting foreign mission matters to a board to administer? Graves said that the scriptural method would be to follow the example of Paul: let local churches unite informally to send a missionary to a foreign field and remit funds by a commercial house, thus eliminating the present nonscriptural plan of allowing a board or convention to override autonomous Baptist churches on the foreign field.

An ominous note was sounded in February, 1859, just a few months before the biennial meeting of the Convention at Richmond. Graves reflected his animosity toward the president of the Convention, R. B. C. Howell, and his dissatisfaction with the Foreign Mission Board. He wrote in his paper:

---

[48] *The Tennessee Baptist* (Nashville), September 4, 1858.

There are elements at work that threaten the disruption of the relation of the Convention and the Foreign Mission Board to the body of the Southern Baptists. There are schemes of consolidation and centralization now urged by certain Brethren who exercise a controlling influence in the Biennial Convention which, if they succeed in consummating, will as certainly destroy the present union of Southern Baptists in Foreign Missions as the Convention meets in May next. And there is a determination on the part of some, moved more by partisan than missionary zeal, to make the next Biennial Convention an ecclesiastical Court and to force its decision into antagonism with Churches and Associations.[49]

Graves came to the Convention at Richmond in May, 1859, determined to have his Nashville minority seated as the true First Baptist Church to prevent the reelection of R. B. C. Howell as Convention president, to kill the Bible Board from which A. C. Dayton had been forced out as president, and to confront the Foreign Mission Board. It was indeed unfortunate for the Landmark faction that the Convention was meeting in Virginia, the center of anti-Landmark leadership. Because of the location, there were 241 delegates from Virginia alone, more than from all of the Landmark states put together. When the ninety-seven from North and South Carolina were added these three anti-Landmark states always had a majority of the 574 delegates attending the 1859 session. It is no wonder that Graves failed in most of his objectives. Howell's group was seated at the Convention, and Howell was reelected president on the first ballot. Recognizing however, that Graves had enough popular support to embarrass if not to split the Convention (as Graves had openly threatened if Howell were elected) Howell promptly declined the office, and after three ballots Richard Fuller, universally beloved and not actively engaged in the controversy, was named to the presidency. The strength of the Landmark faction may be glimpsed when motions to invite ministers of other denominations to seats or to invite them "to witness our proceedings" could not be passed.

Although Graves also failed in his efforts to abolish the Bible Board, he had more success in his confrontation with the Foreign Mission Board. He was given ample opportunity to present every objection and

---

[49] *The Tennessee Baptist* February 5, 1859, 2, col. 4.

did so eloquently and with fervor. After a full day of debate, Graves met with the two secretaries of the board, J. B. Taylor and A. A. Poindexter, and discussed the issues until the "east was glowing and the roosters crowing."[50] As a result, a committee was appointed to inquire about improving the system of missions and missionary operations. In their report, this committee recommended that no change be made in the existing plans of missionary operation, but that if

> any churches, associations, or other bodies entitled to representation in the Convention, should prefer to appoint their own missionaries, and assume the responsibility of defraying their salaries and entire expenses, that the respective Boards are authorized, under our present organization and fundamental rules to become disbursing agents of the bodies so appointing missionaries and appropriating funds..., provided such expenses of forwarding the money, as have to be specially incurred, be borne by the contributors.[51]

Such were the evidences of personal and ideological antagonism that the final action of this 1859 Convention urged that "personal controversies among pastors, editors, and brethren, should, from this time forth, be more than ever avoided." On motion of I. T. Tichenor, it was agreed that all Baptist papers be instructed to publish this resolution.

About two weeks after the close of this Convention, Graves' paper contained an editorial which said:

> There is no reason why our denomination my not co-operate harmoniously in missionary matters. All those who prefer that the Board at Richmond shall have the appointing power and be held responsible for its exercise, can throw their funds unconditionally into its treasury. Those Associations and Churches that prefer appointing their own missionaries can do so, and the Board will transmit their funds, while the missionaries will be amenable to the Associations and Churches sending them forth. Here are two plans of operation submitted to the brethren. Let them make their election. Let them remember that they have no good excuse for

---

[50]For this story, see Barnes, *The Southern Baptist Convention*, 110-12.
[51]Baker, *Source Book*, 145-146.

doing nothing. The missionary spirit enters essentially into a Church organized according to the gospel.[52]

However, still embroiled in the controversy with Howell and the First Baptist Church of Nashville, Graves spent the fall and winter of 1859 touring Alabama, Arkansas, Georgia, Louisiana, Mississippi, Texas, Virginia, and perhaps other states, pressing his cause and seeking vindication. It appeared that he was trying to bring about a schism in the denomination. He won many followers in these states. In May, 1860, as an example, the Mississippi state Baptist convention appointed a committee to attempt to mediate between Graves and the First Baptist Church of Nashville. A light note was injected into the deliberations of the Mississippi body over Landmarkism when T. C. Teasdale, one of their eminent leaders,

> prayed for the peace of Zion with a bias to one side of the mooted question manifested in his prayer; and when he had completed his prayer, someone moved that one be appointed by the chair to answer Dr. Teasdale's prayer.[53]

At the very close of this period in 1860, Graves and his lieutenants were powerful and popular. Their fortunes were radically affected by the outbreak of war, as will be described in the next period under study.

---

[52] *The Tennessee Baptist*, May 21 and May 28, 1859, 2, col. 1.
[53] Cox, ed. *Encyclopedia,* I, 583-84.

# Chapter 9 - From the Civil War Through the Reconstruction Years

In retrospect, one feels a sense of unreality as he watches the rapid outbreak in 1861 of the bloodiest war yet fought, sometimes involving brother against brother. Differing constitutional interpretations, constantly irritated by every sectional issue that arose, caused men to abandon reason and turn to violence. On April 9, 1861, the troops of South Carolina fired on Fort Sumter, and less than a week later war had begun. It continued almost exactly four years, ending with the surrender of Lee at Appomattox on April 9, 1865. Reconstruction was the name given to the painful military, economic, social, and political control of the South during the following twelve years, ending with the final withdrawal of troops from the South in 1877.

Little needs to be said about the war itself, which the South had hoped to win with her cotton. The antebellum culture was totally destroyed, and Lincoln's plan of restoring the seceding states was scrapped after his assassination. President Andrew Johnson was bludgeoned at every point. By one vote a bill of impeachment against him failed. The South was divided into five military districts, with commissioners appointed to determine who could vote. The financial position of many southern states temporarily ruined reckless bonding programs which provided northern control at a fraction of the actual value of posted securities. The sharecropper system became an extension of the control of northern capital. Abolitionist idealism was replaced by economics and politics. Intelligent blacks noticed that not one of their number had been appointed to a federal office in the North and none had a place in a northern state legislature. When Reconstruction became politically ineffective, it was brought to a close.

The economic situation of the South improved slowly during the period. Five years after the close of the war the yield of cotton and tobacco, the "money crops" of the South, was still barely over half of what it was in 1860. Cotton production was 5,387,052 bales in 1860 and 3,011,996 bales in 1870; tobacco had dropped from 434,209,461 pounds in 1860 to 262,735,341 pounds in 1870. "You have no idea of the total prostration of everything in Virginia. Our people are the subjects of great suffering." wrote James B. Taylor in 1866 to President William Carey Crane of Baylor University in Texas. Such was true in most southern states.

## The Civil War (1861-65)

Practically every Baptist state convention in the South passed resolutions favoring the Confederate cause after the outbreak of hostilities.[1] The Southern Baptist Convention meeting in Savannah in 1861 issued a strong declaration justifying the formation of the Confederate States of America, and altered its name to recognize the political change. When the Convention met at Augusta in 1863, it heard a very gloomy report on the disruption of its work because of the war.

> Colleges have suspended, some of them indefinitely. Doctor Talbird, President of Howard College, has raised a company and gone to the wars, and the students of most of our colleges have enlisted in the Confederate army. The Revision Association is prostrate, and we presume the whole work of Revision is indefinitely suspended. Our female schools, in several localities, show signs of distress. Some six or seven Baptist papers have gone down in the past six months, while the Mississippi Baptists and the Texas Baptists issue half sheets, and the Tennessee Baptist is cut down in size to one-third less than the Western Recorder. Added to this gloomy picture, our Foreign Missions are paralyzed, our Home Missions almost suspended, and our State organizations unable to carry on their work. Ministers have been forced through stern necessity to leave their fields of usefulness in order to provide bread for their families.[2]

It will be recalled that when the war began, Southern Baptists had three benevolent boards in the structure of their Convention: one at Richmond, Virginia, for foreign missions; one at Marion, Alabama, for domestic and Indian Missions; and the Bible Board at Nashville, Tennessee. Loosely related to the Convention were the seminary at

---

[1] See, for example, *Minutes of Georgia Baptist Convention*, 1861, 5-6.
[2] *Annual*, Southern Baptist Convention, 1863, 34-35.

Greenville, South Carolina, which closed temporarily in 1862, the Southern Baptist Publication Society, Charleston, South Carolina, and the Southern Baptist Sunday School Union, Nashville, Tennessee. The last two named bodies were permanent casualties of the war, although the records of their demise are incomplete. The Bible Board was abolished by the Convention in 1863 after Nashville was captured by the Union armies.[3]

**Foreign Mission Board.** Mission work in China and Africa limped along during the American war. The Brazilian mission briefly conducted by Thomas J. Bowen, was abandoned early in 1864 because of Bowen's ill health. The board faced many problems during the war. In 1863 it reported to the Convention that it had not been able to meet during the previous year; that the two periodicals, the *Home and Foreign Journal and The Commission,* had been suspended; that there were no agents in the field to help raise mission funds; and that civil war in China and the outbreak of Asiatic cholera there had brought much suffering and death on that field. Receipts in 1863 were $51,000 for the previous two years; at the next meeting in 1866 the boarded reported $68,000 had been raised during that period.

The board experienced difficulty both in raising money for the foreign mission cause and in getting money to the fields. Quite early in the war, Richmond was cut off from land contact with northern ports, and the Union fleet blockaded the southern coast to keep ships carrying cotton to other nations. The board devised several means of raising and sending funds. (1) Under a flag truce the board in Richmond forwarded the money that it had collected to Baltimore, where it was then shipped to the missionaries. This means of communication failed as the war progressed. (2) Isaac T. Smith, the financial agent of the Foreign Mission Board in New York, anticipating the very difficulty which they faced, had already made advances to the missionaries. (3) In the fall of 1862, a Provisional Board was constituted at Baltimore, and foreign missions contributions were received from Maryland, District of Columbia, Kentucky, and Missouri, as well as from friends in northern cities. (4) A rather unique means of financing missions in China and Africa involved the running of the Union blockade. The board invested about $1,500 in bales of sea-island

---

[3] Baker, *Source Book*, 128-29 has the documents.

cotton. After the ship on which it was loaded had successfully run the blockade, the cotton netted nearly $5,000 in England, and this sum was credited there to the account of the missionaries in China and Africa. (5) Some of the missionaries, particularly in China, were able to secure secular work on their fields.   Matthew T. Yates, for example, became an interpreter for the United States government and also made wise investments in land near Shanghai. (6) Some foreign residents in China, noting the need of the missionaries that were cut off from the States, made contributions to them to assist in the work.  Even missionary societies of other denominations assisted the Baptist missionaries in China.   All indebtedness incurred during the war in the foreign mission program was paid shortly after the close of hostilities.

Courageous men and women served well in China during this period.  Roswell P. Grave, M.D., had come to South China through the appeals of J. Lewis Shuck and was for a considerable time alone in the important work at Canton.   In Central China, the imminent Matthew T. Yates, and his wife continued throughout all of this period.  In North China, J. L. Holmes, and his wife arrived in 1860 to open mission work in Chefoo. In the following year Holmes was murdered by bandits. Mr. and Mrs. J. B. Hartwell and Mr. and Mrs. T. P. Crawford performed important service in this field during the period.  An attempt was made to open the mission field in Japan in 1860, but two missionaries were lost at sea and others, were not appointed because of the war and lack of finances.

Throughout all the critical war period, James B. Taylor served as corresponding secretary of the board.  His arduous labors took their toll on his health.

**Domestic and Indian Mission Board.** The home field was devastated by war.  Work with the blacks, Chinese, Germans, English speaking whites and city population promptly ceased with the outbreak of war.  There had been over 150 missionaries serving in the home field before the war, but their work was promptly suspended. The Indian work, in particular, suffered severely.   Southern Baptist schools in Indian Territory, for which the United States government had appropriated $75.00 per year per pupil, were closed.   Many Southern Baptist missionaries and ministers became chaplains or colporteurs in the Confederate army. The several states, as well as the board, were zealous in supplying tracts and Bibles for the soldiers.  In 1863, for example,

Virginia alone provided 5,000,000 pages of tracts for distribution in the Confederate army through the colporteurs. W. W. Barnes felt that "there was never an army in which a greater religious work was done than in the Army of Northern Virginia," where revival occurred on several occasions. When federal troops gained control of the Mississippi River, the board sent J. B. Link, one of their agents in Mississippi to Texas to serve as an arm of the board in raising and distributing home mission funds. The executive committee of Louisiana was similarly empowered.

In the fall of 1863, the Home Mission Society in New York, through its president, United States Senator Ira Harris, applied to the War Department for authority to seize abandoned Southern Baptist meetinghouses in the areas overrun by troops of the Union army. The war department granted them more than they asked, and ordered its commanding officers to seize and deliver to the society "all houses of worship belonging to the Baptists Churches South, in which a loyal minister of said church does not now officiate."[4] The society explained that this was an effort to protect Baptist property in the South from marauders and, in some cases, from "others than Baptists" who had denied the society's right to use them. The society went on to say that the whole object of this move was to occupy the property and save it from being destroyed or passing into other than Baptist hands, reserving it as an inheritance for future Baptists to own and occupy. J. W. Parker of Boston was appointed to head this program and during the first four months of 1864 about thirty Southern Baptist structures were seized. Some of them, as in the case of the Coliseum Place Baptist Church of New Orleans, had not been abandoned, but were seized from Southern Baptists by force. While their motives were good, the society embittered many Southern Baptists in carrying out this program.

As armies of the North captured southern areas, the Home Mission Society sent its missionaries into those areas to labor. In 1862, there were three such missionaries in South Carolina and one in Missouri; in 1863, one each in Kentucky, Louisiana, and Tennessee, two in Virginia, three in Missouri, and four in South Carolina, four in Virginia, six in Missouri, and seven in Tennessee; while in 1865, there were one each in Alabama, Arkansas, and Kentucky, two each in Louisiana, and Mississippi, four

---

[4]*Ibid.*, p. 126.

each in Georgia, and South Carolina, five in North Carolina, seven each in Tennessee and Virginia, and twenty-three in Missouri. Most of these were working among the blacks in those states.[5]

The receipts of the southern board during the war were greatly affected by the inflation of the Confederate currency. In 1860 gifts amounted to $37,659.34; in 1861, $35,274.50. From 1862 to 1865 receipts were in Confederate currency and dropped to $14,996.73 in 1862, but inflation began to appear in 1863 when $29,072.12 was secured. In 1864 receipts totaled $118,937.91, while in 1865, they were shown at $156,491.76, most of it in almost worthless Confederate currency.

Russell Holman returned for his second stint as corresponding secretary in 1857 and served until 1862. He was succeeded by M.T. Sumner.

**Bible Board.** The third of the existing boards when the war began was the Bible Board, which had been established in 1851. The Convention appointed a special committee in 1861 to look in to the condition of this board. When the Convention met again in 1863, the headquarters of the board at Nashville was in the hands of the northern army and the Convention promptly abolished it. Its death prepared the way for the organization of the first Sunday School Board.

**First Sunday School Board.** In the very midst of the dark days of the war, a new board was organized which, both in its own ministry and in the long shadow it cast toward the future, rendered a significant service. After the vote of the Southern Baptist Convention in 1863 abolishing the Bible Board, Basil Manly, Jr., introduced a resolution calling for a committee to look into the need for a board to promote Sunday Schools. As chairman of the committee, Manly wrote in most eloquent language the first apologetic for the Sunday School movement ever adopted by the Southern Baptist Convention.

> All of us have felt that the Sunday School is the nursery of the Church, the camp of instruction for her young soldiers, the great missionary to the future. While our other benevolent agencies relate primarily to the present, this goes to meet and bless the

---

[5] Baker, *Relations*, 90.

generation that is coming, to win them from ignorance and sin, to train future laborers, when our places shall know us no more.[6]

Despite many strong objections, Manly and his supporters were able to secure the organization of the first Sunday School Board in 1863. He was named president of the new board, with headquarters in South Carolina, and inaugurated an ambitious program providing books and for enlisting volunteer agents for each state. In that fall a second great name was attached to the history of the board, that of John A. Broadus. Like Manly, he had been professor in the first southwide seminary in Greenville, South Carolina, which had closed its doors in 1862 because of the war. The amount of work done by these two men was remarkable. Broadus said in his report to the Convention in 1866 that the work they had accomplished was "sadly little," but he was mistaken. Hymnbooks, children's question books and catechisms, teacher's, and pupil's class books, and other printed helps of various sorts were provide in large numbers for the Sunday School in the South. Outstanding men in many southern states served voluntarily to promote the work of the board.[7]

In his report in 1866 Broadus described the beginning of a small monthly paper entitled, *Kind Words for the Sunday School Children.*

> The plan adopted was to issue a small sheet and at a very low price. Children are rather pleased than otherwise that theirs should be a *little* paper, strikingly different from the papers for grown people.

This little paper for children became "the golden thread" that linked this first Sunday School Board with the second board that was organized in 1891. In his closing word Broadus appealed for "the lively sympathy and the liberal support of all that love Him who loves little children."

## The Reconstruction Period (1868-77)

**Progress in Several States.** Before describing numerical gains made across the Southland during these tumultuous days, mention should be made of two events which brought large excisions from the ranks of Southern Baptists. The adoption of the Virginia Secession Ordinance

---

[6] *Annual*, Southern Baptist Convention, 1863, 45.
[7] For the detailed story, see Baker, *The Story of the Sunday School Board*, 16-20.

constituted the breaking point between eastern and western Virginia as the culmination of a number of economic, social, and political tensions, and on June 20, 1863, the new state of West Virginia was formed. In 1868 nearly 15,000 members in 249 churches left the General Association of Virginia to form the West Virginia General Association. The other event was the withdrawal from the white Baptist churches by most of the black Baptists in the South in order to form their own church bodies. Perhaps around 400,000 Baptists were in this way removed from the rolls of white churches. This excision was encouraged by the northern Home Mission Society and the military force stationed in the South, and of course was very appealing to the blacks themselves as an evidence of their total freedom.

The reaction of white Southern Baptists to this withdrawal was fairly uniform. As a rule, this withdrawal was expected and accepted along the seaboard, but farther west the feeling seemed to exist that blacks were not yet sufficiently trained and grounded in the basic Baptist doctrines to the point that they could carry on Baptist church life without some supervision and assistance from the whites. As early as September, 1865, the Dover Association of Virginia discussed the separation of the black churches to form an independent black association, and that action took place by seven black churches in Richmond, Manchester, and Petersburg. Several white associations in Virginia published the view that separate organizations "should neither be required nor encouraged," but this did not slow down the pace of the withdrawal. By 1868 there were three black associations with 129 churches and almost 39,000 members. A black state body was organized in May 1868.

The Tar River Association of North Carolina mentioned that during the first few years after the war, such excisions were numerous.[8] In 1866 the South Carolina State Convention noted the formation of separate organizations by the blacks and urged that the whites be helpful and sympathetic in dealing with them.[9] Between 1872 and 1876, the black membership in the white churches of South Carolina diminished rapidly.[10]

---

[8] Cox-Woolley, eds., *Encyclopedia*, III, 1953.
[9] *Minutes of the 45th and 46th Anniversaries f the State Convention of the Baptist Denomination in South Carolina*, held in July, 1865, and July, 1866 (Greenville: C. E. Elford's Job Press, 1866), 238-41.
[10] See, for example, *Minutes of the Edgefield Baptist Association*, 1871, 3-4.

In Georgia the statistics show the beginning of rather rapid excision from churches after 1867. A black association was shown in 1868 with 2,335 members, which had been organized in 1866.[11] Two additional black associations, both organized in 1866, were shown in the minutes of 1870. By 1875, there were only 3,295 blacks remaining in the 34 white associations in Georgia out of a total membership of 74,545.

In Alabama, reference was made quite early in the war to the possibility of separate churches by the blacks, which the whites felt should be discouraged. In 1865, while recognizing the right of the blacks to withdraw from white churches, it was urged that their highest good would be subserved by maintaining their relationship in the churches with those that know and love them. However, evidently after 1868 the blacks were withdrawing rapidly, and reference was made to their churches which were separate from the white churches. In 1868 the state body urged that wherever possible that white assistance be given to any organization of black churches.[12]

In Mississippi the state body made reference in 1867 to aiding the blacks in organizing their churches.[13] The parting of blacks in Kentucky occurred shortly after the war; while in Texas, between 1865 and 1870, there was a drop in black church membership in the white churches from 35% to 7.7% in ten associations selected for study.[14]

On the whole, the division was an amicable one. In some cases the white churches gave their buildings to the blacks and moved elsewhere to build their own; often the white churches provided financial aid to black Baptists as they attempted to construct their churches. Even during Reconstruction and while experiencing the losses just described, Southern Baptists made substantial numerical progress.

The war was disastrous in its effect upon Baptists in southern seaboard states in particular. Virginia, for example was almost prostrate at

---

[11] See *Minutes of the Forty-Sixth Anniversary of the Georgia Baptist State Convention,* 1868, 27.
[12] *Minutes of the Forty-Sixth Annual Session of the Alabama Baptist State Convention,* 1868, 11-12.
[13] *Proceedings of the Twenty-Eighth Session of the Mississippi Baptist State Convention*, 1867, 20-21.
[14] Paul W. Stripling, *The Negro Excision from Baptist Churches in Texas (1861-1870)*, unpublished Th.D. dissertation, Southwestern Baptist Theological Seminary, Ft. Worth, Texas, May, 1967, 218 ff.

the close of hostilities. The land was devastated. Garnett Ryland, the Virginia Baptist historian, named over two dozen Baptist meetinghouses damaged or destroyed by Union troop; he mourned the execution of Albert C. Willis, a young preacher in the Shiloh Association, and noted the imprisonment of eight other ministers. Men and boys from sixteen to sixty had been called into the Confederate army, and ministering by colporteurs to soldiers became the principal organized activity of Virginia Baptists. Richmond College had been stripped of its library, scientific apparatus, and everything else portable by marauding troops. The endowment of the school was worthless. The entire plant of the *Religious Herald* had been destroyed. President Ryland of Richmond College milked his own cow and sold the milk to sustain his family, making personal deliveries morning and evening.

After the war closed, Baptists in this region resolutely set about to repair the extensive physical damage. A constructive attitude was reflected in the renewed meetings of the state bodies. In Virginia, for example, promptly after the war ended, the General Association adopted a resolution earnestly recommending to brethren throughout the state "to prove themselves to be loyal citizens of the United States; and enter with zeal and activity upon discharge of the responsibilities devolved on them by their new social and civic relations."

The minutes of each state body reflected a desire to begin immediately the significant benevolent ministries interrupted by war. State missions, Sunday School promotion and leadership, ministerial relief, rehabilitation of the schools, and cooperation with the south-wide Baptist body were topics which were discussed in every state. Hardly any annual session of a state body during all this period went beyond the first day without someone earnestly presenting the needs of the blacks and appealing for an active witness to them. Every state in this region took steps to restructure its convention or general association during this period to unify the several programs in the state or to make the body more efficient.

The several state minutes provide inspiring examples of perseverance amidst difficulties. The postwar convention meetings in Florida, for example, were poorly attended and the financial picture was bleak. Kinsey Chambers began work as a part-time state evangelist in 1873 in an effort to turn the tide. His report for five months showed that he traveled 1,688 miles, spoke 105 times, made 54 family visits, helped 1 church, baptized 7, and collected $68.95. His expenses for these five months were shown as $10.75.

A new permanent educational institution was begun by Georgia Baptists in 1873, although it did not come under the control of the state body until 1902. Alfred Shorter, a Baptist in Rome, Georgia, organized a private stock company to sustain a liberal arts college for girls in his community, stipulating that its trustees should always be members in good standing of some Baptist church.

Old Mercer University was moved in 1871 from Penfield to Macon, Georgia, in an effort to improve its financial condition and enlarge its enrollment.

There were varying attitudes toward state organizations. In Kentucky and Arkansas, for example, undoubtedly through the influence of Landmarkism, fierce struggles took place between those who rejected the concept of state structures and those who favored such organizations. In Kentucky the fear of centralization was very strong all during this era, and the district associations looked upon the general body as a competitor rather than a channel of work. In 1869 the General Association reaffirmed its aims, which included better understanding and cooperation, assistance for feeble churches, the use of experienced evangelists in the state, and an effort to reach neglected areas, especially in the mountains of eastern Kentucky. The functioning agency of the General Association was a General Executive Board, later named the State Board of Missions. In 1866 the title of the General Agent, as he had been called, was changed to Corresponding Secretary, which was filled at this time by annual election.

Arkansas Baptists, likewise, had an active controversy over the centralized authority involved in the use of a state structure and an authoritative board whose functions appeared to jeopardize the autonomy of the churches, some thought. It will be recalled that Tennessee had not been successful in establishing a permanent state body during the previous period. On April 10, 1874, through the cooperation of leaders in the three sectional bodies in the state, a unified state structure was organized at Murfreesboro, but the de facto unification of the state was a process requiring many years beyond this period. Mississippi Baptists began refining their state body shortly after the close of the war. In 1871, not satisfied with the structure, a complete reorganization took place; this was repeated in 1873. At the close of the period these Baptists were still struggling with the proper structure of the state body. Texas Baptists still had two rival state bodies at the opening of the period, and additional sectional organizations soon began to organize in various areas of this vast state. Alabama Baptists modified their convention to emphasize the growing Sunday School movement.

Several educational advances were reported during this period. In 1873 the distinguished Confederate officer, Mark. P. Lowrey, with the aid of his two daughters, opened Blue Mountain Female Institute, later to become Blue Mountain College. It was operated as a private school until 1919, when the Mississippi Baptist Convention assumed control of it. Foundations were laid for what became Belmont College in Nashville, Tennessee, when a female school called Ward Seminary was established in 1865.

Texas Baptists during this period of war and Reconstruction faced serious problems in their educational work. In 1861, in open hostility, Rufus C. Burleson, president of Baylor University at Independence, resigned and took his entire senior class to Waco University. Throughout the remainder of the Reconstruction period both Baylor at Independence and Waco University kept open their doors. In 1866 the Female Department of Baylor became a separate institution and moved its campus to Belton, Texas. The rivalry between the school at Independence and the one at Waco was lively during the remainder of the Reconstruction era.

Missouri underwent serious internal convulsions during this period. This state had been almost evenly divided during the war between those loyal to the North and those favoring the South. As a result, in 1865 a separate Baptist body was formed by those desiring to work with the North. However, through the efforts of A. H. Burlingham, members of this new body returned to the older general association three years later. In order to promote harmony, the general association eliminated from its constitution the statement that the body would be auxiliary to the Southern Baptist Convention. As a result, Missouri Baptists, while in the same state body, divided in their support of a general body. In 1878 the executive board was consolidated with the board of the Sunday School convention. This constituted the Missouri structure during all of this period.

**The Southern Baptist Convention.** The period of Reconstruction was one of continuing struggle for the Convention and its boards. The crop failures of the late 1860's, the financial panic of 1873, and the political agitation that led to the withdrawal of the troops from the South in 1877 affected all of the activities of the several agencies of the Convention. Presidents of the body in these critical years were Richard Fuller (1861-63), P. H. Mell (1863-72), and James P. Boyce (1872-79).

Since the societies in the North had so enthusiastically supported the Union cause and the Southern Baptist Convention had vigorously defended the Confederacy, it was unlikely that either side would be interested in the question of reunion during the war period from 1861 to 1865. However, even before the close of the war, the American Baptist Home Mission Society of New York was sending its workers into the occupied areas of the South to do missionary work, primarily among the blacks. After Appomattox and the elimination of the "peculiar institution" that had played such a large part in the sectional quarrels between the North and South, the whole question of reunion was broached. The initiative came from the Home Mission Society, but Southern Baptist state bodies that met in 1865 were practically unanimous in voting nonaffiliation with this society and the foreign mission body in the North. The South was still embittered because of the seizing of church property in the South by the society, calling this action unbaptistic and illegal. Angry words were published, adding to the sectional alienation. The Virginia Baptists General Association, for example, urged its churches "to decline any co-operation or fellowship with any missionaries, ministers, or agents of the American Baptist Home Mission Society." Completely impatient with this attitude, Secretary J. S. Backus of the Home Mission Society wrote a vigorous article, a part of which said:

> And now if it is politically and morally wrong to support "the Southern Confederacy," how can it be religiously right to support "the Southern Baptist Convention?" If the Government is to be one, why should not the Baptist denomination be one, and, as a united people, give their influence and example in support of a united Government? Is not the spirit which would have it otherwise, disloyal? Would not the spirit which seek now to

perpetuate the Southern Baptist Convention, were it in its power, reproduce and sustain the Southern Baptist Confederacy?[15]

The Southern Baptist Convention did not meet in 1865, but in 1866 it went about its work on the assumption that it would continue its operations as before. In 1868, 1870, 1871, 1875, and implicitly in other years, the Southern Baptist Convention vigorously took the position that "separate action in general denominational enterprises is the policy of true peace and surest progress."[16] Although this issue was to come up again in the next period, there never was the slightest suggestion that Southern Baptists seriously favored scrapping their denominational body, different in kind from the several independent and autonomous societies of the North as it was, and returning to the old arrangement. Basically, apart from differences in ecclesiology and sectional temper, there were four reasons given by Southern Baptists for remaining apart organically, even though fellowship was resumed: (1) the combined body would be too large (note that this conceived of a single convention rather than a series of societies); (2) at convention time, few cities in the North and none in the South would be able to accommodate a meeting of the size required; (3) distances were so great that few from the South would be able to attend the meetings in others sections of the country; (4) a separate body in the South would allow southern leadership to develop and bring familiarity by the members of the southern churches with their leader, thus deepening their interests.

**The Domestic and Indian Mission Board.** The Domestic and Indian Mission Board labored arduously on its field "from Maryland to Texas" during the Reconstruction era. Under the leadership of M. T. Sumner (1862-75), the program reflected the oscillation of mission gifts. When the funds were provided, the board eagerly commissioned missionaries to the blacks, to the Indians, and to destitute fields across the South. With dismal regularity, however, a year of good offerings was followed by one with decreased funds, necessitating a cutback in the program and the discouragement of indebtedness. When Sumner resigned in 1875, he was succeeded by W.H. McIntosh, who served during the remainder of this period.

---

[15] See Baker, *Relations*, 95-96.
[16] *Annual*, 1870, 35-36.

This board (called the Home Mission Board after 1874) was caught up in the agitation about the use of agents for raising funds. Stoutly supporting this practice, the board emphasized that as expensive as this method of collecting was, much more money was received for missions by use of agents than without them. Nearly half of all the offerings until almost the very close of this period was used for collection and administration. In 1876, for example, the board collected $19,359.81. Of this, amount, 44% or $8,518.32 was needed for administration, leaving $10,841.49 for the principal task. Another cause of agitation was the assertion by some of the state bodies that a home mission board was not really needed, since the various states could take care of their own needs with their own state mission boards. In 1873, for example, the receipts of the Convention's board were $27,199.20; in this same year, seven states reported having expended $18,367.68 on their own fields. By the close of this era in 1877, the states were spending more money on their fields than the receipts of the Home Mission Board. The reports of the board constantly called for the cooperation of the various states. With respect to the use of the agents in 1876 when it was reported that more than 53% of the collections was used for paying the agents, the board was ordered to dispense with the use of agents for collecting funds. The drop in the receipts shown for 1877 was caused, said the board, by the continuing economic depression that had begun four years before and the adoption of the policy of not using agents on a percentage basis to collect funds.

This critical financial dilemma of the board was greatly compounded by developments in the Baptist Home Mission Society of New York. In 1862, after the society had surveyed the missionary needs in the Virginia peninsula around Fortress Monroe, then occupied by Union armies, the question of providing missionaries there was discussed at the meeting of the full society. The first response of the society was that its financial resources were "inadequate to the necessities of any new territory," and asserted that no justification could be found for "attempting such extension of operations."[17] The attitude was replaced however, by an enthusiasm that swept the society "to the occupancy of a field broader, more important, more promising than has ever yet invited our toils." A resolution was passed providing that steps should be taken immediately to

---

[17] *Annual Report*, American Baptist Home Mission Society, 1862, 21.

send missionaries and teachers both to the free and to the slaves throughout the whole southern section. In justifying the extension of operations into the South, the society later asserted that the withdrawal from the older states of the South after 1845 was simply expediency, while the return of the South was the assertion of the society's "original birthright to the cultivation of this entire continent."[18]

The society was reorganized to include a Southern District, which comprised all of the territory south of New York, A special Freedman's Fund was provided to secure collections for this work in the South. The society sent Edward Lathrop on a tour of the churches, both white and black, along the southern Atlantic coast with a resolution urging Southern Baptists to cooperate with the society in spreading the gospel. Most of the white churches did not welcome him, but the society said that their mission remained unchanged. "The work must not be stopped by State lines, nor sectional hatreds, nor complexion of man."[19] Missionaries rapidly began following the advancing Union armies, so that by 1865 the society reported sixty missionaries in twelve southern states. This included one each in Alabama, Arkansas, and Kentucky; two each in Louisiana, and Mississippi; three in New Mexico; four each in Georgia and South Carolina; five in North Carolina; seven each in Tennessee and Virginia; and twenty-three in Missouri.[20]

Thereafter, the society engaged in considerable activity in three areas of work in the South—evangelism, education, and assistance in constructing church buildings. By 1867, the society had almost a hundred missionaries in twelve states of the South, of whom perhaps fifty-nine were teachers, although the records are not explicit. In addition, loans for building church edifices had been made in Missouri to both white and black churches, as well as in South Carolina to churches of both races and doubtless elsewhere, although the records are not complete.

The Southern Baptist Convention took note of the society's activity in 1867 and defined what it considered to be basis of rapprochement with the society by resolving:

---

[18] See *Home Mission Monthly* (of American Baptist Home Mission Society, New York), VI, 225 f.
[19] *Annual Report*, American Baptist Home Mission Society, 1864, 20 f.
[20] Baker, *Relations*, 90.

> That this Convention having learned, though informally and unofficially, that the American Baptist Home Mission Society is desirous of aiding the religious instruction of this class of our population (the Negroes), the Domestic Mission Board be directed to make known to that Society our willingness to receive aid in this work, by appropriations made to the Boards of this Convention.[21]

In the following year (1868), a committee from the society visited the Southern Baptist Convention and offered a resolution of amity and fellowship. The Convention welcomed the "brethren from abroad—brethren laboring in their own field" and said:

> Could the Home Mission Board (the Society), while conforming to its constitutional obligations, render us assistance here, we are sure that much good might be effected so far as this class is concerned.... Conscious of the risk of being misunderstood and restricted in utterance by a sense of the proper and the becoming, we yet feel constrained by the great interests at stake to renew the suggestion made in the concluding report of the Minutes of 1867. The Domestic Mission Board have [sic] peculiar advantages for prosecuting this work—experience, proximity to the field interest in the people, and they are willing to receive aid in its conduct.[22]

The Southern Baptist Convention appointed representatives to meet with the society in 1868. The chairman of the group was J. B. Jeter and with him were John A. Broadus, Richard Fuller, Basil Manly, Jr., J. R. Graves, and H. A. Tupper, some of the ablest veterans of the Convention. During the exercises, Broadus (who was known in the North of his conciliatory views) addressed the society relative to the freedman task and suggested that only missionaries selected by the southern board be sent among the southern people; or if such missionaries were selected by the society, they should be approved by the southern board. The society officially replied that they were unwilling to operate in this fashion; that they had a right and an obligation to Christ to send their missionaries to

---

[21] *Annual*, 1867, 79.
[22] *Annual*, 1868, 20 f.

any point without endorsement by the South; and if they restricted themselves according to the desires of the South the sources of their benevolence would dry up, for their supporters would be unwilling to make contributions for a program of this kind. Thirty years later, Secretary H. L. Morehouse of the society approvingly pointed to this assertion by leaders of the society during this period as being the immediate response to the requests of the South for the society to make appropriations to the boards in the South or to secure the Convention's approval of missionaries sent to the South.[23]

The issue, then, was joined. The society refused to recognize the Southern Baptist Convention as a territorial general body which had supervision of Baptist work south of the Mason-Dixon Line. The Southern Baptist Convention, on the other hand, demanded that it should be considered the only general organization for missions within the territorial limits of the South, and insisted that any work done by "brethren from abroad" should be channeled through its Domestic Mission Board. Its attitude was expressed by Basil Manly, Jr., who said in an address before the society: "We ask for help and co-operation, but if you repel our confidence, our heart of love which we proffer, we will at least not oppose whatever you may choose to do."[24]

A twofold conflict, which had been implicit from the very organization of the Southern Baptist Convention in 1845, was revealed in the contrasting views. The first conflict was ideological. It will be recalled that the three principal societies in the North were organized in such fashion as to minimize denominationalism while emphasizing the appeal of a particular benevolence. The society method stressed connectionalism or denominationalism. The later related those supporting its program to all of the interest promoted by the denomination. The associational or convention type of structure chosen by Southern Baptists in 1845 was actually a new *kind* of general organization, in that it was a throwback to the associational missionary philosophy used by associational bodies before 1803 and partly utilized by the General Missionary Convention between 1817 and 1820. The organization by Southern Baptists of a convention with separate boards for benevolent activity, sowed seeds for

---

[23] *Home Mission Monthly*, XVI, 406.
[24] Morehouse, *Baptist Home Missions,* 427 f.

this ideological conflict. Had the South simply formed separate benevolent societies for each type of activity, it would have been possible for the various societies conceived as they were, to relate to one another on the basis of their common task, whether located in the North or the South. It is doubtful that a denominational rigidity would have developed. Any church might have had individuals contributing to two or more societies doing the same type of work, depending entirely upon the sympathy of the individual for the general aims and attitudes of the societies involved. The organization of a territorial convention, on the other hand, brought a geographical consciousness and a total denominational loyalty, still intensified by sectional passions, into structured form in the South.

The second conflict was geographical. The constitution of the Home Mission Society, adopted in 1832, provided that its field was all of North America. The constitution of the Southern Baptist Convention, endeavoring to reproduce the General Missionary Convention's constitution of 1814, named the United States as the area of its constituency. This meant that there was a complete geographical overlapping of the territory to be cultivated by the two bodies. This geographical tension did not develop immediately after separation in 1845 for several reasons. For one thing, the cohesive force resident in the institution of slavery, binding together a distinctive geographical area in a cultural, social, and economic unity (combined with the preference of northern missionaries not to work in the South), brought a territorial consciousness to the new convention. The Home Mission Board of the Convention constantly reiterated that its field was the South during all of the period from 1845 throughout the remainder of the Reconstruction era. Furthermore, the voluntary withdrawal of the Home Mission Society from the older states of the South between 1845 and 1862 gave impetus to the conception of a distant geographical division. When the Home Mission Society briefly sent a missionary to Texas after having withdrawn from the field when separation came, the South's Domestic Mission Board secretary referred to Texas as "our territory," as over against the northwestern area which was looked upon as the society's territory. In addition, the normal development of the southern body was abruptly interrupted by the war in 1861 before it could be determined how far the organization would go toward carrying out the constitutional definition of its field. Reconstruction projected this situation for more than a decade after the war. Finally, the different organizational character of the new southern body tended to magnify territorial ideas more than a society type would have. The convention type of organization encouraged denominational unity involving all benevolences, rather than a benevolent unity that divided the constituency into groups loyal to one or more particular phase of activity. The new kind of organization encouraged *intensive* or multi-benevolent development in a given geographical area rather than an *extensive* promotion of a single benevolence in any geographical area.

For these and perhaps other reasons, the geographical tension did not display itself until the renewed activity of the society led it to send missionaries to the South during and after the civil war.

During all of this period from 1860 to 1877, the Home Mission Society endeavored to secure organic union of Northern and Southern Baptists, but the Convention consistently refused to take this step. As a result, the American Baptist Home Mission Society simply bypassed the Convention and worked in and with various states of the South. Between 1867 and 1877, when Reconstruction closed, the society made 686 annual appointments in the South covering 22,402 weeks of missionary labor in an average of 14 states of the South each year. Much of this work was among whites. In addition, in educational work between 1872 (when specific figures are first available) and 1877, the society conducted 7 schools for blacks and Indians in that many states of the South, employing 20 teachers in 1872 whose number increased to 41 in 1877. Pupils in these schools averaged about 800 each year, with 871 enrolling in 1877.[25]

Thus, in the closing decade of this period, an open rivalry developed between the older Home Mission Society of New York and the Home Mission Board of the Convention. The society's work in the South grew rapidly and prospered; its leaders announced that it was ministering to all races in the South in every type of missions, and that they saw no need for Southern Baptist even to have a board for home missions. At the same time, the Home Mission Board was in dire straits. It finances were less than half as much in 1877 as in 1867. Even some Southern Baptists were calling for the elimination of this board from the work of the

---

[25] Baker, *Relations*, 119.

Convention. In addition, the death of the first Sunday School Board in 1873 in the early stages of a severe financial depression caused the Convention to assign the debts and work of that agency to the Home Mission Board. This was well-nigh a last straw for the struggling home mission body.[26]

**The Death of the First Sunday School Board.** After the close of the war, the Sunday School Board secured C. C. Bitting as its corresponding secretary. He worked strenuously to improve the financial condition of the board, but came to the 1868 Convention with an $1,800 indebtedness for that year. He was conscious of the antagonism that such a debt aroused in the convention, and in justifying the situation he presented a melancholy picture:

> This board has existed only five years. Part of this time, a desolating war raged over all our territory, and the remaining time has witnessed the great poverty and oppression of our people. The postal facilities were almost the only means of communication in our business, and these were greatly diminished, while those existing were deranged and irresponsible. In the states where we are located there were, even this year, only about 141 in all, where in 1862, there were 478 offices. During this brief and disastrous period; without experience; without one dollar of permanent capital; dependent only on uncertain and small receipts; without the general and active interest among our brethren which is so beneficial and important, this Board has issued *fourteen publications,* and of these, over 200,000 copies, besides the establishment and improvement of a monthly Sunday-school paper of large circulation and at a cheaper rate than any other such paper known to us. It has aided and established many Sunday-schools. It has circulated many copies of the Word of God. Through its officers, missionaries, publications and appeals, it has contributed, not a little, to the awakening of that increased and general interest in the Sunday-school work which now prevails among our brethren.[27]

---

[26] Ibid., 153-165.
[27] Baker, *The Story of the Sunday School Board,* 22.

The Convention voted to move the board to Memphis, thinking perhaps its financial state might be improved in the West. However, the removal was disastrous for Secretary Bitting, for he was totally unknown in the West. He resigned in 1869. Later in the year Thomas C. Teasdale replaced him and for three years struggled with the financial crisis. During Teasdale's secretaryship, some of the tension that had lingered below the surface in the relations between the southern Sunday School Board and the northern American Baptist Publication Society's work in the same area began to appear. In his first report to the Convention, Teasdale noted with considerable impatience that some Southern Baptists were purchasing their literature from the northern publication society, and acidly remarked:

> If we can command the general patronage of our own Southern people, we will give them a Sunday School paper, at once most excellent and attractive, which shall be alike free from offensive sectionalism and unsound theology; and which shall be in every respect adapted to the peculiar civilization of the South, and the scriptural piety of our people.

In the following year, the Publication Society answered his request for free books by suggesting that if the churches asked for them, such requests should be referred to the Publication Society, Teasdale angrily wrote:

> It was thus made apparent that the American Baptist Publication Society of Philadelphia is not disposed to render aid to the South through the medium of the Sunday School Board of this convention. If it shall do anything to aid our people, it would seem that it must be done independently of any of our Southern organizations. Until this policy of that society in this regard shall have been modified, we must abandon all hope of co-operation with it on such terms as will not compromise the self-respect of our people, nor interfere with the integrity of the Boards of this Convention.[28]

In the fall of 1872 he resigned and the board could not find a replacement. Samuel Boykin was elected secretary pro tem, but when the Convention met in 1873, the board was abolished and its work and debts

---

[28] *Annual*, 1871, 16 of Appendix.

were transferred to the Domestic and Indian Mission Board, whose name was changed in the following year to the Home Mission Board. This competition for selling Sunday School and other publications to the churches smoldered during the period of Reconstruction, but in the next period it broke into flame.

**The Foreign Mission Board.** The Foreign Mission Board promptly resumed its work in Africa and China after the war. A new field was opened in Rome, Italy, in 1870. William N. Cote was the pioneer there, but in the following year he was replaced by George B. Taylor, son of the executive secretary of the board. An appeal for missionary cooperation came from São Paulo, Brazil, in 1873, where some of the Confederate leaders had migrated after the war, but there was a delay of almost a decade before the challenge was answered.

The corresponding secretary of the board, as pointed out, was James B. Taylor, whose distinguished service safely guided the foreign mission venture through the difficult days of beginning and of civil war. He resigned in December, 1871, shortly before his death, and was replaced by Henry Allen Tupper, who continued in that office during the remainder of this period.

The *Home and Foreign Journal* was begun again as the promotional periodical of the boards. During this period there was considerable discussion at the meetings of the Convention concerning the use of agents to raise money for the several boards. In 1871, for example, even though the agent could keep 20% of what he collected for foreign missions, the board felt that his services were indispensable. In 1874 the Foreign Mission Board reported that agents were costing about 25% of what they collected. During the Reconstruction period women began their local and state organizations in a movement that was destined to bless the foreign mission program during the years to come. Lottie Moon had gone to China to be there a brief period with her sister, Edmonia, who had to return to the States in 1877 because of her health.

In the closing year of the period, a glimpse of a struggle to come was seen in a message delivered by T. P. Crawford, one of the missionaries in China, in May, 1877, at a mission conference. Crawford spoke on the advantages and disadvantages of the employment of native agents. He was so impressed by the disadvantages of such employment that he was thrown into controversy with the Foreign Mission Board itself, and during the following decades he was the principal figure in the Gospel Mission controversy.

**Theological Education.** The Southern Baptist Theological Seminary at Greenville, South Carolina, found it necessary to close in June, 1862, after its third session. Most of the faculty and student body became chaplains or soldiers in the confederate army. After the war, the four stalwarts constituting the faculty (Boyce, Broadus, Williams, and Manly) vowed that they would die before letting the seminary die, despite almost hopeless conditions. The seminary reopened on November 1, 1865, with seven students. It soon became evident that South Carolina, so severely mauled by the war, could not support the school. Plans were set in motion early in the 1870's to move to a more favorable location and secure endowment, but the Panic of 1873 inhibited this. In 1877 the seminary was moved to new quarters in Louisville, Kentucky. Baptists in that state made herculean efforts to provide cash and pledges to insure its survival. At the close of this period the issue was still in doubt.

**The Women's Work.** Baptist women in the South, of course, had been active in missionary societies since before the forming of the General Missionary Convention in 1814. In fact, many female societies sent funds for foreign missions to the General Convention between 1814 and 1844, and were permitted on the basis of these contributions to appoint men to represent them at the triennial meetings.

A large step toward organizational articulation came when Mrs. Ann J. Graves of Baltimore, whose son, R. H. Graves, had been appointed by the Foreign Mission Board of southern body in 1855 to China, began to call informal meetings of Baptist women of Baltimore together to hear letters from her son who was working in Canton. Perhaps the initial convention-related meeting of record occurred in 1868 when the Southern Baptist Convention convened in Baltimore. Promptly the women of several states began to organize to forward the missionary enterprise. Baltimore Baptists sent a circular throughout the South appealing to the women of Baptist churches to become active in the missionary enterprise. In this circular the women of Baltimore said that they had adopted a plan of having mission boxes in their homes, each member pledging to put at least two cents a week into this box, preferably on Sunday. The circular also suggested the organization of societies in each state to attend to business, and regular meetings in each church or neighboring churches, for prayer and dissemination of missionary intelligence. By 1874, the Foreign Mission Board recommended that an executive or central committee for women's work be appointed for each state. At first the board made these appointments in consultation with brethren in the state concerned, but within ten years the women's committees became self-perpetuating. In 1875 the Southern Baptist Convention commended the significant work of "these gentle and loving servants of Jesus." By the close of the reconstruction era, the Convention was urging that a female missionary society be organized in every church. The exhortation is 1877 was prophetic of things to come.

> Let the Christian women of our Churches generally, adopt some such plan, and press it with zeal and energy, and like the rock smitten by the Prophet's rod, the dry places shall become fountains of blessing to the needy.[29]

## The Fortunes of Landmarkism

Civil war and reconstruction were quiet hurtful to the Landmark movement. Homer L. Grice remarked: "The war brought at least one great blessing to Southern Baptists: It ended the greatest controversy that ever afflicted them." It is true that Landmarkism never again had strength enough to confront the Southern Baptists Convention as it did in 1859 at Richmond, but the movement was far from terminated at the close of the war. The fall of Nashville to Union forces in February, 1862, in which J. R. Graves lost everything—book stock, press, and equipment—was only the first of many blows that wasted him. The postwar yellow fever epidemic claimed his mother and his wife. He accepted the pastorate of the First Baptist Church, Memphis, in 1867, leaving the familiar and beloved environs of Nashville. He was able to begin the publication of *The Baptist* at Memphis, but he was defeated again and again in his struggle to establish a publication agency. His paper was quiet popular in what James E. Tull termed "the Landmark belt"—Tennessee, Arkansas, Mississippi, Texas, Louisiana, and North Alabama. With the close of the war, Graves began a strenuous decade of preaching, lecturing, and writing. "All was energy, toil and frequent physical breakdowns." Perhaps his own

---

[29] *Annual*, 1877, 59.

trials brought a kindlier spirit to Graves. Late in this period he wrote in his paper:

> It has been a long time since anything of a personal character appeared in this paper.... The older we grow the more we are convinced that it were better to let the most bitter things pass unnoticed.[30]

Homer L. Grice wrote that many Graves' followers

> were not willing to help split associations, state convention, and the Southern Baptist Convention on the personal and denominational issues he had stressed, for they knew what the Campbellite and antimission splits had done to Southern Baptist life. Increasingly, they tired of warfare and yearned for peace.[31]

In addition, Grice felt that Southern Baptists, "suffering sorely from the ravages of the Civil War and grappling with the many difficult problems of the reconstruction era had other things to think about than the Graves-Howell controversy."[32]

However, despite this improved spirit by Graves and the quiescence of his followers, the ecclesiology views of such an influential man as J. R. Graves (and he never relinquished them) continued to develop polarities in churches, state bodies, and the Convention itself. Strong Landmark leadership was a significant factor in several spin-offs just before and after Graves's death in 1893. At the same time, as James E. Tull pointed out, Landmark doctrines were entering the bloodstream of Southern Baptists. Second-generation Landmarkers adopted those aspects of Graves' system that they preferred, and overlooked others. Consequently, Landmarkism, apart from Graves himself, exhibited no monolithic character, even among the original triumvirate. This will be glimpsed more clearly in the next period when various controversies commanded the general support of all types of Landmark followers; and despite the fact that at least two of them, embodying basically the thrust of Graves, appeared at precisely the same time, there was little coalescence in the controversies because of their varying emphases.

---

[30] On April 24, 1875. Quoted in Tull, *Southern Baptist Landmarkism*, 499.
[31] Cox, ed., *Encyclopedia*, I, 684.
[32] Ibid., 584-585.

# Chapter 10 - The Struggle to Live

The post-Reconstruction decades were crucial for Southern Baptists. Some of their difficulties developed from internal and inter-Baptist rivalries growing out of doctrinal or sectional ideologies. On the other hand, many of their problems were thrust upon them by the kind of world in which they lived in the forty years between 1877 and 1917. In many respects these years were most remarkable, defying any attempt to unravel their complex components. The aspects of the world that were most influential on the growth and life of the Southern Baptist Convention may be described in general terms. The rapid growth of the population in the United States (from 47,141,000 in 1877 to 103,414,000 in 1917) challenged Southern Baptists with potential converts. Immigration reached new heights, totaling more than 23,000,000 people during these years. In fact, between 1905 and 1914, six of the ten years showed immigration exceeding 1,000,000 each year, while the lowest number of immigrants in the other years was 751,786. The frontier to the west ceased to exist by about 1890, due partly to extensive purchase of western land by speculators, and partly by achieving control of the Indians in the West by eliminating their basic meat supply through destroying the huge buffalo herds and by establishing reservations for them. At the same time the development of the railroads provided more rapid and convenient transportation. In 1860 total trackage was 30,625 miles. This figure grew steadily until 1920, when total track mileage approximated 260,000. Southern Baptists spread rapidly to the southwestern and western areas, affecting the sectional nature of their general body and bringing additional missionary activity to the new settlements along the railroads. Better communication was secured by the invention of the telephone to supplement the telegraph, while the automobile and even the flying machine had their beginnings in this period.

Technological improvements helped the United States become the world leader in many areas. The typewriter, the linotype (accelerating effective journalism), the phonograph, and the electric light were only a few of the significant inventions. The refinement of agricultural implements had revolutionized the operation of farms. Industry kept pace. Before the turn of the century the United States had surpassed England and Germany in the production of iron and steel and was the leading industrial nation. Mass production that inhibited individual craftsmanship and creativity in work already was well under way. The number of wage earners engaged in manufacturing more than trebled between 1869 and 1914. The gross value of manufactured products rose at the same time from about $3,400,000,000 to $24,200,000,000. The American labor movement became effectively organized for the first time in this period. This was the age of giant corporations, huge personal fortunes, and unbelievable corruption in financial and political life. Monopolies brought government intervention in industry. The only interruption in the spiraling prosperity of this period was the panic of 1893. Reflecting instability in the British market in 1890, foreign capital movement to America was stopped, bringing a market collapse in New York and substantial exports of gold. The inflexible banking system was helpless to stop the completion of the cycle, and a severe financial panic gripped the nation from about 1893 to 1897. The effects of this depression were reflected in every Baptist institution or activity during that important decade.

As southerners returned to the national political arena, they found that northern financial and industrial leaders, without the opposition in Congress by southern planters, had utilized the Federal Government to forward and protect their sectional interests; but by the close of this period, the South was involved in the new nationalism that had developed rapidly after the Spanish-American War and the new enthusiastic idealism that accompanied the First World War. The Spanish-American War in 1898 catapulted the United States into the position of a world power. After its close the United States annexed Hawaii on July 7, 1898, and on December 10, 1898, received the Philippines, Puerto Rico, and Guam from Spain. At the very close of the period, World War I was fought to make the world safe for democracy. War was declared on April 6, 1917, and peace was signed on November 11, 1918.

The greatest influence on Southern Baptists, of course, came from the religious climate during this period. In both European and American religious life the baneful carry-over of rationalism and skepticism from an earlier period formed a foundation for religious confrontations in all denominations. The nineteenth century was characterized both in Europe and the United States by a strong anti-supernaturalistic thrust. The French Revolution inaugurated forms of free thought and liberalism that radically affected politics, culture, and religion in the following century. Successive blows were aimed, in particular, at the basic supernaturalism that undergirded the Christian movement. Scientific thought was used to erode the theological assertions of a creative and providential God, and indeed, the necessity of his existence. In 1859 Charles Darwin published his *Origin of Species*, which developed the theme that human life evolved from lower forms through the survival of the fittest: this was projected into religious and metaphysical structures to undermine man of the most evident arguments for the existence and providence of God. Historical and radical literary critics attempted to reconstruct the Scriptures in such fashion as to eliminate the meaning of biblical inspiration. Loisy and Tyrrell in the Roman Catholic Church and Wellhausen and Strauss of the Protestant community published radical works in this vein. An increased sociological emphasis, interpreting Christianity in humanitarian terms rather than individualistic regeneration, resulted in extensive application of the "this-worldly" social gospel in the place of an "other-worldly" individual-redeeming gospel. A part of the move toward church unity and ecumenism stemmed from not only the needs of the mission fields but from the attempt by Christian liberals to unify all Christian denominations in the struggle against hostile critics. Philosophy, taking its cue from the upward direction of the evolutionary process in the hypothesis of Darwin, began to reflect an optimistic attitude toward the future and potentiality of man, who indeed might evolve into deity.[33]

These scientific, literary, sociological, ecumenical, and philosophical trends formed the religious community in the world of Southern Baptists from 1877 to 1917. All of them appear in some aspect of Southern Baptist life.

The critical internal and inter-Baptist attacks against the Convention during this period occurred precisely at those points where this body broke with the old society-type ideology in 1845 when organizing

---

[33] For a summary of these developments, see Clyde L. Manschreck, *A History of Christianity-Reformation to the Present* (Englewood Cliffs, New Jersey: Prentice-Hall, Inc., 1964), pp. 315ff, and 411 ff.

on the associational or convention concept: (1) opposition to the effort to establish a specific geographical base; (2) opposition to the effort to sustain a multibenevolent ministry; and (3) opposition to the effort to "elicit, combine, and direct" the energies of all Southern Baptists in a united denominational thrust. The first two attacks stemmed from the desire of the older societies (for home missions and for publication) in the North to retain the geographical field and the publication ministry in the South that had been theirs before the organization of the Southern Baptist body. The third attack was launched by the Landmark movement within the Southern Baptist Convention as a protest against the centralization of denominational life in general bodies to the detriment of the authority of the local churches. Had the Convention failed to survive any of these confrontations, it would have been badly mutilated or utterly destroyed.

## Establishing a Geographical Base

As mentioned heretofore, the convention ideology differed radically from the society plan in that the former desired a geographically-based denominational body that would assume leadership in all of the benevolences the constituency might desire to cultivate. Each society, on the other hand, was benevolence-centered. It functioned for one benevolence only, minimized geography and denominational unity in favor of widespread financial support, and ignored all other denominational emphases as being the province of other societies. Consequently, from the very time that the Southern Baptist Convention was organized in 1845 there was a potential confrontation between the Domestic Mission Board of the new body and the older Home Mission Society of New York relative to the geographical base each would cultivate. Not only so, but the increasing home mission programs of the several associations and state bodies in the South presented rivals for funds to the Home Mission Board (so called after 1874) of the Convention.[34]

**Rivalry by Southern States.** The rivalry with the state bodies in the South not only radically diminished the receipts of the southern board but also closed many areas of work to it. It was reported at the meeting of the Convention in 1881 that because of this rivalry the only areas of mission service left in the hand of the Home Mission Board were

---

[34] For this story, see Baker, *Relations*, pp. 158-59.

Florida, Arkansas, Louisiana, Texas, Indian Territory, and California. W. H. McIntosh, secretary of the board, remarked at the Convention's session in the following year that the geographical area which constituted the largest resources of the board and in which the greatest results had been accomplished—the older southern states—had been taken over by the state boards, thereby diminishing the contributions to the southwide board "whose labors are bestowed upon regions that need assistance and can give but little." As a matter of fact, the board was denied the right of collecting funds and prosecuting mission in some of these states by official action of the state conventions.[35]

**Confrontation by the Home Mission Society.** But the paucity of receipts from its constituency was not the severest trial of the Home Mission Board. At this very time, the Baptist Home Mission Society of New York, under the able leadership of Henry L. Morehouse, disregarding protests by Convention leaders, was aggressively striving to supplant the Convention's Home Mission Board entirely. The society was not only pressing a mission program in the older states of the South, but was rapidly enlarging its work in the few states and territories left in the hands of the southern board because of southern state convention rivalry.[36]

When the receipts of the board plunged to a new low of $12,960.43 in 1878 and the Home Mission Society of New York continued its domination of the southern home field, Southern Baptists began to debate seriously both in the Convention sessions and elsewhere whether a southern Home Mission Board was really needed, since the associations and state bodies in the South and the northern society were so active in the work. The year 1882 was critical. This marked the fiftieth anniversary of the northern society, and it used its great resources and history to call for additional cooperation by the South. In that year, for example, the society had 67 missionaries in 13 states of the South in their evangelistic program, 13 schools with 78 teachers and 2,329 pupils (principally black) in the South, and had provided extensive assistance to churches of all races in the constructing of church buildings. Baptist state bodies in Texas, Arkansas, Georgia, and Mississippi were in more or less formal alliance with the society in its southern work, and financial support was given the

---

[35] *Annual*, Southern Baptist Convention, 1892, p. xi of Appendix A.
[36] For this story in some detail, see Baker, *Relations*, pp. 154 ff.

society by Baptists in other southern states without formal alignment.[37] The society's receipts during the previous ten years had amounted to almost $2,000,000. In contrast with this, the Convention's home mission receipts during the same period were less than $225,000 (of which perhaps 40% was probably used for collecting agents and administration).

**A New Location and Secretary.** On the second day of the 1882 session of the Convention, Joshua Levering of Maryland offered a resolution that a committee consisting of one from each state be appointed to study the Home Mission Board and make such recommendations as might "promote its usefulness to the enlargement of the work committed to its trust." Two days later the committee appointed made the following report:

> Your Committee to whom was referred the consideration of the present condition, prospects and enlargement of the Home Mission work of this Convention, beg leave to report that we find a want of enthusiasm on the part of the denomination in the work of this Board, and since from the experience of a series of years, it seems impossible to arouse this enthusiasm without making material changes, your Committee feel constrained, as on the whole promising the best results, to recommend the following resolutions, viz;
>
> 1st. That the Home Mission Board be removed from Marion, Alabama, to Atlanta, Georgia, as soon after the adjournment of this Convention as such transfer can be made.
>
> 2nd. That the Board be instructed to employ a Corresponding Secretary, and in addition thereto, one or more district Secretaries, if found best for the efficient prosecution of its work.
>
> 3rd. That the Committee on Nomination of new Boards be instructed to render their report in accordance with the foregoing resolutions.
>
> Your Committee desire, in presenting the above recommendations, to state distinctly and emphatically, that in all their inquiries, they have heard no word of complaint against any of the brethren composing the present Board, but, on the contrary, only words of commendation and praise for their faithful attention

---

[37] Ibid., 134 ff.

to the work committed to their trust, and they cannot close this report without recommending the adoption of the following resolution, viz:

"That the earnest and sincere thanks of this Convention be and are hereby tendered to the Home Mission Board, at Marion, Alabama, and to its Corresponding Secretary, and to each member thereof, for long and faithful services rendered so willingly and gratuitously."[38]

Pursuant to these instructions, the Home Mission Board elected I. T. Tichenor as the successor to McIntosh, and moved the headquarters of the board to Atlanta, Georgia. Tichenor faced what he called later "a great defeat and a lost cause."

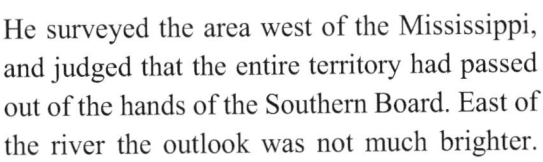

I. T. Tichenor, the man who is credited with saving the Home Mission Board (Photo courtesy of Southern Baptist Historical Library and Archives)

He surveyed the area west of the Mississippi, and judged that the entire territory had passed out of the hands of the Southern Board. East of the river the outlook was not much brighter. Mississippi was allied with the Publication Society of the North, Georgia was cooperating with the Home Mission Society in freedman missions, while Florida was seriously considering an official alignment with the Home Mission Society. Tennessee Baptists also were studying the possibility of Northern alignment. Indian Territory and Louisiana were the only areas that offered the possibility of alignment with the Southern Convention, and in the former the Home Mission Society was pressing an aggressive campaign.[39]

Tichenor promptly began to challenge the Home Mission Society. During the next five years he made an intensive effort to attend meetings of all state bodies in the South and as many of the associational gatherings as time and strength permitted. In August, 1882, President E. T. Winkler of the Home Mission Board wrote an article that was widely publicized in many periodicals, in which he openly questioned the propriety of the

---

[38] *Annual,* Southern Baptist Convention, 1882, 29.
[39] Baker, *Relations,* 160.

aggressive program of the Home Mission Society in the South. Probably for the first time this article alerted many Southern Baptists to the issues involved in the extensive program of the northern society in the South. Winkler noted the several plans of cooperation between the Home Mission Society and various southern states, and pointed to the announced new program of the society which would greatly affect the work of Home Mission Board if it succeeded. He concluded his article by saying:

> Every one of the border States of the South is occupied by the Home Mission Society; and most of our older States are in cooperative alliance with the American Baptist Publication Society in colportage and Sunday School work.... The missionaries employed in the South by the Home Mission Society is 120—just three times the number of those under commission of our own Home Mission Board. The total expenditures of the Northern Society at the South, for regular missionary and educational work and school buildings, during the past year, was over $84,000, while on the other hand, the entire contribution of Southern Baptists to their Home Mission Board did not amount to $29,000.[40]

This article by Winkler was the beginning of a widespread newspaper controversy over the right of the society to work in the South, which the Southern Baptist Convention called its territory. Corresponding Secretary H. L. Morehouse of the Home Mission Society affirmed that the society was in the South to stay, and said vigorously that in its constitution the society named North America as its field, which, of course, included the South. The *Religious Herald* of Virginia and the *Foreign Mission Journal* of the Convention openly debated this question with the *Home Mission Monthly* of the society. In 1887 the Home Mission Society published an article in its journal which remarked:

> We observe that some influential Southern Baptists are openly asserting that the Home Mission Board of the Southern Baptist Convention is a superfluity and ought to be dispensed with entirely. Its field is covered by old and efficient State conventions, the only new mission fields to which it devotes attention being

---

[40] Ibid., 161.

portions of Florida and Texas. It is felt that a special organization for such limited work is not now called for, whatever may have been the demands for it in the past.[41]

Tichenor worked strenuously to overcome the lethargy of Southern Baptists in their home mission program. His vision was large. Year after year he challenged the Convention with significant programs couched in appealing terms. In 1885, for example, he said to the Convention:

> For once let us try what united energies of this Convention can accomplish when it determines to do a deed of noble daring for our kindred, and for our Saviour's cause. Long enough we have been creeping timidly along the shore. Let us launch out into the great deep of human necessity, and let down the gospel net where the thousands are perishing. For forty years we have been pursuing a policy which has distrusted our God and been hurtful to ourselves. We are weary of following every other Christian host into battle for the world's deliverance. We want to move up the front, and as good soldiers bear our full part in the conflict.[42]

His vision encompassed many new facets of work, including schools, hospitals, homes for orphans and for the aged and infirm, and "indeed all those means which lift up our humanity from the degradation of the fall, and prepare it for the work of God in this life, and to dwell with Him in the life to come." His eloquence was stirring.

> The breath of the Divine Spirit can dissipate the mists of worldliness that bedim the vision of His people, and show us even now that both duty and happiness require such consecration. A new Pentecost, with its disported tongues of fire, may impart new life, even in our day, to His children.... A mighty revolution, shaking as with the might of an earthquake, the sleeping Christians of our time, may break upon us as a meteor breaks through the midnight sky. The voice of the Almighty may call to this valley of dry bones, "O, ye dry bones, hear the word of the Lord," and

---

[41] Ibid., 164.
[42] *Annual*, Southern Baptist Convention, 1885, xv-xvi.

starting from their long slumbers they may stand up an exceeding great army, prepared for the conquest of the world.[43]

He found it difficult to stir his comrades. In 1891, for example, he expressed disappointment at the meager funds received for carrying on the work, describing extensively the economic and material development of the South that should cause Southern Baptists to advance. He closed by exclaiming,

> Brethren of this Convention, you have laid this work upon us. Its vastness has awed our souls. Its sore pressing needs have touched our spirits. Its crying wants have moved our hearts to pity, and sometimes to tears. Its boundless opportunities have excited our enthusiasm. We want to do the work you have assigned us, but how can we when we are trammeled by the slowness of our churches and the scantiness of our resources. Take from hands that are eager to do what we see so plainly needs to done these shackles that restrain our efforts and limit our action.[44]

Despite such expressions of disappointment, Tichenor accomplished much. Perhaps he more than any other single person should be credited with saving the home field. As a result of his energetic policy,

> in five years (after he took office in 1882) there was not a missionary to the white people of the South who did not bear commission from either the Home Mission Board of the Southern Baptist Convention, or one of our State Boards in alliance with it.[45]

Even in the troublesome border states of Missouri and Indian Territory, where the controversy between the Home Mission Society and the Home Mission Board was so vigorously waged, Tichenor was able to negotiate a settlement. In Missouri, committees from the two general bodies worked out a compromise by which they shared this important field of service, but in 1890, so unsatisfactory was the arrangement that the state body asked both of the home mission bodies to withdraw and permit the state forces

---

[43] Ibid., xvii.
[44] Ibid., xliv.
[45] Ibid., 1892, xl of Appendix A.

to collect and divide home mission funds.⁴⁶ This arrangement seemed to please all participants. In Indian Territory, J. W. Murrow, the venerable missionary of the southern board, disagreed with Tichenor's aggressive pro-southern policies and in 1891 was forced to resign. He was promptly appointed by the society as their missionary and continued his work.⁴⁷ Thenceforth, Tichenor worked actively in Indian Territory for southern interests.

During Tichenor's last year as secretary in 1899, 671 missionaries were supported jointly with the state boards. Alabama, Arkansas, Florida, Georgia, Indian Territory, Kentucky, Louisiana, Maryland, Missouri, Mississippi, North Carolina, Oklahoma Territory, Tennessee, Texas, and Virginia were cooperating with the board in part or all of their work. The receipts of 1899 were $79,366.68.

Joe W. Burton has suggested ten significant contributions made by Tichenor, as follows: (1) he saved the Southern Baptist Convention through saving the Home Mission Board; (2) he laid the foundations for the Cooperative Program through his plea for systematic giving; (3) he established a church building department; (4) he fostered and built up the Sunday School work; (5) he inaugurated the board's work in Cuba; (6) he actively promoted city missions; (7) he assisted blacks through conducting institutes and training them for efficient service; (8) he inaugurated the chain of mountain mission schools; (9) he promoted direct missions on the frontier, among the Indians and among the foreigners; and (10) he led Baptists to see the South as a base for world missions.⁴⁸

**The Beginning of Comity Agreements.** At the 1894, meeting of the Convention, T. T. Eaton, Kentucky Baptist editor, submitted the following resolution, which was approved.

> *Resolved,* That a committee of five be appointed to confer with a similar committee to be appointed by the American Baptist Home Mission Society with reference—

---

[46] *Annual Report*, American Baptist Home Mission Society, 1890, 23.
[47] See William A. Carlton, "Not Yours But You"- The Life of Joseph Samuel Murrow (unpublished dissertation, Southwestern Baptist Theological Seminary, Ft. Worth, Texas, 1945), 98.
[48] Joe W. Burton, *Epochs of Home Missions* (Atlanta: Home Mission Board, 1945), 77-84.

1. To cooperation between our Home Board and the Society in work among the colored people of the South; and

2. With reference to a more definite understanding in regard to the territorial limits of the work of the Board and the Society among the native white people, the Indians and the foreign populations of the country.[49]

*The Fortress Monroe Conference.* The Convention appointed a committee consisting of T. T. Eaton, H. H. Harris, I. T. Tichenor, J. B. Gambrell, T. P. Bell, Noah K. Davis, and O. F. Gregory. The society named James L. Howard, T. J. Morgan, H. L. Morehouse, J. B. Thomas, E. H. Johnson, A. S. Hobart, Nathan E. Wood, and, by invitation, M. MacVicar. The combined committee met at Fortress Monroe, Virginia, on September 12, 1894, where Howard was elected chairman and Gregory and Wood were named secretaries. Despite the fact that on each of these committees were those who had been strenuously opposed to the work of the other body, an excellent spirit prevailed. After two days of deliberation, the group unanimously adopted two items, and a third one which was proposed by the South, was reported favorably, although the northern committee had no instructions about approving it. The first item concerned schools among the black people. It was unanimously agreed that the Home Mission Board should appoint a local advisory committee at each point where a school was controlled by the society; that control of the schools shall remain in the hands of the society, but these local advisory committees shall make recommendations to the society concerning any changes needed for the school; that the board and the Southern Baptist Convention shall appeal to Baptists of the South for moral and financial support of these schools and encourage promising young black people as students. The second item concerned mission work among the blacks. It was unanimously recommended that the two bodies cooperate in the mission work among the black people of the South in connection with the Baptist state bodies, white and black, in the joint appointment of general missionaries, in holding Ministers' and Deacons' Institutes, and in the better organization of the missionary work of black Baptists. The third item concerned territorial limits. The committee of the society referred to their board (which subsequently approved it) the

---

[49] *Annual*, Southern Baptist Convention, 1894, 16.

proposition of the committee of the Southern Baptist Convention, which read as follows:

> We believe that, for the promotion of fraternal feeling and of the best interests of the Redeemer's kingdom, it is inexpedient for two different organizations of Baptists to solicit contributions, or to establish missions in the same localities, and for this reason we recommend to the Home Mission Board of the Southern Baptist Convention and to the American Baptist Home Mission Society, that in the prosecution of their work already begun on contiguous fields, or on the same field, that all antagonisms be avoided, and that their officers and employees be instructed to co-operate in all practical ways in the spirit of Christ. That we further recommend to these bodies and their agents, in opening new work, to direct their efforts to localities not already occupied by the other.[50]

Despite the fine words and good spirit of the Fortress Monroe Conference, however, the agreement was not effective. Some white Baptist state conventions refused to enter into it, while black Baptists generally either showed little interest or in many cases were so separated by factions within the states that they could not agree on any program. The Home Mission Board seriously and energetically endeavored to make the program a success. It refused to aid black Baptists who would not cooperate with the society, and turned away from educational activities among the blacks since the society was majoring in that field. However, the program increasingly became less effective, and within a decade many felt that it was no longer operative.

*The Washington Conference.* Another comity agreement was attempted after the opening of the twentieth century. The Home Mission Board had been receiving frequent requests for aid from churches composed of Southern Baptists in New Mexico. At the Southern Baptist Convention in 1894 a Texan offered a resolution that New Mexico should be entered as a mission field, and the Convention approved. However, after the resolution that led to the Fortress Monroe Conference was approved later in the same session, the Home Mission Board was directed not to enter New Mexico until after the conference with the society had

---

[50] Baker, *Source Book*, 161-62.

been held. The requests for aid from churches composed of Southern Baptists in New Mexico were especially numerous and urgent in 1907 and 1908. When the Convention began looking favorably toward assisting these churches, Secretary H. L. Morehouse of the society protested and cited the Fortress Monroe agreement. The southern board again requested a conference with the society to settle this question. A conference was held in Washington, D. C., on April 15, 1909, and before beginning their new discussions, all parties agreed that the Fortress Monroe agreement had expired and that its stipulations were not now in force or binding.

The combined committee recommended that the southern board, with the consent of the New Mexico Convention, take over all the work of the society in New Mexico and that any question of territorial adjustment on the part of both boards be considered settled for a period of at least five years.[51] When this recommendation came to the Southern Baptist Convention, however, J. B. Gambrell of Texas added a statement declaring that nothing in the agreement should be construed to limit any church, association, or other Baptist body in the free exercise of the inalienable right to make such alignments for cooperation as will, in its judgment, be for its own good and for the furtherance of its work.[52] The society was unwilling to accept this qualification and refused to approve the recommendations of the Washington Conference.

*Old Point Comfort-Hot Springs Conference.* Agitation in New Mexico, which had initiated the Washington Conference, continued, and their state body split in two, one portion affiliating with the society and one with the board of the southern convention. At the request of the northern brethren, on September 27-28, 1911, a meeting of committees appointed by the Northern and Southern Baptist Convention took place at Old Point Comfort, Virginia, and later at Hot Springs, Arkansas. With reference to New Mexico, this committee recommended that a new state body be organized, composed of the two existing rival conventions, and that the new convention should affiliate solely with the southern board and convention. This plan was subsequently adopted by the society, the Home Mission Board, the two New Mexico conventions, and the Northern and Southern Baptist Conventions. The Northern Baptist Convention had been

---

[51] Ibid., 162-63 for this agreement.
[52] *Annual*, Southern Baptist Convention, 1909, 31-32.

organized in 1907, but the Home Mission Society still retained its former functions.

In addition to settling the New Mexico problem, the joint committee in 1911-12 also set forth some principles of comity that have continued to be recognized to the present time. The committee asserted its belief in the independence of local Baptist churches, and in the advisory nature of all denominational bodies. Based upon these fundamental principles, the joint committee formulated three comity statements that were subsequently unanimously approved, as follows: (1) the giving of financial aid by a denominational body should not impair the autonomy of any church; (2) denominational organizations should carefully regard the rights of sister organizations and of the churches, to the end that unity and harmony and respect for the liberties of others should be promoted; and (3) Baptist bodies should never in any way injure the work of any other Baptist group.[53]

*The Oklahoma Decision.* Growing directly out of the New Mexico decision by the joint committee from Northern and Southern Baptists, came another territorial adjustment during this period. Both Northern and Southern Baptists had worked in Indian and Oklahoma Territory for many years. At times there were four or five sectional bodies organized, each affiliating with either the North or the South in carrying on their programs, and in general ignoring the other bodies. However, beginning in March, 1901, a series of harmonious conferences among the several bodies in Indian and Oklahoma Territory took place. These conferences resulted in the formation of the Baptist General Convention of Oklahoma in 1906. In the following year, Oklahoma became the forty-sixth state of the Union. The new Baptist General Convention of Oklahoma adopted dual alignment, sending funds both to the society and to the board.

The question of alignment had plagued Oklahoma Baptists for years. The predominantly southern population of Oklahoma was constantly being augmented by new southern immigrants. The settlement by the joint committee from both Northern and Southern Baptists in New Mexico was the decisive factor in causing Oklahoma Baptists to change their affiliation. The chief consideration for asking New Mexico Baptists to cooperate with the Southern Baptist Convention, the joint committee

---

[53] Baker, *Source Book*, 163 ff has this document.

had said, "was the fact that the tide of immigration into New Mexico from Texas and other Southern States in recent years had been so great. The result has been that the population of New Mexico has become largely Southern in tradition and sympathy and preference."[54] A committee of Oklahoma Baptists, facing the same problem in that state, said that every reason given for New Mexico being turned to the Southern Baptist Convention applied with more weight to them. Consequently, in November, 1914, the Oklahoma body voted to adopt single alignment with the Southern Baptist Convention. No question of doctrine was involved.

> The reasons assigned for the action were that it was best in Oklahoma, as it was in New Mexico, for a State Convention to be affiliated with only one general society and that the preponderating sectional element in the denomination in the State should determine which one it should be.[55]

Thus, by the close of this period in 1917, the Convention had established its geographical base and in its struggle to accomplish this, had begun the development of a denominational consciousness that substantially deepened the loyalty of its constituents.[56] This loyalty would soon result in the reassessment of the geographical base when southern people, accustomed to their affiliation with the Southern Baptist Convention, moved into every section of the nation and preferred their old affiliation.

## Sustaining a Multibenevolence Ministry

The second crucial struggle of the Southern Baptist Convention in this period developed from its ideology that conceived of all denominational and benevolent activity in the geographical area of its work as being properly a part of its mission. At this point there was a growing rivalry between the American Baptist Publication Society of Philadelphia, which had been faithful in providing Sunday School publications for Southern Baptists since 1840, and Southern Baptist leaders who desired to incorporate this ministry in the structured work of their Convention. It will be recalled that the first Sunday School Board of

---

[54] *Annual*, Southern Baptist Convention, 1912, 46 ff.
[55] Baker, *Relations*, 198.
[56] Ibid., 168-69.

the southern body survived only from 1863 to 1873, after which, because of financial difficulties, its duties were assigned to the Domestic or Home Mission Board, along with a debt of $6,565. This was the situation in 1877.

**The Home Mission Board Period.** The financial panic of 1873, which brought the demise of the first Sunday School Board, caused the Convention to instruct its Home Mission Board to incur no additional debts whatsoever on the Sunday School publications. Consequently, the Home Mission Board let a contract with J. W. Burke and Company to publish *Kind Words* and lessons leaflets, with the understanding that there would be no expense of any kind to the board and any profits would accrue to the publisher. Later, because of the profit made by this contract, J. W. Burke and Company allowed a royalty of $800 a year under a new contract, which was increased on June 1, 1881, to $1,000 a year. Burke had been publishing over 100,000 copies of *Kind Words* each month, together with lesson leaflets in the number of about 40,000 a month. The old Sunday School debt had been pared down to about $3,000. By January, 1884, all of the old debt of the first Sunday School Board was paid off through these royalties.

The financial profit shown in the publication of the Sunday School material did not go unnoticed. In 1885 a committee of the Convention complimented the board for the paper, but went on to say the following:

> Neither brother Boykin nor any other man can supply all the demands of the literature essential to efficient Sunday-school work. The very best writers of our denomination are needed to supply, in adequate measure, what is now needed. If, therefore, we expect to meet these varied demands, we must very materially increase the facilities for producing this literature. Multitudes of our churches are already ordering their publications from Northern and Western publishing houses, not only on account of their cheapness, but because of the ability with which they are prepared, as many of their ablest men are editing these publications. Whether we can, under present circumstances, compete with these houses in these respects, is a question to be determined. On some accounts it may be well to make the experiment. We only speak what we all feel when we say that no one man can supply the demands of this service. We must have

something adapted to all stages of mental and moral development—a graded series reaching from our infant classes to mature age.

In view of the early expiration of the contract for the publication of *Kind Words*, we suggest to the Home Board to mature some plan by which these growing demands may be met. With Rev. Samuel Boykin as chief, supported by such talent as can be found in our midst, this paper would meet all the demands of the case, and none of our people would look either North or West for any Sabbath-school literature.[57]

The "Northern publishing house" referred to in this report was, of course, the American Baptist Publication Society, the principal publisher of Sunday School materials in both northern and southern Baptist life. In that same year Secretary I. T. Tichenor of the Home Mission Board bluntly urged the Convention to consider enlarging the area of Sunday School literature to provide all Baptist churches in the South with needed materials. When the committee report suggested that the board "mature some plan by which these growing demands may be met," Tichenor promptly responded. In the following year he reported to the Convention that the board was "fully convinced that it was the duty of the Board and Convention, if possible, to supply the Sunday-school needs of its constituents." He said that he had awarded a five-year contract to publish several editions of *Kind Words*, and in addition to publish a full grade of *Quarterlies* in the number of three, and a *Magazine for Teachers*. The board would receive an annual royalty of $1,000 without assuming any risk under the contract. The Convention approved this without a word of opposition or dissenting voice. With this approval of a series of Sunday School publications, there developed what Tichenor called "the heaviest denominational conflict of the century." The northern publication society enjoyed a large and profitable business among the Baptist churches in the South, and was not willing to give up this business without a struggle. For the next several years the rivalry rocked along quietly, but there were evidences of it. For example, in 1887 Tichenor reported that outstanding Southern Baptist writers like Basil Manly, Jr., F. H. Kerfoot, J. M. Frost, H. H. Harris, and Samuel Boykin had contributed material, and that the

---

[57] *Annual*, Southern Baptist Convention, 1885, 24-25.

patronage was so gratifying that the publisher had been forced to enlarge his facilities materially. On the back of the Convention *Annual* in 1887 was an advertisement for the series, including weekly *Kind Words*, the semimonthly *Kind Words*, the monthly *Kind Words*, lesson leaflets, the *Child's Gem*, *Kind Words* quarterlies for three age groups (primary, intermediate, and advanced), and the *Kind Words Teacher*. The board reported in 1888 that the total issues of the series promised to reached 5,000,000 during that year.

The tension was apparent at the 1889 Convention meeting in Memphis. A committee appointed to confer with the American Baptist Publication Society during the previous year reported that they could not reach an agreement on points of difference in the prosecution of their work.[58] The board's report on *Kind Words* was rather brief and seemingly harmless, but the subject was so sensitive that a motion was passed referring the whole publication question to a special committee, with the understanding that any question or comment about publications would be referred without debate to that committee. When the committee reported, it simply pointed out that the contract with the publisher of the series would not expire until June, 1891, so that nothing could be done by the Convention until that time.

All of this agitation greatly aroused James M. Frost, a mature and experience pastor in Richmond, Virginia.

> Frost was deeply stirred by the issues involved. He had the insight to perceive that this was no mere squabble over finances. The future of the Southern Baptist Convention and all its work were involved in the right answer. His conviction was deepened by a chance visit with Dr. Tichenor. Frost described later how he and Tichenor had met at Selma, Alabama (perhaps in 1889 when the Alabama State Convention met there). Tichenor had attended the deliberations of the State Mission Board; he and Frost stood at the front gate of the house where Tichenor was staying and for two hours they talked. "Rather he talked and I listened. I was sympathetic, but unable to follow his sweep of thought in outlining the future, showing what the Baptists of the South might

---

[58] Ibid., 1888, 28.

accomplish, and the imperative need that a people make their own literature."⁵⁹

What else Tichenor said to Frost on this occasion has not been revealed, but it is significant that among the first to commend Frost for moving toward providing a board for Sunday School work was I. T. Tichenor. On February 27, 1890, Frost published in the *Religious Herald* of Virginia an announcement that when the Convention next met he planned to offer resolutions to the effect that a new board should be organized for publication work. Strangely enough, Frost at this time did not know that there had formerly been such a board. However, he soon learned of this fact and pored over the story of the earlier movement. He later remarked:

> I saw at once that without knowing it I had in my proposition only gathered up the broken threads of history as if knitting them together again. Manifestly the unseen hand that touched the heart and mind in the night time was weaving the life plan for Southern Baptists.⁶⁰

Frost presented his resolutions, which were referred to a committee of one from each state and Frost as chairman. The committee could not agree, but the majority report by Frost was adopted. It provided that a standing committee of nine be appointed to take over all the interests of the Sunday School promotion and publications from the Home Mission Board. Frost later remarked that with only two exceptions, every denominational paper in the South opposed his proposition.

**The Sunday School Committee.** The attitude of I. T. Tichenor was significant. He reported to the Convention that these publications had attained a success most gratifying to the Home Mission Board. He praised their writers, their teachings, and their rapidly enlarging circulation. Their value, he said, had increased six fold in the previous three years. However, he concluded, if the Convention should commit this

> great and growing interest to a separate Board, we will rejoice that the success it has attained in our hands has made such a separation

---

⁵⁹ Baker, *The Story of the Sunday School Board*, 38.
⁶⁰ J. M. Frost, *Sunday School Board History and Work* (Nashville: Sunday School Board, 1914), 11.

an act of wisdom, and we will heartily co-operate with the new Board in the work of the Convention. Should the Convention continue these publications in our hands we will, as heretofore, comply with its instructions and use our best endeavors to increase their circulation and their usefulness.[61]

Such a spirit on the part of Tichenor revealed the greatness of the man, for this growing, prosperous, and influential ministry of the Convention was one which any board would have been glad to retain under its control.

The Sunday School Committee authorized by the Convention in 1890 carried on the publication work for one year, and then reported that the needs of the denomination required either a considerable enlargement of the powers of this committee or, preferably, the appointment of a board to whom these great interests could be entrusted. This report was referred to a committee composed of one representative from each state. They soon learned that the members could not agree, so with considerable acumen, they chose one representative from each party to act as a sub-committee to recommend to them a report for the Convention. J. B. Gambrell of Mississippi, who did not favor the separate board at this time, and J. M. Frost of Virginia were appointed to work out some kind of report. They spent the day in the hotel room discussing what kind of report to make to the full committee. Twenty years later Frost wrote that Gambrell proposed to let Frost write the report and even name the location of a proposed board, provided Gambrell could write the closing paragraph. Frost agreed, with the proposal that he be allowed to add one sentence. The report was written under these circumstances. It recommended that a new board be created to be called the Sunday School Board of the Southern Baptist Convention and be located at Nashville, Tennessee. At the close of this report, Gambrell wrote his paragraph mentioning that "there are widely divergent views held among us by brethren equally earnest, consecrated, and devoted to the best interest of the Master's Kingdom." It was recommended, therefore, that

J. B. Gambrell who did not favor the establishment of a Sunday School Board (Photo courtesty Southern Baptist Historical Library and Archives)

---

[61] *Annual*, Southern Baptist Convention, 1890, vii-viii.

the fullest freedom of choice be accorded to everyone as to which literature he would use or support without any disparagement "on account of what he may do in the exercise of his right as Christ's freeman." Frost added his final sentence urging all brethren to give the board a fair consideration and not to obstruct it in the great work assigned to it by the Convention.[62]

When the report was read to the Convention, men in every part of the congregation were ready to speak for or against it. John A. Broadus, however, the patriarch at Southern Baptist Theological Seminary, quickly moved to the rostrum and with deep emotion requested there be no debate, but that immediately the Convention take its vote on the report. With only thirteen dissenting votes, the board was approved. A. T. Robertson wrote later on:

> And even as I write, the tears come unbidden, as I think of the old veteran sitting there, his head buried in his hands and his whole frame heaving with emotion, which, if I mistake not, found relief in sobs.[63]

Thus, the Home Mission Board, which had conserved this significant ministry from 1873 until 1890, was relieved of the privilege and task of publication work as the new board was founded.

**The Rebirth of the Sunday School Board.** The problems facing the new Sunday School Board authorized by the Convention at Birmingham in 1891 were many and large. There was still a great deal of opposition within the Southern Baptist Convention to a separate board; the headquarters must be moved from Atlanta, Georgia, to Nashville, Tennessee; the trustees of the new board were totally inexperienced in this kind of operation; a new secretary would have to be secured; and, although there were many signs of its coming, few people recognized the scope and extent of the financial panic that had its birth in the same year as the Sunday School Board. To face this situation, the new board had practically no resources; indeed, until the sale of periodicals provided funds in December, 1891, the only finances available to the board came from two short-term loans amounting to about $1,200 from a Nashville bank on endorsements by members of the board.

---

[62] Baker, *Source Book*, 149-51.
[63] A. T. Robertson, *Life and Letters of John A. Broadus* (Philadelphia: American Baptist Publication Society, 1901), 394.

Only ten trustees were in attendance out of the forty making up the board when the first meeting took place on May 26, 1891. When their first choice for corresponding secretary declined, the board met two weeks later to elect James M. Frost who, after severe personal struggles, accepted the post on July 1, 1891.

The committee report adopted by the Birmingham Convention spelled out the work of the new board. Its task was to publish the Sunday School series, doing its best to improve them and increase the circulation, but to assume no other publication work except the proposed catechisms of John A. Broadus; to assume the Sunday School interests in the territory of the Convention informed in matters of Sunday School work; to enter into a printing contract rather than follow the leasing system in the publication of the Sunday School series; to prepare a list of books for recommendation to the various Sunday Schools; to aid mission Sunday Schools by contributions of literature and money through state organizations, with the understanding that no system of state or sub-agencies should be organized; and to take over the work of the Sunday School Committee after the issuance of the third quarter's series of literature. With his own private desk, money secured from his wife, and a small office borrowed from the Tennessee state paper, Frost began his work.

The first year was a critical one. Frost knew, as did everyone else, that if the new board failed to show a profit during this first year, it would likely be dissolved. Frost arranged for the transfer of Samuel Boykin, who had been editing the Sunday School literature for the Home Mission Board in Atlanta, and Boykin arrived in Nashville on January 1, 1892. Frost negotiated a printing contract for the following year, which brought comfortable quarters for the board without charge, and then busied himself as editor, writer, promoter, and business manager during the remainder of the first year.

As he reported to the Convention in May, 1892, Frost eloquently related the new board to the golden days when Basil Manly, Jr., and John A. Broadus produced the *Kind Words* series from Greenville, South Carolina. He then announced that the new board had a balance of over $1,000 after paying all operating expenses for the previous year, and capitalizing on this achievement, he called for the increased use of the periodicals of the board. He closed with a challenging word: "We stand in the present, but we speak for the future; we work in the present, but shall gather and garner our harvest in the centuries and the ages and the eternities."⁶⁴

In a surprising move, Frost resigned on January 1, 1893, to become pastor of the First Baptist Church Nashville. His successor was Theodore P. Bell, a staunch southerner in his thinking, who accepted the post on March 16, 1893. During this three-year secretaryship Bell rendered outstanding service. In the midst of a deepening financial panic the receipts of the board increased year by year, climbing to $63,141.12 in 1896, with a reserve fund of $2,500.

One of the most important of Bell's contributions was the nurturing of the new movement for the training of young people in Baptist life. The Christian Endeavor movement had been begun in 1881 among the Congregationalists and quickly began to cut across denominational lines to claim young people. The various American denominations recognized the danger of losing their young people and glimpsed at the same time the opportunity of enlisting this group in active service. In 1891 the Baptist Young People's Union of America was organized in Chicago and began to attract many Southern Baptist young people. In 1893 the Southern Baptist Convention adopted a resolution which marked the beginning of this program in its structure. The resolution recommended that young people form societies that were "strictly Baptist and denominational and be under the sole authority of the local church without interdenominational affiliation." It also suggested that the Sunday School Board provide literature for the churches to forward this work. Isaac J. Van Ness was secured to lead this movement in the board, and promptly showed great ability. After considerable Convention-wide discussion, the Baptist Young People's Union, Auxiliary to the Southern Baptist Convention, was formed at Atlanta, Georgia, on November 21-22, 1895. This was at first an independent body, not organically related to the Convention, but year by year its relationship became closer.

It is likely that T. P. Bell was influenced to move to another area of denominational life by the continuous friction between himself and the American Baptist Publication Society of Philadelphia. His correspondence was filled with emotional resentment against the Philadelphia body. More

---

⁶⁴ *Annual*, Southern Baptist Convention, 1892, lxiv.

than once he wrote that the purpose of the Publication Society was to destroy the Sunday School Board. Just a few weeks before his resignation Bell remarked in a letter to a friend that perhaps he (Bell) was "too strongly *Southern* Baptist" in his sentiment, and that the time had come when he had better let others of a broader spirit take the lead in some things. On January 22, 1896, Bell purchased *The Christian Index*, the Georgia Baptist paper. He resigned from the board the following week to become editor of the paper.[65]

After Bell resigned the board enthusiastically elected J. M. Frost as corresponding secretary again. Frost made it clear that he was now burning his bridges behind him so far as leaving the secretaryship was concerned; that he was setting his face and heart to the future of the board. It was well that he dedicated himself to the task, for the twenty years left to him were filled with strenuous labors.

**Rivalry with the American Baptist Publication Society.** The immediate struggle in which Frost became engaged involved the very existence of the board itself. The American Baptist Publication Society had befriended the first Sunday School Board in the 1860's and 1870's, but increasingly in the 1880's and the 1890's it had become aware of the large amount of its business that was being secured by the Sunday School Board of the South. Under a new secretary the society determined to challenge the board, knowing that many in the South would for various motives support the society against the board. Secretary A. J. Rowland of the society wrote Frost early in February, 1896, suggesting that there be a closer relationship between the two bodies. On February 11, 1896, Frost replied to Rowland that if the suggestions of Rowland were carried out, it would be a serious threat to the very life of the board. Despite this, on March 18, Rowland sent a series of propositions which, in essence, simply meant the swallowing up of the southern Sunday School Board by the society. On April 1, Frost replied that the board was unwilling to accept this proposition because it involved "not only the integrity and efficiency of the Board but its very existence, and contemplates the destruction of our own Sunday school periodicals." Rowland then threatened to take the matter to the floor of the Southern Baptist Convention. Frost later on

---

[65] Baker, *The Story of the Sunday School Board,* 70.

recorded the dramatic scene that took place at the Convention meeting in 1897 in these words:

> Prior to Chattanooga the Society had first proposed to the Sunday School Board to absorb its life and business, and when this was declined, it then circularized the Baptists of the South to make the offer effective through the approaching session of the Convention. I had just returned to the secretaryship to encounter this new phase of the opposition, but it failed to get any public consideration, though the situation was painful in private circles.
>
> At Wilmington, however, a year later the opposition got into the open and produced a scene well-nigh dramatic. It was commonly reported that the Society had seventeen officials and employees in attendance. One of them made an open attack from the platform on the Sunday School Board, especially on its Bible work in a lengthy and elaborate speech... It created a stir of resentment in the audience as could be easily seen. At its close many men made an effort to get to the floor. I never saw so many heavy guns unlimber so quickly and get ready for action. Dr. William E. Hatcher, of Virginia, got the floor, and in twenty-five minutes made a speech that was a marvel even for him. All of his powers with an audience came into play in that short time. He told how he had not favored making the Board at first; how it had won its place in the denomination; how the Baptists of the South had set it out as their policy; ... Can anyone who was present ever forget how he stirred and swept the people as he turned with a mighty sweep in declaration: "I have been a life-long friend of the Publication Society, but it must not come here to interfere with our work."[66]

This was the climax of the struggle. Increasingly the leadership and the constituency of the Southern Baptist Convention turned their support to the Sunday School Board, and by the close of the period its manifold ministry was writing new chapters in Southern Baptist history.

---

[66]Frost, *The Sunday School Board*, 81-82.

## Eliciting, Combining, and Directing the Denomination

The third crisis involving the life of the Convention stemmed basically from the Landmark movement of J. R. Graves. It will be recalled that Graves' attacks on the functions of the Convention when it met in 1859 reflected his view that general bodies among Baptists must not assume spiritual or denominational authority which was granted only to local Baptist churches by the New Testament. He was partially mollified in 1859 when the Convention said that churches or groups of churches may send their own home or foreign missionaries independently of the Convention's boards, and the Convention even agreed to assist in forwarding funds to foreign missionaries so independently engaged.[67] It has been mentioned that Landmarkism was relatively quiet during this period between the civil war and the end of Reconstruction. James E. Tull felt that this happened because the movement had become "engulfed in the general impoverishment and paralysis of Southern life and culture" during Reconstruction and so had little vitality to incite controversy during that period. In fact, the personal losses of Graves himself in the war and thereafter would complement this suggestion. Homer L. Grice attributed the noncombative spirit of the movement to another significant factor—the mellowing of Graves himself.

> A reading of his writing in *The Baptist* after 1877, the year his publication society failed, reveals that the man of thunder and conflict had subsided and a man of gentler and sweeter spirit was developing. He gave much less attention to controversial matters and dealt much more gently with those who did not agree with him. He magnified the doctrines of grace and preached with tenderness and love, becoming a revered and widely loved man. It is this Graves his friends and admirers, and their descendants, largely remember.[68]

It is also undoubtedly true that Landmarkism had no monolithic pattern that was widely accepted. Even the original Landmark triumvirate of Graves, J. M. Pendleton, and A. C. Dayton never really agreed on a unified system of landmark doctrine. Indeed, Tull makes it plain that

---

[67] Baker, *Source Book*, 145-46.
[68] Cox, ed., *Encyclopedia*, I, 577.

Graves himself had critical doctrinal tensions which, if generally known, would have alienated many Baptists from him.[69] The tendency, of Landmarkism was to create small islands of "mild," "moderate," "radical," or "schismatic" Landmarkers and this was the pattern that developed between 1877 and 1917. It is significant that when the Landmark resurgence came in this period, each appearance was triggered in a historical situation that did not involve the entire Landmark syndrome as such. In each case, however, the controversy led unerringly back to the taproot of Landmarkism: the sacrosanct nature of the authoritative local congregation.

Why was there a resurgence of Landmarkism in the 1880's and 1890's after the quiescence of the 1860's and 1870's? Tull interpreted it in terms of four factors: (1) the shift of regional dominance to the Southwest in the Southern Baptist Convention precipitated the most strongly Landmark area of the Convention into a position of ascendency and brought newly located Convention agencies under intensive Landmark cultivation; (2) the continuing influence of Graves radiating out from Memphis provided a vital infusion of strength; (3) denominational newspapers, the majority of whom were sympathetic to Landmarkism, spread the Landmark doctrines among the people; and (4) the intellectual currents of the denomination showed that Landmarkism was still a "virile, grass-roots, people's movement."[70] Another considerable element was the immediate historical context of the four aspects of the landmark resurgence. The four began completely independently, and although without question they interacted on one another, the initial thrust of each had its own peculiar characteristics and emphases. The contextual coloration gave each movement a somewhat individualistic character, and caused its focus to shift perceptibly. They related to one another because of their Landmark base, despite differences in historical milieu.

The out-croppings of various aspects of Landmarkism in the 1880's and 1890's were the Gospel Mission movement and the Whitsitt controversy.

**The Gospel Mission Movement.** The founder of this movement was T. P. Crawford (1821-1902), a missionary to China for fifty years,

---

[69] Tull, *Landmarkism.*, 519 ff.
[70] Ibid., 486 f.

forty of which were under the Foreign Mission Board of the Southern Baptist Convention. He arrived at Shanghai in March, 1852, to begin his long service, but in 1863 he and his wife transferred to North China and made Tengchow their center for thirty years. His first impression of the missionary methods in China was unfavorable. When he and his wife arrived at Hong Kong, a scandalous situation involving a Presbyterian missionary in China was brought to his attention. This missionary employed a hundred native assistants whom he sent to different cities not accessible to foreigners and provided them with Scriptures and tracts, purchased from a Chinese printer, to be distributed free. Instead, however, most of these assistants were selling the Bibles to the Chinese printer at a reduced price, who resold them again and again to the missionary. This had gone on for years, and the native assistants provided excellent statistics on Bible distribution. From this time until 1886, Crawford recorded his distaste for the employment of native workers with foreign funds on the grounds that it contributed to making them insincere, dishonest, cheats, and parasitic. Undoubtedly his visit to the United States in 1859 greatly influenced Crawford to sharpen his weapons and perhaps forge new ones. He attended the Convention at Richmond in that year when J. R. Graves spoke at length against the authority of the Foreign Mission Board to examine, choose, support, and direct the missionaries on the foreign field. These prerogatives, said Graves, belonged only to churches or groups of churches, and not to boards.[71] W. W. Barnes noted:

> The Gospel Missioners made the same attack on the Convention and its boards that the antimissionaries and J. R. Graves,... had previously made; they proposed the same methods in the homeland and on the foreign field.[72]

This similarity is not surprising. Crawford's exposure in 1859 to Graves provided him with considerable grist for the mill, although he may have come into contact with Graves in Tennessee before he left for the mission field. His Quaker inheritance from his mother's side doubtless demanded that his inner light on mission methodology be revealed; his judicious investments in China provided him with financial stability apart

---

[71] See Graves's assertions in Chapter X.
[72] Barnes, *The Southern Baptist Convention*, 115.

from the board's salary; and his independent nature chafed at every hindrance to carrying out his long-standing ideas. In 1878 he visited the United States and on a leisurely tour of about five months, propagated his views North and South, climaxing it with an address at the 1879 Convention. After he returned to China, Crawford increasingly demanded that foreign fields be self-supporting and that indigenous churches be autonomous. In 1881 he disbanded the mission boarding schools because he felt that the young men educated in them were unfit to make their way among their countrymen and could not subsist without foreign employment. Curiously enough, the Foreign Mission Board was partly responsible for the stepped-up activity of Crawford. In 1885 the board had mailed to their missionaries a copy of the book of C. H. Carpenter, *Self-Support, Illustrated in the History of the Bassein Karen Mission from 1840 to 1880*, thinking it would be of interest and encouragement. Crawford evidently thought that the board might be weakening in its opposition to his views on self-support. He devoured this book and writings by J. L. Nevius, a Presbyterian missionary in China who advocated "self-supporting and self-propagating" indigenous churches.

In March, 1885, Crawford again returned to the United States, this time without informing the board of what he was about to do. He finally visited the board on October 12 and demanded that a committee be appointed to hear him express his views. Missionaries from Africa and Rome were present, and other missionaries expressed their views in letters. On November 6, 1885, this committee agreed that self-support was the end toward which the missionary should work, but recognized that it might not be possible to adopt it quickly on every mission field. Three reasons were given for this position: first, that the original agreement with the missionaries now in the field involved using native workers, and their program would be radically upset to make a change; second, the circumstances and conditions were not the same on every mission field, and a general law against native employees would be very hurtful in some areas; and third, to adopt this principle would be to affirm that the gospel cannot lift the Chinese or Africans above the corrupting influences of money.

After this committee had reported, the board suggested to Crawford that he return to his field, but he would not go. He spent several months traveling and making speeches derogatory to the interests of the board. He attended the Convention in May, 1886, and addressed that body on the work in China, but was not supported in his appeal to change the decision of the board. At the 1887 meeting of the Convention, resolutions were adopted providing for a review of mission methods of the board, but the committee that reported in 1888 recommended that existing methods not be changed.

From 1886 to 1889, Crawford had no communication with the board although he continued to draw a salary. In 1890, with three other missionaries and four Chinese Christians, Crawford organized the first Gospel Mission Association in North China. There is no record that this association met after it was organized until 1893.

The climax came in 1892 when Crawford published a small fourteen-page tract entitled *Churches to the Front!* In this his Landmark views were clearly expressed. He attacked the centralization involved in the board system which would overthrow the independence and self-respect of the churches and reduce them to mere "tributary appendages." All ecclesiastical bodies except churches are encroaching upon the prerogatives of the "only religious organizations recognized in the New Testament." Baptists are different from other denominations.

> Centralization and ring-government may suit the policy of other denominations. They do not suit ours, but are deadly hostile to it. Yet, strange to say, this dangerous element was first introduced among us with the first session of the Old Triennial Convention in 1814; and, stranger, still, the Northern Baptist Union and the Southern Baptist Convention have continued it down to the present day. Their Boards are...self-perpetuating, irresponsible central bodies with unlimited permission to grow in power by absorbing the prerogatives and resources of our Churches, as the old Roman hierarchy grew by absorbing those in the early ages of Christianity.[73]

As a result of this frontal attack on the Convention and its boards, Crawford was removed from the list of missionaries. A few other missionaries followed him, but the movement never gained the support

---

[73] See Baker, *Source Book*, 177-180 for excerpts from this work.

one would have supposed Crawford's direct appeal to solid Landmark doctrines would have created.

**The Whitsitt Controversy.** The second of the movements involving Landmarkism was occasioned by the views of W. H. Whitsitt (1841-1911), who was professor of church history and president of Southern Baptist Theological Seminary when the agitation arose in the 1890's. Based principally upon information from the so-called "Kiffin" manuscript and the minutes of the Jessey church in England, Whitsitt had come to the conclusion that Baptists both in England and in America had not baptized by immersion before the year 1641. He published two anonymous editorials in a Congregationalist weekly of New York (*The Independent*) on September 2 and September 9, 1880, advocating this position. In 1895 he wrote the article on Baptists in *Johnson's Universal Cyclopaedia* over his own name and asserted these same views. Led by T. T. Eaton, who was one of the trustees of the seminary, pastor in Louisville, and editor of the *Western Recorder*, a storm of protests took place. It is curious that Eaton had antecedents that were anti-Landmark, his gifted father was strongly anti-Landmark, and the son himself had been pastor in Petersburg, Virginia, a strongly anti-Landmark atmosphere, for over a decade before coming to Louisville. In the following year (1896) Whitsitt published *A Question in Baptist History*, which reviewed his research and conclusions about the use of immersion by Baptists. In this article on Whitsitt, W. O. Carver remarked that

**William H. Whitsitt who was dismissed as president of Southern Seminary, primarily as a result of the Landmark influence**
(Photo courtesy of Southern Baptist Historical Library and Archives)

the fight was carried on all across Convention territory—in associations, state bodies, and at the Southern Baptist Convention.[74] In addition to Eaton, John T. Christian and S. H. Ford vigorously opposed Whitsitt's view. This controversy, aimed as it was at a central tenet of Landmarkism (Baptist church succession), infuriated the disciples of Graves (who had died in 1893). The climax took place in May, 1898, when Whitsitt

---

[74] See W. O. Carver, "William Heth Whitsitt: The Seminary's Martyr," *Review and Expositor* (Louisville), October, 1954, 450.

submitted his resignation as president and professor to the trustees of the seminary and retired to Virginia.

The Landmarkers felt that they had won the Whitsitt controversy. The controversies occurred almost simultaneously and involved different aspects of the Landmark viewpoint, thus dissipating a possible concentrated attack by all Landmarkers. Landmarkers themselves were divided in the nature and intensity of their views. For example, in Texas some of the leaders James E. Tull identified as Landmarkers were on the Convention side of the several controversies. J. B. Gambrell is an illustration of this. Gambrel took the Convention side of the Crawford controversy; he defended Whitsitt's right to historical research by strongly asserting that no man could be called non-Baptistic or heretical because of his views on history.[75] The conservative position of men like this and the opposition they displayed to Landmark agitation doubtless influenced their many admirers to turn away from schismatic ideas. There were other factors: the severe financial depression of the 1890's demanded that principal attention be turned to keeping alive; the formation of the second Sunday School Board in 1891 and its victory at Wilmington over the American Baptist Publication Society were strong blows to true Landmarkers; a generation of experience with the convention-type pattern had convinced many that Graves was wrong in 1859 in prophesying that the churches would be overwhelmed by this kind of general body; a new nationalism was everywhere apparent even in religious circles after the Spanish-American War in 1898 and the turn of the century; the victory of the Convention in its severe struggles with the northern benevolent societies had embodied a new loyalty to the general body; and perhaps even the mellowing of J. R. Graves and his death in 1893 as a faithful member of the southern Baptist fellowship had some influence in strengthening the place of the Convention. James E. Tull is probably correct in suggesting that Landmark ideas had filtered into the bloodstream of Southern Baptists, for some of them are still evident; but the radical denominational enlargement and concentration beyond the local church level that took place in the early decades of the twentieth century in the structure and functions of the Southern Baptist Convention point unerringly to the disintegration and overbalancing of Landmark views. A

---

[75] See the *Baptist Standard* (Texas), June 11, 1896.

strong Landmark undercurrent would have rendered impossible what took place in Southern Baptist organizational life between 1917 and 1972.

# Chapter 11 - The Convention Claiming Its Birthright

While the struggle for existence described in the previous chapter was the most dramatic episode in the history of the Convention during this period, of parallel importance were the week-by-week ministries of the three boards, the enlarging areas of service within the Convention, and the continuous efforts to modify the structure of the general body to provide a better instrument for the work Southern Baptists were trying to do.

## The Ministry of the Three Boards

During all of this period the Foreign and Home Mission Boards, in addition to their struggles to preserve their existence, steadfastly pursued their main tasks, and before the period closed in 1917 showed excellent advances in their work. The Sunday School Board, founded in 1891, also made large strides in achieving the goals set for it by its founder.

**Foreign Mission Board.** The period of Reconstruction had thoroughly tested the dedication of the missionaries on the foreign field as well as the foreign mission leadership at home, for both faced trying circumstances.

*The Field in 1877.* The stresses experienced at home were clearly reflected in the skeletal staff on the mission fields at the close of Reconstruction. These have been termed the "lonely days" on the foreign field, due to the fact that missionaries were few and for the most part isolated. Three fields were sustained during the rigorous days through which the South had gone. In Africa the missionaries were W. J. David at Abeokuta and W. W. Colley, a black missionary, at Lagos. This mission was facing very knotty problems and would experience dark days during the next decade. The second field was China, the oldest mission effort by Southern Baptists. In North China at Tengchow, Mr. and Mrs. T. P. Crawford, Mrs. S. H. Holmes, and Miss Lottie Moon were the mission staff. In Central China at Shanghai, Mr. and Mrs. Matthew T. Yates were the only missionaries. In South China at Canton, R. H. Graves, his wife, Miss Lulu Whilden, along with E. Z. and Maggie Simmons, were the mission staff. In Italy at Rome, George B. Taylor, assisted by native pastors, carried on the work. Despite the extension of the panic of 1873, the offerings from the states for foreign mission in 1877 amounted to $31,789.42.

*Progress by Three Secretaries.* It will be recalled that the great patriarch of the Foreign Mission Board, James B. Taylor, died at the close of 1871, and Henry A. Tupper was elected his successor in 1872. Tupper served effectively until 1893, and many advances were made in the work of the board during his secretaryship. In 1887, Lottie Moon wrote from China to suggest that Southern Baptist women set apart a week just before Christmas as a time of prayer and offering for world missions. In 1888 Tupper presented the challenge of Lottie Moon to the Woman's Missionary Union, which had just been organized in Richmond, Virginia. They set their goal for $2,000, but typical of many later goals, it was exceeded by the women, and $3,315.26 was given. During the administration of Tupper, 147 missionaries were appointed, new stations were established in China and Nigeria, and new fields were opened in Mexico, Brazil and Japan. In these years a total of $1,330,747.27 was given by Southern Baptists for foreign missions.

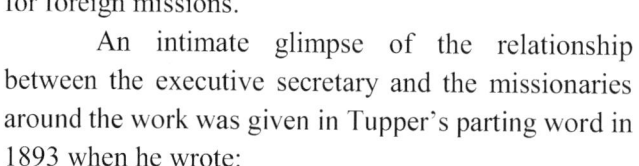

**Charlotte "Lottie" Moon, missionary to China** (Photo courtesy of Southern Baptist Historical Library and Archives)

An intimate glimpse of the relationship between the executive secretary and the missionaries around the work was given in Tupper's parting word in 1893 when he wrote:

> I feel as if I were saying good-bye to a great family, loved as life itself. We have had many joys together and many sorrows. My soul is knit to them as to my own flesh and blood. I love and honor every one of them. A braver band never fought the Lord's battles. I rejoice in the crowns awaiting them, as a father rejoices in the glory of his children![1]

---

[1] *The Foreign Mission Journal* (Richmond), XXIV (July, 1893), 353-54.

R. J. Willingham was elected corresponding secretary to succeed Tupper, and promptly began an aggressive program of outreach. This was made possible partly by the rapid improvement of the financial situation of the board. Its annual income increased from $110,000 in 1893 to $600,000 in 1914. The number of missionaries grew from 92 to 298 during the same period. Three new countries—Argentina (1903), Macao (1910), and Uruguay (1911)—were entered, and many new mission stations were begun on old mission fields. Willingham was an avid builder of schools and other institutions. During his tenure, six hospitals were built in China; the first building was secured for the seminary in Canton, China; theological schools (in some instances, both a college and a seminary) were established in Nigeria, Italy, Mexico, Brazil, China, Japan, and Argentina; and Baptist publishing houses were established in China, Brazil, Japan, and Mexico. Willingham became ill in 1913, and died in December, 1914.

J. F. Love succeeded Willingham as a corresponding secretary in 1915. By 1917, when this period closed, Love had already given evidence of his outstanding ability. Work was opened in Chile in 1917. Cash receipts for current support in 1917 were $852,923.73, and Love remarked that "Southern Baptists have put more money into the regular work during the past twelve months than they have contributed to current support in any previous year of the seventy-three of the Board's history." For the first time in ten years the board reported that they were totally out of debt. Typical of the increasing magnitude of the work on the field, Love reported that during 1917 there had been 6,290 baptisms, 6 churches constituted, contributions of $152,874.16 by the native Christians, 26 churches becoming self-supporting, and treatment of patients numbering 102,271 by medical missionaries. During the year of 1917, Women's Missionary Union contributed over $250,000 in cash to foreign missions, while the new Laymen's Movement involving men had raised $6,000 for a special project. In 1917 the board reported 172 missionaries in China, 16 in Africa, 19 in Japan, 4 in Italy, 29 in Mexico, 58 in Brazil, 16 in Argentina, and 2 in Chile. This made a grand total of 316 missionaries in 8 countries.

**Home Mission Board.** During the period between 1877 and 1917 the Home Mission Board carried on eight distinct ministries. Most of these had been originally outlined in 1845 as the task of the board when it was constituted by the Convention, but additional areas of service were entrusted to it during this period.

One of the principal ministries of the board was the founding of new churches and missions. Even in the older states, a committee reported in 1889 that there were many important towns without a Baptist ministry in them. A careful study of the *Annuals* of the Convention indicates that year by year a strong emphasis was made during this period upon constituting new churches and missions. In many reports the exact number is not shown, but typically there were 244 churches constituted in 1891, 133 in 1894, 195 in 1900, and 213 during 1917. As a part of this movement, strenuous efforts were made during the 1880's to establish an active church building department, but this did not receive the support of the people, and the effort was abandoned for the time. Under the leadership of Women's Missionary Union, in 1903 a campaign was launched to raise a building and loan fund honoring I. T. Tichenor, and in 1908 the $20,000 goal was reached. In reporting this to the Convention in 1910, the amazing statement was made by the board that one or more of what were then the strongest churches in the capital city of every southern state had been helped by the Home Mission Board.[2] At the very close of this period, with a new Department of Church Extension, Louis B. Warren led in what would be a very successful drive for funds to lend to churches that needed to build.

A second major area of ministry looked to the winning of the cities. The board had always used some of its meager resources in this ministry. New Orleans, for example, repeatedly appears as an area of service during the first fifty years of Convention life. A new thrust was in 1905 to increase this assistance to cities with their peculiar problems. Typical of the need for this ministry, in 1907 it was pointed out that there were thirty-six white Baptist churches in the three cities of Baltimore, St. Louis, and New Orleans. Of these churches, twenty were able to make their own way, but sixteen of them were being assisted by the state mission boards and the Home Mission Board, and could not continue to exist without this assistance. The population of these cities was increasing 177 times as fast as the membership of the Baptist churches.

---

[2] *Annual*, Southern Baptist Convention, 1910, 251.

During this period the board began an active program of reaching the mountain people of the Southeast. In cooperation with Baptists of western North Carolina the board carried on a joint mission program in the mountainous areas in the 1880's, and in addition, began the development in 1905 of a system of mountain schools in cooperation with other Baptist groups.

The frontier mission program was a fourth area of the board's work during this period. As the western frontier slowly receded, the board sent many missionaries to the frontier. In the 1880's and 1890's in particular, the interest of the Convention in frontier missions was high. In 1905 a field secretary was appointed for the western territory. By 1910, there were over 700 missionaries at work west of the Mississippi River in this frontier category.

The blacks, both during and after their days of bondage, were the object of the ministry of the board. As pointed out before, most of the blacks withdrew from the white churches shortly after the Civil War. Black Baptists began organizing their first conventions in 1880, and by 1895 three separate bodies became the National Baptist Convention of the United States of America. However, in 1915 this body divided into two organizations, one the National Baptist Convention, U.S.A., Incorporated, and the other the National Baptist Convention of America. In 1905 the Home Mission Board entered into a joint program with the National Baptist Convention, involving an outlay of a maximum of $15,000 per year by each board. When the division in this black Baptist body took place in 1915, after some confusion, the board primarily carried on its cooperation with the National Baptist Convention, U.S.A., Incorporated.

One extremely valuable ministry of the board to black Baptists during the period from 1877 to 1917 was what has been called Ministers' Institutes, although subsequently deacons and other leaders of the blacks were involved in the program. These institutes aimed to gather a group of uneducated ministers for a short study, usually about ten days, of fundamental doctrines. Evidently it was begun by E. W. Warren, of Atlanta, Georgia, whose work along this line was enthusiastically described in northern Baptist newspapers as early as May, 1873.[3] The

---

[3] See Baker, *Relations*, 115-16. Note reference to these in *The National Baptist* (Philadelphia, 1865-1894), May 27, 1873.

Southern Baptist Convention endorsed his program in 1875, and in the following year the Home Mission Board began conducting institutes of this sort across the South. Three years later the Home Mission Society of the North voted to cooperate with the Southern Baptist Convention in providing these institutes. In the first full year after this program was begun, it was reported that 1,119 ministers and deacons had participated in 33 institutes, and that every southern state had been reached with one institute or more of about three days' duration.[4] In a touching and significant move, W. H. McIntosh, formerly the executive secretary of the board, was appointed in 1883 as missionary to the blacks.

Directly as a result of the Fortress Monroe agreement of 1894, the board worked with the Home Mission Society of New York in what was called the New Era Plan. After nine years, this plan was modified and called the Enlarged Plan of Negro Work, in a closer cooperative arrangement between the Home Mission Board and the similar board in the National Baptist Convention. In implementing this plan, the Southern Baptist Convention named A. J. Barton as its first field secretary for Negro work in 1904. The board provided matching contributions from National Baptists to a maximum of $15,000 the first year. In 1906, there were thirty-three missionaries employed jointly by the cooperating boards. Two years later there were thirty-seven missionaries jointly employed. By 1914, there were forty-seven. The division in the following year in the National Baptist Convention interrupted the significant growth of this program.[5]

Although not departmentalized in earlier years, the next large division of the work of the Home Mission Board could be described as language missions. Reference to this work in the earlier periods had already been made. Between 1877 and 1917, however, the language mission program enlarged greatly. During this period some of the great names in Indian mission work in Indian Territory and Oklahoma Territory were H. F. Buckner, Joseph S. Murrow, and E. Lee Compere.

Work was begun among the Germans in earlier periods, but the need for this distinctive program disappeared after World War I. One outstanding name in German missions in Baltimore was Marie Buhlmaier, who served for about twenty-five years beginning in 1893. The opening

---

[4] *Annual Report*, American Baptist Home Mission Society, 1880, 37.
[5] Rutledge, *Mission to America*, 135.

wedge for Baptist work among the French in Louisiana was the conversion of Adolphe Stagg, who made an outstanding contribution. Work was begun among the Italians in Florida in 1908, one of the chief names in leadership being J. F. Plainfield.

Reference had already been made to the work of the board in California under J. Lewis Shuck and B. W. Whilden. During the period under study, J. B. Hartwell, veteran Chinese missionary, served in San Francisco and helped constitute the first Chinese Baptist church of that city in 1880.

An active ministry to the deaf began in 1906 when John W. Michaels, a deaf mute, was appointed to this field.

One of the significant challenges in language missions has been those speaking Spanish who immigrated to the United States from Spain, Mexico, Cuba, Puerto Rico, or some other South or Central American country. In 1881 a mission was begun in San Antonio as the first permanent Spanish Baptist work in Texas. In 1884, a beginning was made in Florida among this group, also. Charles D. Daniel, foreign missionary to Brazil and Cuba, was appointed general superintendent of the Spanish-language missions in Texas in 1906, and under his leadership, the Mexican Baptist Convention of Texas was constituted in 1910.

As early as 1879 appeals had come from Cuba for missionaries. In 1886 the Convention voted that the Home Mission Board should be the agency for Cuban work, rather than the Foreign Mission Board. Both Secretaries Tichenor and Gray became enthusiastically involved in Cuban missions. The outstanding name in this area was M. N. McCall, who began his work in 1905 in Havana. In 1906 a seminary was begun, and the churches were organized into the Western Cuba Convention.

Work was begun in the Panama Canal Zone in 1906. Under the leadership of J. K. Wise, advance was slow, partly because the construction of the canal, completed in 1914, encouraged a transient population.

The military chaplaincy had engaged the board, as described earlier, during the civil war, but for over half a century thereafter the board had no need for these services. In 1916, with the involvement of the United States in World War I, the Convention called for men to serve as chaplains to the men in the armed forces. At the very close of the period the board inaugurated a program of camp ministries, with George Green as director.

The eighth thrust of the board was all-encompassing; that is, it was the basic principle involved in all the ministries of the board. In 1906, after a careful study by the Convention, the board was instructed to create a Department of Evangelism. This was not achieved before a tense and critical battle on the floor of the Southern Baptist Convention. In the midst of the struggle, B. H. Carroll of Texas turned the tide in an eloquent address.

> If I were the secretary of this [Home Mission] board, I would come before this body in humility and tears and say: "Brethren, give me evangelists. Deny not fins to things that swim against the tide, nor wings to things that must fly against the wind."[6]

W. W. Hamilton was elected as the first general evangelist. Everywhere this work met with favor because it was so primary in the entire program of Southern Baptists. Throughout the remainder of this period, this department served well and was mainly self-supporting through the offerings given to the evangelists. In 1917, for example, there were 20 evangelists who reported over 9,000 baptisms and 11,000 additions, as well as almost 1,100 volunteers for special service, all of which was performed at a net cost of about $18,000.

Although not distinctly set out as one of the programs of the board, one of the most important supporting services was the use of publications to inform and inspire the people about the work of the board. It will be recalled that the two mission boards shared the *Southern Baptist Missionary Journal* under several names until about 1874. During most of the period under study the official organ, *Our Home Field*, was used with slight variations of title to publicize the work of the board. For the most part the corresponding secretaries carried the editorial load of publishing these magazines. In 1909 the board established a Publicity Department and employed Victor I. Masters as its first editorial secretary in charge of publicity. He continued this service throughout the remainder of this period.

After the retirement of I. T. Tichenor in 1899, F. H. Kerfoot became secretary of the Home Mission Board until 1901; F. M. McConnell, from 1901 to 1903; and B. D. Gray, from 1903 to 1928. The

---

[6] *Baptist Standard* (Texas), May 31, 1906, 2.

report for 1917, under the last-named secretary, showed cash receipts of $474,375. Forty-five Baptist camp pastors were supported to work in the United States Army after the outbreak of war in Germany. Twenty evangelists, twenty workers encouraging enlistment of the home field, an active department for church extension, thirty-five workers in Cuba, and three workers in Panama Canal Zone were reported. An enrollment of 5,190 was shown in mountain schools in Virginia, Kentucky, Tennessee, North Carolina, South Carolina, Georgia, Alabama, Arkansas, and Missouri, which had 210 teachers. An active Publicity Department was spreading tracts and books on home missions. Much credit for the excellent progress during the closing years of this period should go to B. D. Gray, whose policy of expansion and cooperation was reaching its climax before the difficult days of the 1920's.

**Sunday School Board.** When J. M. Frost began his work in 1891, the Home Mission Board had operated eight types of programs of Sunday School work. The principal effort, of course, had been the publication of church literature. It had been the success of this program that prompted the organization of the new board in 1891. The seven related programs of Sunday School promotion, cooperative work with state boards, church music publishing, the production of church supplies, church library service, research and statistical analysis, and the distribution of religious books can be glimpsed in the work of the Home Mission Board before 1891. During the three-year service of T. P. Bell, two additional programs were developed: Training Union promotion and Convention support. These ten programs of work were enlarged and strengthened during the second secretaryship of Frost between 1896 and 1916. In addition, a very significant organizational advance took place at the turn of the century. Frost secured Bernard W. Spilman, a strong and experienced Sunday School leader in North Carolina, as the first field secretary of the board in order to provide a direct tie with the field. For two years Spilman served alone, making passenger trains his office. During the next decade eleven additional field workers were added. Between 1896 and 1916 a remarkable increase in the percentage of Southern Baptist church members enrolled in Sunday School took place, rising from 38 percent in the former year to 65 percent in the latter. Great advances were made in grading the Sunday School, providing standards for measuring the quality of work, the training of Sunday School teacher, the integration of the Sunday School program, the providing of assistance in methodology for busy lay workers, and the upgrading of the quality of Sunday School lessons.

In addition to these ten programs of work continued from previous years, when Frost began his second term as secretary, he introduced six additional activities; some of which, while not altogether new, were enlarged or restructured.

One of the most significant of these new programs concerned the publication of books. It will be recalled that for more than half a century Southern Baptists had plainly said they did not desire to go into the field of book publication. Frost understood the objections to this activity. The Landmarkers had opposed it on the grounds that a denominational board should not be in the book publishing business; the opening of a new area of competition with the Publication Society of Philadelphia distressed some; a large body of Southern Baptists objected to book publishing because of the financial risks involved. Now, however, J. R. Graves, the leader of Landmarkism, was dead, and there had come a recession of Landmark influence. The confrontation at the Convention in 1897 between the Publication Society and Sunday School Board had won many Southern Baptists to the support of the board's activities in every sphere. Frost planned to limit the financial risk by establishing a book fund. On December 31, 1897, the board authorized the setting aside of a $500 fund for publishing the life of Matthew T. Yates, the pioneer Chinese missionary, a manuscript for which had already been prepared by President Charles E. Taylor of Wake Forest College. Frost published this book on his own initiative after writing many of the important leaders of the Convention. In 1898 Frost reported publishing the book and "asked to be allowed liberty in this, using for its advancement such money as we can appropriate from the business, or such as may be given to the Board for this purpose." The committee of the Convention reporting this recommended that the board be allowed to publish books as a part of its work, noting the far-reaching significance of this advance, but expressing its confidence in the board for this enlargement of its work.[7] The climax came in 1910. T. P. Bell, editor of *The Christian Index* of Georgia, learned that the Publication Society of Philadelphia had closed its branch houses

---

[7] *Annual*, Southern Baptist Convention, 1898, 24.

in the South. He presented a resolution authorizing the board to supply the churches with "books, tracts, hymn and song books, and indeed all supplies for churches, Sunday schools, missionary societies, Young People's unions, such as are suitable and desirable." The vote was unanimous by the Convention. Frost responded with deep emotion that he counted this the greatest hour of his life.[8]

In addition to this new enterprise, under the leadership of Frost the board enlarged its ministry in Bible and general tract distribution, organized a Home Department "to carry into the home all the influences of the Sunday-school in the way of religious training," provided assistance in church architecture, began a new thrust in student work, donated funds to Southern Baptist Theological Seminary to provide teaching in Sunday School work, and saw the Convention establish a Baptist assembly ground at Ridgecrest, North Carolina, which subsequently assumed a large place in the training program of Southern Baptist for lay leaders and workers in the churches.

Frost died on October 30, 1916, ending the pioneer era in the life of this board. The impact of these first twenty-five years of the Sunday School Board was many-sided. In its initial thrust of promoting Sunday Schools it had fared remarkably well. In 1891 there were approximately 8,600 Sunday Schools in Southern Baptist churches; by 1917 this number had increased to 18,134 schools, enrolling 1,835,811. Training Unions numbered 4,827 by 1917. Receipts of the board were over $450,000 when Frost died and in the following year were reported as $537,695.14. Resources were fixed at over $700,000 in 1917. Perhaps even beyond this impressive growth in long-time influence were the new methodology and unifying thrust of the new board. Standardized methods and uniform, structural patterns were developed by talented men in leadership and exploited through financial assistance to seminaries and state bodies, magnified in the literature used by almost every Southern Baptist church, and promoted through field workers, study courses, state papers, an all other media of Southern Baptist information. The effect on the life of Southern Baptists can hardly be estimated. New direct leadership was provided at the Convention level and channeled through parallel structures developed in the states and associations for each benevolence (i.e., Sunday

---

[8] Baker, *The Story of the Sunday School Board*, 89.

School, Training Union, Vacation Bible School, etc.) so that churches were provided patterns, motivation, and nearby assistance in the promotion of all of these areas of service. These were large factors in developing the denominational consciousness of Southern Baptists that tied them to the structures, methods, and doctrines of the Southern Baptist Convention.

## Expanding Horizons

The larger economic, social, political, and religious world described at the opening of the previous chapter brought new challenges to the Southern Baptist Convention in the two-score years after Reconstruction closed. The true significance of the denominational-type organization adopted by Southern Baptists in 1845 began to be displayed. In addition to directing the activity of its three functional boards, the Convention expanded its ministry in several additional areas.

**The Enlistment and Organization of Lay Constituency.** Interacting with the developments in the religious community, the Convention found itself faced with a multitude of women who desired to serve their Lord in the best possible fashion; became conscious of the world of young people, both in the local churches and in university settings, who were competent and eager to play a larger part in Christian service; recognized the vast potential involved in the enlistment of laymen for a larger participation in the Kingdom enterprise; and gave consideration to Christian schools and an assembly for training of leadership.

*Women.* Reference has been made to the increasing interest of Southern Baptist women in the foreign mission enterprise before 1877. In 1875, at the close of the previous period, the Convention for the first time took official cognizance of the "enlarged zeal and practical wisdom" of Southern Baptist women in the cause of foreign missions, and commended their unusual qualifications for this ministry.[9] But the women did not need the urging of the Convention to meet, pray, and give. They were rapidly forming missionary societies in all of the territory of the Convention, fostering home as well as foreign missions.

---

[9] *Annual*, 1875, 71.

In 1878 the Convention's committee on women's work urged the organization of central committees of women in each state, and this marked a large step toward a convention-wide structure for women. As early as 1883, women began holding meetings for their group at the annual sessions of the Convention. The men made it rather plain that women were not entitled to be seated officially as Convention messengers.[10] Not until 1918 were they so seated. The year 1887 brought crystallization of the desires of many of the women leaders to provide a convention-wide structure. Under the leadership of Miss Martha McIntosh of South Carolina and Miss Annie W. Armstrong of Maryland, resolutions were adopted which urged each central committee in the several states to appoint three lady delegates "to meet during the next session of the Southern Baptist Convention, to decide upon the advisability of organizing a general committee; and if advisable, to provide for the appointment, location, and duties thereof."[11]

On May 11, 1888, in the basement of the Broad Street Methodist Church, Richmond, Virginia, thirty-two delegates from twelve states and other women from three more states met to discuss a general organization. This meeting differed from any other one held heretofore in that it contained official representation from the several states and had come to discuss the possibility of general organization. When it appeared that most representatives would vote for such an organization, the formal program was set aside and a committee reported and the constitution was adopted, with Baltimore selected as the site of the executive committee.[12] Martha McIntosh was elected first president; ten vice-presidents (one from each of the original states) were named; Annie W. Armstrong became corresponding secretary; and nine residents of Baltimore composed the

Annie Armstrong, first Corresponding Secretary of the WMU, she worked closely with the Foreign Mission Board in raising funds, for foreign missions (Photo courtesy of Southern Baptist Historical Library and Archives)

---

[10] Barnes, *The Southern Baptist Convention*, 181 ff gives the story.
[11] Baker, *Source Book,* 151, for this document.
[12] Ibid., 152-53.

executive committee. The name originally adopted was changed two years later to Woman's Missionary Union, Auxiliary to the Southern Baptist Convention, and this has remained unaltered since that time.

Several factors distinguished the new organization from other denominational woman's organizations. It combined home, foreign and state mission interests in one body. Through its auxiliary relation to the Southern Baptist Convention, it would not handle money and duplicate mission boards; its collected money would be disbursed by Convention boards; it would not independently appoint its own missionaries. The Convention was relieved.[13]

The organizational structure was enlarged during the remainder of this period. In 1896 the Union assumed responsibility for the Sunbeam Band (now called Mission Friends), which had been initiated by George B. Taylor in 1886 in Virginia, to provide missionary education for children under nine years of age. In 1907 the name "Young Women's Auxiliary" (now called Baptist Women) was adopted for the specific program of the Union for young women. In 1908 the Union began promotion of the Order of Royal Ambassadors as an organization for missionary education for boys. In 1913 a new department was created to provide training for girls between the ages of the Sunbeams and the Young Woman's Auxiliary and given the name Girls' Auxiliary (now called Girls in Action and Acteens). Miss Lottie Moon, missionary in China, suggested in 1887 that Southern Baptist women institute a week of prayer and offering for foreign mission in connection with Christmas. This plan was adopted and shortly after the close of this period the offering was name the Lottie Moon Christmas Offering for Foreign Missions. The goal set in 1888 was $2,000 and over $3,000 was raised, this overreaching of challenging goals has been the pattern year by year as the annual offerings have been counted in millions of dollars. In 1894 a Week of Self-Denial was structured to pray and give to home missions, and not long after the close of this period, became the annual Annie W. Armstrong Offering for Home Missions. From almost the very beginning of Woman's Missionary Union, the four fundamentals of its program have been promotion of mission study, stewardship,

---

[13] Cox, ed., *Encyclopedia*, II, 1513.

community missions, and prayer; and these were formally adopted in 1913.

Recognizing the need for the training of women missionaries for the foreign field, some of the women of Louisville, Kentucky, rented a private house in 1904 where single young ladies could live while attending seminary classes. As the number of applicants grew, the local committee appealed to the Union for assistance. In 1907 the trustees of the seminary surrendered to the Union the management and control of the Women's Training School and offered the young ladies the privilege of attending their classes. The Union adopted this project, and with the aid of a gift from the Sunday school Board, a building was purchased and occupied during the remainder of this period.

Another significant missionary ministry of the Woman's Missionary Union began in 1904 with the establishment of a fund to provide a home for children of missionaries. This became the Margaret Fund, named after the mother of the donor. For ten years this provided a home in Greenville, South Carolina, but in 1914 the home was sold and the funds invested for use in educating missionaries' children. The first scholarship was awarded just after the close of the period.

The executive secretaries of Woman's Missionary Union during this period were Annie W. Armstrong (1888-1906), Elizabeth Crane (1907-12), and Kathleen Mallory (1912-48). The presidents of the Union were Martha E. McIntosh (1888-92), Fannie Exile Scudder Heck (1892-94, 1895-99, and 1906-15), Mrs. Abby Manley Gwathmey (1894-95), Mrs. Charles Stakley (1899-1903), Mrs. J. A. Barker (1903-06), and Mrs. W. C. James (1915-25).

*Youth.* Another large part of the Southern Baptist constituency—the young people—were rarely seen or heard before the Civil War. The development of organized groups of young people for fellowship and religious training slowly took place after the war, particularly in the North, in several denominations. The founding of the Christian Endeavor societies among the Congregationalists in 1881 accelerated this movement, and by the 1890's practically all major denominations in the United States were involved in providing unions, leagues, or societies for their young people.

Baptists North and South had provided such organizations under various names by 1891. To pull these together into a single Baptist organization, the Baptist Young People's Union of America was formed in July, 1891, at Chicago, specifically noting that the local group could call itself by whatever name it chose. The society plan necessarily was involved in the organization of this national Baptist youth body, since none of the existing Baptist societies in the North fostered this type of work or even favored it. Young Baptists from the South were grouped as one department in the national body.

In 1893 the Southern Baptist Convention took note of the movement, urging that Baptist young people's societies of this sort in the South be "strictly Baptistic and denominational," and that they be under the authority of the local church without interdenominational affiliation. The Sunday School Board was asked to provide literature for their use.[14] After considerable wrangling during the next two years, a consultative meeting was held on November 21, 1895, at Atlanta, Georgia, consisting of 236 delegates from 10 states ( Alabama, Georgia, Mississippi, and Tennessee provided 210 of these). This body organized the Baptist Young People's Union, Auxiliary to the Southern Baptist Convention. This action was approved by the Southern Baptist Convention in the following year, although at that time it was simply an independent society of Southern Baptists. However, by 1901 the minutes of this union were printed with those to the southern convention; after 1909 the officers and executive committee were elected by the Southern Baptist Convention; and in 1918, just after the close of this period, this body was disbanded and the work assumed by the Sunday School Board of the Convention.[15] In that year the enrollment in the various unions in the South was shown as 230,540.

What became the Baptist Student Union in the next period had its beginnings during these years. Southern Baptist leaders recognized that there was a definite need for some program to cultivate the religious life of young people who had gone away to colleges and universities. As early as 1914 Baptist educators discussed the problem and possible solutions. Under the leadership of Charles T. Ball, professor of missions in Southwestern Seminary, the Baptist Student Missionary Movement of North America was formed on November 16, 1914. Ball was without doubt greatly influenced by the interdenominational Student Volunteer

---

[14] *Annual*, 1893, 44 f.

[15] Barnes, *The Southern Baptist Convention*, 181 ff gives the story.

Movement and the Laymen's Missionary Movement. The aim of the body, as the name suggested, was specifically missionary, but it did desire to reach all Baptist students to pray, to give, and to promote at home and abroad the missionary enterprise. The movement was still developing at the close of the period, but within a few years it would be swallowed up into a new student organization with wider objectives.[16]

*Laymen.* This period found many strong Baptist laymen in the South. Indeed, in the forty years from 1877 to 1917, laymen served as presidents of the Southern Baptist Convention for no fewer than nineteen of these sessions. A new impetus was given to their enlistment in 1906-07 by interdenominational attention to the Student Volunteer Movement and a commemoration of the one hundredth anniversary of the Williams College haystack prayer meeting that triggered organized foreign mission work in the first decade of the nineteenth century. On November 13-14, 1906, a group of prominent laymen of several denominations met in New York to pray and face the challenge of missions. From this conference the Laymen's Missionary Movement was launched, which was defined as being an effort to enlist laymen to participate in and promote the foreign mission cause in their own denomination. In 1907 Joshua Levering and W. J. Northen led in a conference of "some two hundred" Baptist laymen meeting the day before the Richmond session of the Southern Baptist Convention. This conference recommended that the Convention express "its hearty approval of the spirit and purpose of the Laymen's Missionary Movement."[17] Such was done, together with the approval of a proposed executive committee for the Laymen's Missionary Movement of Southern Baptists.

In 1907 J. T. Henderson was elected general secretary for the movement and began his work the following year. Following the direction of the interdenominational movement, the thrust of this body in the early years was missions only, and the concept of a general denominational body for men was disavowed. The centripetal nature of the Southern Baptist Convention, however, slowly pulled this body toward the organizational structure and the ideals of the Convention, and in the next period this development can be discerned more distinctly. During the

---

[16] Ibid., 192 ff.
[17] *Annual*, Southern Baptist Convention, 1907, 46.

remainder of the present period the Laymen's Missionary Movement of the Convention provided Convention-wide leadership, inspiration, and guidance. Organization in the various states developed slowly, sparked by several annual "conventions of men" after 1912. Headquarters of the group was moved from Baltimore to Chattanooga, Tennessee, in 1914. There are no statistics available for the period closing in 1917.

*Christian Education.* At the meeting of the Southern Baptist Convention in 1913, a resolution was presented in behalf of forming a Board of Education, principally because Southern Baptist involvement in Christian education at many levels was increasing rapidly and needed to be correlated and because "practically all large Christian bodies have some general agency for promoting this work."[18] In 1915 the Convention authorized its president to appoint a committee of one from each state to be called the Education Commission of the Southern Baptist Convention. In 1916 this commission presented a survey of the involvement of Southern Baptists in educational programs and made four recommendations, which were adopted, as follows: (1) that an effort be made to arouse the people to importance of Christian education; (2) that a literature be created for use by the various state education boards and commissions; (3) that with the cooperation of the Sunday School Board of the Convention authorize an Education Day in Sunday Schools of the South; and (4) that adequate statistics of Southern Baptist educational institutions be gathered.[19] The implementing of these goals was still being attempted at the close of this period.

*Ridgecrest.* The Convention became mildly involved in another distinct movement during this period which would subsequently become a significant factor in lay organization and enlistment. When B. W. Spilman was Sunday School leader in North Carolina in 1895, he earnestly desired a Baptist assembly for promotion and inspiration. In 1907, at the suggestion of Spilman, the North Carolina Baptist Convention purchased almost 1,000 acres of land in the Swannanoa Gap area, and the Southern Baptist Convention endorsed this type of ministry. In 1909 Spilman, who had been named the first general secretary of the Ridgecrest Baptist Assembly (although that name was not adopted until 1912), held the first

---

[18] Ibid., 1916, 51.
[19] Ibid., 50-56.

conference on these grounds with emphasis on all types of denominational activity. Although sorely tried during the early years of its operation by financial difficulties, fires, hurricanes, and lawsuits, this assembly was making its place in Southern Baptist life at the close of the period.

## Theological Education

A second area of enlargement in the ministries of the Southern Baptist Convention during this period was theological education.

**Southern Baptist Theological Seminary.** It will be recalled that the seminary moved from Greenville, South Carolina, to Louisville, Kentucky, in 1877 at the very close of the previous period. As John A. Broadus remarked humorously:

> It was physically no great task to remove the Seminary from Greenville to Louisville. There was nothing to move, except the library of a few thousand volumes, and three professors,— Broadus, Toy, and Whitsitt,—only one of whom had a family.[20]

James P. Boyce, the other faculty member and its chairman, lived in Louisville from 1872 to 1877 and endeavored to raise an endowment to enable the move from Greenville to take place. Only eighty-nine students were enrolled during the first session in Louisville, but the number almost doubled by the second year. Endowment, so diligently sought, reached $400,000 about 1891.

The fist professor to be added to the original distinguished four faculty at the seminary had been Crawford H. Toy.[21] In May, 1869, President Boyce persuaded the trustees to appoint another member for the faculty, and Toy was elected as professor of Old Testament. He had volunteered as a missionary to Japan, but was prevented from going by the Civil War, and instead had studied for two years in Belin. During his first session as teacher at the seminary in 1869, however, he revealed that in his German training he had accepted Darwin's evolutionary hypothesis and favored Kuenen-Wellhausen theory of Pentateuchal criticism.[22]

---

[20] Quoted in William A. Mueller, *A History of Southern Baptist Theological Seminary* (Nashville: Broadman Press, 1959), 42.
[21] Jesse Fletcher has an outstanding discussion of the Toy Incident in *The Southern Baptist Convention*.
[22] See Broadus, *Memoir of J. P. Boyce*, 259 ff.

When Toy refused to desist from these teachings, he was dismissed in May, 1879, by the trustees.[23]

The pioneer James P. Boyce died in 1888. Previously called chairman of the faculty, he had been elected the first president of the school seven months before his death. In May, 1889, John A. Broadus was elected president by the trustees and served until his death in 1895. Although there were but six faculty members when both Boyce and Broadus died, the catalogs from 1895 through the remainder of this period mentioned that the student body was larger than that of any other theological seminary in America.

Upon the death of Broadus, William H. Whitsitt became president and served for four years. The controversy that has already been described forced him to resign in 1899, when E. Y. Mullins succeeded him as president. At this time the faculty numbered seven. Several important achievements came during the remaining years of the period after Mullins became president. In 1901 the Sunday School Board founded a Sunday School lecture series, in 1906 the Home Mission Board began an evangelism lecture series, and in 1910 the George W. Norton lectures were endowed by Norton. *The Review and Expositor*, at that time the only Baptist theological quarterly published in the South, was begun in 1904. In 1907 the Woman's Missionary Union Training School opened near the seminary, and women were taught in

Crawford H. Toy who had fallen in love and was at one point engaged to Lottie Moon. Moon eventually broke off the engagement and focused on her language studies and foreign missions commitment. After his termination, Toy took a teaching position at Harvard and eventually became a Unitarian (Photo courtesy of Southern Baptist Historical Library and Archives)

Edgar Young Mullins who followed Whitsitt as president of Southern Seminary (Photo courtesy of Southern Baptist Historical Library and Archives)

---

[23] Baker, *Source Book*, 168-72 has this document.

seminary classes along with the men. At the close of this period in 1917, the enrollment consisted of 292 men and 91 women, and a faculty of 12.

**Southwestern Baptist Theological Seminary.** A new Southern Baptist seminary was formed in Texas during this period. It developed from the theological department of Baylor University. In 1901 B. H. Carroll became head of that department at Waco, Texas. In 1905 this department was enlarged into the Baylor Theological Seminary with Carroll as dean. By private appeal he had raised an emergency fund of $30,000 to support the new school for three years. At the end of these years Baylor University and the seminary were separated, and on March 14, 1908, the new institution was chartered. The trustees were to be appointed by the Baptist General Convention of Texas unless other states desired to assist in supporting the school. Ten state bodies indicated their desire to help and were permitted to name trustees. In the first year as a separate school, the seminary enrolled 188 men and 26 women and graduated 21 men. The faculty consisted of B. H. Carroll, A. H. Newman, C. B. Williams, Calvin Goodspeed, J. D. Ray, J. J. Reeve, and L. R. Scarborough. Carroll was president and Newman was dean.

The trustees appointed a committee on location of the new seminary. After examining several offers and visiting possible sites, this committee recommended on November 2, 1909, that the seminary be located in Fort Worth. The first session in Fort Worth began in a partially completed building on October 3, 1910, with 201 enrolled throughout the year. Of these, 171 were ministers and 30 were women, and 15 were graduated. The faculty was the same as in 1908 with the addition of W. T. Connor and two special lecturers (Henry. C. Mabie and J. B. Gambrell). Carroll continued to serve as president until his death on November 11, 1914, when he was succeeded by L. R. Scarborough, professor of evangelism.

**Benjamin H. Carroll, first president of Southwestern Seminary** (Photo courtesy of Southern Baptist Historical Library and Archives)

Southwestern Seminary was coeducational from its founding. In 1914 ground was broken for a building to house the Woman's Missionary Training School and the following year it was occupied. The women of

Texas contributed $110,000 toward its cost. From the beginning women were admitted to all degree programs, including the doctorate, on the same basis as men. In 1915 a full department of religious education was established, and John M. Price was secured to head it. In the same year, I. E. Reynolds was named head of the department of gospel music. The beginning of these two departments resulted in the admission of more women and laymen to the student body. At the close of this period in 1917, the seminary enrolled 188 men, 135 women, and 14 laymen, and graduated 38 (26 ministers, 11 women, and 1 layman). The faculty in 1917 had changed considerably. Scarborough was president and teacher, and with him were C. B. Williams, Charles T. Ball, W. W. Barnes, J. B. Weatherspoon, W. T. Connor, J. M. Price, and I. E. Reynolds.

## Relations with Other Christian Groups

New or enlarged relations with other Christian bodies began to develop during this period. The story of cooperation with black Baptist organizations is told in connection with the work of the Home Mission Board. Two other groups, one Baptist and the other interdenominational, became a part of Southern Baptist interest during this period.

**Baptist World Alliance.** Suggestions had been made on several occasions that Baptists around the world should have common organization for fellowship and inspiration.[24] J. N. Prestridge, editor of *The Baptist Argus*, Louisville, Kentucky, evidently was responsible for the initial call by the paper in 1904 for a world conference of Baptists. At the Convention in that year he introduced a resolution calling for the appointment of a committee to study the best means of accomplishing this. In October, 1904, British Baptist leaders invited Baptists of the world to meet in London on July 11-18, 1905, and representatives from twenty-three nations responded. On July 17 a plan of organization and a proposed constitution were adopted. The preamble magnified fellowship "in the Lord Jesus Christ as their God and Saviour of the Churches of the Baptist order and faith" and disclaimed the exercise of functions of any existing organization. Article 2 limited the membership to any "general Union, Convention or Association of Baptist churches," so individuals and

---

[24] Cox, ed. *Encyclopedia*, I, 127 ff. See also Barnes, *The Southern Baptist Convention*, 268, for this background.

churches related to the body only through organized general structures with which they might affiliate. Meetings every five years were suggested. Principal direction of the alliance was entrusted to a general secretary. During the remainder of this period this office was held by John H. Shakespeare, who was the secretary of the British Baptist Union. The second session met at Philadelphia in 1911; the third, delayed by World War I, did not convene until 1923 at Stockholm, after the close of the period. The proceedings of each congress have been published in detail after each meeting. They reflect the great inspiration and international fellowship that always accompany such meetings.

## Structural Tensions in the Convention

The language of the founding fathers of the Southern Baptist Convention shows that they deliberately chose to organize in a way different from the society pattern, preferring instead to copy the older associational-type of structure.[25] They wanted a "judicious concentration" of all benevolent activity into one convention

> embodying the whole Denomination together with separate and distinct Boards for each object of benevolent enterprise, located at different places, and all amenable to the Convention.[26]

They felt that this kind of structure would be more effective, more responsive and representative, and more denominationally unifying than the separate and independent benevolent societies with which they had been affiliated between 1814 and 1845.[27] They recognized that the old society method was fundamentally antidenominational at several points. First, the zealous regard by each of the completely autonomous societies for its own benevolence brought a rivalry with the other Baptist societies in the collection of funds and in the magnitude of each program. This was one of the basic factors that led to the abandonment of the society method by northern Baptists in 1907. Second, the society pattern brought a neglect of many areas of denominational concern which were not specifically

---

[25] Baker, *Source Book*, 24 ff.
[26] Ibid., 114.
[27] This "convention-type" organization was rejected by the leaders of Northern Baptists in the 1820's. See Baker, *Relations*, 15-16, and Hudson, *Baptist Concepts of the Church*.

related to the immediate program of any of the societies. Third, the autonomous nature of each of the triennial bodies allowed no holistic concept or true denominational representation. The denomination was pared into benevolent slices that overlapped but were not united. The possibility that such judicious concentration might threaten the autonomy of the churches did not trouble Southern Baptists, as has already been pointed out, and the history of the body during this period from 1877 to 1917 confirmed their view.

However, the grand denominational concept of W. B. Johnson was crippled radically at the initial meeting in 1845. The Preamble and Article V of the constitution provided for it—one body to direct all benevolent societies that Southern Baptists might wish to promote. Yet Johnson himself did not realize that when they retained some of the old society characteristics in the structure of the new body, they were introducing antidenominational elements to set in motion ideological and functional tensions that would ultimately need to be confronted. Some of these society characteristics that were structured into the new body by the founding fathers were the priority of the benevolence over denominational solidarity, the use of designated giving for support of the benevolences, financial gifts as the basis of representation in the Convention, and the widespread concept that the functional existence of the Convention ceased when the triennial meeting adjourned.

During the period between 1877 and 1917 Southern Baptists began to recognize that these society characteristics, imbedded into a convention-type structure, inhibited the development of those denominational goals which had initially moved the founders of the Convention to leave the old society method; namely, the desire to form an effectively functioning, responsive and representative, and denominationally unitying body. The efforts to achieve these goals through modifying the structure during this period will be described briefly.

**Making the Convention More Responsive and Representative.** The adoption of the society financial plan for determining the basis of representation in the Southern Baptist Convention in 1845 brought to this body one of the basic weaknesses of the society plan; namely, a structure for benevolent work of the denomination that was neither representative of nor responsive to the denomination itself. As early as 1824 Francis Wayland, who was to become the most influential figure for a long generation among American Baptists, remarked concerning the society plan of carrying on benevolent work:

> The convention at present is composed of delegates from missionary societies, and of course must, in its very nature, be mostly composed of persons elected from the vicinity of its place of meeting. And besides, were the meeting ever so universally attended, its foundation is radically defective. A missionary society is not a representative body, nor can any number of them speak the language of a whole denomination.[28]

It was this society plan of operation with respect to constituency and support that was adopted by the Southern Baptist Convention in 1845. While this structure provided a committed constituency, in contrast with the earlier associational plan which in many cases did not, the adoption of this plan by the Convention in 1845 made it impossible to unite the whole denomination in the manner desired by W. B. Johnson, the principle architect.

The truth of Wayland's comment was demonstrated in the years between 1877 and 1917. Not only was the basic nature of the society opposed to true representation of the denomination, but a number of specific elements enhanced the problem. The increasing size of the constituency of the Convention soon lessened the ratio of the decision-making as meetings became so large that sober deliberation was completely impossible. The agenda was so crowded with reports of work done and recommendations for work to be done that the Convention did not have enough time to give even brief consideration to many of them in the four or five days meeting. The location of the Convention meeting place became overwhelmingly important. Nearby people would attend in large number and vote for any sectional issue that was favorable to them or pleased them. Resolutions were introduced that reflected the interests of a small sectional group, so that by reason of the time and location of the meeting, the well-being of the whole body was adversely affected. New plans and programs were often introduced at the meetings, and because of the lack of prior time to study them and judge their effects, the messengers

---

[28] Baker, *Source Book*, 70-71.

were forced to vote on illogically conceived or improperly developed schemes that were foredoomed to failure. These and many more weaknesses in the operation of the Convention during this period were stressed by various leaders across the South.[29]

Almost every year during this period between 1877 and 1917 someone raised the question from the floor of the Convention relative to changing the method of representation. Changes actually were made half-a-dozen times. Despite this chronic tampering with the basis of representation, however, there was little consensus among Southern Baptists as to the proper method of determine the constituency in order to make it both representative and responsive. Serious consideration was given to four types of representation, even without financial contributions to the Convention, was permitted during most of this period. Several attempts were made to eliminate this kind of representation in order to reduce the size of the Convention, but its popularity was such that this provision was retained and became a principal area of representation.

Support for state representation in the Southern Baptist Convention was surprisingly strong. In 1878 specific states were authorized to send messengers on a financial basis, and the state as a basis for general representation was seriously discussed in later years.

The numerical basis of representation was suggested many times. In 1891 and again in 1893 proposals from the floor were made to follow this plan. In the latter year, a large committee composed of some of the most important members of the Convention recommended that the basis of representation be changed either to a numerical basis or to a combined numerical-financial basis. The numerical plan suggested ten representatives from each cooperating state, plus one representative for each four thousand white Baptist membership within these states, and one representative from each cooperating district association. This plan was not adopted. In 1894, 1902, and after the close of this period, the numerical basis was stoutly championed. The most persuasive argument for this kind of representation was the assertion that most of the state conventions and other Baptist bodies had a numerical basis of representation. However, the effort to secure this kind of representation failed during this period.

---

[29] See, for example, the critique of the committee of E. Y. Mullins, *Annual*, Southern Baptist Convention, 1926, 31-32.

The church basis of representation was most widely urged. As might be expected, J. R. Graves of Tennessee was one of its early champions. He wanted to limit the representation to membership of the churches only, and suggested that each Baptist church contributing any sum to the boards of the Convention should be allowed one delegate (in his terminology), and an additional delegate for each hundred dollars given. His point of view was reflected in 1905 at the Kansas City meeting of the Convention when a communication was presented to the Convention. The principal demand of this memorial said:

> We want the money and the associational basis of representation eliminated from the Constitution and a purely church basis substituted instead.... The numerical basis is objectionable because such a basis carries with it the idea that the commission was given to the individual as such and not to the churches as such. Nothing short of exclusive church representation will satisfy us. We ask that you eliminate all other bases and adopt the church basis of representation.[30]

When the Convention refused this request, the Landmark group under B. M. Bogard and others withdrew from Convention and state cooperation.

However, this call for the church basis of representation was not limited to aggressive Landmarkers alone. A few weeks after the 1901 session of the Convention, the *World and Way* of Missouri published an article on "Representatives of What?" The writer said in part:

> So far as I could see from the minutes of the Convention there was not a single church on the roll as being represented. The representatives were from the local association and those appointed by the State boards.... Is it any wonder that there is a hue and cry about ten thousand churches that do not co-operate with the Convention and its work? The basis of membership in the Convention is $250 for each messenger. This puts the Convention where not one church in five hundred can reach it. ... Any regular Baptist church should be allowed to be represented in our

---

[30] Baker, *Source Book*, 174, has this document.

associations and conventions.... Baptists believe in co-operation but not in centralization.[31]

A clear distinction should be made between the Landmark position of *delegated* church representation and the position of many non-Landmarkers which might be termed a *designated* church representation. The Landmarkers viewed the Convention as a body composed of autonomous and scripturally authoritative local churches officially represented through their delegates. Their ecclesiological theory asserted that otherwise there would be no basis for the general body even to exist, since the local church was the only scriptural and authoritative body among Baptists. The other view denied both the necessity and the advantage of projecting the authority of local churches into general bodies. Instead, an anti-Landmark concept conceived of general bodies as mass meetings of representative Baptists composed of messengers *designated* by the churches, but who did not officially represent their churches, nor possess any delegated authority from the churches, nor corporately exercise any authority of the Convention stemmed from fraternal and widespread denominational consensus, not from the authority of the churches. In essence, this meant that all general bodies—associational, state, and convention-wide—were mass meetings of Baptists, not officially delegated bodies with any power over the churches that sent the messengers.

After the Convention refused to change its society-type of financial representation in 1905 at the demand of the Landmark group, it continued to ponder and debate the best way to secure a more representative and responsive basis. However, at the end of this period in 1917, Article V on membership still provided that the Convention should consist of (1) messengers who contribute funds, or were elected by Baptist bodies contributing funds on the basis of one messenger for every $250 paid into the treasuries of the boards and (2) one representative elected from each of the district associations cooperating with the Convention.

**Deepening a Denominational Consciousness.** A cursory glance at the appeals of W. B. Johnson in 1845 makes it plain that he desired more than simply an effective and responsive general body when he urged the adoption of a plan to "elicit, combine, and direct" all Southern

---

[31] Baker, *Relations*, 168.

Baptists in a concerted effort. Underlying all of this was the desire to unify Southern Baptists in such fashion that the tenuous "ropes of straw" holding together autonomous and sometimes non-cooperative Baptist churches would be strengthened by a strong denominational loyalty as a means of supporting the domestic and foreign programs consistently and conscientiously. The South had always had a distinctive sectional cohesiveness. Social, economic, political, and linguistic patterns were different from those in the North. The presence of slavery after 1619 accentuated this sectional uniqueness. The struggles for religious liberty and the union of Regular and Separate Baptists brought a sense of southern unity. The strong blows of Primitivism and Campbellism severely affected Southern Baptists before their organization in 1845 and instilled a battle-field type of solidarity. The events of 1861 to 1877 deepened the southern sectional feelings.

Yet, in the period between 1877 and 1917, the Convention experienced the fiercest struggles it had known at this precise point: loyalty to the Convention. Doubtless the organization of benevolent work outside of the Convention was not intended to disparage the Convention's purpose of becoming the structural body for all southern benevolences, but the lack of consensus for structuring such benevolences as publications, theological education, and a Sunday School union within the Convention structure, for reasons already suggested, could have destroyed the effectiveness of the southwide body. The severity of the struggles with the Home Mission Society of New York over the home field and the American Baptist Publication Society of Philadelphia relative to the multipurpose nature of the Convention, along with the several Landmark attacks involving the right of the Convention to carry on its work, showed the depth of the lack of loyalty to the Convention in the 1880's and 1890's. But it was in these very struggles that a strong denominational consciousness was developed. The vision of southern leaders like I. T. Tichenor challenged the Convention's constituency to rally to the cause. The second Sunday School Board, organized in 1891, had a strong unifying effect through its literature and promotional activity. The tensions between the southwide and state programs lessened perceptibly by the turn of the century. The remarkable growth in several directions accelerated this denominational consciousness. When Southern Baptists moved to other states, they longed for the old ties and familiar denominational structures. This was the basic reason for the geographical expansion into other states during this and the following period. In this period Southern Baptists in New Mexico, southern Illinois, and Oklahoma sought ties with the southern convention from their new localities. It is likely that the appeals of Oregon Baptists in 1894 were unheard because of the territorial consciousness of the Convention at that time; but when Southern Baptist people began to swarm into all areas of the nation, territorial limitations could not stand in the face of the denominational consciousness displayed by them wherever they might live. The inability of the strong resurgence of Landmarkism in the 1890's to bring extensive schism in the Convention (despite some very strong attacks at many points) and the relative aloofness of the Southern Baptists to the ecumenical movement probably resulted from the sense of identity developed in the convention-type structure of the South.

Thus, by 1917 the Southern Baptist Convention had totally recovered from the trauma of war and Reconstruction. Its ministry had been enlarged to three effective boards; it had greatly expanded its areas of service; and its organizational structure was being tested at the point of denominational effectiveness and responsiveness.

# PERIOD THREE: THE MODERN ERA (1917-2012)

*From the Formation of the First Executive Committee to the Great Commission Resurgence*

## Chapter 12 - Denominational Changes

After the controversies brought on by Landmarkism, the denomination approached the beginning of the new century with a new sense of denominational identity and pride. While the Landmarkers had basically been defeated, their influence was left behind in the form of Fundamentalism and in a strong sense of emphasis on the local church. However, they had lost the battle for a unified denomination. I. T. Tichenor had helped Southern Baptists develop a sense of pride in themselves as a denomination and had successfully worked for a stronger missions emphasis in North America.

In 1898, there were three permanent boards at work and the Women's Missionary Union was busy promoting missions to Southern Baptist churches. It was this sense of optimism that saw resolutions from the State Convention of Georgia presented through the Home Mission Board which read, in part,

> Whereas, The nineteenth century...has witnessed such marvelous progress among our Baptist People, not only in numbers but in every qualification which fits them to be a mighty agency in the hand of our redeemer in his purpose to give his gospel to every creature, be it
> 
> *Resolved*, That this Convention respectfully suggests to the Southern Baptist Convention that it recommend the observance of the year 1900 as a year of thanksgiving by our Baptist churches in which special efforts be made to more fully inform them of the

gracious fullness of the Divine blessing received during this century, and to better organize and equip them for the mighty work which lies before them in the century to come.

## Committee on Co-operation

A committee was appointed that consisted of one representative from each state, as well as the secretaries of the Boards. They were to carry out the suggestions of the Georgia resolutions.[1] The Centennial Celebration was observed at the annual meeting of the Southern Baptist Convention in Hot Springs, Arkansas in May 1900. Their work was evaluated and suggestions and recommendations were made to the Convention for future progress, that the work already done not be lost. Among other things, the recommendation was made for the formation of a joint Committee of Co-operation, consisting of committees of three appointed by the three separate Boards. This joint committee was to have the authority to employ a "Secretary of Co-operation and such other agencies as may be deemed necessary to do the work herein contemplated. The expenses of this work shall be borne equally by the three Boards."[2]

The report was adopted, and the Committee on Co-operation gave a full report in 1901. Among other suggestions, the Committee recommended

> a special agency be employed to be known as the Committee on Co-operation of the Southern Baptist Convention, composed of the following fifteen brethren and located in Baltimore.... We recommend further that this committee be authorized to employ a secretary, fix his remuneration, and also provide such other agencies as in their judgment may be necessary.[3]

After discussion, the Convention rejected five of the seven recommendations, including the one quoted above. The only remaining recommendations was a call to continue to focus on the proclamation of the gospel and to encourage every "State Association or Convention, and every State Board, to co-operate with us in a vigorous, specific movement

---

[1] Home Mission Board Report, *Annual,* 1898, LXVI, 35.
[2] *Annual,* 1899, 31 ff.
[3] Baltimore churches had made a financial offer to the Convention, on condition that the Committee on Co-operation be located there. *Annual,* 1901, 14,33 ff.

of this kind along such lines of co-operation as can be mutually agreed upon in each state."[4]

While many of the leaders of the various Boards understood the need for a central, unifying and coordinating body, there was not enough of a perception of need felt among the churches in the South. After the positive reports from the Boards, apparently the sentiment among Southern Baptists attending the meeting was that of positive contentment.

Even though the decision was made not to establish a permanent coordinating agency, there was still a persistent feeling that a need existed to streamline Southern Baptist work. Perhaps this was due to the influence of the era when scientific processes were being applied to many aspects of life in an attempt to systematically improve processes. It could also be a result of the improved economic conditions and transportation facilities throughout the South, which resulted in increased attendance at the annual meetings. The increase in attendance even affected the character of the meetings themselves. An editorial in the *Religious Herald* pointed out the impact this had on the deliberation of matters at the Convention:

> It must be frankly admitted, however, that the real work of the Convention is no longer done by the Convention itself. It is practically impossible, with the present organization and methods, and in the physical conditions in which the Convention is frequently forced to meet, to deliberate about anything. So it has come to pass that debate is practically unknown and conference is out of the question. We are rapidly coming to the place, if we have not already reached it, when we must rely wholly upon the Boards and standing committees to do our thinking for us. This is to some extent both desirable and inevitable. At the same time we cannot suppress the conviction that it is not best for us, or for the interests which we seek to promote, that our great representative body should denigrate into a mere celebration, a place for set and formal reports and addresses, a sort of spectacular gathering, full of holy enthusiasm, it may be but lacking utterly the deliberative element.[5]

---

[4] *Annual*, 1901.
[5] *Religious Herald*, May 20, 1909, 10.

## Improving the Convention's Effectiveness

The potential effectiveness of the new Convention was markedly reduced in 1845 when the founding fathers retained at least three of the society's antidenominational characteristics in the structure of the new body. For one thing, the old society concept of the nature of general bodies was retained. They were viewed as aristocratic, inspirational gatherings somewhat aloof from the total life of the denomination, having no corporate or functional existence between sessions. The fact that each society fostered only one benevolence resulted in partitioning the denomination in such fashion as to exclude a holistic conception. The meetings of the societies occurred only once every three years, and each society took cognizance only of its own benevolence. Each benevolence took precedence over the denominational emphasis. In the second place, W. B. Johnson's scheme for structuring all benevolent activities under one convention was rejected, and some benevolences were organized outside the structure of the Convention. In the third place, support for the benevolences of the Convention came from designated giving to specific benevolences, and the method of securing these funds was quite haphazard.

These basically antidenominational society characteristics, which were placed in the structure of the new denominational Convention by Southern Baptists in 1845, resisted any major change for over half a century. There were four principal reasons for this. For one thing, many Southern Baptists, particularly in the border states, clung to the hope that reunion of all American Baptists might be achieved. They desired to hold the new body to a limited program of benevolences lest there should come further alienation with Baptists in the North. When Georgia Baptists suggested that the southern body immediately adopt all benevolences for the South, Editor John Waller of the *Western Baptist Review* of Kentucky wrote a sharp reply in which he vigorously opposed any more divisions between the northern and southern Baptist bodies "merely because their Boards are located north of Mason and Dixon's line."[6] A second deterrent to any rapid move toward the convention ideal of promoting all benevolences was introduce after 1851 by J. R. Graves and the Landmarkers, who opposed authorizing any nonlocal body to enlarge the

---

[6] John Waller, ed., *Western Baptist Review*, I, 57 ff.

area of its benevolent work. Third, many Southern Baptists doubted their financial ability to promote all benevolences desired by the southern constituency through one denominational body, as demonstrated by their lengthy refusal to enter into the book publishing enterprise. Finally, the heterogeneous nature of Baptist life in the South, heightened by difficulties in communication and transportation, blunted the efforts of leaders to elicit, combine, and direct the energies of the whole denomination in one sacred effort through the new Convention.

In this ambivalent context, then, it is no wonder that the grand design of the Southern Baptist Convention to become an effective, all-inclusive denominational body to promote all benevolent activity of Southern Baptists was almost obliterated, and the Convention was often called "the missionary convention," suggesting the old society emphasis, during this period. It had no funds of its own, even to print minutes of the sessions, so designated mission funds were conscripted for this purposed. There was even a debate about where to keep the Convention minute book and records, since the Convention had no de facto existence or headquarters.

However, the very nature of the new Convention challenged these society characteristics. Four steps illustrating the struggle of the convention thrust may be distinctly observed. First, there were demands for more frequent meetings of the Convention. The many denominational emphases that went beyond missions required sessions more often than every three years. In 1851 the meetings of the Convention were changed from triennial to biennial, and in 1866 they became annual. Second, there were repeated efforts to bring all benevolences into the structure of the Convention. Four benevolences were structured within the Convention during the first twenty years of its history: a foreign mission body, a domestic mission body, a Bible Board, and a Sunday School Board. Three additional major benevolences were developed outside of the Convention following the old society pattern: a publication society in 1847, a Sunday School Union in 1857, and a south-wide theological seminary in 1859. These external benevolences, however, were so formed as to recognize the Convention and relate rather loosely to it. Third, in 1891 a significant and spectacular development occurred, although most Southern Baptists did not recognize it as such. In that year the second Sunday School Board was formed and this board represented a large step toward bridging the gap between the old program of supporting a few basic benevolences and the total denominational thrust of the new southern convention. The new agency was able to carry on a large number of additional denominational functions, moving perceptibly toward the ideal of Article V of the original constitution. At the same time, this new agency provided a source of finances for the denomination over and above the expenses required for its operation. Thus, the Convention was now able to give leadership in many benevolent undertakings that could not have been fostered before 1891 because of financial limitation and designation. In part because the new board possessed these funds, it was assigned leadership in Sunday School and Training Union work, architectural assistance to the churches, periodical and book publishing, production of church supplies for every type of use in the churches, training in church budgeting, cooperative work with state boards, and many similar denominational programs. In addition, this board provided financial assistance to about a dozen denominational agencies in connection with its own distinctive program, which would not have been possible without this revenue.

## Formation of the Executive Committee

In 1913 the Convention bluntly instructed a commission to study the structure, plans, and methods of the Convention to determine whether or not they *were* best adapted for "eliciting, combining and directing the energies of Southern Baptists and for securing the highest efficiency of our forces and the fullest possible enlistment of our people for the work of the Kingdom."[7] This was denominational language. The climax came in 1916 when M. H. Wolfe of Texas proposed the creation of a strong Executive Board "which shall direct all of the work and enterprises fostered and promoted by this Convention." A committee was appointed to study this matter. A minority report, interestingly enough, proposed a plan of consolidation calling for all the boards and agencies to be merged into a corporation, the Southern Baptist Convention, which should have a Board of Directors composed of the secretaries of the state conventions. This board would hold all of the property and direct all of the work of the Convention.[8]

---

[7] *Annual,* Southern Baptist Convention, 1913, 69 f.
[8] Barnes, *The Southern Baptist Convention,* 178.

The majority recommendation carried and a small executive Committee of seven was named. One can detect a note of caution in the initial allocation of a few duties to this body. It was to have oversight of arrangements for the meetings of the Convention; to act *ad interim* on general business not otherwise provided for; to serve as an advisory group when requested to do so by one or more of the boards; and "this committee shall have no further duties except as other things may be specifically committed to it by the Convention itself at its annual meeting."[9] Yet even in the 1917 session, several additional matters for study and recommendation were referred to this committee.[10]

This represented an important turning point for the Convention. Before 1917 each of the Boards had been, for all practical purposes, autonomous. While it is accurate to say that the Southern Baptist Convention exists only during its annual convention, prior to the establishment of the Executive Committee, it largely became dormant during the remainder of the year. With the formation of the Executive Committee, it now became possible to have a means to coordinate the work of the Convention between annual meetings. In effect, it shifted from being a voluntary affiliation society, to a coordinating denomination.

This original committee of 1917 was not particularly imposing in its size or functions, but in its development it revolutionized the nature and operation of the Southern Baptist Convention and brought a denominational solidarity never achieved under the older society pattern. As a limited Executive Committee of seven members was formed, it quickly proved its value. In 1918 the committee was enlarged to twenty-four members (including one from each state), and in 1921 women were added to it.

Sensitivity relative to centralization in the Convention began to disappear rapidly during the 1920's. The increasing financial stringency following the Seventy-five Million Campaign, the overwhelming number of committee reports in any annual session (there were fifty-four committee reports in 1925), the painfully visible evidence of disunity in the work of the increasing number of agencies of the Convention, and the recognized need for a Convention "watchdog" to maintain the integrity of

---

[9] *Annual*, Southern Baptist Convention, 1917, 33 f.
[10] *Annual*, 1918, 109.

the body brought the appointment of a Committee Correlation in 1923 and a Committee on Business Efficiency in 1925. The latter committee made an intensive survey of the work of the Convention and were convinced

> that the constituency of this convention is becoming insistent that the work of the agencies of the convention shall be more closely correlated, and that the agencies themselves shall be brought into such relations with the convention as will guarantee in advance both efficiency of administration and prevention of incurring any indebtedness, except for current expenses between the meetings of the convention.[11]

As a result, the Executive Committee was given additional powers in 1926, and in 1927 its structure was strengthened substantially to provide it with strong organizational functions. It became the fiduciary, fiscal, and executive agency of the Convention in all of its affairs not specifically committed to some other board or agency. It represented a de facto year-round corporate voice for the Convention. New structural unity was achieved, and denominational solidarity was magnified more than simply benevolent activity.

## An Improved Basis of Representation

It will be recalled that the one of the tensions introduced into the structure of the Southern Baptist Convention from the society method in 1845 involved the financial basis of representation. The continuous agitation of this question brought no change during the previous period, but was discussed almost exhaustively until 1927, when a strong Committee on the Basis of Representation, headed by E. Y. Mullins, severely criticized the existing structure and functions. Two years later a memorial from the District of Columbia echoed these sentiments. A Committee on Changes in the Constitution brought an extensive report in 1931. Relative to the basis of representation, it recommended that Article III be changed at several points, but that the financial basis of representation be retained. When this item was presented to the Convention, E. C. Routh of Oklahoma offered a substitute article which was adopted, providing a modified church basis of representation.[12] As

---

[11] *Annual,* 1926, 19.
[12] *Annual,* 1924, 65-68.

subsequently refined, this article said that the Convention shall consist of messengers who are members of missionary Baptist churches cooperating with the Convention on the basis of one messenger from each church in friendly cooperation and sympathetic with its purposes and work, and has during the fiscal year preceding been a bona fide contributor to the Convention's work; that one additional messenger may be elected from each church for every 250 members or for each $250 paid to the work of the Convention during the fiscal year preceding the annual meeting; that the maximum number of messengers from any church is ten, and each messenger must be a member of the church by which he is appointed.[13] It should be recalled that this was not the Landmark position of *delegated* church representation, but was a *designated* church representation. The Routh article conceived of general bodies as mass meetings of representative Baptists composed of messengers designated by the churches, but who did not officially represent their churches nor possess any delegated authority from the churches. According to this view, the authority of the Convention stemmed from fraternal and widespread denominational consensus, not from any projection of the authority of the churches. This will explain why the Convention could consistently and heatedly refuse the Landmark church basis of representation between 1900 and 1930, and then in 1931, adopt the substitute article of Routh.

It should be observed that this change increased the visibility of churches by using them to provide the distribution of messengers at the annual meeting, but this was not a church delegate base after the Landmark pattern. It gave additional messengers on a numerical basis for the larger churches; and it rewarded the church by additional messengers when they increased their financial gifts to the Convention. Undue influence by large and wealthy churches was minimized by limiting the maximum number of messengers from any church. Thus, by 1931, the old society financial basis of representation was modified to provide denominational consensus with a wide base, while additional visibility and a sense of immediate participation were given to each affiliating Southern Baptist church.

---

[13] *Annual,* 1972, 30.

# A Supplementary Structure for Decision-Making

Closely related to the question of the basis of representation at the Convention was the problem of the size of the body. This Pandora's Box doubtless had several bases: the increasing number of benevolences promoted by the Convention brought numerous adherents from each one to the general meeting; the rapid growth of the constituency between 1845 and the turn of the century tended to increase the size of the annual meeting; the opportunities for fellowship and information at the Convention were a drawing point; and the rapid development of transportation facilities, especially the railroads, made attendance much more convenient. One reason for the constant tampering with the basis of representation, as well as the numerous suggestions for changing it, had been the recognition that the annual meetings were becoming unwieldy in their size, particularly when important issues were being decided from the floor of the Convention. In 1891 the largest building in Birmingham, Alabama, was so crowded with messengers that the speaker had to be boosted through a window and led by a devious route to the platform because of the press of the crowd. The numerical basis of representation was suggested in 1891 and again in 1893 in a deliberate attempt to control the size of the body. In 1893 a large committee composed of some of the most important members of the Convention recommended that the basis of representation be changed either to a numerical basis or to a combined numerical-financial basis. The numerical plan suggested ten representatives from each cooperating state, plus one representative for each 4,000 white Baptist membership within these states, and one representative from each cooperating district association. In 1894, 1902, 1919, and numerous other times, the numerical basis was stoutly championed, particularly because "practically all of the State Conventions and other Baptist bodies have a numerical basis of representation."

The dilemma of the size of the body at its annual meeting was dramatically illustrated in 1920 when the Convention convened at Washington, D. C. Twenty-five years before, when the Convention had met there, the messengers had numbered 870; in 1920, the messengers numbered 8,359. J. R. Graves would have stirred uneasily in his resting place had he known that in the 1920 session his son-in-law, O. L. Hailey, presented a resolution bewailing the size of the meeting and asking that a committee be appointed to consider several matters including "the number of messengers who may be appointed from each State." At the 1927 meeting of the Convention, E. Y. Mullins headed a committee to study the basis of representation. His report to the Convention listed the weaknesses of the existing plan: the immensely enlarged membership; the difficulties of deliberation; the great increase in the number of reports (which in 1845, he said, consisted of two or three missionary subjects, but now involved reports by over fifty committees on a variety of subjects); the ignorance of the messengers concerning new policies recommended, due to the absence of advance knowledge; the shortness of the Convention period, covering from three to five days only; the preponderance of those coming from the locality near the meeting place of the Convention with a consequent lack of balanced judgment from all geographical sections in reaching important decisions; the danger of sectional initiative in introducing new measures which might be lacking in proper coordination with other interests and activities, etc. The principle remedy suggested by Mullins was to utilize a numerical basis of representation so that the Convention would consist of a few hundred messengers, with 1,000 as the maximum, and virtually empowering an enlarged Executive Committee, along with a small but authoritative triennial Convention, to operate the affairs of the body.[14]

The Convention, however, after considerable deliberation, turned away from the suggestion that its annual session should be arbitrarily diminished in size to a few hundred messengers or representatives. In so doing the Convention had almost exhausted the possibilities suggested for reducing the size of the annual gathering which had been put forward during the past half century. It had ruled out the strictly financial basis of representation, numerical representation, and "presbygational" representation on both an associational and state level. Instead, the Convention approached the problem obliquely. The main concern of the Convention in taking this new direction was to meet an immediate situation rather than to grapple with the many problems involved in the size of the annual gathering. In the constitutional revision of 1931, the Convention introduced a bylaw to put into their formal structure a principle that had been informally followed since the beginning days of the Convention. From the very first years after 1845, when important decisions were to be made, the Convention regularly appointed

---

[14] *Annual*, 1926, 32 ff.

committees composed of one or more representatives from each state cooperating with the Convention, in order to insure widespread distribution in the makeup of the committee. In 1931 a small group of Baptists in Arizona had asked for the privilege of having representation from their state on the boards of the Convention. The Convention passed Bylaw 17 which formally defined how a state could secure representation on the boards and the executive committee of the Convention. This bylaw said:

> Any state desiring representation on any board of the Executive Committee of this Convention shall make formal application for the representation desired, stating the number of Baptists in the state who are co-operating with this Convention and the total amount of money given to the Convention objects the preceding year. The Convention shall then make such investigation as it may desire and shall upon the basis of the information obtained vote on the question of representation on each board and the Executive Committee upon which representation is sought and the question shall be decided by a majority vote.[15]

Some refinements have subsequently been made by this bylaw, which will be discussed later.

This action took care of the immediate petition of Arizona, but it did more than that. By the formal adoption of the principle of state representation on boards, commissions, and standing committees of the Convention, an official substructure on a decision-making level had been provided. As early as 1909 it had been recognized that the character of the Convention was already being altered by the substructure of boards and committees. The *Religious Herald* of Virginia remarked in an editorial in that year:

> It must be frankly admitted, however, that the real work of the Convention is no longer done by the Convention itself. It is practically impossible, with the present organization and methods, and in the physical conditions in which the Convention is frequently forced to meet, to deliberate about anything. So it has

---

[15] *Annual*, 1931, 102.

come to pass that debate is practically unknown and conference is out of the question. We are coming rapidly to the place, if we have not already reached it, when we must rely wholly upon the Boards and standing committees to do our thinking for us. This is to some extent both desirable and inevitable.[16]

The editor did express the wish, however, that the annual meeting could retain some of its deliberative element. This statement and wish foreshadowed the actual development put into formal articulation in 1931: an extensive system of boards, commissions, and committees to do most of the study and make recommendations to the annual meeting, which, in turn determines the principles of operation. Thus, instead of an intermittent tampering with the basis of representation as a means of securing smaller annual gatherings, the Convention chose to operate through a dual representation: one on a state basis being penultimate in authority, aristocratic in make-up, widely representative, consisting of state membership as trustees on boards, commissions, committees, and institutions; the other being the Convention session itself—ultimate in authority, democratic in make-up, totally available for members of all cooperating churches, and less representative because of the size and place of the annual meeting, economic conditions, the intensity of issues confronting the Convention, etc. A sweeping constitutional revision in 1946 confirmed this dual representation as the desired organizational structure and focused on safeguarding the makeup of the trustees of these boards, commissions, committees, and institutions as important substructures of the Convention. The qualifications, election, and rotation of these representatives were carefully spelled out in the constitution and bylaws of the Convention. They were to be chosen specifically "to represent the constituency of the Convention, rather than the staff of the agency."

It is interesting to notice that the 1927 Mullins committee suggested that the annual session of the Convention should consist of only a few hundred messengers, with 1,000 as the maximum. Had the Convention actually set up such a limited basis for forming the annual meeting, the whole system of decision-making would have had serious

---

[16] See *Religious Herald* (Virginia), May 20, 1909, 10, col. 1. See also *Annual*, 1912, 77-78.

deficiencies that do not appear in the present dual system. Many of the objections of the Mullins committee to the old system have been met by this dual structure of representation. The large attendance from points near the meeting place and sectional initiative in presenting programs to the Convention are minimized by the broad nature of the trustees of the boards, commissions, committees, and institutions, for they are representative of every state related to Convention life. The many values involved in messengers from each church being free to attend the Convention and vote have been conserved, and even deliberative functions on major matters are still exercised by the annual meeting. Committees have not supplanted the authoritative Convention, but have evolved into technical and deliberative subsections of Convention life to bring recommendations to the whole body, thus supplementing the Convention. This combined aristocratic-democratic structure has solved many of the problems involved in the size of the annual meetings of the Convention.

# Chapter 13 - The Beginning of the Modern Era to World War II

The period between the two World Wars has combined paradoxical elements. On the one hand, Southern Baptists have never known a period of greater financial crisis and continuing threats of bankruptcy. Conditions were so difficult that one prominent Southern Baptist writer called these "the dark ages" in Southern Baptist life. Yet, on the other hand, these very harsh years were among the most creative and progressive the Southern Baptist Convention ever experienced.

The principal events characterizing the history of the Convention between the wars were the struggle to carry on its ministry despite the severe and continuing financial crisis, the impact of the attacks of liberals, the attempts to revise the structure of the Convention in order to provide an effective vehicle for the work of the denomination, the response of Southern Baptists to ecumenical efforts, and the substantial growth effected in the midst of a complex evolving culture.

## The Seventy-five Million Campaign

At the close of World War I on November 11, 1918, Southern Baptists shared with the entire nation the jubilant optimism of a challenging and an unhindered future, since the war to make the world safe for democracy had been won. Clearly the time was ripe for lengthening the cords of service. Inspired by the united military effort in World War I, the overwhelming success of mammoth financial campaigns by Red Cross and Community Chest leaders, and idealistic proposals from religious leaders of several denominations for spectacular campaigns in behalf of the cause of Christ, Southern Baptists enthusiastically heard suggestions from Rufus W. Weaver to raise $100,000,000 for Jesus in five years; from their Education Commission to raise $15,000,000 in five years for Christian Education; and from their ministerial relief and annuity leaders calling for a $5,000,000 campaign for their work. In 1918 the Convention created a committee to make plans for raising vast sums to promote all benevolences through the cooperation of all of its constituency. During the following year, Southern Baptist leaders uniformly appealed for the adoption of a great and challenging program.

On the opening morning of the 1919 session of the Convention at Atlanta, Georgia, President J. B. Gambrell set the tone for what would follow. He said:

> It is my deep conviction that this Convention ought to adopt a program for work commensurate with the reasonable demands on us and summon ourselves and our people to a new demonstration of the value of orthodoxy in free action.
>
> It is, moreover, a conviction as deep as my soul that this Convention, representing the sentiments and convictions of millions of Christ's baptized people, ought to send out to our fellow Baptists everywhere a rallying call to unite to make effective in all lands the unique message of Christ.[1]

Committees were appointed to translate this word into action. A committee on Financial Aspect of the Enlarged Program recommended that the Convention undertake to raise $75,000,000 during the next five years. As later modified, the plan called for the appointment of a commission of fifteen members to lay plans and launch the campaign.[2] George W. Truett of Texas was appointed chairman of the Financial Campaign Committee, together with one member from each state. Promptly this committee met with the Executive Committee and the executive secretaries of the general and state boards. The Sunday School Board, Nashville, provided headquarters for the campaign; L. R. Scarborough, president of Southwestern Seminary, became general director; and I. J. Van Ness was named treasurer. Quotas were established for each state, and the proceeds were budgeted for missions, education, ministerial relief, orphanages, and hospitals. The seven remaining months of 1919 were designated to promote some aspect of the campaign: preparation, information, intercession, enlistment, stewardship, and Victory Week in December.

---

[1] *Annual*, 1919, 23.
[2] Ibid. 22.

In May, 1920, it was reported that $92,630,923 had been subscribed, and $12,237,827 had been paid, despite very adverse conditions such as a major coal strike, almost incessant rain during a period of seventy-five days in more than one-half of the territory of the Convention, and the shortness of time for preparation.[3] But dark days were in the offing. In the last half of 1920 the most severe depression since the 1890's struck the nation. Perhaps hardest hit was the farmer, the mainstay of Southern Baptist support, who was submerged in depression until the late 1930's. Seven million unemployed Americans walked the streets in 1921. National income fell from $75,000,000,000 in 1920 to $59,000,000,000 in 1921.[4] Southern Baptists, with 23,143 rural churches (out of a total of less than 26,000), were greatly hurt.[5]

George W. Truett who assisted the Convention in paying off the debt incurred during the $75 Million Campaign (Photo courtesy of Southern Baptist Historical Library and Archives)

As a consequence, the receipts for all causes—state and southwide—began declining sharply in the second year of the campaign. At the end of the five years, only $58,591,713.69 was raised, over $34,000,000 less than was pledged. However, state, home, and foreign mission programs had already been rapidly enlarged to take advantage of the funds that had been promised. By 1926 the Convention alone had a staggering debt of approximately $6,500,000, not to speak of the debts compounded in the states.

## Struggle for Financial Integrity

Depression continued to plague the agricultural and rural areas in the mid-twenties, adding to the burdens remaining from the Seventy-five Million Campaign. In his financial analysis in 1930 E. P. Aldredge remarked that the severe local and state needs were clearly reflected in the giving trends of the previous five years. Gifts to state convention objects rose from $3,568,483 in 1925 to $5,515,040 in 1929, while gifts to the

---

[3] George W. McDaniel, *The Southwestern Evangel* (Ft. Worth), 89-91.
[4] O. T. Barck and N. M. Blake, *Since 1900* (New York: The Macmillan Co., 1947), 393.
[5] See *Southern Baptist Handbook* (Nashville), 57.

southern body dropped from $4,686,952 in 1925 to $2,227,290 in 1929.[6] But the trials of Southern Baptists had just begun. The stock market crash of 1929 was preceded by a shocking theft from the Home Mission Board in 1928 by Clinton S. Carnes, treasurer for almost a decade, aming to $909,461 in principal and interest. This board's debt promptly rose to $2,257,453,[7] and the severest part of the depression was yet to come. The plight of the Convention's two mission boards illustrated the grim prognosis for their future. When C. E. Maddry took office on January 1, 1933, the Foreign Mission Board owed $1,110,000 to four banks in Richmond, together with $249,000 additional debt incurred by the missionaries on the fields. The banks notified the board it must immediately pay the $67,000 interest due in 1933 and at least $150,000 on the principal. Maddry said that this would be disastrous to the foreign mission work, whose budget for the year was only $600,000. He reminded the bankers that in the ninety years of the board's history their institutions had not lost a cent in principal interest, and pledged that they would ultimately receive all of their money if the board was permitted to use enough of its $600,000 budget to operate its foreign mission program. The bankers finally agreed, and Maddry was successful in maintaining a missionary staff on the field while striving to pay off these debts. In the six years before 1932, the board lost 127 missionaries, one fourth of its peak force up to that time. Beginning in 1933 the retrenchment on the mission fields stopped, and the number of missionaries slowly rose until the close of the period.[8]

Meanwhile, the Home Mission Board also secured a new leader in J. B. Lawrence. He set the tone for Southern Baptists. When the creditors demanded the more than two and one-quarter million dollars, he faced them with honesty and integrity. They were sympathetic and offered to discount the debts in substantial amounts if the board would pay them promptly. His reply was, "We do not desire to receive a discount on our just debts. We will pay them in full. Just give us a little time and you will not lose one dollar." As the long depression decade of the 1930's approached its close, the integrity of Lawrence and Southern Baptists had

---

[6] *Annual*, 1930, 100.
[7] Rutledge, *Mission to America*, 56.
[8] Cauthen, *Southern Baptist Foreign Missions*, 39-41.

been so demonstrated that the banks holding mortgages on their property were eager to refinance their loans at better interest rates and lift the mortgages promptly.[9] The debts were not finally paid until 1943, but the outbreak of war in late 1941 broke the strength of the depression period.

Of great importance also during these stressful times was the work of the Executive Committee. Its enlargement in 1927 came partly as a result of the evident need for effective leadership in financial matters and efficient operation. In 1929 the Executive Committee recommended a belt-tightening financial plan that greatly aided in conserving the fiscal resources of the Convention. Again in 1938 the Executive Committee proposed sweeping recommendations, embodying developments evolved during the darkest days of the depression, which aimed to acquaint the denomination with the business methods of the Convention and to maintain the highest efficiency in fiscal matters.[10]

Perhaps the most effective effort to meet the crisis of huge debts and mounting interest was the Baptist Hundred Thousand Club. There had been prior campaigns to raise funds, such as Honor Day, the Emergency Mission Relief Campaign, and the Crucible Service Campaign, and some of these had been effective. On April 12-13, 1933, the Executive Committee considered a number of plans for some practicable and continuing program to reduce the Convention's debts, and adopted the one proposed by Frank Tripp. It was approved by the Convention at Washington in 1933, and Tripp became the director of the movement. The plan was simple: each member of the Hundred Thousand Club pledged to give $1.00 per month over and about his regular gifts through his church.[11] Through the faithful efforts of these Baptists, the debt was retired in 1944.

## The Cooperative Program

A tension in the structure of the Southern Baptist Convention resulted from the continuance in 1845 of the old society plan financing benevolent work by promoting designated giving to particular benevolences. It was too much to expect that the grand denominational scope of the preamble to the constitution, as reflected in Article V, would be immediately grasped in a single historical act. The gulf between the

---

[9] *Annual*, 1942, 64-65.
[10] *Annual*, 1929, 73; and *Annual*, 1939, 41-43.
[11] *Annual*, 1933, 57.

society concept of supporting only *designated* benevolences and the fully developed convention program of financing *all* benevolences was too wide to leap in a single bound. To be consistent with the convention ideal, it would have been necessary in 1845 to abandon designated giving to particular benevolences and, instead, to provide undesignated financial support to the Convention, which should in turn foster all the benevolences the Convention might wish to promote. Such a radical break with the familiar and successful traditional financial pattern, however, was unthinkable. There was no hint in the minutes of the new Convention, in the denominational newspaper accounts, or in the several reminiscences by actors in the drama that any other form of financing was even suggested.

This society pattern of financing that was imbedded into a convention-type structure proved to have numerous weaknesses. For one thing, there was a critical need for better support of the benevolences promoted by the Convention; i.e., foreign and home missions. The demise of the Bible Board and the first Sunday School Board for lack of finances illustrated this problem. Secondly, at almost each session of the Convention it was recognized that there were many additional areas of service that needed to be penetrated but could not be because of financial stress. Finally, the collection of funds under the old society philosophy was completely haphazard. Once or twice a year a church would be visited by a representative of one of the benevolences and an offering for that particular benevolence would be taken. The whims of the people and of nature itself were involved: a lengthy rainy season in a particular area when benevolent offerings were being taken could almost eliminate these gifts. Under such a procedure, there could be no systematic planning either by the benevolent boards or the Convention itself. It became necessary, for example, for the two mission boards to borrow money from banks month by month in anticipation of receipts that might or might not come in a special campaign during the ensuing year. After the turn of the century, in particular, many resolutions were passed and numerous committees were appointed at Convention sessions to correct the situation.

The financial success of the Sunday School Board after 1891 provided some assistance to the beleaguered Convention, while the organization of the first Executive Committee in 1917 brought increased efficiency in the handling of funds that were secured; but it became desperately clear that better financial methods both in securing and in handling funds were imperatively needed. It took a crisis to bring a change; that crisis was the Seventy-five Million Campaign. Although it precipitated a financial crisis, this campaign was not simply a failure. For one thing, it marked a period of greatly expanded receipts which were put to good use. Frank E. Burkhalter wrote:

> It should be remembered that the campaign did raise $58,000,000 in cash for Baptist missionary, educational, and benevolent causes. This was several times what the same people were giving previous to the campaign. In five years state and associational missions received $9,900,785 from the campaign. Home missions received $6,622,725, as compared with only $8,188,730 in the preceding 74 years of its history. Foreign mission received $11,615,327, as compared with about $12,500,000 in the preceding 74 years. Seminaries, schools, and colleges received $16,087,942, or nearly as much as in all their years preceding.[12]

Furthermore, the campaign lifted the sights of the Baptist people concerning their potential in mission and stewardship. For the first time, the average Southern Baptist was called upon to make a significant gift to missions and education. In addition, the emphasis on "calling out the called," which accompanied this campaign, brought many vocational workers into active Christian service during this period. Finally, the experience gained from this campaign caused the Convention to confront seriously for the first time the ambivalence in their structure relative to finances, and turned them in a new direction. "Budget" became a large word; improved methods of enlistment and stewardship promotion were developed; and the Convention adopted a financial program designed to provide undesignated gifts "for eliciting, combining and directing the energies of the whole denomination in one sacred effort."

---

[12] Cox, ed., *Encyclopedia*, II, 1197.

The critical debt remaining from the Seventy-five Million Campaign forced the Convention to give immediate attention to financial methods. Studies of various sorts had been made and committees appointed for over a decade, but the combination of debt and depression in 1924 worked a change. A Conservation Commission had been named at the beginning of the Seventy-five Million Campaign to promote collection of campaign pledges. In 1923 a new Committee on Future Program was appointed to plan for the direction to be taken after the close of the campaign. M. E. Dodd was chairman of this committee and is generally considered the architect of what came to be known as the Cooperative Program. In 1924 this committee recommended that a simultaneous every-member canvass be made in every Baptist church in the South from November 30 to December 7, 1924, to cover budgeted denominational needs for 1925. An appeal was made for all Southern Baptists to adopt the biblical principles of stewardship and tithing, and systematic giving week-by-week, rather than to follow the older pattern of two huge financial campaigns each year for benevolent work.[13] In 1925 the committee recommended the adoption of this "Co-Operative Program" of Southern Baptists, urging

**M. E. Dodd, the architect of the Cooperative Program** (Photo courtesy of Southern Baptist Historical Library and Archives)

> that there be a general committee, with headquarters in Nashville, for the promotion of the Co-Operative Program, consisting of seventeen members chosen from the South at large, together with the general secretaries, state secretaries, secretary of Laymen's Movement, president and secretary and three members of the Women's Missionary Union, and presidents of the three Southwide educational institutions.[14]

This program was adopted, and J. E. Dillard was named chairman of the new commission, holding that office until his death. In 1927 the new structural form adopted by the Convention in 1917 (the Executive

---

[13] *Annual*, 1924, 65-68.
[14] *Annual*, 1925, 36.

Committee) and the improved financial program adopted in 1925 (the Cooperative Program) were combined. The Executive Committee was enlarged and given widely expanded duties: to prepare a detailed, combined budget for consideration by the Convention each year, to act as agent of the Convention to conclude all agreements with cooperating state agencies for handling southwide funds, to recommend percentages of southwide funds to be allocated to each cause or agency, and to serve in general as the fiscal agency of the Convention.[15] A Promotional Committee for raising funds sought in the annual budgets was named, but in 1929 its work was assumed by the Executive Committee.

Essentially the Cooperative Program involved the relationship between the Convention and the several state bodies related to the Convention. Each state body prepared a budget for the work of the following year, including its own financial needs and a proposed percentage for Convention needs. The percentage of distributable funds retained by the state and those sent to the Convention differed in each state. Some divided on a 50-50 basis, some on a 60-40 basis, and some (particularly in new areas) on a 75-25 basis- 75% for the state and 25% for the Convention.

> The Cooperative Program includes all distributable funds, all designated funds, and all special offerings, such as the Women's Missionary Union Lottie Moon Offering for foreign missions, the Annie Armstrong Offering for home missions, offering for state missions, etc. In reality, all funds received for any cause included in the Cooperative Program, whether they be distributable, designated, or special funds, belong to the Cooperative Program. Designated funds and special offerings for a cause cannot be divided. They must go according to the wish of the donor.[16]

The significance of the adoption of the Cooperative Program in 1925 resides in its correction of the ambivalence in the financial methods carried over from the society plan in 1845 and its exploiting of the genius of the convention-type program. The Cooperative Program brought the goal of the original constitution of 1845 closer to realization; i.e., the

---

[15] *Annual*, 1927, 12 ff.
[16] Cox, ed., *Encyclopedia*, I, 323.

formation of a body to carry on all types of benevolent work desired by its constituency. The old society type of designated financing only was replaced by one which allowed designation but provided support for all benevolences, whether popular or otherwise. By this plan, each state became an active participant in both fostering appeals for benevolent objects promoted by the Convention and in the financial well-being of the Convention itself. This fusion between the state programs and the Convention's activities brought a new denominational unity to Southern Baptists.

## A Confession of Faith

Until this time, Southern Baptists had never adopted a confession of faith. Baptists in the South had usually adhered to the 1742 Philadelphia Confession, gradually replacing it with the 1833 New Hampshire Confession which had been promoted throughout the South by the Northern Baptist Publication Society. This was about to change.[17]

After World War I, J. B Gambrell had taken the War Department to task for placing Baptist chaplains into the broad category of Protestants. The general consensus among Baptists, possibly as a result of the influence of Landmarkers, agreed that Baptists were a category apart from true Protestants. J. F. Love called for a committee of five to be appointed to prepare a fraternal address to other Christians who were of like mind and faith. The committee was chaired by E. Y. Mullins, and included L. R. Scarborough, who was fully involved in planning the Seventy-five Million Campaign, J. B. Gambrell, Z. T. Cody, and William Ellyson. Their work was completed in just a few months, but never adopted by the Convention.[18]

In 1920, Love and the Foreign Mission Board presented it as a statement of beliefs to be affirmed by foreign missionaries. It was accepted without comment as a part of the Foreign Mission Board report. At that same convention, J. C. White, a delegate from the Inter-Church Movement, was allowed to address the Convention, although there were strong feelings of opposition to the movement. After his address, J. B.

---

[17] H. Leon McBeth, *The Baptist Heritage: Four Centuries of Baptist Witness.* (Nashville: Broadman Press), 1987, 677.
[18] Jesse C. Fletcher, *The Southern Baptist Convention: A Sesquicentennial History.* (Nashville: Broadman & Holman), 1994, 135.

Gambrell met him at the podium and said, "Baptists do not have pope. They never put anybody where they can't put him down...and another thing: Baptists never ride a horse without a bridle."[19]

In 1922, a joint meeting was held between representatives of the Northern and Southern Conventions to explore the possibility of issuing a joint confession of faith. Despite strong support from both sides, the idea was rejected. The largest opposition to the joint statement was in the anti-creedal northern majority.[20]

Giving impetus to the adoption of a formal confession came in the form of J. Frank Norris, Pastor of Fort Worth's First Baptist Church and the primary leader of the Fundamentalist Movement. He had once been a strong SBC loyalist, but split from the convention over the Seventy-Five Million Campaign. He used his pulpit to rail against Southern Baptists for allegedly teaching biological evolution in their colleges, tolerating "modernistic" views of Scripture in their seminaries, and making an idol of the denomination in their churches.[21]

Despite President E. Y. Mullins' attempts to mollify critics, the battle continued to heat up. To make matters worse, the Education Association denied that the Bible could be taken literally. The 1924 meeting in Atlanta rejected a call for a binding doctrinal statement, but formed a committee to consider a statement related to the Baptist Faith and Message. The committee was chaired by Mullins. They rejected Southern Seminary's Abstract of Principles, referred to the Foreign Mission Board's 1919 Statement of Beliefs, but ultimately adapted the 1833 New Hampshire Confession of Faith with some additions.[22] There was an attempt to include an article concerning evolution, but that effort failed.[23]

The 1925 confession was met with almost total silence, although people were found on both sides. Some people felt there was nothing wrong with it; there simply was no reason for it. Others felt that adopting it was the first step on the road to creedalism. They also felt that it would turn Baptist attention away from the Bible to human doctrinal statements.

---

[19] Reported in Fletcher, *The Southern Baptist Convention*, 136.
[20] Ibid., 141.
[21] McBeth, *The Baptist Heritage,* 677.
[22] Fletcher, *The Southern Baptist Convention*, 142.
[23] Ibid., 678.

²⁴ The 1925 confession would be revised in 1963 as a result of events surrounding the Elliot Controversy, which will be discussed in the next chapter.

## The Commissions

Leon McBeth pointed out that for reasons that are unclear, the Convention has chosen to call its smaller agencies *commissions* rather than *boards*. While they have the same relationship to the Convention as the boards, and they are funded in the same manner, they are smaller and more specific in their scope. Initially, all but two of the commissions were located in Nashville; the Brotherhood Commission was located in Memphis, and the Radio and Television Commission was located in Fort Worth, Texas.

**Education Commission.** While Southern Baptists had supported Southern Baptist Theological Seminary over the years, some of the controversies at that school, including the incident over firing of C. H. Toy, and later the firing of William Whitsitt, encouraged Baptists in the Southwest to consider the formation of their own seminary. Almost entirely due to the efforts of B. H. Carroll, Southwestern Baptist Theological Seminary was formed in 1908. [25]

At its formation, Southwestern pioneered four areas in theological training among Southern Baptists. First, it accepted women in all courses of study and degree programs on equal terms with the men. It was a co-ed institution with twenty-six women enrolling during its first year. Second, it focused on training the laity for Christian service instead of training only vocational clergy. Third, it pioneered a Religious Education department with the hiring of J. M. Price in 1915. Fourth, it pioneered the field of church music, which began that same year with the hiring of I. E. Reynolds. [26]

It was against this backdrop that while states had their own colleges, there was a need for more coordination and planning. The Education Commission was formed in 1915, and the new Commission promptly launched plans to raise fifteen million dollars for Baptist schools. This was eventually expanded and taken in as a part of the Seventy-Five

---

[24] Ibid., 678
[25] Fletcher, *The Southern Baptist Convention*, 115.
[26] Ibid., 118.

Million Campaign. The Commission was raised to Board status in 1918, but when the Seventy-Five Million Campaign failed, finances were in disarray and the Education Board was abolished in 1928. It was restored in 1931, and reorganized in 1951.[27] It continued to function until it was abolished in 1997.[28]

Related to the Education Commission was the formation of a training school for ministers in New Orleans. The idea was posed in 1914 by P. I. Lipsey, editor of the Mississippi *Baptist Record*. The idea had come up previously, but no action had been taken, especially in light of the fact that Southwestern Baptist Theological Seminary had been established.[29]

In 1915, a feasibility committee was established with participation by the Home Mission Board, and the Louisiana and Mississippi state conventions. In 1917, the Convention instructed the Sunday School and Home Mission Boards to cooperate in establishing a Baptist missionary training school in New Orleans.[30]

This school would be distinctive from the two established seminaries. While one focused on producing an educated ministry, and the newer of the seminaries focused on training preachers, the new Bible Institute was to have a missions motif. The school began holding classes in 1918. In 1925, the Baptist Bible Institute came under the full ownership of the Southern Baptist Convention. In that same year, Southwestern Seminary was ceded to the Convention by Texas Baptists. The New Orleans school became New Orleans Baptist Theological Seminary in 1946.[31]

**Southern Baptist Commission on the American Baptist Theological Seminary.** Early in the twentieth century, it was apparent that black Baptists in the south needed theological training to supplement that which they received in the black colleges. The National Baptists had committed themselves to the formation of a seminary for this purpose and, in 1913, the Convention approved a proposal by E. Y Mullins to appoint a

---

[27] McBeth, *The Baptist Heritage*, 653.
[28] http://www.sbcec.net/legal/OMRevisions.asp
[29] Fletcher, *The Southern Baptist Convention*, 129.
[30] Ibid. 130.
[31] Ibid.

committee to work with them. In 1914, Southern Baptists voted to raise fifty thousand dollars toward the establishment of such a school.[32]

After many delays and a split in the National Baptist Convention, the American Baptist Seminary finally opened in 1924 and was located in Nashville.[33] Southern Baptists continued to support the seminary until the following motion was made in 1995:

> WHEREAS, Since 1924, the Southern Baptist Convention has, along with the National Baptist Convention, U.S.A., Inc., jointly supported The American Baptist Theological Seminary; and
>
> W H E R E A S , In the years since 1924, America has moved from a racially segregated society and an era of white patronage of black institutions to a time when the colleges and seminaries of Southern Baptist general bodies are open to all who would study there without regard to race, and to a time when the undergraduate programs of the denomination's colleges and seminaries are equipped to provide African-Americans who have been called to the ministry of Jesus Christ with the preparation prerequisite to seminary training; and
>
> W H E R E A S, Leaders of the National Baptist Convention, U.S.A., Inc., have expressed an interest in assuming full responsibility for selecting trustees to govern the Seminary;
>
> Now, Therefore be it enacted that:
>
> 1. The Southern Baptist Convention surrenders all its rights in regard to The American Baptist Theological Seminary, including any rights it may have to participate in the governance of the Seminary and any rights to the property of The American Baptist Theological Seminary.
>
> 2. The amendments to the charter of The American Baptist Theological Seminary adopted by the Seminary's board of trustees on May 5, 1995, are approved.
>
> 3. The Southern Baptist Commission on The American Baptist Theological Seminary shall be dissolved, subject to

---

[32] *Annual*, 1914, 27.
[33] McBeth, *The Baptist Heritage*, 654.

approval of the dissolution by the 1996 Southern Baptist Convention.[34]

**The Brotherhood Commission.** Women have been very effective in focusing attention on missions, and their success led men to have a desire for a similar agency. In 1907 the Laymen's Missionary Movement was begun and it continued under that name until 1926, when it was called the Baptist Brotherhood of the South. In 1950, it became the Brotherhood Commission. Since 1936 its headquarters became Memphis, Tennessee and remained there until the agency was absorbed into the North American Mission Board (NAMB).

The original purpose of the movement was to involve men in the support of missions. Over the years, it assumed other purposes, eventually leading to a blurring of the actual purpose of the organization. In 1954, the Royal Ambassadors was transferred from the WMU to the Brotherhood.[35]

Royal Ambassadors did not enjoy the success under the sponsorship of the Brotherhood that it did under the WMU. They gradually shifted their emphasis from missions education and gave more attention to crafts, camping, outings, and other activities. The organization was discontinued in 1997 as a result of the 1995 vote by the Convention.[36] Its work was absorbed by NAMB and the men's group was renamed simply Baptist Men.[37] Men of the convention seem to have placed more emphasis in recent years to activities such as disaster relief. They have excelled in this regard, making the Southern Baptist Disaster Relief teams easily identifiable nationwide.

**The Social Service Commission.** The temperance movement had been active for a number of years in Baptist life, but in 1908 a standing Temperance Committee was established. Southern Baptists eventually became a strong voice in bringing about the national prohibition of alcoholic beverages.[38]

---

[34] *Annual*, 1995, 294,
[35] McBeth, *The Baptist Heritage*, 657.
[36] Ibid.
[37] http://www.sbcec.net/legal/OMRevisions.asp
[38] McBeth, *The Baptist Heritage*, 656.

By 1913, many leaders began to see the value in bringing pressure from the Convention to bring about social change. In 1914, the Social Service Commission was formed, but most of its attention was devoted to continuing the work of the Temperance Committee. Many of the more progressive members were eventually dropped from the committee, silencing them on many of the reform issues, but they continued to speak out on alcohol abuse and lynching.[39]

In 1947 the Commission was strengthened and a full-time director was employed. The name was later changed to the Christian Life Commission (CLC). In the 1960s, they were assigned two primary functions; they were to assist churches in understanding the moral demands of the gospel and to help Southern Baptists apply Christian principles to moral and social problems.[40] This will be discussed further in a subsequent chapter.

## Relief and Annuity Board

Southern Baptists did not keep pace with other denominations when it came to providing some sort of pension for ministers. During the early days of the denomination, many ministers received no stated salary, although churches generally provided some sort of support. Churches simply felt no sense of responsibility in this regard. This is not because they did not care; in the nineteenth century, there was simply no concept of retirement. People worked all of their lives or until they were forced to cease their labors due to disability. Ministers were no different from the general population in this regard.[41]

The Foreign Mission Board's policy developed over the years. From the 1850s, it had a harsh policy, but was more benevolent in its practice. In 1859, it had indicated in response to a question as to what the duty of the Board was regarding its support of returned missionaries who were unable to return to the field. The response of the missions entity was that the Board bore no obligation toward them any more than an employer who paid someone to labor for a salary. However, they softened that policy

---

[39] Ibid.
[40] Ibid.
[41] Ibid, 650.

by agreeing that a missionary who lost his health in service should be entitled to some sort of financial support.[42]

By 1914 a Nashville pastor, William Lunsford, became deeply concerned about the plight of ministers who had labored selflessly in a lifetime of service to end their days in abject poverty. Convinced that this was in itself immoral, he presented this to the Nashville Pastor's Conference in 1916. Since he served with several other pastors on the Sunday School Board, he was successful in getting a hearing. He was able to persuade the Baptist Sunday School Board to set aside $100,000 for ministerial relief and in 1917 the Southern Baptist Convention appointed a commission to study the matter. In 1918, the group presented a report to the Convention that a Board of Ministerial Relief and Annuities be established, with their headquarters in Birmingham, Alabama. The Convention approved the report with one change: the headquarters was to be located in Dallas, Texas. This was possibly in response to the fact that the Education Board was located in Birmingham, and this would be the first agency located west of the Mississippi River.[43]

Not surprisingly, William Lunsford was elected as the first secretary and he served in that position until 1927. As early as 1923, the Board had assets of $1,490,193.59.[44]

## The Great Depression

It was in the context of an economic depression that Austin Crouch accepted his new leadership role at the Executive Committee. In September 1930, Southern Baptists were struggling so badly that L. R. Scarborough, President of Southwestern Baptist Theological Seminary, broken-heartedly reported that it appeared that the seminary must close. He reported that faculty members had gone unpaid and there was no money to even pay expenses. Offering his resignation, he stated that he believed the seminary property would need to be sold off so that the debts could be paid.[45]

After a stunned silence, Southern Seminary president, John R. Sampey stated that Southern Seminary had some money as a result of

---

[42] Ibid.
[43] Fletcher, *The Southern Baptist Convention*, 131.
[44] Ibid.
[45] Fletcher, *The Southern Baptist Convention*, 156.

endowment and that they could meet their expenses. In an unparalleled statement of generosity he said, "I move that Southern Seminary's apportionment be cut and the difference given to Southwestern."[46] Even though the problems continued, that act probably kept Southwestern from closing its doors.

The struggle was just as severe at the Foreign Mission Board. It was reported in 1927 that their treasurer, G. N. Sanders, had embezzled a little over $103,000. As they struggled to recover financially from this defalcation, their leader, J. F. Love died from exhaustion in May of 1928. In 1929, one of Love's associates, T. B. Ray took over as leader of the struggling Board.[47]

In the three years prior, eighty-two overseas missionaries had resigned from service and nine others had died. Even though only twelve new missionaries were appointed, the Board continued to incur greater debt, receive fewer gifts, and face a dismal future. Then in October 1931, Ray was asked to step down as executive secretary and again accept a staff assignment.[48]

After nearly a year, Charles E. Maddry agreed to accept the position. He was a graduate of Southern Seminary, had served as a pastor, as the general secretary of Baptists in North Carolina, and had served as executive secretary of a special promotion committee to help with the Cooperative Program. He began in January 1933. It took until 1936 before they could resume more normal operations and Maddry began reorganizing the functioning of the Foreign Mission Board.[49]

J. B. Lawrence was dealing with very similar issues at the Home Mission Board. They had always lagged behind the Foreign Mission Board, as a result of early fierce competition from the American Baptists' Home Missionary Society, a lack of good leadership in its early years, and a lack of clarity in its roles. After it reorganized under the capable leadership of I. T. Tichenor, the man credited with saving the Home Mission Board, it finally began to turn around. Then, with the embezzlement of nearly a million dollars by Clinton Carnes, the treasurer, combined with other debts, the Home Mission Board found itself with a

---

[46] Reported in Fletcher, *The Southern Baptist Convention*. 156.
[47] Ibid.
[48] Ibid.
[49] Ibid.

debt totaling approximately $2.5 million. Nevertheless, in spite of the obstacles, Lawrence served as chief executive of the Home Mission Board for a quarter of a century and fought resolutely to restore integrity at the Board.[50]

The missionary force fell to 106 in 1930 before the long, slow recovery could begin. By 1936, even with Cooperative Program giving down, Lawrence had been able to demonstrate Southern Baptists' commitment to evangelism by reestablishing the Department of Evangelism.[51]

Even with the nation struggling through the depression, Southern Baptists continued to persist in their efforts. In 1925, money given by Southern Baptists reached $39 million. They fell to $32,000,600 in 1930, and then fell to $29,000,188 in 1935. On the other hand, membership had grown from 3.6 million members in 1925 to 4.3 million in 1935. However, it is possible that some people were counted more than once as members moved west in search of work. There would have been a reluctance to drop someone from the membership rolls of their original church, even though they had left town.[52]

While Southern Baptists were blessed to have strong leaders such as Austin Crouch at the Executive Committee, J. B. Lawrence at the Home Mission Board, and Charles E. Maddry at the Foreign Mission Board, in 1935, I. J. Van Ness stepped down as the head of the Baptist Sunday School Board (BSSB).

The Sunday School Board was a late-comer to Southern Baptist life. Founded in 1891 with J. M. Frost at the head, many people thought it would be impossible to persuade Southern Baptists to support a Sunday School. In 1901, Frost wisely hired Bernard W. Spilman as its first "field worker." He visited countless churches, convincing them to form Sunday Schools, adopt more uniform standards, and persuaded them to use BSSB literature. In doing so, he helped tie them securely to the denomination.[53]

One book that has helped shape the Southern Baptist version of the Sunday School more than any other is Arthur Flake's *Building a Standard Sunday School* (1919). Flake had been an active layman in

---

[50] Ibid., 148.
[51] Ibid., 158.
[52] Ibid., 161.
[53] McBeth, *The Baptist Heritage*, 645.

Sunday School before joining the staff of the Sunday School Board. His famous "Flake's Formula for Sunday School Success" has become almost legendary among Southern Baptists, even being taught in the seminaries as late as the 1980s.[54]

The formula was surprising in its simplicity, yet proven in its success. It had five simple points: (1) discover prospects, (2) organize to reach the people, (3) enlist and train workers, (4) provide space, and (5) visit and enlist the prospects. Flake insisted that outreach and evangelism ranked as legitimate purposes, adding "reach" to the purpose of "teach" to Sunday School's purpose.[55]

Primarily due to the strength of Sunday Schools in the churches, the Sunday School Board had managed to remain in the black during the dark years of the depression. Another factor is probably because much of what was published was ordered in advance. Also, the BSSB did not continue to print new materials in hopes that the old materials would soon be sold. They operated primarily on a supply and demand basis as any other business would. Additionally, they were selling their items for a profit, an advantage other Southern Baptist boards and agencies did not have.

Arthur Flake, a Baptist layman who joined the Sunday School Board and revolutionized the concept of Sunday School growth. (Photo courtesy of Southern Baptist Historical Library and Archives)

When I. J. Van Ness retired in 1935, even though the BSSB was stronger than ever, Van Ness's latter years were marred by a power struggle with W. F. Powell, pastor of First Baptist Church, Nashville, and chairman of the elected Board. Even so, it was during Van Ness's tenure that the Sunday School Board took over responsibility for the Baptist Young People's Union, assumed the retreat property of Ridgecrest, North Carolina, and helped innumerable times with the needs of both of the missionary boards.[56]

---

[54] The author studied Flake's Formula while a student at New Orleans Baptist Theological Seminary. The author cannot say from direct experience whether it continued to be taught beyond that point, but there is no reason to think it would be quickly discarded.
[55] McBeth, *The Baptist Heritage*, 645.
[56] Fletcher, *The Southern Baptist Convention*, 162.

As Van Ness retired, Thomas Luther Holcomb took the reins. Standing just over five feet tall, he was not short on experience leading large organizations. He had served as pastor of First Baptist Church of Oklahoma City and a member of the Sunday School Board at the time he was elected.[57]

Quickly establishing himself as the person in charge, he soon hit the road as no one had since J. M. Frost had done in his first year of service. He soon established a five-year plan which would culminate in 1941 to coincide with the Board's fiftieth anniversary. He promoted his plan and the Board utilizing associations and volunteer workers.[58]

At the end of his five year plan, Southern Baptists had added 1,839 new Sunday Schools, as well as two thousand new training unions. This had a significant impact on the publishing revenues, so that even in the depression era, the Sunday School Board was able to produce dramatic results.[59]

**I. J. Van Ness, former head of the Sunday School Board**
(Photo courtesy of Southern Baptist Historical Library and Archives)

---

[57] Ibid.
[58] Ibid. 163.
[59] Ibid.

# Chapter 14 - The Influence of Liberalism: From World War II to 1960

In this period of the story of Southern Baptist life, the Convention faced problems and tensions of a magnitude and an intensity never before experienced in its history. More than ever before Southern Baptists interacted explicitly with the political, social, economic, and ecclesiological currents about them. These currents have been very complex, and as always, Southern Baptists did not present a unified response to them. As a result, many of the issues have been divisive, a few of them have been critical, and some of them have been fruitless.

Practically every writer has described the years since 1942 as revolutionary. Perhaps this era commenced when the first atomic bomb was dropped on Hiroshima on August 6, 1945, to bring a rapid end to World War II. It has been characterized by the extensive growth of disaffection and cynicism toward authority; the eroding of traditional moral and social restraints; violent confrontations to correct real or fancied wrongs, end wars, stop discrimination, diminish pollution, and air many other grievances; the impassioned search for identity; and the development of remarkable scientific and medical exploits, ranging from putting a man on the moon to the transplanting of human hearts. Editorials in Baptist newspapers and even references in *Annuals* of the Southern Baptist Convention to the fast-moving events of these three decades testified that Southern Baptists in the modern era were no longer isolated from the most secular aspects of daily living. Less than a century before, the Convention had refused even to hear a resolution on temperance in one of its sessions.[60] Now it interacted with almost everything. World War II (1941-45), the Korean War (1950-53), and the war in Southeast Asia (about 1964-73) affected the enrollment in the auxiliaries of the Convention and involved moral questions that Southern Baptists discussed extensively. They reacted to the formation of the United Nations in 1945; to the cold war

---

[60]Barnes, *The Southern Baptist Convention*, 246.

with the Soviet Union after President Truman enunciated his position in 1947; to the appointment by Truman of a personal ambassador to the Vatican, the formation of the National Council of Churches, the renaming of northern Baptists (the American Baptist Convention), the declaration of the dogma on the assumption of Mary in 1950, and the somber take-over of China by Communists in the same year; to the accelerating racial struggles of the 1950's and 1960's; to the launching of the first Soviet satellite to inaugurate the space race in 1957; to the Bay of Pigs fiasco by President Kennedy in 1961, and the war scare of 1962 when the Soviets were forced to withdraw their missiles from Cuba; to the terrible assassinations of the two Kennedys and Martin Luther King, Jr.; to the runaway inflation of the 1960's; and to the political scandals of the early 1970's.

Meanwhile, the Convention instituted challenging programs of advance for its constituency. Due to the exigencies of war, Convention sessions in 1943 and 1945 were not held. A generous offering for world relief was promoted in 1946; simultaneous evangelistic campaigns were held in 1950 west of the Mississippi River, and in the following year, east of the river; a Jubilee Advance was promoted between 1959 and 1964 in cooperation with other Baptist groups in America, commemorating the 150th anniversary of the first Baptist general body in America; participation in a North American Baptist Fellowship was begun in 1965; and in that same year approval was given to the Crusades of the Americas, a movement involving fellowship and joint evangelistic efforts by Baptists of North, Central, and South America with a widespread evangelistic thrust in 1969. The principal areas of Convention preoccupation during this period, however, involved its continuing growth; its expanded geographical base to include all of the United States; its vexing controversies; and its intensive study of its own structure as a means of providing a better vehicle for achieving its goals.

When the world became fully involved in what has become known as World War II, the economic depression finally came to an end, but other changes began to take place in society. These had a profound impact on Southern Baptist life. World War I had introduced mechanized warfare to the world, but World War II took it to a new level. Soon, the influences of war would carry over into every aspect of life.

As a result of the high demand for manpower to fill the swelling military force, men left their jobs in the factories, on the farms, and pulpits to don the uniforms of the armed services. Many, either because of age or physical condition, remained at home. However, the number of men who remained behind was not sufficient to produce the number of tanks, airplanes, jeeps, and guns that were in higher demand than ever before. Women now stepped out of the home and into the factories to fill roles that had previously been open to only men. This, in itself, was to have a long-lasting impact on society and the church.

## Sociological Changes

**Women's Issues.** Women have long been on the cutting edge of Southern Baptist life. Women began some of the early missionary societies in the United States. Later, women in southern Baptist churches pooled their butter and egg money in order to finance missionary work at home and abroad. Later, Edmonia and Charlotte (Lottie) Moon had to work hard to persuade the Foreign Mission Board to let them, single women, serve as career missionaries. Even after Edmonia had to return to the States due to poor health, Lottie remained on the field working faithfully, even to her own deteriorating health. Ultimately, there was no question of women's faithfulness or ability to serve the Lord, even overseas as missionaries.

In 1885, the issue came up as to whether or not women should be allowed to vote as members of the Southern Baptist Convention. The argument was made that the Convention's Constitution Article 3 stated that the Convention was made up of members of Southern Baptist churches. Apparently, the question had come up that since women were members, should they not be allowed to participate in deliberations and to vote?

The following was offered by J. W. Jones, Virginia:

Whereas, There has arisen some question as to the eligibility of women to seats as delegates in this Convention; therefore be it

> Resolved, That this whole question be transferred to a committee of one from each State to report to this meeting of the Convention such action as may be deemed expedient.[61]

On the fourth day of the Convention, the final item of business in the morning session was the report back from this committee:

> J. W. Jones, Virginia, from the committee, reported the following on
>
> ### FEMALE REPRESENTATON
>
> Your committee, to whom was referred the whole question of the eligibility of women to seats as delegates in this body, have considered the matter, and have unanimously agreed to the following:
>
> As some doubt has arisen to the proper construction of the Constitution, we recommend the following amendment: In Art. 3 of the Constitution strike out the word "members," in the first line, and insert instead thereof the word "brethren."[62]

The report was adopted by a vote of 131 in the affirmative and 42 in the negative. It went in to effect immediately, as the Constitution which is contained in the opening pages of the Annual, contained the word, "brethren."[63]

In all likelihood, it was a response to this that led women to meet in Richmond, Virginia in 1888 and organize the Women's Missionary Union (WMU) as an auxiliary to the Southern Baptist Convention. By existing as an auxiliary, they are affiliated with the Convention, but are not controlled by it and are completely self-governing.[64] Among the organizers of the WMU was Annie Armstrong of Maryland, who was elected as the first Corresponding Secretary. The WMU was established on May 14, 1888 with its offices located in Baltimore, Maryland.[65] The

---

[61] Annual, 1885, 14.
[62] Ibid., 30.
[63] Ibid., 3.
[64] Interestingly enough, even though they exist at the national level as an Auxiliary and receive no funding from the Convention, they operate as a part of many state conventions and receive funding from them at the state level.
[65] Fletcher, *The Southern Baptist Convention*, 95.

offices were relocated to Birmingham, Alabama in 1921 when the WMU decided it wanted a more "central location."[66]

Jesse Fletcher is probably correct in his assessment that Southern Baptist missions would not have enjoyed the level of progress that they had were it not for the efforts of the women's organization. The WMU remained focused on its passion for calling churches back to what it felt was its fundamental task: missions. While the organization never intended to send missionaries itself, it would remain independent and free to function according to their own stated priorities.[67]

It was the WMU that supported H. A. Tupper in adopting a special offering to relieve Lottie Moon for one year. The offering which became an annual affair and was named for Lottie Moon, was championed by Recording Secretary Annie Armstrong.

With the advent of World War II, women contributed to the war effort by filling roles that previously had been limited to men. After the war, many men returned home to find their wives working. Other wives, widowed by the war, now found themselves as the sole means of financial support for their families. Also, many of the men returned from the war with emotional scars that they did not feel at liberty to discuss. A great many of these found solace in alcohol, or in extramarital relationships or otherwise abusive relationships.

Socially, divorce was still considered a scandalous occurrence, mentioned only in whispered tones. Yet, it is hard to imagine that the consideration of such extreme actions did not enter into the minds of these women, many of whom had learned to provide for their families in non-traditional roles.

**Racial Issues.** Southern Baptists, like all denominations, did little about unsophisticated discrimination against blacks before World War II. David Reimers remarked that until then "the basic approach of Protestantism to a solution to the race problem still consisted of evangelism and Negro education."[68] The many "pronouncements" on race relations by the several denominations in the 1930's were relatively

---

[66] McBeth, *The Baptist Heritage*, 662.
[67] Fletcher, *The Southern Baptist Convention*, 95.
[68] David Reimers, *White Protestantism and the Negro* (New York: Oxford University Press, 1965), 95.

harmless.[69] Reimers counted the resolution adopted in March, 1946, by the Federal Council of Churches of Christ as being a major step toward confronting the evils of racial discrimination. Segregation was denounced as unnecessary and undesirable and a violation of the gospel of love and human brotherhood. In Reimers' words, this was

> the first time in history of American Protestantism that a major interdenominational group committed itself to fight the traditional practices of racism, practices that had existed since colonial times.[70]

The initial thrusts toward Southern Baptist participation in this spirit were spearheaded by the Christian Life Commission, referred to during the previous period. When the Supreme Court declared in 1954 that segregation of the races was unconstitutional, the Southern Baptist Convention under the leadership of its Christian Life Commission adopted a resolution reading in part as follows:

> 1. That we recognize that fact that this Supreme Court decision is in harmony with the constitutional guarantee of equal freedom to all citizens, and with the Christian principles of equal justice and love for all men.
>
> . . . . . .
>
> 5. That we urge Christian statesmen and leaders in our churches to use their leadership in positive thought and planning to the end that this crisis in our national history shall not be made the occasion for new bitter prejudices, but a movement toward a united nation embodying and proclaiming a democracy that will commend freedom to all peoples.[71]

Despite vigorous attempts during the following several years to hobble the active efforts of the Christian Life Commission to implement this resolution, Southern Baptists made progress toward overcoming attitudes and customs held for more than a century.

---

[69] Ibid., 96.
[70] Ibid., 112-13.
[71] *Annual*, Southern Baptist Convention, 1954, 56.

## Ecclesiological Struggles

Since the earliest cries for separation of church and state by Baptists in England and the United States, the perplexing question continually has come—how separate can they be? A survey of the *report from the Capital*, the informative news bulletin of the Baptist Joint Committee on Public Affairs, reveals the amazingly complex extensive nature of church-state tensions. Among items involved since 1956 were the authority of school boards to prescribe or require prayer or devotions; the power of military leaders to prescribe worship and require attendance; tax exemption for houses of worship as a judicial issue; tax support for religious elementary and secondary schools; college dormitory loans to religious institutions from government credit agencies; loans to college students in religious institutions from public funds; the use of Peace Corps personnel in religious schools in foreign nations; exports of surplus food to feed needy populations; government food surpluses given to church youth camps; federal and state hospital grants for religiously owned hospitals; religious texts for public office and for candidates; and government rehabilitation contacts with church-related agencies.[72] The controversy over prayer in public schools (with many influential Southern Baptists on both sides of the issue) was particularly long and painful. Similarly, on the issue of federal aid to Baptist institutions, important Baptist names were found in each party to the discussion. Some state Baptist bodies refused to grant permission for their colleges to receive federal grants or loans, while others permitted this. Several hospitals were released from state convention control to permit them to accept such grants. The Southern Baptist Convention was affected by these developments, and in 1970 and 1971 two consecutive sessions voted to release the two hospitals at New Orleans, Louisiana, and Jacksonville, Florida, from Convention control and operation.[73]

One of the most perilous areas of church-state relations in its far-reaching significance for Southern Baptist life concerned decisions made by state courts in litigation over church property. The earliest state courts in the United States were forced to pioneer in litigation of this ort, since

---

[72] Cox-Woolley, eds., *Encyclopedia*, III, 1926.
[73] For the specific actions in 1970 and 1971, see *Annual*, Southern Baptist Convention, 1970, 65-66; and ibid., 1971, 55.

the principle of separation of church and state in the new nation confounded most precedents. The problem was twofold. First, in view of the principle of separation of church and state, to what extent do courts have jurisdiction to some degree, what legal principle would apply to assure equity to the widely differing systems of ecclesiastical government found in American religious life?

Considerable care was given to the answer of the first question. The position finally established has been summed up the Supreme Court of North Carolina, as follows:

> The legal or temporal tribunals of the State have no jurisdiction over, and no concern with, purely ecclesiastical questions and controversies, for there is a constitutional guarantee of freedom of religious profession and worship, as well as an equally firmly established separation of church and state, but the courts do have jurisdiction, as to civil, contract and property rights which are involved in, or arise from, a church controversy.... This principle may be tersely expressed by saying religious societies have double aspects, the one spiritual, with which legal courts have no concern, and the other temporal, which is subject to judicial control.[74]

The second problem involving the equitable principle of adjudication was given a forthright answer. In order to deal fairly with the various types of church government involved (from Roman Catholicism with its rigid episcopal control, to Quakers with practically none), it was determined that each religious denomination be a law to itself. Thus, in cases involving the Roman Catholic Church the secular courts would attempt to apply the principles of that Church to the litigation at hand. Were a Congregational church involved in litigation, Congregational ecclesiology would be followed. Examples of this may be seen in the case of Father Francis Fromm in the Fifth Circuit Court of Pennsylvania in 1798, where Roman Catholic principles were used to determine the verdict, and the famous Dedham case of 1820 in Massachusetts, where the Supreme Court followed the ecclesiology of the Congregational churches.

---

[74]Supreme Court of North Carolina, *Reid v. Johnston*, 241 N. C. 201, 85 S. E. 2d 1114 (1954).

The development of these basic principles did not automatically solve the problem of the proper decision in church litigation. In addition to determining the facts in a controversy, it became necessary for a court to distinguish the dominant ecclesiological factor of the particular denomination involved in the litigation. In Baptist life this was not easy. What is the unifying or dominant principle of Baptist life—majority rule by the congregation, or is it adherence to traditional Baptist doctrine?

One of the first legal cases of this sort among American Baptists pointed to the Baptist doctrine as the distinctive element in a Baptist church, taking precedence even over majority rule. In 1781 the First Baptist Church of Philadelphia was involved in a bitter controversy. Because of the shortage of Baptist ministers in America, the church had extended a call to Elhanan Winchester to become its pastor without first investigating his theological views. After assuming his office, Winchester began preaching the doctrines of Universalism which, to say the least, the Baptists in the church believed were detrimental to the dignity and work of Jesus Christ. The leaders in the church were troubled, but many people flocked to hear Winchester and throngs joined the church under his preaching.

In a long address, the church appealed to other Baptist churches to stand by it. The language was vigorous.

> The method taken by him, at first, to propagate this wicked tenent [sic], was by "creeping into houses, and leading captive persons of weak capacities" wherein he met with too much encouragement. Alarmed at this authenticated report, he was, at different times, privately conversed with on the subject, by several of the members;—he did not presume to contradict it fully, and yet his confession was, by no means, satisfactory. Upon these occasions he would frequently intimate his intention of *going away*, provided the smallest division took place on his account; while at the same juncture, as opportunity served, he failed not to use argument in order to gain proselytes. Such conduct gave an early disgust to several, who, leaving their seats among us, went elsewhere to worship God.... Ruin began to stare us in the face! Hereupon many of the brethren, in a church capacity, called upon Mr. Winchester; and, with affectionate concern, intreated [sic]

him, in case he held so dangerous a sentiment, by no means to promulgate it as it was totally repugnant to our principles: He acknowledged his holding the sentiment, but promised he would not advance it in public, without the church's approbation. Contrary to *their* expectation [sic], and *his* verbal engagement, he not long after, at different times and sundry places, spake openly and explicitly thereupon, to the grief of some and injury of others, as numbers can testify.[75]

Finally, the deacons of the church demanded that Winchester resign for preaching false doctrine. He declined. When the quarrel was brought before the church in conference, a majority sustained Winchester. It appeared that the First Baptist Church of Philadelphia would now become the First Universalist Church of Philadelphia. Winchester, it should be said, was one of the founders of the Universalist movement in both America and England.

The Universalist majority began litigation to secure control of the church property, but on July 9, 1784, the court held for the Baptist minority on the ground that it was "the rightful church."[76] Subsequent decisions of various state courts established the principle that

> ...a majority in a Baptist church is supreme, or a "law unto itself," so long as it remains a Baptist church, or true to the fundamental usages, customs, doctrine, practice, and organization of Baptists. For instance, if a majority of a Baptist church should attempt to combine with a Methodist or Presbyterian church, or in any manner depart from the fundamental faiths, usages, and customs, which are distinctively Baptist, and which mark out that denomination as a separate entity from all others, then, in such case, the majority could not take the church property with them

---

[75] *Address from the Baptist Church in Philadelphia, to their Sister Churches of the Same Denomination, through the Confederated States of North America* (Philadelphia: Printed by Robert Atkin, at Pope's Head, 1781), np.

[76] See William W. Keen, ed., *The Bi-Centennial Celebration of the Founding of the First Baptist Church of the City of Philadelphia* (Philadelphia: American Baptist Publication Society, 1899), 66-69.

for the reason that they would not be acting in accordance with distinctively Baptist principles.[77]

In the Philadelphia decision one can glimpse the element of trust (which secular courts hold sacred). Baptist money and life had been put into this property. The court viewed the contending parties, not as majority or minority, but simply as corporate litigants. The decision was reached, not by counting the number on each side, but through determining which party could be identified with the undivided church before there was disagreement or schism. Since the minority remained Baptist and the majority adopted Universalist views, the property was awarded to the Baptist minority.

Thus, this early case suggested the principle that the unifying or dominant element in Baptist life is not majority rule but the continuity of Baptist doctrine. This principle had been followed regularly in many state courts. In fact, the Supreme Court of Illinois in the old case of *Ferraria v. Vasconcellos* ruled that those who abandon "the tenets and doctrines" of a given "denomination" forfeit their rights to the use of the property "although but a single member adhere to the original faith and doctrine of the church." Before the year 1900, Baptist litigation in Texas followed this principle regularly.[78]

However, there has been another point of view expressed by courts in various states concerning the unifying or dominant principle in Baptist life. Instead of viewing *Baptist doctrine* as the major principle in a Baptist church, they have held that *Baptist church government* should take precedence. In a denomination in which the church congregation is the governing authority, say proponents of this view, the majority always rules, regardless of the nature of the disagreement. Thus, if 100 members out of 150 in a Baptist church vote to change *anything*—affiliation, liturgy, even doctrine itself—there can be no legal recourse by the minority to secure property. This was the decision of the Supreme Court of Texas in 1900 in a case involving the First Baptist Church of Paris, Texas. The

---

[77] Supreme Court of North Carolina, *Dix v. Pruitt*, 192 N. C. 829, 135 S. E. 851 (1926).
[78] B. F. Fuller, *History of Texas Baptists* (Louisville: Baptist Book Concern, 1900), 431-466. See Supreme Court of Illinois, *Ferraria v. Vasconcelles* (sic) 23 Ill. 456 (1860); *Ferraria v. Vasconcellos*, 31 Ill. 25 (1863).

majority had abandoned the doctrines and practices of the undivided church, but secured the property on the ground that it was the majority and that this alone justified any action that might be taken. One Baptist historian in Texas wrote that the adoption of this principle was a great "menace" to all Baptist churches.[79]

This dual interpretation of Baptist life has continued in the decisions of various state courts. Some award property to the majority without giving recognition to the "faithful minority." Others probe the practices and doctrines of the undivided church to determine which part remained true to the doctrines and practices followed before disagreement and schism.

It is evident that the dual application of Baptist principles discussed heretofore does not in itself constitute any danger to the independence of Baptist churches. Whether the majority riles or the faithful minority remaining Baptist secures the property, both principle and equity support the verdict. When the majority rules, little needs to be said concerning church autonomy.

More problems are involved, however, in awarding the property to the faithful minority. The basic principle is equitable. If a majority in a Baptist church should turn to Presbyterian views, it appears reasonable that the true Baptists in the minority should retain the property which has been accumulated by Baptists through the years. But what shall be done in the case of a Baptist church which has a schism and *both sides*, majority and minority, remain Baptist? How much deviation from the practices of the undivided church constitutes ground for awarding the property to the minority? Even this question can be answered satisfactorily when there has been a *radical* break with the past by the majority; but what if the majority should remain distinctively Baptist and make only *mild* alterations in its program?

It is at this point that the danger of appealing to a secular court is apparent. The court ostensibly rules only on property matters; yet to arrive at that decision a secular court must sift the religious beliefs and practices of the two parties in a Baptist church and determine the most sensitive and vital point of Baptist life: the being or essence of a true Baptist church. This means that a secular judge must do something which even the wisest

---

[79] Fuller, *History of Texas Baptists*, 465.

Baptist, steeped in Baptist history and doctrine, could never do. He must decide which group in the schism constitutes the true church and which are "the Nicolaitans." The opening wedge comes in the adjudication of property rights; but property rights must necessarily involve the identification by a secular court of the true church.

One of the outstanding cases along this line involved the North Rocky Mount Baptist Church in North Carolina. On August 9, 1953, at a properly called business conference of the church, a vote was taken concerning whether to remain affiliated with the Southern Baptist Convention and its related state and associational bodies or to withdraw. A majority of 241 favored withdrawal under leadership of the pastor; 144 were opposed to withdrawal; while 200 abstained from voting. In a lengthy and bitter trial, both sides used various denominational leaders to testify about the "fundamental usages, customs, doctrine, practice, and organization of missionary Baptists." The superior court allowed this testimony and awarded the property to the minority. The majority appealed, insisting that withdrawal from the Southern Baptist Convention did not constitute any change in the fundamental usages, customs, doctrine, etc., of the church. The decision was upheld by the Supreme Court of North Carolina, but a significant emendation was made. In essence, the supreme court said that all denominational testimony was to be eliminated; that denominational affiliation or the lack of it was not the principal issue in the case; and that the decision to uphold the superior court was not based upon whether the North Rocky Mount Baptist Church remained in or withdrew from affiliation with the Southern Baptist Convention and its related bodies. The decision, it was said, rested only upon changes in the local church in fundamental usages, customs, doctrines, etc., *without reference to denominational affiliation and based solely upon testimony from the local body.* This was very significant clarification by able judges and followed the ancient and original principle.[80]

However, the very point emphasized in this North Carolina Supreme Court emendation has been ignored in other litigation. The First Baptist Church of Normal, Illinois, by majority vote, decided to leave the American Baptist Convention and join the Conservative Baptist

---

[80] *Reid v. Johnston.*

Association of America. The Circuit Court of McLean County held for the majority, but the Appellate Court of the Third District of Illinois reversed this decision and said: "Severing relations with the American Baptist Convention was a distinct departure from the doctrines, beliefs, and a practice theretofore followed by the congregation and appears to have been so understood by both groups."[81] A change in inter-Baptist denominational affiliation alone was the ground for awarding property to the minority.

In another case, the First Baptist Church of Wichita, Kansas, in March, 1960, voted 1,074 to 235 to withdraw from affiliation with the American Baptist Convention, the Kansas Baptist Convention, and the Wichita Association of Baptist Churches. The church gave no indication that it would affiliate with any other group thereafter. Ten members of the minority brought suit, but the district court held for the majority. The Supreme Court reversed this decision. Now, the fact of the reversal by the Supreme Court is in itself not a matter of concern, for, as pointed out previously, the minority has often been awarded the property in church litigation.

But the ground of the reversal was radical. Its principle can destroy voluntary cooperation by Baptist churches which cherish their independence. The Supreme Court quoted an earlier opinion that

> repudiation by the defendants of the national, state and local associations maintained by the churches of the Baptist faith constituted a departure from the original principles, rules and practices of church government recognized by the united body prior to the occurrence of any schism therein.[82]

The Supreme Court then added: "We hold that not even in an autonomous Baptist church may the denomination of the church be changed by a mere majority vote." It should be noted that there was no evidence that this majority group planned to affiliate with any other general body. Subsequently, however, the majority constituted itself a distinct congregation on August 12, 1962, and voted to cooperate with the Southern Baptist Convention on November 11, 1962. It is now known as

---

[81] *Sorrenson v. Logan*, 32 Ill. App. 2 d 294.
[82] Supreme Court of Kansas, *Huber v. Thorn*, 371 P2d 1943 (1962).

the Metropolitan Baptist Church. The withdrawal from a general body by a majority in a church evidently was considered grounds for awarding church property to the minority.

What does this decision mean? It means simply that in those states where this precedent is followed, the general denominational bodies (national, sectional, state, or district association) have an interest in the property of every Baptist church affiliated with them. Even a disavowal of this by the general bodies themselves (as is true in the constitution of the Kansas state body affiliated with the Southern Baptist Convention) probably could not, in the eyes of the courts, bind the minority in any local church. Denominational affiliation within Baptist ranks has replaced fundamental doctrines and practices of the undivided church as the criterion for awarding church property to the minority in cases where this precedent is followed. In essence, this decision robs an autonomous church of its autonomy.

## Enlarged Geographical Base

Along with this numerical increase has also come a startling geographical expansion by churches and other bodies affiliating with the Southern Baptist Convention. As described previously, the geographical base of the Southern Baptist Convention in 1845 was described as embracing "fourteen States, with an aggregate area of 955,664 square miles, and a population of about eight millions."[83] Between 1845 and 1942 (over ninety-five years), only six additional states were added to Convention affiliation—Arizona, California, Illinois, New Mexico, Oklahoma, and Texas. But in less than thirty years that followed, the Southern Baptist geographic base was expanded to include the other thirty states of the Union.

In the decade following the Second World War, three new Southern Baptist seminaries were established in California, North Carolina, and Missouri. During this period, Southwestern Seminary outgrew its older counterpart in Kentucky, and became the largest of the three previously existing seminaries. New Orleans was third in size, after Southern Seminary.[84]

---

[83]Baker, *Source Book*, 125-26.
[84] Fletcher, *The Southern Baptist Convention*, 193.

Golden Gate Baptist Theological Seminary began in the latter part of 1944 with the California Baptist Convention assuming responsibility for the institution the following year. In 1950 during the Southern Baptist Convention meeting in Chicago, the Convention voted to accept ownership and support of the seminary.[85] While the area has grown economically, the seminary has never grown significantly in size, even though it has expanded its programs.

In 1950, in addition to accepting ownership of Golden Gate Seminary, the Convention also recommended the establishment of the Southeastern Baptist Theological Seminary in Wake Forest, North Carolina. It became the first seminary that was begun by the Convention itself. Each of the other seminaries had been started by other entities and later accepted by the Convention. The seminary took over the facilities of old Wake Forest College when they moved to Winston Salem, North Carolina. Work began at Southeastern Seminary in 1951.

Southeastern's president, Sydnor Stealey, assembled a faculty that was, for the most part, trained at Southern Seminary. He was the son of C. P. Stealey, a loyal follower of J. Frank Norris and an active participant in the Fundamentalist movement. The younger Stealey, however, was not heir to his father's beliefs. In 1961 he warned that the Convention was moving too much toward a more conservative position. He thought that Southeastern Seminary should represent a more progressive environment. One of its early graduates was Edwin Young who would later be president of the Southern Baptist Convention and who would react against the school's liberal teachings. Young helped reshape the seminary in the 1990s.[86]

The Convention's assumption of ownership of Golden Gate Seminary and beginning Southeastern Seminary in 1950 seemed to demonstrate the Convention's commitment to providing seminaries in the geographical vicinity of churches that would use their students and graduates as pastors. As a result of a Convention study showing an increase in college students studying for the ministry, and with a perception of a growing need for seminary training in the western area of the Convention, a serious discussion took place with Central Baptist

---

[85] Ibid., 194.
[86] Ibid., 194-195.

Theological Seminary in Kansas City, Kansas. Central began as an independent school with a missional emphasis. When it aligned itself with the American Baptist Convention, a number of their Southern Baptist professors, trustees, and students left. In 1957, Southern Baptists voted to establish another seminary in the same city. Trustees were elected and Millard J. Berquist was appointed as the first president. The first professor hired by Berquist was Ralph. H. Elliott.[87]

## Structural Refinements

The historical summary of the agencies of the Convention in the next section of this chapter will describe most of the important changes and additions to the organizational structure, but a specific reference should be made to some of the basic conceptual patterns retained in the Convention structure during these years.

Increasingly the Executive Committee began to assume its power function, and it has become the organizational pivot of Southern Baptist Convention work. Mainly through its initiative, some procedural alterations have been made in the general structure: more laymen were included on the boards, commissions, and committees (1958, 1961); two consecutive Conventions must vote before an agency is discontinued or the constitution is altered (1960, 1963); and more careful supervision of registration and voting with computer cards were introduced (1965). Two major constitutional revisions were made in 1946 and 1958. The constitution was entirely rewritten in 1946 (utilizing professional assistance in its study), and changes were made to clarify the meaning, eliminate unnecessary verbiage, use more constitutional rather than popular language, and make the document as accurate, precise, and concise as possible.[88]

Significantly, the extensive constitutional revision of 1946 explicitly approved the dual decision-making structure inaugurated formally in 1931 by refining the methodology for naming the trustees of the various boards, commissions, and committees. These were to be rotated regularly to provide wider representation. Another change attempted to decentralize the appointment of these trustees by providing

---

[87] Ibid., 196.
[88] *Annual*, Southern Baptist Convention, 1946, 66.

that the Committee on Boards be elected from nominees chosen by a caucus of the messengers from each state in the Convention. After two years this plan was scrapped and the Committee on Boards was named the Committee on Committees. Sensitive to the difference in the number of constituents in each state, the Convention voted that each state having 500,000 members should receive an additional member on each board, plus another one for each 250,000 members beyond the 500,000. In 1953 this same provision was extended to include membership on the Executive Committee, except that the first additional number was granted for 250,000 Baptists in a state instead of 500,000, and a total limit of five additional members was set. However, in 1967, an attempt to reduce the proportion of membership for trustees on all boards and agencies from smaller state conventions was voted down by the Convention.

The extensive 1958 changes in the constitution followed the appointment in 1956 of a Committee to Study the Total Baptist Program, headed by Douglas M. Branch. W. L. Howse judged one aspect of their work as "a major turning point in Southern Baptist life. It is doubtful whether the Convention at any time in its history has taken an action more far reaching than this."[89] He was referring to the correlation and coordination of Southern Baptist programs. He noted that since the opening of the twentieth century there had been a striving to fulfill at least three basic needs of the Convention: (1) to define denominational programs better; (2) to correlate and coordinate denominational programming and long-range planning; and (3) to develop knowledge and skills in programming and long-range planning. A recommendation in this area by the Total Study Committee urged that the Executive Committee should

> maintain an official organization manual defining the responsibilities of each agency of the Convention for conducting specific programs and for performing other functions. The manual shall cite the action of the Convention that assisted the programs and other functions to the agency. The Executive Committee shall present to the Convention recommendations required to clarify the responsibilities of the agencies for programs and other functions, to eliminate overlapping assignments or responsibility, and to

---

[89]Cox-Woolley, eds., *Encyclopedia*, III, 1918.

> authorize the assignment of new responsibilities for programs or functions to agencies.[90]

This was made a bylaw of the Convention in 1960.

Each agency of the Convention worked in its own area of program budgeting and moved toward correlating programs, curricula, and meetings of the various Southern Baptist Convention agencies affecting the local churches as the main center or basic unit of all programs.

> The Inter-Agency Council was enlarged and strengthened to provide the structure through which the Convention agencies could work to correlate their program efforts. Between 1960 and 1967 the Convention adopted a program statement for each agency, describing the work assigned to it. Agency programs were designed to prevent unnecessary overlapping of work, to lessen tensions between agencies, and to make possible a more objective study of budget needs.[91]

Another meaningful result of the Total Study Committee was the construction of a separate Southern Baptist Convention building in Nashville to house the Executive Committee and smaller agencies of the Convention. The Southern Baptist Convention Building was occupied in 1963 by the Executive Committee, Baptist Foundation, Stewardship Commission, Education Commission, and Christian Life Commissions. The Seminary Extension offices were moved there from Jackson, Mississippi, the same year.

Also in 1958 a new by-law pointed to the increasing desire by the Convention for wider representation in their trustees of boards and other agencies of the body requiring that all Convention committees, boards, and commissions include both laymen and ordained persons, with neither contributing more than two thirds. In 1961 even more lay participation was structured: the Committee on Boards, Commissions, and Standing Committees was doubled in size to include two members from each state, one a layman. The first woman vice-president of the Convention was elected in 1963, Mrs. R. L. Mathis. In 1968 the Convention voted that

---

[90] Ibid.
[91] Ibid., 1965-66.

young people should have broader participation in decision-making processes of Southern Baptists at all levels.[92]

It is worthy of notice that Southern Baptists made no basic alterations in the four significant structural concepts they had adopted between 1917 and 1942; namely, an Executive Committee to serve between sessions of the Convention, a Cooperative Program for financing all budgeted areas of work, a new widely-based plan of representation whose authority stemmed from consensus, and the formal articulation of a dual system of decision-making—trustees from states and the Convention sessions. Each of these has become a distinctive area of strength in the structure of the Convention. Hardly a session was held between 1967 and 1970, for example, that the messengers did not heartily praise the Cooperative Program as the best channel for supporting the work of the body. They reflected the flowery language of the 1939 Executive Committee reported:

> The Cooperative Program is the greatest step forward in Kingdom finance Southern Baptists have ever taken. It was slow and gradual in its formation. It arose out of the desires and efforts of pastors and churches to find a plan whereby all worthy denominational causes might be cared for fully and fairly without conflicting with the necessary programs and work in the churches themselves. It is believed to be sane, scriptural, comprehensive, unifying, equitable, economical and thoroughly workable. It is based upon the assumption that all denominational causes will be included, that all agencies and institutions will co-operate in its promotion, that all pastors will represent and present all causes and seek to secure regular, proportionate and adequate support by putting on the Every Member Canvas every year. In this way all occasions for rivalries and conflicts and overlapping are removed, the offerings will come in regularly and each cause will receive and each contributing member will make fifty-two offerings a year instead of one. It is the best plan we know and it is hoped that it

---

[92]Ibid., 1967.

will increasingly receive the hearty and enthusiastic support of all our people.[93]

In 1956 the principles of cooperation between the state conventions and the Southern Baptist Convention relative to the Cooperative Program were reaffirmed (as set out in the 1934 and 1951 *Annuals*), with the added word that each state had the right to deduct or not to deduct any items from Cooperative Program receipts before setting the percentages of division. Cooperative Program undesignated receipts for Southern Baptist Convention causes had grown to $29,970,527 in 1971.[94]

## The Liberal-Fundamentalist Encounter

The 1920's brought to a climax for Southern Baptists their corporate reaction to some of the fierce theological confrontations experienced by other denominations earlier in the century. Professor Crawford H. Toy of Southern Baptist Theological Seminary, who had studied under liberal European theological teachers in German universities in 1867-69, had been forced to resign in 1879 because he was teaching these views in his seminary classes.[95] Other Southern Baptist teachers and schools felt the impact of these new ideas and events.

> During the early years of the century, an increasing number of ministers and theological seminaries were accepting the critical approach to the Scriptures, together with a liberal theology which minimized or rejected the doctrine of the deity of Christ, weakened the orthodox teaching of depravity and sin, deplored the view of the atonement as divine satisfaction or vicarious substitution for the sinner, and particularly rejected belief in the visible return of Christ to establish his kingdom.[96]

Among northern Baptists and in other denominations the opposition to this liberal theology was manifested in Bible conferences and pungent literary responses in the closing decades of the nineteenth century. The conservative movement secured its name and united its forces

---

[93] *Annual*, Southern Baptist Convention, 1939, 28-29.
[94] The statistics of the Executive Committee for 1972 covered only nine months, due to a change in fiscal year, so this is the closest relevant figure.
[95] Baker, *Source Book*, 168-172 has the document.
[96] Cox-Woolley, eds., *Encyclopedia*, I, 516.

about 1910 when two wealthy laymen financed the publication of twelve small volumes or pamphlets entitled *The Fundamentals: A Testimony of the Truth*. These pamphlets brought the name "Fundamentalists" to those holding to such views and asserted the five basic doctrines that characterized the Fundamentalist movement: the virgin birth, the bodily resurrection of Christ and his followers, the verbal inspiration of the Scriptures, the substitutionary theory of the atonement, and the imminent, physical second coming of Christ in the millennial reign. Some of the contributors to this series were Southern Baptists, including Professors J. J. Reeve and C. B. Williams of Southwestern Baptist Theological Seminary, and E. Y. Mullins, president of Southern Baptist Theological Seminary. Robert G. Torbet wrote that most Baptists probably accepted the theological views set forth by the fundamentalists, but their rigid creedalism, rationalization of faith, and most of all, their harsh and militant spirit alienated many who were sympathetic with their conservative doctrinal stance.[97] The World's Christian Fundamentals Association was formed in 1919 with members from Presbyterians, Methodists, Disciples, and Baptists included in their number.[98]

Among Southern Baptists the leading fundamentalist figure was J. Frank Norris of Fort Worth, Texas. He participated in the World's Christian Fundamentals Conference of 1919, and helped form the Baptist Bible Union of America four years later. Because of the overwhelmingly conservative nature of Southern Baptists, he and his group found it difficult to establish doctrinal grounds for attacking the Convention and its agencies. Norris, however, used fundamentalism as a platform for personal controversy and to further his ambitions. Although he had previously exercised his considerable gifts in forwarding the organized work of Texas and Southern Baptists, he began during this period to use his newspaper to attack the Seventy-five Million Campaign, Baylor University, Southwestern Seminary, Texas Baptists, and the Southern Baptist Convention. He was expelled from Tarrant County Baptist Association in 1922 and 1924 and by the Baptist General Convention of

---

[97] Torbet, *History of the Baptists*, 427.
[98] For old but still valuable books on this subject, see S. G. Cole, *The History of Fundamentalism* (London: Archon Books, 1931), and Norman F. Furniss, *The Fundamentalist Controversy 1918-1931* (New Haven: Yale University Press, 1954).

Texas in 1923 and 1924. He continued to harass the Southern Convention until his death in 1952.[99]

The growth of Fundamentalism in Southern Baptist life will be critical in shaping the significant controversies of the next chapter and will be instrumental in bringing about what has become known as the Conservative Resurgence.

Related to the rise in Fundamentalism was the evolutionary confrontation. Inspired by Charles Darwin's seminal work, *The Origin of Species*, in 1859, many theories were developed during the following decades by scientists and liberal theologians tending to discredit the Genesis account of creation and advancing an evolutionary hypothesis to account for the existence and nature of man. Perhaps the climax to this tension between the two sides in this controversy occurred in the South with the passing of a statute on March 21, 1925, in Tennessee which forbade any educational institution supported by public funds "to teach the theory that denies the story of the divine creation of man as taught in the Bible." John T. Scopes, a biology teacher in Dayton, Tennessee, provided a test case and was brought to trial. This attracted worldwide attention, and although he was convicted, his sentence was set aside by the supreme court on a technicality. In the midst of these exciting events the Southern Baptist Convention at Memphis, Tennessee, in 1925, and the question of evolution spilled over into the deliberations of the Convention. Already the Convention had spoken on the issue. In 1922 and again in 1923 E. Y. Mullins had decried the attacks upon religion because of discoveries or alleged discoveries in physical nature; the use of such sciences as psychology, biology, and geology to deny the supernatural in the Christian religion as if they were necessarily relevant; and the teaching of mere hypotheses as though they were facts.[100] The Convention adopted this statement as its views. However, at Memphis in 1925, growing out of the continuing agitation over the question of evolution, the Convention adopted a confession of faith, not, they said, as a final or infallible statement of belief, or an authoritative creed, or an attempt to hamper

---

[99]See a critical description of Norris' disruptive tactics in Baker, *Source Book*, 196-97.
[100]*Annual*, Southern Baptist Convention, 1923, p. 19.

freedom of thought; but to serve as a consensus of opinion by this particular session to assist in the interpretation of the Scriptures.[101]

The adoption of a confession of faith, however, did not bring an end to the discussion of evolution in the Convention. Many of the conservatives felt the confession had not been clear and specific in its denunciation of the evolutionary hypothesis. In the 1926 Convention, George E. McDaniel, in concluding his presidential address, purposely headed off an impending controversial debate by asserting:

> This Convention accepts Genesis as teaching that man was the special creation of God, and rejects every theory, evolution or other, which teaches that man originated in, or came by way of, a lower animal ancestry.[102]

By previous arrangement a motion was promptly made to the effect that this statement be the sentiment of the Convention, "and that from this point on no further consideration be given to this subject, and that the Convention go forward with the consideration of the main kingdom causes to which God has set our hearts and hands." This was adopted. However, on the fourth day of the Convention, S. E. Tull introduced a resolution asking that all of the Convention's institutions, boards, missionary representatives be requested to acquiesce to McDaniel's statement. The resolution was adopted.[103]

A rather curious constitutional situation grew out of this last resolution. On November 10, 1926, the Baptist General Convention of Oklahoma voted to withhold undesignated funds of the Cooperative Program from Southern Baptist seminaries whose faculties refused to sign the McDaniel statement; they took the same action in 1927. The funds were released in 1928.

Meanwhile, however, the constitutional question had occupied the minds of Southern Baptist leaders. In 1927 the Convention instructed the Executive Committee to prepare a statement on the basis of cooperation between the Convention and state bodies. At two points, in particular, the committee was asked to clarify the relationship: a definition of the duties, functions, and limitations of state conventions and boards as collecting

---

[101] Ibid., 1925, 76. The document is in Baker, *Source Book*, 200 ff.
[102] *Annual*, 1926, 18.
[103] Ibid., 1926, 98.

agencies for the Convention; and the safeguarding of Convention funds in the hands of state bodies. The latter point touched directly upon the action of the Oklahoma body and also upon the practice of other state bodies that had withheld funds for Convention-wide objects. In 1928 the Executive Committee presented a detailed statement on relations between the Convention and state bodies that has become the basis of their relations. The report began by noting that the Convention "is not an ecclesiastical body composed of churches, nor a federal body composed of state conventions." All cooperation with the Convention is on a voluntary basis, and churches, associations, unions, and conventions are self-determining in their own spheres and activities. The Convention totally disclaimed any authority over state bodies, but set out four principles in relation to its own identity. (1) The cooperative relations between the Convention and state bodies includes the recognition that the state boards are collecting agencies for southwide as well as state funds, although this relationship is simply a matter of convenience and economy and may be changed at any time. (2) Even though the state bodies handle first the funds collected for the southwide body, the Convention retains as "inalienable and inherent" the right or first appeal to the churches for funds; and in matters other than raising money, the Convention retains complete control of its own affairs, with the right to fix its own objectives and to determine the amounts of money allocated to its various objects. (3) The power of appointing members of all committees and boards of the Convention resided in the Convention itself, although the Convention may, if it desires, consult the state or territorial subdivisions in this matter. (4) Neither the Convention nor a state body may impose its will upon the other in any manner or degree at any time. The Convention "has no authority to allocate funds or to divert funds from any object included in a state budget. In like manner no state body has any authority to allocate funds to or divert from any object included in the Southwide budget."[104] It will be observed that this last sentence dealt with the action taken by the Oklahoma convention in 1926.

---

[104]Ibid., 1928, 32-33.

# Chapter 15 – The Conservative Resurgence

The events that took place that are described in this chapter were a collection of events that really had a common thread. It consists of precipitating events and background motivations, which set in motion a ten year process that has become known as the Conservative Resurgence.

## Growing Revolutions

After the societal changes of World War II, Southern Baptists began to see changes in their denomination and the beginnings of a tremendous struggle. With the sociological shifts that took place in the United States, the religious communities varied in their reactions. Southern Baptists did not always cope well with the changes, but usually made some attempt at a response.

At the end of the Korean War, Southern Baptists saw changes occurring all around them. There were racial conflicts, and Southern Baptists, who had long been associated with their legacy of association with slavery and sectionalism, realized that there was a need to address this very sensitive issue. This task was given to the Social Service Commission which was led at that time by Hugh H. Brimm. In 1953, A. C. Miller took over from Brimm and the agency was renamed the Christian Life Commission.[1]

In 1954, the Supreme Court struck down segregation in the landmark *Brown vs. Board of Education*. Southern Baptists met just a few weeks later for the annual meeting and became the first major religious group to endorse the decision. The Christian Life Commission began to expand its role, not just in understanding their place with regard to race relations, but also began to address women's issues and the growing threat of Communism.[2] However, as is often the case, the tendency to be on the

---

[1] Fletcher, *The Southern Baptist Convention*, 200.
[2] Ibid.

cutting edge in dealing with difficult issue is the fact that those who are addressing these things often become so focused on the issues with which they are dealing that they lose touch with those who make up the greatest part of the denomination.

Foy Valentine took over the Commission in 1960 and became more aggressive in dealing with more contemporary concerns, but not without opposition from the culturally anchored churches of the Deep South. Since many of the social struggles, such as the Women's Liberation Movement, ran counter to the beliefs and practices of many Southern Baptists, it would not be long before the leadership would be considered among those who were considered a part of the liberal faction of the denomination.[3]

One of the parallels of the Women's Liberation Movement in Southern Baptist life was the increasing number of women attending seminary and first taking assignments with the mission boards, and also holding various positions in church work. This seemed to enjoy the support of the WMU under the leadership of Alma Hunt, who succeeded Kathleen Mallory in 1948.[4]

## The Elliot Controversy

While Southern Baptists had been preoccupied with the struggles taking place outside of the denomination, events were taking place within the denomination's seminaries that would soon rock Baptists across the South. Many would be completely appalled at what was taking place within Southern Baptists seminaries; others would be appalled at their reactions.

Ralph Elliott was a graduate of Southern Baptist Theological Seminary and had been a protégé of J. J. Owens, a professor of Old Testament there. When Elliott became caught up in a controversy with President Duke McCall over faculty contributions to a book McCall published, Elliott was able to escape by being the first professor to join the

---

[3] Ibid., 201.
[4] Ibid., 205.

faculty of the new Midwestern Baptist Theological Seminary in Kansas City in 1958.⁵

In 1961, Elliott was invited by the Sunday School Board's Broadman Press, to write a book, *The Message of Genesis*. Many of Elliott's views, including the documentary hypothesis and questioning not only the Mosaic authorship of the Pentateuch, but also the historicity of many passages of some of the narrative portions of Genesis, brought into the light openly what was being taught in the seminaries. Baptist beliefs on much of this had not changed since C. H. Toy was dismissed from teaching at Southern Seminary in 1879.⁶

W. A. Criswell, pastor of First Baptist Church of Dallas, quickly became a spokesperson for the conservative reaction. When the Convention met in San Francisco in 1962, the Elliot controversy had heated up to a critical point, with many Baptist papers already fueling the issue. Herschel H. Hobbs, pastor of the First Baptist Church of Oklahoma City, had been elected President of the Convention the previous year in St. Louis.⁷

K. Owen White, pastor of the First Baptist Church of Houston, led the attack. He had published an article called "Death in the Pot," which was based on 2 Kings 4:40. He had sent the article to all Baptist state papers, to the seminary presidents, the Sunday School Board, and to other denominational leaders. In the article, he described Elliott's work as undermining the historical accuracy of the Bible. Soon, conservatives began organizing to address the issue of liberalism in Southern Baptist life. It was significant that the book was written by a professor teaching at a Southern Baptist seminary and had been published by the publishing arm of the Southern Baptist Sunday School Board. ⁸

**K. Owen White, former pastor of First Baptist Church, Houston**
(Photo courtesy of Southern Baptist Historical Library and Archives)

---

⁵ Ralph Elliott, *The "Genesis Controversy" and Continuity in South Baptist Chaos—A Eulogy for a Great Tradition* (Macon: Mercer University Press, 2005), 3-5.
⁶ Fletcher, *The Southern Baptist Convention*, 206.
⁷ Ibid.
⁸ Ibid.

Initially, Midwestern's President Millard Berquist and the trustees supported Elliott. Broadman Press recalled all unsold copies of the book and reassigned the copyright to Elliott. Finally, the pressure became so great that the trustees asked Elliott to promise that he would not allow his book to be reprinted. When he refused, he was fired for insubordination. He was eventually hired at Crozer Theological Seminary, a school affiliated with the American Baptist Convention.[9]

**Herschell H. Hobbs, former pastor of First Baptist Church, Oklahoma City and SBC president**
(Photo courtesy of Southern Baptist Historical Library and Archives)

As far as Baptists on both sides of the controversy were concerned, the issue was not settled. Midwestern Seminary had not fired Elliott for what Conservative Southern Baptists considered heresy. In other words, they did not feel there was anything wrong with what he published; they simply wanted the pressure taken off of the institution.

At the 1962 Convention, Hobbs successfully handled motions to minimize damage. In Spring, 1963, Hobbs met with Porter Routh, Executive Secretary of the Executive Committee since 1951, and Routh's associate, Albert McClellan, and the three together decided to make a proposal to the Executive Committee. In this proposal, a special committee would be appointed to study the 1925 *Baptist Faith and Message*. They felt that if the issuance of a statement of faith was sufficient to settle issues in 1925, surely the same would be true for the controversy that was drawing the attention of Southern Baptists in the 1960s. They proposed the committee include the seminary presidents, but there was strong opposition to this since the seminaries were the source of the problem. The result was a Committee of State Convention Presidents to be chaired by Hobbs to bring a report to the 1963 Convention.[10]

The Committee considered three options: a new statement, a reaffirmation of the 1925 statement, or a revision to the 1925 statement. They opted for the last choice. They spent a great deal of time on a

---

[9] Ibid., 207.
[10] Ibid., 208.

preamble. They added statements to some of the articles. Some articles were combined with others.¹¹

The 1963 document was presented to the meeting in Kansas City in May 1963. There was some debate triggered by the concerns of some of the Landmarkers, but in the end, the Convention voted, not unanimously, to approve the 1963 *Baptist Faith and Message* as presented. Believing the issue to be settled, the leader of the opposition to Elliot, K. Owen White, was elected president. Possibly in an attempt to make sure both sides were appeased, WMU President Marie Mathis was elected as one of the Convention's vice-presidents.¹² Ultimately, this would not be a show of solidarity of the two sides, but would typify the growing factions within the denomination.

## *Broadman Bible Commentary*

Another symptom of the influence of more liberal thinking within the Convention is seen in the publication of the *Broadman Bible Commentary*. Volume I was released in 1969 and G. Henton Davies, a scholar in England, had been recruited to author the work. Davies espoused the JEPD documentary hypothesis and used the historical-critical method of interpretation.¹³

This in itself, while alarming to many Southern Baptists, should not have been a surprise to many. The Baptist Sunday School Board had added Church Study Course materials as early as 1902, but had grown significantly over the years. They produced the eight volume *Bible Survey Series* beginning in 1969, with the eighth volume released in 1971. Volume 3, *A Nation in the Making*, was released in 1969, the same year Volume I of the *Broadman Bible Commentary* was released. In the *Bible Book Series* Volume 3, Page Kelley, Associate Professor of Old Testament Interpretation at Southern Baptist Theological Seminary, spent four paragraphs discussing the Mosaic authorship of the Pentateuch. In this discussion, he basically presented Moses as the "author" in the sense that he was responsible for it, having collected the already existing sections,

---

¹¹ Ibid.
¹² Ibid., 210.
¹³ McBeth, *The Baptist Heritage*, 680.

and serving as an editor of the work.[14] Kelley then spent the next four pages describing the JEPD documentary hypothesis. In his discussion, he likened it to the four Gospel writers, each presenting a different point of view. He attached dates to the four threads, all dated hundreds of years after the date of the Exodus and the life of Moses, effectively making the Mosaic authorship of any section of it impossible.[15]

The greatest controversy in the Davies commentary concerned Genesis 22 where the author called into question whether God really commanded Abraham to kill Isaac. The conflict heated up prior to the 1970 Denver meeting and discussion raged during the convention. Finally, the Convention voted by a wide margin to direct the Sunday School Board to recall volume 1 and have it rewritten to reflect more conservative Southern Baptist perspectives.[16]

When the elected board asked Davies to rewrite the book, he refused. They went to Clyde Francisco, Old Testament professor at Southern Seminary, and he undertook the task. The new work was published in 1973 and was released as "Volume 1, Revised." Conservative opponents felt that while the language was slightly more accommodating, most of the changes were relatively minor and there was not a significant improvement to the work.[17]

Other volumes of the commentary which were released a little later than the first volume did not exactly approach the Scripture from a conservative standpoint. For example, volume 5 dealt with the authorship of the book of Isaiah. In it, Page Kelley, the same author who had penned the Bible Book Series volume discussed previously, began by saying,

> In attempting to examine the problem of the unity and authorship of Isaiah we are in no way calling into question the inspiration of any part of the book. Nor are we suggesting that the sections judged to be later than Isaiah contain less of the revealed truth of God. As a matter of fact, it is precisely in those chapters the authorship of which is most widely debated that we are led

---

[14] Page H. Kelley, *Bible Survey Series Volume 3: A Nation in the Making.* (Nashville: Convention Press, 1969), 10-11.
[15] Ibid., 11-14.
[16] McBeth, *The Baptist Heritage*, 680-681.
[17] Ibid., 681.

into the very heart of the Old Testament. Whoever the human author, or authors, may have been, this book, both in its entirety and in its various parts, belongs to the enduring word of God (40:8).[18]

Kelley then went on to fully discuss the Deutero- and Trito-Isaianic authorship theories, concluding that while it is possible that one person wrote the entire work, it is far more likely that it was a composite work.[19]

## Women's Ordination

Another divisive issue was the role of women in ministry and their ordination. While there had been some historical precedent for women serving in areas of ministry, there is no evidence that ordination had been a part of the process. Shubal Stearns' sister, Martha, the wife of Daniel Marshall, was known to preach and pray in public.[20] Later, the First Baptist Church of Waco appointed (rather than ordained) women to serve as deaconesses as early as 1877,[21] though the practice never became widespread.

In 1964, Watts Street Baptist Church of Durham, North Carolina ordained Addie Davis, a 1963 graduate of Southern Seminary, to the gospel ministry. While there was some early opposition to this, Davis soon accepted a church in Vermont, and so removed herself from the center of attention. Additionally, Baptists respected the autonomy of the local church and were reluctant to interfere in what was obviously a local church decision.[22]

While there is no record of another woman being ordained until 1971, the practice soon began to gain some momentum. While there were probably no more than fifty women ordained by 1978, the number later increased rapidly. In even greater numbers, churches were ordaining women as deacons or deaconesses. By 1976, the opposition to the practice had become solidified enough that Black River Association in Arkansas passed a resolution in 1976, calling the practice "unbiblical" and

---

[18] Page L. Kelley, *The Broadman Bible Commentary, Volume 5: Proverbs – Isaiah* (Nashville: Broadman Press, 1971), 159-160.
[19] Ibid., 160-163.
[20] Reported in McBeth, *The Baptist Heritage*, 690.
[21] Reported in Fletcher, *The Southern Baptist Convention*, 226.
[22] Ibid. 225.

criticizing Charles Ashcraft, the Arkansas Executive Secretary, for his public support of the practice. The following year, the Arkansas Convention passed a resolution criticizing the Home Mission Board for their appointment of an ordained woman, Suzanne Coyle, to work in a Philadelphia Mission. Oklahoma had already passed a resolution condemning the practice of ordination of women as deacons and ministers.[23]

While it was never clearly stated by parties on either side, the issue of the practice of the ordination of women was only symptomatic of a deeper concern. The greater issue was not whether or not Southern Baptists should ordain women. Instead it was whether or not the Bible permitted the practice. However, in order to ascertain that, parties on each side of the debate interpreted the Bible differently. It became a battle based on semantics. Each side used much of the same terminology, but they held completely different meanings to the terms they used. This will be clearly seen in the next section.

## Inerrancy

The underlying conflict between the two factions in the denomination rose to the surface in 1979 in the form of a single word: *inerrancy*. This new herald helped coalesce the conservative contingent and neutralize their opposition. Both sides declared that the Bible was inspired and infallible, but the word *inerrant* was soon claimed by the conservatives alone.

Inerrancy was not a term that was unique to Southern Baptists. It had previously been used by the Lutheran Church, Missouri Synod, when that denomination struggled with similar issues. That led to the formation of the International Council on Biblical Inerrancy in 1977.[24]

The Southern Baptist argument around the word *inerrancy* centered on the idea that the original manuscripts, generally referred to as "autographs," were without error and that the Bible is true in all respects. The difficulty is that none of the autographs are known to exist, making it an argument impossible to prove. One camp was quick to express that what was really important was that the truths by which Scripture was to be

---

[23] Ibid. 226-227.
[24] Ibid., 252.

interpreted were essentially true and the presence of apparent inaccuracies in Scripture did not impact the truths of the Bible. Inerrantists, on the other hand, held that there was no error in the Scripture except those that had crept in as a result of faulty translation or human error subsequent to the original writings.[25]

Some faithful Christians felt that this was a simple contest between those who held to a literal interpretation of the Scriptures, and those who preferred a nonliteral interpretation.[26] In reality, it went far deeper than that. It ultimately came down to not just how Southern Baptists interpreted Scripture; it came down to how the Bible was seen overall.

Later, a book was written by a former staff member of the Home Mission Board. He had been terminated and eventually left the denomination. He wrote a book called *The Fundamentalist Takeover in the Southern Baptist Convention: A Brief History*. In the introduction to that book, Editor James Shoopman tried to state that the issue was not really over inerrancy; instead, he said that it was over the issue of the Priesthood of the Believer.[27] While he saw this as a completely separate issue, in reality, they were related. According to Shoopman, the concept of Priesthood of the Believer was the right to interpret Scripture according to the believer's own conscience and in light of the best scholarship. Conservatives used that term to describe the belief that each believer has the privilege to come directly to God without need of a human mediator or priest. Christians have Christ as their High Priest who, with the Holy Spirit, makes intercession before God's Throne of Grace. In other words, the moderates, as those opposed to the conservatives came to be called, felt that inerrancy was not an issue as long as they could interpret Scripture according to their own understanding.[28] Inerrantists felt that the Christian should always use the question, "But what does the Bible *say*?"

---

[25] Ibid.
[26] Ibid.
[27] Rob James and Gary Leazer, *The Fundamentalist Takeover in the Southern Baptist Convention: A Brief History*. (Timisoara, Romania: Impact Media, 1999), 6
[28] When this author was an undergraduate student, his Greek Professor, Dr. Vernon G. Davidson, told the class, "Boys, when you translate the Scripture, you need to do so after prayer and under leadership of the Holy Spirit. Then, do the best you can to translate taking into consideration you own level of bias,

The term *inerrancy* came to be the way the conservatives identified themselves to each other. It came to be loudly used in the 1979 at the SBC meeting in Houston. During the meeting preceding the Convention, at the Southern Baptist Pastor's Conference, conservative speakers had openly criticized the seminaries as being the breeding ground of liberalism in the Convention. This was the opening shot on what was to eventually become the Southern Baptist Convention's Civil War.[29]

## Missions in the Middle

While the battle raged between the two sides for more than a decade, there were many Southern Baptists who felt that they had been caught in the middle. For many of them, they continued to do their jobs, anxious to see what the ultimate outcome would be and what would happen to them as a result. These were the people of the agencies of the Southern Baptist Convention.

In the 1960s, the Home Mission Board joined forces with the Foreign Mission Board in what was called the "Crusade of the Americas." This ambitious project trained Spanish-language missionaries to work among the Hispanic populations in the United States and North America, with the hope of evangelizing North and South America.[30] The Home Mission Board had been under the leadership of Arthur Rutledge since 1964, and under the leadership of Samuel Redford from 1953 until he stepped down in favor of Rutledge. Rutledge retired in 1976, dying one year later. He was succeeded by William Tanner, who was a skilled denominationalist.[31] Unfortunately, he became very frustrated with the growing polarization of the Convention and left in 1986 to lead the Oklahoma Baptist Convention.[32]

In 1978, the Southern Baptist Convention concluded a study of nearly a decade where a new missions initiative was formulated. The program was called Bold Mission Thrust. The program was almost lost amid the fighting within the denomination. In 1977, the Convention had

---

prejudice, background and ignorance." This writer has found that to be true time and again.
[29] McBeth, *The Baptist Heritage*, 681.
[30] Fletcher, *The Southern Baptist Convention*, 214.
[31] Ibid., 256.
[32] Ibid., 266.

approved a plan to double three times by 2000 the combined receipts of the state conventions and the Cooperative Program. This would extend bold missions programs and called for five thousand lay persons to serve for one or two years at home and on foreign mission fields. The Executive Committee was to have oversight of this program. It called on people to focus on discipleship and commitment and increase personal giving toward a double-tithe by A.D. 2000.[33]

The Foreign Mission Board also experienced a change in leadership. Baker James Cauthen stepped down after twenty-five years at the helm of that organization. Keith Parks was elected as his successor. Just like Jerry Rankin and Cauthen before him, he had practical experience as a missionary. However, effectiveness in an organization does not always translate to effectiveness in leading an organization, a lesson Parks learned painfully. He would eventually resign after repeated conflicts with the conservative board of trustees.

## Other Changes in Leadership

The seminaries had been the center of the struggle within the Convention. Some concerned Southern Baptists were not certain the necessary correction could ever come about fully. Gray Allison, a former missionary, decided to establish an alternative to the liberalism that had invaded the seminaries. In 1972, he established Mid-America Baptist Theological Seminary. While it was initially established in Little Rock, it eventually moved to Memphis, Tennessee and came under the protection of Adrian Rogers, the successor to R. G. Lee as pastor of Bellevue Baptist Church.[34] The seminary has remained independent of Convention ownership as a means of ensuring that it did not become another battleground or a place where liberalism is fostered.

R. G. Lee, former pastor of Bellevue Baptist Church, Memphis and SBC president (Photo courtesy of Southern Baptist Historical Library and Archives)

Lloyd Elder had been president of the Baptist Sunday School Board since Grady Cothen had retired. There were efforts to fire him in

---

[33] Ibid., 251.
[34] Ibid., 242.

1989, but that was delayed after agreements with some of the leaders of the convention. He left that position in 1991.

## Battle for the Gavel

While previous attempts to stop the drift away from conservatism had largely failed, a new battle line was being formed. A Texas lawyer and judge, Paul Pressler, had become greatly alarmed at the teaching he heard in Baptist churches, while in college and law school, and later, after he returned to Texas. Pressler was aware that their views were a result of the training they had received in Southern Baptist seminaries. In March, 1967, Pressler met a New Orleans seminary student from Texas, Paige Patterson.[35]

Mutual friends had assured Pressler that Patterson shared a conservative view similar to Pressler's. They met for coffee at Café du Monde and discussed their mutual concern for their denomination. According to Patterson, they did not develop a plan, but they came away with a commitment to discover why previous attempts to advance conservatism in the Convention had failed, and to become thoroughly familiar with the bylaws of the convention, so that they could follow the process correctly. What they eventually discovered was that this was going to be a lengthy process and that they could not do this alone. While a majority of Southern Baptists were conservative, they did not control the leadership positions of the denomination. This would have to change.[36]

The pair estimated that it would be a ten year process. According to Patterson, it took twice that.[37] The reason it would be such a lengthy process was simply because of the bureaucratic process that would be involved. First, they would have to identify a potential candidate for President of the Southern Baptist Convention who (1) shared the conservative view, (2) was willing to be a visible spokesperson during what would become a very ugly struggle, and (3) could actually get elected at the Convention.

---

[35] Fletcher, *The Southern Baptist Convention*, 244.
[36] Paige Patterson, "Roping the Whirlwind–A Renaissance Plan," paper delivered at the Northeast Region Evangelical Theological Society Meeting, April 2010. Copy furnished to the author by Dr. Patterson.
[37] Ibid.

Patterson identified four distinct groups in the Convention: "movement" conservatives, "intuitive" conservatives, denominationalists, and liberals. He acknowledges that the last group consisted of few actual liberals; the majority were neo-orthodox professors and denominational leaders who were committed to historical-critical scholarship. Denominationalists were primarily conservative to the extent that theology and hermeneutical methods matters, but were above all committed to maintaining the denominational status quo. The denomination had been good to them and they did not want to run the risk of upsetting the establishment. Movement conservatives were conservative in their theology, understood the relationship between political process and leadership in a free-church denomination, and believed the issue was critical enough that they were willing to suffer for the necessity of the cause. Intuitive conservatives made up a majority of the denomination. They were conservative in their theology, but tended to believe the best about their leaders, though they began having doubts of their own.[38]

In 1978, a group of pastors and laymen met at the Atlanta Airport Ramada for a meeting to discuss what needed to be done to return the denomination to its proper course. After the meeting, the participants began to inform Baptists in their states about the state of the denomination, especially the seminaries. As they had developed the plan, the decision was made to protect those who served as pastors of congregations as long as possible. Further, those who would be put up as nominees for convention president would be excluded from all meetings and strategic planning.[39]

The process [40] that was to take place is as follows: Each cooperating Southern Baptist church is permitted to appoint up to ten

---

[38] Paige Patterson, *Anatomy of a Reformation: The Southern Baptist Convention, 1978-2004* (Fort Worth, Texas: Seminary Hill Press, ND), 3.
[39] Ibid., 4.
[40] Numerous works have been published that describe the struggle for the life of the denomination in great detail. Paige Patterson goes into greater description and analysis in his publication that is cited here, so that information will not be duplicated. Also, James C. Hefley produced a 5 volume work called, *The Truth in Crisis*, and a sixth volume, *The Conservative Resurgence in the Southern Baptist Convention* that are worthy of consideration. Additionally Jerry Sutton produced a book called *The Baptist Reformation*. Finally, Jesse Fletcher devotes several chapters to the struggle in *The Southern Baptist Convention*. The reader

messengers to the annual meeting of the Southern Baptist Convention, although most churches send far fewer than this, if any at all. The messengers elect a president of the Southern Baptist Convention who appoints a Committee on Committees consisting of two people, usually one pastor and one layperson, from each state. In turn, the Committee on Committees nominates a Committee on Boards, which is subsequently elected by the Convention in session. This committee is also made up of two people from each state. The Committee on Boards then recommends to the Convention a slate of nominees, including the trustees of the various agencies, boards, and institutions of the denomination. Since trustees of the various agencies serve no more than ten years, with various members rotating off each year, it is anticipated that it will take approximately ten years for the presidents to consistently appoint conservative members to the Committee on Committees who will consistently nominate a conservative Committee on Boards who will, in turn, nominate conservative trustees. In order to accomplish this, the election of presidents who were committed to the conservative cause for at least ten consecutive years was absolutely essential. Should a moderate president be elected at any point during this time, it would draw the conflict out even longer. It began with the election of Adrian Rogers, pastor of Bellevue Baptist Church in Memphis, Tennessee, as president of the Convention in 1979.[41]

After Rogers' election, he joined Larry Lewis in pressing Wayne Dehoney and Herschel Hobbs to clarify the meaning of the *Baptist Faith and Message* article on Scripture. They wanted assurance that the purpose of the article was to affirm inerrancy. While the answer they were given was sufficient for them, subsequent *Baptist Press* releases did not include the assurances they had been given. The inerrantist position supported a strong conservative social and political agenda, a strict moral standard, and generally opposed women taking leadership positions in religious life.[42]

The practice had become that a president was elected and it was expected that the incumbent would run virtually unopposed for the second term. In all likelihood, the moderates were focusing on the in 1981 election

---

is strongly encouraged to consult these works for further information on the Conservative Resurgence.
[41] Ibid., 6.
[42] Fletcher, *The Southern Baptist Convention*, 260-262.

which was to be held in Los Angeles, California. They had not prepared to put forth a candidate in 1980 when Adrian Rogers announced that he would not run for a second term. Instead, Bailey Smith, an inerrantist pastor from Del City, Oklahoma was nominated and easily won on the first ballot. He was reelected the following year in Los Angeles.[43]

After Smith's election, the Committee on Resolutions which had been appointed the previous year by Rogers was able to move a resolution for doctrinal integrity to the floor after it had been passed over the previous year at Houston. Hobbs, who was the unofficial spokesperson for Southern Baptist beliefs, took a moment of personal privilege. He had been the architect of the 1963 Baptist Faith and Message and had ably handled the Genesis controversy. He urged the Convention to make a renewed commitment to the common denominational task of evangelism and missions, and he cautioned the gathering against creeping creedalism. Sadly, he was booed for his efforts.[44]

In spite of the public debates between high profile members of the two factions, conservatives continued to fill vacancies on the boards of the various Southern Baptist agencies. Moderates successfully challenged some of the nominees, but it was soon apparent that the conservatives had gained momentum and that they resonated with a majority of Southern Baptist messengers.[45]

At the end of Smith's second term as president, moderates put forth retiring president of Southern Seminary, Duke McCall as their candidate. Conservatives nominated James Draper, pastor of First Baptist Church of Euless, Texas. Draper defeated McCall in a runoff with 56.97 percent of the vote. Draper tried to work with moderate leaders and agency heads of the various agencies. He was reelected in Pittsburg in 1983.[46]

After Draper's election, moderates began producing moderate oriented publications and organizations for the purpose of countering the conservative resurgence. It is interesting to note that many of the leaders among the moderates had previously held leadership positions in many of the Convention's agencies.[47]

---

[43] Ibid., 268.
[44] Ibid.
[45] Ibid.
[46] Ibid., 270-271.
[47] Ibid., 279-280.

In 1984 when the Convention met in Kansas City, moderates placed retiring Sunday School Board president Grady Cothen as their candidate against Charles Stanley, pastor of First Baptist Church of Atlanta. While Stanley was elected president, Russell Dilday, president of Southwestern Seminary became the last moderate to preach the Convention sermon. In it, he made a passionate appeal for Southern Baptists to abandon the direction it was headed under the conservatives. He was joined by Roy Honeycutt of Southern Seminary and in 1985, Keith Parks, president of the Foreign Mission Board openly opposed Stanley's reelection. In spite of the opposition by the moderates, Stanley was reelected in 1985. Winfred Moore, after his defeat by Stanley, was elected as first vice-president over incumbent Zig Ziglar.[48]

After the reelection of Stanley, a twenty-two person Peace Committee was appointed to look into the roots of the division and propose a path to reconciliation. This committee was made up of twenty men and two women, with both Stanley and Moore serving as *ex-officio* members. The assignment was for two years with an interim report to be given in Atlanta after one year of work. The committee was chaired by Charles Filler of First Baptist Church, Roanoke, Virginia.[49]

Prior to the 1986 Atlanta meeting, the Peace Committee announced that investigation into the six seminaries and five agencies found significant theological diversity. Furthermore, they referred to both sides as being guilty of political activities and using language toward each other that caused further division between the sides, rather than reaching toward reconciliation. They even accused denominational and independent publications of choosing sides.[50]

At the Atlanta meeting, Adrian Rogers was again placed in nomination for Convention president, pitted against Winfred Moore. Rogers was elected with 55 percent of the vote. Rogers had been the undisputed leader of the conservative majority on the Peace Committee and he was clearly now the leader of the conservative movement.[51]

Now possessing a majority on the Home Mission Board and the Christian Life Commission, conservatives were now able to elect a

---

[48] Ibid., 281.
[49] Ibid., 284.
[50] Ibid., 284-285.
[51] Ibid.

conservative chairman of each of those organizations. The chairman of the Home Mission Board trustees had already been successful in securing the resignations of the moderate-dominated Search Committee, which had been appointed to find a replacement for William Tanner, who was stepping down as president to become Executive-Treasurer of the Oklahoma Baptist Convention. There was no question in anyone's mind that the Search Committee would be finding a conservative chief executive.[52]

The Christian Life Commission was a different story. Foy Valentine had already stepped down as head of that organization and the moderate-dominated commission had selected Larry Baker, a former professor at Midwestern Seminary as his replacement. Conservatives vowed that his tenure there would not be lengthy.[53]

In 1986, the Peace Committee requested a meeting with all of the seminary presidents at Glorieta Baptist Conference Center to take place in October of that year. They had come under tremendous fire over several faculty members, as well as some of the presidents themselves over their roles in the conflict. Attempting to strike a conciliatory chord, Randall Lolley of Southeastern Seminary drafted a report from the presidents; it included a statement taken from Fuller Seminary that used language that they felt was middle ground. In it, they stated that the Bible was not errant "in any area of reality." In their statement, they also pledged to fill their faculties with conservative professors to balance the ones who currently held positions. When it was released by the Peace Committee, the presidents' statement was referred to as the Glorieta Statement. When Lolley and Honeycutt returned to their schools, they were met by concerned faculties. Any attempt to explain further only made matters worse. It was apparent that the conservatives had won and the presidents knew it.[54]

In 1987, the Peace Committee report was adopted in St. Louis. It affirmed all of the issues that the conservatives wanted and was consistent with the concept of inerrancy and gave many agencies fears that it would be treated as a creed. At the same meeting, Larry L. Lewis, who had led

---

[52] Ibid.
[53] Ibid.
[54] Ibid. 286.

many of the early conservative fights, was presented as the newly elected president of the Home Mission Board. Under his direction, the Home Mission Board soon refused to give financial support to support women pastors and moved to stricter enforcement on the appointment of divorced persons. While the Home Mission Board was now under conservative control, the Foreign Mission Board continued to remain under moderate leadership in the person of R. Keith Parks and continued to come under fire. In protest to many of the changes, Southeastern president Randall Lolley resigned, followed by his dean and three other administrators. He was soon replaced by inerrantist Lewis Drummond.[55]

When it was time for the 1988 Convention in San Antonio, conservatives hoped to build on the success of the previous eight years, while moderates hoped to make a turnaround in the Convention direction. Moderates ran Richard Jackson, a well-known and popular individual and the leader of the moderate organization, Baptists Committed. Jerry Vines, co-pastor of the First Baptist Church of Jacksonville, Florida had been an articulator for several years of the conservative position, put was not as nearly well-known. There was a strong push for Vines at the Pastor's Conference, especially by well recognized W. A. Criswell, pastor of First Baptist Church of Dallas. It was the narrowest vote in Southern Baptist History, with Vines winning by a mere 692 votes out of more than 32,000 votes cast. At the same convention, a controversial resolution was passed that affirmed the authority of the pastor with regard to the spiritual leadership of his church. It passed by a margin of roughly 11,000 to 9,000. Moderates were incensed as they thought this eroded the belief in the priesthood of the believer. In protest, moderates followed Randall Lolley to the Alamo where they burned their Convention ballots in protest.[56]

In December of 1988, moderates decided to launch a major concerted effort to defeat the candidates of the conservatives and formed "Baptists Committed to the SBC." It consisted of members of the moderate organizations, Southern Baptist Alliance and Women in Ministry, as well as other moderates. Winfred Moore became chairman of the group. They worked to organize chapters in several southern states.[57]

---

[55] Ibid., 287-288.
[56] Ibid., 290.
[57] Ibid., 294.

At the 1989 Convention in Las Vegas, Morris Chapman vocalized in the Convention Sermon a growing concern over state convention-affiliated colleges and universities with regard to their doctrinal integrity. While these institutions of higher education are affiliated with the state conventions and have no direct connection with the Southern Baptist Convention, they continued to be a battleground even after the end of the SBC Conservative Resurgence.[58]

At that same meeting, the moderates put forth Dan Vestal as their candidate for president. Vestal was the well-liked pastor who had served churches in Texas and in Georgia. He was considered a conservative, and had been influenced by Paul Pressler. Ultimately, Vestal lost to Vines' reelection. He lost to Vines by greater than a 13 percent margin.[59]

Coming to New Orleans for the 1990 Convention, messengers and leaders of both sides felt that this might be considered the last battle between conservatives and moderates. Before the Convention met, Morris Chapman was chosen to be the candidate for the conservatives. Vestal ran again, this time with the support of Carolyn Weatherford Crumpler, who had recently resigned as Executive Director of the Women's Missionary Union. Chapman won with nearly 58 percent of the vote[60] while Crumpler lost with an even greater margin.[61] After conservatives dominated so many of the votes on issues that people on both sides made a great exodus from the Convention, leaving less than a quorum present to conduct business. Having no choice, a series of reports was given after which Vines adjourned the meeting.[62] The battle was over and the conservatives had won.

---

[58] Ibid., 298.
[59] *Annual*, 1989, 45.
[60] *Annual*, 1990, 56.
[61] Ibid., 59.
[62] Ibid., 66.

# Chapter 16 – Since the Conservative Resurgence

After the struggle for denominational control ended, it quickly became apparent to the moderates that any voice they had remaining in the Convention would only be as a dissenting minority. They would soon take steps to completely withdraw from the Convention and establish a denomination of their own, even though many of their numbers denied at the time that this was taking place.[1] At the same time, the conservatives began efforts to move beyond appointing trustees to the seminaries to restaffing the agency leadership positions, and then moving on to state conventions.

## The Cooperative Baptist Fellowship

In July 1990, Dan Vestal and other leaders of Baptists Committed, called for a national meeting to deal with their lack of denominational voice. They earnestly believed that they were in the majority in the Convention. Even so, they only expected about five hundred people to attend the meeting in Atlanta. To everyone's surprise, more than three thousand people registered for the meeting, with representatives from moderate groups such as Baptists Committed, the Forum, *SBC Today*, and Women in Ministry. At the end of the meeting, a new charter for an alternative funding program which by-passed the Executive Committee was in place. The charter for the tax-exempt status had been taken out by Duke McCall, Grady Cothen, Hettie Johnson, and others prior to the call

---

[1] This author was on active duty in the military as a Chaplain under the endorsement of the Home Mission Board. One his closest friends who eventually went with the Cooperative Baptist Fellowship, at the time of the formation of the new organization stated that he believed that it was not going to be another denomination, but would be an alternative for the moderates within the denomination.

for the meeting.² It was not long before other moderate organizations came into being, such as the Associated Baptist Press.³

In 1992, the Cooperative Baptist Fellowship (CBF) Executive Committee met near the Dallas-Fort Worth Airport to consider electing an Executive Secretary. They had already begun funding some organizations that had been defunded by the Southern Baptist Convention. Cecil Sherman, who had resigned from the Peace Committee in protest and had been serving as pastor of First Baptist Church of Ashville, North Carolina and was at that time serving as Pastor of Broadway Baptist Church in Fort Worth, was approached and finally agreed.⁴ Later that year, the CBF appointed its first missionary couple and hired Keith Parks as global missions coordinator. In 1994, the Southern Baptist Convention quit accepting funds from the fellowship. The CBF adopted a formal mission statement in 1995.⁵ With its acceptance into the Baptist World Alliance in 1993, they became a separate denomination apart from the Southern Baptist Convention.

## Battles in the States

Simply because the battle for the control of the national convention was over does not mean that all of the struggles ceased. In fact, in some areas it intensified. The attention shifted to the states where it met with varying degrees of success. Some states were gained by conservatives while in others the moderates remained in control. Some state conventions began to be controlled by conservatives while the colleges and universities in those states were moderate-dominated.

Moderates won in Virginia, though not initially by a great majority. In 1989, Ray Spence was elected as president of that state convention. They also passed a resolution in favor of support of Lloyd Elder and Russell Dilday. Another resolution instructed a committee to explore an alternative news agency to the Baptist Press, as it was coming

---

² Fletcher, *The Southern Baptist Convention*, 308.
³ Ibid. 309.
⁴ Ibid., 318.
⁵ Cooperative Baptist Fellowship website, http://www.thefellowship.info/About-Us/FAQ,

under the control of the conservatives.⁶ Struggles continued until 1993 when conservatives in Virginia formed the Southern Baptist Convention of Virginia.

Texas was the other singular great loss for conservatives. The Baptist General Convention of Texas remained in the hands of moderates, as well as the schools owned by that convention. Taking a cue from the moderates' playbook, conservatives in Texas formed the Conservative Baptist Fellowship of Texas in 1995, but in 1998 officially began their own state convention called the Southern Baptist Convention of Texas (SBCT). Two colleges in Texas are affiliated with that Convention, Criswell College and Jacksonville College, though neither is owned by the SBCT.

South Carolina had remained a more conservative convention than North Carolina, but in 1991, Furman University had indicated a desire to elect its own trustees. The state convention failed to support such a move. The situation continued to remain unresolved until a group of thirty-four South Carolina pastors met and recommended that the Convention sever all ties to Furman. Their suggestion was seconded by Furman and a special meeting of the South Carolina Convention was called to deal with the matter. In June 1992, Furman was made independent of the state convention.⁷

Without going into detail in the various other states, the greatest evidence of the struggles taking place in the states is seen in the colleges and universities that are owned or affiliated with the various state conventions. In the state of Georgia, for example, Mercer University severed its ties with the Georgia Baptist Convention. The other colleges remained, but were widely known to lean toward the moderate position. In recent years, the state convention has made an attempt to bring them back into line consistent with their congregations, a process that has proven to be extremely painful for all concerned. The Georgia Baptist Convention went to court over who exactly was in control of Shorter College (now Shorter University). When the Convention won, it made the decision to move it back to the right. When Shorter's president informed

---

⁶ James. C. Hefley, *The Conservative Resurgence in the Southern Baptist Convention* (Hannibal, Missouri: Hannibal Books, 1991), 125.
⁷ Fletcher, The Southern Baptist Convention, 317-318.

the faculty that they would have to sign lifestyle statements, affirming a conservative lifestyle and rejecting homosexuality, public drinking and other behaviors, more than fifty faculty and staff members either resigned or signaled their intent to leave, including one who stated that he was openly gay.[8]

The battle in other states has been more low-key. In Alabama, Samford University openly affiliates with the Cooperative Baptist Fellowship, granting minister's dependent scholarships to children of either Southern Baptist or Cooperative Baptist Fellowship ministers.[9] It has even formed its own divinity school, Beeson Divinity School, which boasts a broad, ecumenical approach to theological education.[10]

## Under the Executive Committee

*The Sunday School Board.* Jerry Sutton stated that the Baptist Sunday School Board, and its affiliated Broadman Press, was known as a bastion of moderate/liberal influence. It was the publisher of *The Message of Genesis*, the Broadman Bible Commentary, and other controversial publications. According to Sutton, it began under the leadership of James Sullivan, president 1953-1975, and continued under Grady Cothen, 1975-1983. After Cothen's departure, he authored a book, *What Happened to the Southern Baptist Convention?* which was published by Smyth and Helwys, a publisher of materials used and authored by moderate writers.[11]

Lloyd Elder, president from 1983 to 1991, resisted efforts to bring the Sunday School Board to a more conservative position. The Convention voted in 1985 to produce a new conservative commentary, which represented the inerrantist view. Elder stalled this for more than a year until the August 1986 plenary session of the Sunday School Board when the trustees voted to publish the commentary series over Elder's opposition. As early as 1987 the trustees were informing Elder as to their dissatisfaction. As Elder continued to promote a moderate agenda, conflict with the trustees intensified. Elder eventually began to record his

---

[8] http://www.insidehighered.com/news/2012/05/14/shorter-university-faculty-leaving-over-new-lifestyle-statements
[9] http://admission.samford.edu/scholarships/
[10] http://beesondivinity.com/about
[11] Jerry Sutton, The Baptist Reformation: The Conservative Resurgence in the Southern Baptist Convention. (Nashville: Broadman & Holman, 2000), 28.

conversations with trustees and others, and surrounded himself with employees who proved to be less than dependable. Elder was granted early retirement in July 1991.[12]

Upon Elder's retirement, James T. Draper, Jr. assumed the presidency of the Sunday School Board. Draper, a clear conservative, brought the Sunday School Board back to a more conservative position. In 1998, the name of the organization was changed to LifeWay Christian Resources of the Southern Baptist Convention. This move was a means to show that the entity was more than a Sunday School Board; it was the world's largest producer and distributor of religious materials. Some have challenged that this move is simply a decision to eliminate the name "Baptist" in order to make the materials more marketable to the broader Christian community. Regardless, Draper assembled a new team to oversee the LifeWay Christian Bookstores, Broadman and Holman publishers, and other chief operating officers.[13]

*Christian Ethics and Religious Liberty.* At the beginning of the Conservative Resurgence, Foy Valentine was the head of the Christian Life Commission. His openly leftward leaning positions made him an easy target for the conservatives. As Valentine took a more liberal approach on abortion and the Convention took a distinctive pro-life position, Valentine made the decision to retire, expressing his intention in a letter to the trustees in April 1986. Nathan Larry Baker was selected as his replacement, but the trustees were not unanimous in this decision. Conservatives soon began asking for Baker's removal over his position on abortion, capital punishment, and women in ministry. In May 1988, after only fifteen months as head of the Christian Life Commission, Baker resigned to take a pastorate in Louisiana. Richard Land, a staunch conservative, was elected on September 12, 1988 as the new executive director/treasurer.[14]

The executive director of the Baptist Joint Committee on Public Affairs (BJCPA), James E. Wood, Jr., had signed a statement endorsing abortion. Wood was replaced in October 1980 by James Dunn, who soon took positions on issues that were counter to those advocated by the

---

[12] Ibid., 288-307.
[13] Ibid., 307-308.
[14] Ibid., 309-314.

Convention. Opposition to the BJCPA was mounting. It seemed that the more Southern Baptists learned about it, the less credibility it had. In 1984 and in 1986, motions were made to defund the committee. A subcommittee was appointed to study the organization. While some representation on the BJCPA board was changed, the organization was allowed to function as a type of independent board. In 1989 a motion was made to create a Religious Liberty Commission, but that decision was tabled until after the 1989 Southern Baptist Convention. The BJCPA was reduced in its funding in 1990 from $391,000 to $50,000 with the balance being transferred to the Christian Life Commission. The committee was completely defunded in 1991. Responsibilities for all moral and religious liberty issues were assigned to the Christian Life Commission. When the Southern Baptist Convention reorganized in 1997, the agency was renamed the Ethics and Religious Liberty Commission of the Southern Baptist Convention with Richard Land as the head.[15] In more recent years, Richard Land has come under fire for his positions on several emotionally charged issues, resulting in the cancelation of a weekly radio broadcast hosted by him. He was also reprimanded by trustees.[16]

## Domestic Missions

When the Conservative Resurgence officially began in 1979, Bill Tanner was president of the Home Mission Board. By the mid-1980s, conservatives made up a majority of the trustees of the missions agency and their impact began to be felt. He eventually left to take the position of executive director of the Oklahoma Baptist Convention. The original search committee for his replacement was asked to resign so that a more conservative committee could be appointed. All of them resigned except for two who remained on the new committee. As they performed their appointed duty, the trustees took a more hands-on approach to the leadership of the mission board. In October 1986 the trustees voted to cut off any supplemental funding to any church which called a woman as pastor. By late 1986, the conservative Larry Lewis, former president of Hannibal-LaGrange College in Missouri was selected for the post. He assumed those duties in April 1987.[17]

---

[15] Ibid., 317-319.
[16] http://www.bpnews.net/BPnews.asp?ID=38103
[17] Sutton, *The Baptist Reformation*, 258-259.

While the trustees had voted to cease funding to churches with women pastors, they were possibly unaware of the fact that ordained women continued to be endorsed as chaplains. Later, when the issue of women serving as chaplains was addressed to the administration of the Home Mission Board by a group of military chaplains, the point was made to the Chaplaincy Commission that this was contrary to the decision by the Convention not to appoint women as missionaries who were ordained. These chaplains were quietly informed that technically chaplains were endorsed by the Home Mission Board, not appointed or funded as missionaries. Later, when the chaplains continued to press the issue, they were warned that continued actions on their part could result in the removal of their endorsement, forcing them to leave the military service. In spite of the threat, some of the chaplains contacted the trustees in the Home Mission Board directly and informed them as to the practice. When the trustees instructed the Chaplains Commission to cease appointing ordained women as chaplains, it began endorsing women as chaplains who had no ordination. As more chaplains became aware of this, the information was communicated to the trustees. Eventually, there were some personnel changes and the policy was changed to be consistent with the intent of the Convention.[18]

The personnel changes in the Chaplains Commission were only representative of others that took place under Lewis's leadership. However, while Lewis moved the Home Mission Board into a more conservative practice and position, some of his actions drew fire from Southern Baptists. One such incident was when Lewis and Richard Land fixed their signatures to a document entitled "Evangelicals and Catholics Together." Many Southern Baptists were concerned about the doctrinal differences between Baptists and Catholics and had reservations over the action. After the Foreign Mission Board's board of trustees voted to express concern over the document, Land and Lewis agreed to remove their signatures from it.[19]

In 1995, the plans for the restructuring of the Convention were well underway. Lewis asked for a delay in its consideration because of his concerns about its impact on home missions. He had concerns over the

---

[18] Personal knowledge of the author.
[19] Sutton, *The Baptist Reformation*, 262-263.

recommendations to focus primarily in the North and in major cities, as well as several other components of the plan, including the transfer of Canada from the Foreign Mission Board to the Home Mission Board/North American Mission Board. After voicing his frustration over the restructuring and creation of the North American Mission Board, he announced his retirement in September 1996.[20]

The reorganization of the North American Mission Board (NAMB) was to follow a similar model to that which is used in corporate structure, where the organization begins with the mission statement and builds the organization around the functions that work toward the accomplishment of that mission. In the case of NAMB, the process would focus on evangelism and church planting. Robert Reccord, pastor of the First Baptist Church of Norfolk, Virginia, was tapped to lead the redeveloping organization. He began by stating at Glorietta Baptist Conference Center that Bold Mission Thrust's goal of baptizing half a million people by A.D. 2000 is impossible, but continued by saying that what is impossible with men is not impossible with God. He then set a new goal of baptizing a million people by 2005. He explained that this would be done through the local church and placed the local church at the center of everything NAMB did. Additionally, Reccord reaffirmed a commitment to reaching the cities of North America.[21] Under the reorganization, NAMB combined the Home Mission Board, Radio and Television Commission, and the Brotherhood Commission and moved the headquarters to Alpharetta, Georgia.[22] Reccord remained as head of NAMB until 2006 when he resigned. While no improprieties surfaced that led to his resignation, Reccord had been criticized for a perceived lack of relationship with state convention leadership. He had previously been placed under supervision by the trustees and had what he described as philosophical and methodological differences with the trustees. In September 2010, having previously served as pastor of Highview Baptist Church of Louisville, Kentucky, Kevin Ezell was selected to become the next chief executive officer of NAMB.[23]

---

[20] Ibid., 263-265.
[21] http://www.bpnews.net/printerfriendly.asp?ID=23053
[22] http://www.namb.net/history/
[23] http://www.namb.net/Kevin-Ezell/

Since becoming president of NAMB, the mission board has undertaken the challenge of completely reorganizing in an effort to mobilize missionaries and churches for evangelistic church planting. This initiative is called Send North America.[24]

## Foreign Missions

When the Conservative Resurgence began in 1979, Baker James Cauthen had served as executive director of the Foreign Mission Board for almost thirty years. He officially retired on January 7, 1980 and R. Keith Parks assumed the presidency of the Foreign Mission Board. Parks served during most of the time period referred to as the Conservative Resurgence. He was seen as a man of intense loyalty to the Great Commission. During his time there, he reorganized the work of the Board according to a corporate model. He expanded the Convention's understanding of partnership missions and developed a task force approach for responding to opportunities for work which opened on short notice. In 1987, he reorganized the Foreign Mission Board, establishing a Global Strategy Group, with this team replacing the Executive Management Group. In the new organization, there were two significant emphases: First, it surveyed missions to see what institutions could be turned over to Baptists in the countries in which the missionaries served, freeing them up for more evangelistic work with unreached people groups. Second, it established a policy where at least seventy percent of the mission force would spend a minimum of half their time on outreach, new churches, and evangelism.[25]

Until 1985, Parks had remained outside of the controversy in the Southern Baptist Convention, keeping any apprehension he had about the swing in the direction confined to private communications to individual missionaries. In April 1985, however, he wrote openly to Southern Baptist foreign missionaries his belief that he could not support Charles Stanley's reelection as president of the Convention, primarily because he felt that Stanley's church, First Baptist Church of Atlanta, supported so many non-SBC missionaries that he felt that in the long run it would be destructive to the Cooperative Program, as already evidenced by the church's meager support of the funding program.[26]

---

[24] http://www.namb.net/faq/
[25] Sutton, *The Baptist Reformation*, 268-269.
[26] Ibid., 269-270.

The Conservative Resurgence was already having an impact on the FMB. Previously, all SBC missionaries had to have minimum study at an SBC seminary. However, in 1987, the board allowed graduates of Mid-America Baptist Theological Seminary to be appointed as career missionaries. About the same time, there were conflicts involving several missionaries who were either already on the mission field or en route. Several of them had expressed beliefs that seemed to run counter to what Southern Baptists widely believed. Some of the missionaries resigned; others were outright terminated. Things seemed to come to a head with regard to the International Baptist Theological Seminary, in Ruschlikon, Germany. In 1991, the trustees of the Foreign Mission Board made the decision to defund the seminary due to its doctrinal positions. As a result of the defunding, several SBC foreign missionaries resigned, including the president of the Ruschlikon seminary, John David Hopper and his wife, Jo Ann. The Hoppers were immediately employed by the Cooperative Baptist Fellowship in the same capacity. Finally, in April 1992, Parks resigned as president of the Foreign Mission Board.[27]

June 1993 saw Jerry Rankin, a career missionary with the Foreign Mission Board, installed as the new president. Missionaries around the world seemed to be relieved to have one of their own elected. One of his first steps was to phase out the Global Strategy Group and replace it with a vice president for overseas operation. Ten area directors related to the board through the vice president. Rankin soon found himself in conflict with the WMU. First, the WMU was reluctant to allow the mission boards to assume responsibility for their own missions offerings, but the heart of this seemed to lie the issue that the WMU had decided to expand their curriculum and product line to include CBF related pieces.[28]

In 1997, the Foreign Mission Board changed its name to the International Mission Board (IMB). Throughout Rankin's time at the Foreign Mission Board/International Mission Board, Rankin continued to push for churches to faithfully support their foreign missionaries with their Cooperative Program gifts and their prayers, always stressing the work Southern Baptists were doing to advance the Kingdom around the world. Rankin retired July 31, 2010.

---

[27] Ibid., 270-285.
[28] Ibid., 285-286.

In February 2011, Thomas D. (Tom) Eliff was nominated to be president of the IMB. He was elected by the trustees the following month and installed in that office officially in November of that year. Eliff had been president of the Southern Baptist Convention in 1996 and 1997, president of the Pastor's Conference in 1990 and preached the Convention Sermon in Orlando in 1994. He had been pastor of First Southern Baptist Church of Del City, Oklahoma for twenty years, leaving in 2005 to become IMB's senior vice president for spiritual nurture and church relations. At the time of his election, he was 67 years old, but assured Southern Baptists that he was not coming as an interim; he was coming with a vision, vowing to serve as long as God gives him grace and energy.[29]

## Baptist Faith and Message

When the Baptist Faith and Message was adopted in 1925, it was intended as a means by which Southern Baptists would be able to articulate its beliefs to those outside of the denomination, while at the same time, stating clearly to all, both within and without the Convention, while not being a binding creed upon any church or member. It had been used in that capacity until the time of its revision in 1963. With controversies developing in the Convention over theology, the question arose as to whether or not professors at the seminaries were teaching things that were not in concert with what was believed by the majority of Southern Baptists. If they were being supported financially by the churches, their teaching should be consistent with what Southern Baptists believed. When the 1963 version was adopted, it included language that was not to clarify what was believed, but which was made more broad and general so as not to exclude anyone. The difficulty with this was the ability to attach different meanings to words, so that two groups could use the same terminology, but have different meanings. This was central to the issue during the Conservative Resurgence. Finally, in 1999, T. C. Pinkney of Virginia made a motion to the Southern Baptist Convention to ask the president to appoint a committee to consider a revision of the 1963 document. The motion passed, and President Paige Patterson appointed a committee made up of Max Barnett of Oklahoma, Steve Gaines of Alabama, Susie Hawkins

---

[29] http://www.gofbw.com/news.asp?ID=12713

and Rudy A Hernandez, both of Texas, Charles S. Kelley, Jr. and Fred Luter of Louisiana, Heather King of Indiana, Richard D. Land and Adrian Rogers of Tennessee, R. Albert Mohler of Kentucky, T. C. Pinkney of Virginia, Nelson Price of Georgia, Roger Spradlin of California, Simon Tsoi of Arizona, and Jerry Vines of Florida. Adrian Rogers was appointed chairman of the committee.[30]

When the report was presented the following year, there were several proposed amendments to the report, including one by chairman Adrian Rogers. Each of the proposed amendments was debated, with members of the committee speaking against each one. Each proposed amendment failed and the Baptist Faith and Messaged was adopted as it was originally presented.[31]

The adopted confession of faith included a statement from the committee chairman what articulated the authority of the Bible and absolute truth, as well as a desire to clearly state what Southern Baptists believe about specific issues that would not have even been envisioned by previous generations. The committee made a conscious effort to maintain as much of the language in the original confession as possible. No new articles were added to the 1963 document, although statements were added to several of the sections. One specific statement that was adopted would have been controversial had it been presented prior to the Conservative Resurgence. Article VI specifically stated that while both men and women are called to ministry, the office of pastor is limited to men as qualified by Scriptures. The adoption of the new document remains as clear evidence that the conservative values of the churches were publicly articulated by the Convention as a whole.[32]

## Changes in the Seminaries

*Southern Baptist Theological Seminary.* In the minds of many Southern Baptists, no seminary was in greater need of reformation than the denomination's oldest theological institution. When the Conservative Resurgence began, Duke K. McCall was president. He, as well as other seminary presidents, desired to preserve the status quo when the Conservative Resurgence began. In 1982, Dale Moody, who had been a

---

[30] *Annual*, 199, 36-88.
[31] *Annual*, 2000, 75-76.
[32] http://www.sbc.net/bfm/bfmchairman.asp

senior professor of theology and had already retired, yet continued to teach as a contract professor, was forced out when his contract to teach was not renewed. He had already come under fire for some of his teachings that were in contradiction with the 1963 Baptist Faith and Message, as well as the seminary's "Abstract of Principles." That same year, Duke McCall retired, succeeded by Roy L. Honeycutt.[33]

During Honeycutt's time at Southern, the trustees were slowly replaced, with the board taking on an increasingly conservative view. Honeycutt openly entered the fray in 1984 when he preached the Convention sermon, attempting to rally the seminary community and its friends to oppose the conservatives who were taking control of the Convention. Increasingly, Southern's professors came under fire, even to the point that some of them were urged to resign by people outside of the seminary. In 1989, Glenn Hinson was quoted as stating that he would like to see a greater push toward an ecumenical environment in the Southern Baptist Convention. He clearly did not see the unlikelihood of this occurring at Southern or in the Convention. Finally, in 1990, trustees voted to make the 1987 Peace Committee Report a guideline for hiring, promoting, and granting tenure to professors. In 1991, newly elected Provost Larry L. McSwain tried to encourage Southern Seminary to be more tolerant of the conservative view. He stated, "I have never understood how you can claim academic freedom as a value and exclude conservative views from the educational experiences any more than I believe you can claim academic freedom in an institution that refuses to teach its students liberation theology or feminist theology." In 1992, David Dockery was appointed dean of the School of Theology, and within months, several of the professors resigned to take positions at The Baptist Theological Seminary of Virginia. In May 1993, Honeycutt announced his intention to retire. He was replaced in July of that year by 33-year-old R. Albert Mohler, Jr. Mohler was a graduate of Southern with both his masters and doctor of philosophy degrees. He had served on staff in various administrative roles from 1983 until 1989. Mohler was a known conservative and immediately set out to clean house, removing several professors. During nearly two decades at Southern, Mohler has brought evangelical, conservative scholarship back to the seminary. Mohler has

---

[33] Sutton, *The Baptist Reformation*, 340-342.

served as a leader and spokesperson for and to Southern Baptists on numerous issues.[34]

*Southeastern Baptist Theological Seminary.* Southeastern Seminary was probably the most visible evidence for a need for the Conservative Resurgence. It had begun with the intent of being the most progressive of the seminaries. When Randall Lolley became president in 1974, he brought with him Peter Drucker's emphasis on management by objectives, which is a type of shared leadership. The result was a faculty that became strong and nearly unaccountable. During his tenure there, several conservative student-led organizations developed. These groups began working to have a more conservative viewpoint presented in the classrooms and on campus, even arranging to have Paul Pressler invited to the school as a guest speaker at one of their organizations. By the mid-1980s, many of the faculty members had come under harsh criticism for their teachings and publications, some of which were published by the Sunday School Board. A 1986 Peace Committee visit identified specific areas of concern, some of which had been reported by students at Southeastern. As the conflict continued, Randall Lolley decided to resign rather than promote the conservative agenda. His resignation was to take effect in July of 1988, or sooner if his replacement was found. Lewis Drummond was elected president and took office on April 1, 1988.[35]

Two days after his election, Drummond learned that the school's accrediting agencies would be investigating several areas of concern. It was an extremely difficult time for Drummond, but he was successful in managing the school through the exodus of numerous faculty members, while keeping the school off of probation with its accrediting agencies. At the end of four years, the Chairman of trustees informed Drummond that his position was secure at Southeastern, more so than it ever had been. However, Drummond soon received an invitation from his alma mater, Samford University, to come to teach at Beeson Divinity School. Drummond was thrilled at the opportunity to return to the classroom and later reported that he believed he had done what God had brought him to

---

[34] Ibid., 342-362.
[35] Ibid., 324-329.

Southeastern to do and that he had left it a place for a new, younger person to help the seminary begin all over again.[36]

With Drummond's departure scheduled for June 30, 1992, the trustees met and elected Paige Patterson at the seminary's fifth president. He immediately set out to satisfy any remaining accreditation concerns. He also began to restructure the seminary, even removing books from the library that advocated homosexuality and other non-Christian lifestyles. By September 1994, the curriculum was being revised to focus on what was needed to train pastors and others to function effectively in ministry. Enrollment quickly began improving, with enrollment records being set each year from 1996 to 2000. Patterson left Southeastern in 2003 to return to his beloved state of Texas where he became president of Southwestern Baptist Theological Seminary.[37]

Daniel (Danny) Aiken left Southern Seminary in 2004 to become the new president. He had been an associate professor and the Dean of Students at Southeastern 1992-1996, when he left to take a teaching position at Southern Seminary. Akin has continued the conservative direction of the seminary and has placed a great emphasis on Christian living and the biblical view of the family. He has three sons in the ministry and keeps the focus of Southeastern on the purpose of training ministers for service.[38]

*Southwestern Baptist Theological Seminary.* It is probably safe to say that if Russell Dilday had remained silent, the Conservative Resurgence would have never turned its attention to Southwestern Seminary. The school had a reputation for conservatism. Most of Dilday's early public comments defending his faculty were basically a defense when no accusation was being made. As conservatives took aim at Southern and Southeastern, Southwestern was not even considered as a target. In fact, no complaints were ever lodged against any faculty member or their teachings at Southwestern. In spite of this, Dilday became very vocal in his criticism of the conservative movement. He preached his "Higher Ground" sermon at the June 1984 Southern Baptist Convention. In spite of the lack of criticism of his seminary, he continued to defend the

---

[36] Ibid., 329-334.
[37] Ibid., 334-339.
[38] http://www.danielakin.com/?page_id=2

faculty and the school and to openly criticize the conservative movement. Even after the visit by the Peace Committee, while no fault was found with the seminary, Dilday continued to defend the institution. In October 1986, Dilday met with the other seminary presidents and assisted in drafting the Glorieta Statement, which he then signed. He continued to be vocal until 1989 when Ken Lilly, one of Southwestern's chairman of the trustees wrote a letter to the other members of the board expressing concern over Dilday's political activities with regard to the Convention leadership and direction. In 1991, Attorney Jim Bolton, a long-time friend of Dilday's was elected chairman of the trustees. He pledged to work with Dilday in love and that any disagreement would be in private and that in public they would be unified with him. Echoing this, Dilday pledged to remain out of Convention politics. The implication was that the trustees would be supportive of his leadership and that he would leave the politics behind. This was a short-lived promise on Dilday's part, being openly critical of the Convention over the next two years. Finally, in March 1994, the trustees voted twenty-six to seven to dismiss Dilday.[39]

In 1994, Ken Hemphill became President of Southwestern Seminary. His presence had a sort of calming influence on everyone, granting assurance to faculty and trustees alike that the school was on the right track. He built morale among the faculty, students, as well as the national alumni. His greatest challenge was the fact that one of the school's two accrediting agencies, the Association of Theological Schools (ATS) had placed Southwestern on probation, primarily over Dilday's firing. Hemphill decided not to appeal ATS's ruling, but instead simply worked to address all issues they raised. He left in 2003 to become the SBC's national strategist for the Empowering Kingdom Growth program.[40] He was followed that year by Paige Patterson who left his position at Southeastern to lead Southwestern. Patterson continued to expand the programs at the seminary, keeping it completely grounded in conservatism, even though it is in the heart of Cooperative Baptist Fellowship territory.[41]

---

[39] Sutton, *The Baptist Reformation*, 363-380.
[40] http://www.swbts.edu/centennial/hemphill.cfm
[41] http://www.swbts.edu/centennial/patterson.cfm

*Golden Gate Baptist Theological Seminary.* When the Conservative Resurgence began, William M. Pinson, Jr. was president. His greatest concern was that the institutions as a whole were under attack. Yet, under his administration, as well as that of the administration of Franklin D. Pollard, the school was safe from attack.[42] Pollard arrived in 1983, but only served for three years, leaving to become pastor of First Baptist Church, Jackson, Mississippi. During his short time there, the school experienced its largest enrollment gain in its history. William O. Crews, Jr. became president in 1986. Crews was a clear conservative and had been active at the state and national levels of denominational life. He expanded the seminary to campuses in several other western states. Jess Iorg became president in 2004, resigning his position as Executive Director/Treasurer of the Northwest Baptist Convention in Oregon. The seminary is intentional in helping Southern Baptist evangelize the West and the Pacific Rim.[43]

*New Orleans Baptist Theological Seminary.* Like Golden Gate, New Orleans remained unscathed by the Conservative Resurgence. Under the leadership of President Landrum Leavell, the school had taken some criticism over the publication of a book by Fisher Humphreys, but the school was given a clean bill of health by the Peace Committee. Leavell retired in 1995, and in 1996 Charles S. "Chuck" Kelley was selected as the seminary's eighth president.[44] The school has remained a conservative institution. By 2005, New Orleans had become the largest of the six Southern Baptist seminaries, but the campus was flooded when Hurricane Katrina devastated the city. Forced to shift operations to the Atlanta Campus temporarily, the school remained in operation. After a long recovery process, the seminary replaced much of the older student housing that had been damaged beyond repair and acquired properties adjacent to the campus. The school has emerged even more beautiful than it was before the storm.

*Midwestern Baptist Theological Seminary.* Midwestern was the place where much of the Conservative Resurgence began, with the publication of Ralph Elliott's book which was discussed earlier. It was also

---

[42] Sutton, *The Baptist Reformation*, 381.
[43] http://www.ggbts.edu/about/History.aspx
[44] Sutton, *The Baptist Reformation*, 382-382.

the last place to be fully impacted by the move to conservatism, as the conservatives did not gain a majority among the trustees until 1991. By then, many of the moderates at Midwestern had seen the handwriting on the wall and had already sought positions elsewhere. However, in 1983, President Milton Ferguson received complaints concerning the writings of one of his professors, G. Temp Sparkman. He had been accused of believing in universalism, based upon the writings in two of his books. He denied believing in any form of universalism, but when a subcommittee of the SBC Peace Committee visited Midwestern Seminary, they were informed that he was on sabbatical until August of that year. He had already been advised to seek other employment when he returned, even though the trustees had already affirmed that his teachings were within the seminary articles of faith. This seemed to be consistent with the way the Elliott controversy was handled by the trustees. However, in 1991, the conservatives had gained a majority among Midwestern's trustees and were committed to bringing the school to a more conservative stance. Sparkman submitted his resignation in 1992, citing medical reasons. Later, when two professors were being considered for tenure, they had issues with the meaning of certain parts of the Baptist Faith and Message. Ultimately, in spite of the president's lobbying on their behalf, one of them, Wilburn T. Stancil, was denied tenure. After a prolonged battle with the trustees, Ferguson announced his plans to retire as president. In 1995, Mark Coppenger was elected as the third president of the embattled seminary. After the Stancil issue, the ATS made notations in their report about the trustee governance of the institution and its impact on the learning environment. By August 1997, several of the notations had been removed and steady work was being done to remove the others. The last of these had been completed by March 1999.[45] Coppenger resigned in September 1999 and in January 2001, R. Philip Roberts was elected as the fifth president.[46] After eleven years in that position, allegations were made concerning Roberts' misuse of seminary resources and of verbal abuse of seminary staff. In a February 2012 called meeting with trustees, Roberts

---

[45] Ibid., 383-390.
[46] http://www.mbts.edu/about/history/

was in discussion with the trustees, during which he tendered his resignation.[47]

## Calvinistic Resurgence

One of the earliest disagreements among Baptists has been over the issue of God's sovereignty and man's free will. The conflict can be traced back to the differences between the Particular Baptists and the General Baptists, whose major difference seems to be over the limits of the atonement. The differences were even seen in the various confessions; the Philadelphia Confession was strongly Calvinistic while the New Hampshire Confession moderated it somewhat. It was the New Hampshire Confession that gave shape to the 1925 *Baptist Faith and Message*. Specifically among Southern Baptists, James Boyce and Basil Manly, Jr. tended to stricter Calvinism. E. Y. Mullins and W. T. Conner modified the position. However, according to David Dockery, it was Dale Moody, Frank Stagg, and Herschel Hobbs that moved Southern Baptists to the non-Calvinistic positions on atonement, election, and predestination.[48] It is difficult to measure the degree to which the Convention holds to classical Calvinism. By and large, it appears that the pastors who graduate from some seminaries hold to Calvinism more strongly that those who graduate from others. Al Mohler, president of Southern Seminary has been open concerning his Calvinistic views, even being a frequent speaker at Reformed Theological Seminary.[49] Danny Akin, president of Southeastern Seminary, also presents himself as reformed in his theology, although he seems open to working with those who do not agree with him on all points.[50]

Calvinism has traditionally been described by use of the acronym TULIP. Each of the letters of the acronym stands for one of the five points of classical Calvinism. "T" represents the belief in the Total Depravity of Man meaning that man, in his sinful state, is totally blind and deaf to the gospel without God intervening first. "U" stands for Unconditional

---

[47] http://www.bpnews.net/bpnews.asp?id=37155
[48] Reported in Fletcher, *The Southern Baptist Convention*, 372-373.
[49] This author, while not reformed, is a graduate of Reformed Theological Seminary, and sees the reports of Mohler's speaking engagements in alumni periodicals.
[50] http://www.sbclife.org/Articles/2006/04/SLA7.asp

Election, which states that God chose those to whom he was pleased to bring knowledge of himself, not based upon any merit shown by the object of his grace and not based upon his looking forward to discover who would "accept" the offer of the gospel. God has elected, based solely upon the counsel of his own will, some for glory and others for damnation. He had done this act before the foundations of the world. "L," or Limited Atonement, is the most controversial of all of the points of Calvinism. It holds that Christ's atonement was limited to only those to whom God gave Christ to save, the "elect." Only those that God had foreordained to be saved would respond positively to the Gospel message. "I" is for Irresistible Grace and means that when the message of God's grace is presented to members of the elect, they would find his grace irresistible to the point of responding in repentance for their sin. "P" is the single point to which almost all Southern Baptists hold, and which sets them apart from true Arminians. That point is Perseverance of the Saints, sometimes called "once saved, always saved." This is the doctrine that states that when a believer has been regenerated by God, that person will remain in God's hand in a state of grace until that person is glorified at the "last day."[51]

When a group of prominent Southern Baptists signed a document affirming their reformed beliefs,[52] a respondent group articulated their views in a document called "A Statement of the Traditional Southern Baptist Understanding of God's Plan of Salvation."[53] It has been signed by more than 800 Baptists, including Chuck Kelley, president of New Orleans Seminary and Paige Patterson, president Southwestern Seminary, members of the Baptist Faith and Message 2000 Committee, and numerous state executives and past presidents of the Southern Baptist Convention.[54] It is obvious to even the most casual observer that there is strong disagreement within the Convention over the issue of soteriology. Both sides agree that salvation is initiated by God and that it comes only through faith in Christ and in Him alone, but they disagree on other points.

---

[51] http://www.reformed.org/calvinism/index.html
[52] http://www.t4g.org/uploads/pdf/affirmations-denials.pdf
[53] http://sbctoday.com/wp-content/uploads/2012/06/A-Statement-of-Traditional-Southern-Baptist-Soteriology-SBC-Today.pdf
[54] http://sbctoday.com/2012/06/01/list-of-signers-of-%e2%80%9ca-statement-of-the-traditional-southern-baptist-understanding-of-god%e2%80%99s-plan-of-salvation/

The issue is not likely to be resolved soon, but it is clear that Calvinism has experienced a resurgence within the past few years. With godly people of prominence in the seminaries espousing this position, and with godly people of prominence in the seminaries holding to a non-Calvinist position, the disagreement will undoubtedly grow.

## Great Commission Resurgence

In addition to the Conservative Resurgence and the Calvinistic Resurgence that has taken place among Southern Baptists in recent years is the Great Commission Resurgence, a movement that began as a result of a 2005 study by Thom Rainer, who was at the time dean of the Billy Graham School of Missions, Evangelism and Church Growth at Southern Seminary. In the study, Rainer outlined why he believed the Convention has been in a state of decline since the end of the Conservative Resurgence. He also articulated what he believed needed to happen to turn the trend around.[55] Many of his concerns were reiterated in a book compiled by David Dockery called *Southern Baptist Identity: An Evangelical Denomination Faces the Future*.[56] Later, Danny Akin addressed the issue at Southeastern Seminary outlining twelve axioms for a Great Commission Resurgence.[57] Johnny Hunt posted an open letter to Southern Baptists calling for a Great Commission Resurgence.[58] Then, at the 2009 Convention, Al Mohler made a motion that the president of the Convention appoint a Great Commission Task Force (GCRTF) to bring a report the following year "concerning how Southern Baptists can work more faithfully and effectively in serving Christ through the Great Commission." The motion was adopted.[59]

The following year, the Convention met in Orlando. Morris Chapman had already announced his retirement as president of the Executive Committee. He had also been very open about his opposition to the GCRTF's report, even after the preliminary report was made to the Executive Committee in February. While initially he had supported the

---

[55] http://www.floridabaptistwitness.com/sb/4249.article.print
[56] David Dockery, ed. *Southern Baptist Identity: An Evangelical Denomination Faces the Future* (Wheaton, Ill: Crossway Books, 2009), 217 *ff*.
[57] http://www.danielakin.com/?p=1037
[58] http://www.bpnews.net/BPFirstPerson.asp?ID=30531
[59] *Annual*, 2009, 57, 84.

idea of a Great Commission Resurgence, he later came to oppose the work done by the committee appointed by Hunt, even using his last address to the Convention as president of the Executive Committee to strongly oppose adoption of the report.[60] When the proposal was presented to the Convention, there was little debate over several of the points in the recommendation, but one particular point seemed to draw the most opposition. Point three of the motion stated,

> 3. That the messengers to the Southern Baptist Convention, meeting in Orlando, Florida, June 15-16, 2010, request the Executive Committee of the Southern Baptist Convention to consider recommending to the Southern Baptist Convention the adoption of the language and structure of Great Commission Giving as described in this report in order to enhance and celebrate the Cooperative Program and the generous support of Southern Baptists channeled through their churches and to continue to honor and affirm the Cooperative Program as the most effective means of mobilizing our churches and extending our outreach. We further request that the boards of trustees of the International Mission Board and North American Mission Board, in consultation with the Woman's Missionary Union, consider the adoption of the Lottie Moon and Annie Armstrong offering goals as outlined in this report.[61]

There appeared to be a great concern that adoption of the language in favor of "Great Commission Giving" would circumvent the Cooperative Program and would ultimately lead to its failure. The motion was amended to read

> 3. That the messengers to the Southern Baptist Convention, meeting in Orlando, Florida, June 15-16, 2010, request the Executive Committee of the Southern Baptist Convention to consider recommending to the Southern Baptist Convention the adoption of the language and structure of Great Commission Giving as described in this report in order to enhance and celebrate the Cooperative Program and the generous support of Southern

---

[60] http://www.morrischapman.com/article.asp?id=92
[61] *Annual*, 2000, 88.

Baptists channeled through their churches and to continue to honor and affirm the Cooperative Program as the most effective means of mobilizing our churches and extending our outreach. *We affirm that designated gifts to special causes are to be given as a supplement to the Cooperative Program and not as a substitute for Cooperative Program giving.* We further request that the boards of trustees of the International Mission Board and North American Mission Board, in consultation with the Woman's Missionary Union, consider the adoption of the Lottie Moon and Annie Armstrong offering goals as outlined in this report.

The report as amended was adopted overwhelmingly with a showing of ballots.

## A New Era

*A New Descriptor.* Ever since Southern Baptists expanded beyond the limits of the Southeast United States, they have struggled with what to call themselves. It seemed to be a contradiction to have a regional name with a national presence and a global mission. In 1903, the Convention heard a proposal to change the name to "The Baptist Convention of the United States,"[62] but when it was presented the following year the messenger withdrew the original motion and suggested it be referred to a special committee for further study.[63] From the 1950s on, the issue would resurface from time to time, but never passed, even though many people felt that compelling arguments could be made for the need of a name change. The argument that was used most frequently was that the name change would benefit work worldwide or in pioneer areas in the United States. An intensive study was undertaken in 1974 but the SBC voted at that time to keep its present name.[64] The topic still resurfaced in 1983, 1990, and 1998. In 1999, the Convention was asked to conduct a "straw poll" during its meeting that year in Atlanta. The straw poll was defeated on a floor vote. At the 2004 meeting in Indianapolis a motion was made to authorize the SBC president to appoint a committee to study a name

---

[62] *Annual*, 1903, 38.
[63] *Annual*, 1904, 6-7.
[64] McBeth, *The Southern Baptist Heritage*, 631.

change. The motion was defeated on a ballot vote of 44.6 percent yes and 55.4 percent no.[65]

Nevertheless, the issue of a name change continued to resurface. In 2011, SBC President Bryant Wright decided to appoint a special committee to study the feasibility or need for a name change. Without consulting the Executive Committee, he appointed a committee made up of members who served at their own expense. Executive Committee members expressed concern that this was being done without the consent of the Convention, but Wright assured them that after they conducted the study, whatever recommendation they made would have to be approved by the Convention. He asked them to consider four things. "Is it a good idea, that is, is there value in considering a name change? If so, what would be a good name to suggest? What would be the potential legal ramifications of a name change? What would be the potential financial implications?"[66] Wright had his web team activate a website where anyone could submit comments and submit a suggestion for a name if they so desired.[67]

In early 2012, the task force met with the Executive Committee with their recommendation, which was ultimately submitted to the 2012 Convention in New Orleans. The task force recommended the Convention keep its legal name but adopt an informal non-legal name for those who want to use it: "Great Commission Baptists." The recommendation was discussed a great deal prior to the Convention, with comments fairly evenly divided on both sides of the issue. When it was presented to the Convention, the Convention Center was filled, with people standing to hear the discussion. When one messenger called for the vote, a show of ballots indicated that it was too close to call. Ultimately, the motion passed with fifty-three percent voting in favor of the motion. Ultimately, it does not change anything for any church or SBC entity. A church may use the new descriptor if they choose, but since all Southern Baptist churches are

---

[65] http://www.bpnews.net/BPnews.asp?ID=36156
[66] Ibid.
[67] In a History of Southern Baptists class, students were asked to conduct a poll of their churches and see what the feeling of the people were. Most were strongly against considering a name change. One student, Todd Unzicker, suggested the name, "Intergalactic Baptist Convention," stating that that should solve the matter for good.

autonomous, they were free to call themselves by any name or descriptor they desire, regardless. The Convention has now trademarked the name, which presumably allows only cooperating Southern Baptist churches to use the new moniker.

*A New Era in Leadership.* In an historic move at the Southern Baptist Convention, Fred Luter, a black pastor who grew up in New Orleans and had become pastor of Franklin Avenue Baptist Church, a struggling congregation, led the church in growing from fewer than one hundred members in 1986 to a megachurch with membership in excess of seven thousand before the church and New Orleans were flooded during Hurricane Katrina. Since the church reopened, it has grown back to nearly five thousand members. He has been active in Convention life for several years, having been the first African American to serve as first vice-president and the first African American to preach the Convention sermon. He also served on the 2000 Baptist Faith and Message committee.[68] It was significant that he was elected unopposed on June 19th, the day celebrated by African Americans as the anniversary of emancipation from slavery in the United States. During the three minute nomination speech by David Crosby, pastor of First Baptist Church of New Orleans, the audience broke out in applause four times. Since there was no other nominee, it is customary that the SBC recording secretary cast the single ballot. However, Wright said, "This chair on this occasion believes this historic moment should fully belong to the messengers of the Southern Baptist Convention." He instructed that if it was their pleasure that the recording secretary cast the single ballot for Luter, please stand. The crowd rose to its feet in applause as the recording secretary cast the single ballot. Thunderous applause continued as Luter approached the podium, wiping tears of joy from his eyes.[69] Even though the elected president of the Convention has little direct power, he wields great influence, particularly in the area of appointments to strategic committees. It remains to be seen whether the Convention sees this as a sincere reaching out to ethnic groups that have not been seen in large numbers in the predominantly Anglo convention.

---

[68] http://www.sbcannualmeeting.net/sbc12/newsroom/newspage.asp?ID=15
[69] http://www.bpnews.net/bpnews.asp?id=38081

## What Does the Future Hold?

Where the Southern Baptist Convention is concerned, it remains to be seen what lies ahead for the denomination born in slavery. It has every appearance to moving ahead into a very positive future, making inroads in areas where Southern Baptist work has not been strong, or with ethnic groups that may exist as subcultures in areas where Southern Baptists have proliferated, yet failed to reach out to new groups in the area. Much of the neglect has not been intentional; most people simply are reluctant to engage people with whom they are not aware of any common bonds or similarities. One thing that is certain is that Southern Baptists have expressed a commitment to reaching the world for the kingdom, whether that is an unreached people group across the globe or across the backyard fence. How will this be done? That is yet to be determined, but if the denomination remains committed to being Great Commission Baptists, it will be accomplished.

One question that is regularly posed to a professor of Southern Baptist history is the role the small, rural churches will play in the future. Many young prospective ministers seem to believe that the larger churches, those with more than two hundred in members, or mega churches will eliminate the need for the small churches. On the other hand, most small churches, which make up a majority of the Convention, use buildings that have long been paid for and have little overhead expense. While the larger churches are able to provide a wide range of ministries, the small congregations are forced to concentrate on the basics, are not faced with large utility expenses. While large churches have multiple staff members who are very specialized in their functions, the smaller churches have a pastor who has the opportunity to know each family, their struggles and joys, and to see how each family fits into the life of that church. The day of the small church in the Convention is not dead, nor is it on life support. Instead, churches large and small are faithfully cooperating together to send missionaries across North America and around the globe. May Southern Baptists always keep this as their focus and mission.

# Bibliography

The following is a select bibliography to direct attention to the principal materials used in the preparation of this book. Hundreds of other books, particularly in the area of biography, could have been included. The principle source has been the *Annuals* of the Southern Baptist Convention from 1845 to the present. The following additional books have helped.

Aiken, John. G. *A Digest of all of the Laws of Alabama Containing all of the Statutes of a Public and General Nature.* Philadelphia: Alexander Towar, 1833.

*American Baptist Year Book.* Philadelphia: American Baptist Publication Society, 1847, 1862, and 1878.

Ammerman, Nancy Tatum. *Baptist Battles: Social Change and Religious Conflict in the Southern Baptist Convention.* New Brunswick, New Jersey: Rutgers University Press, 1995.

Asplund, John (ed.). *The Annual Register of the Baptist Denomination in North America* (1791-96). Copies on file at Southwestern Baptist Theological Seminary, Fort Worth, Texas.

Bailey, Kenneth K. *Southern White Protestantism in the Twentieth Century.* New York: Harper and Row, 1964.

Baker, Robert A. *A Baptist Source Book, with Particular Reference to Southern Baptists.* Nashville: Broadman Press, 1966.

\_\_\_\_\_. *Relations Between Northern and Southern Baptists.* Fort Worth: 2nd edition, Marvin D. Evans Printing Company, 1954.

\_\_\_\_\_. *The Blossoming Desert: A Concise History of Texas Baptists.* Waco: Word Books, 1970.

\_\_\_\_\_. *The First Southern Baptists.* Nashville: Broadman Press, 1966.

\_\_\_\_\_. *The Story of the Sunday School Board.* Nashville: Convention Press, 1966.

\_\_\_\_\_. *The Thirteenth Check- The Jubilee History of the Annuity Board of the Southern Baptist Convention 1918-68.* Nashville: Broadman Press, 1968.

*Baptist Missionary Magazine* (Boston) under various titles, 1803-1909.

Baptist World Congress *Proceedings* (since 1905).

Barck, Oscar Theodore and Blake, Nelson Manfred. *Since 1900*. New York: The Macmillan Company, 1952.

Barnes, Gilbert H. *The Anti-Slavery Impulse (1830-1844)*. New York: Appleton-Century-Crofts, Inc., 1933.

Barnes, W. W. *The Southern Baptist Convention 1845-1953*. Nashville: Broadman Press, 1954.

Baugh, John F. *The Battle for Baptist Integrity*. Austin: Battle for Baptist Integrity, Inc.

Benedict, David A. *A General History of the Baptist Denomination in America, and Other Parts of the World*. Boston: Lincoln and Edmands, 1813- in two volumes.

_____. *Fifty Years Among the Baptists*. New York: Sheldon and Company, 1859.

Broadus, John A. *A Memoir of James Petigru Boyce*. Nashville: Sunday School Board, 1927.

Burkitt, Lemuel, and Read, Jesse. *A Concise History of the Kehukee Baptist Association*. Halifax: A. Hodge, 1803.

Burroughs, Prince E. *Fifty Fruitful Years*. Nashville: Baptist Sunday School Board, 1941.

Burton, Joe W. *Epochs of Home Missions*. Atlanta: Home Mission Board, 1945.

Campbell, Jesse H. *Georgia Baptist: Historical and Biographical*. Macon: J. W. Burke and Company, rev. 1874.

Carey, S. P. *William Carey*. Philadelphia: The Judson Press, 1923.

Carleton, William A. *"Not Yours But You"- The Life of Joseph Samuel Murrow*. Unpublished Th.D. dissertation, Southwestern Baptist Theological Seminary, Fort Worth, Texas, 1945.

Carroll, B. H. Jr. *The Genesis of American Anti-Missionism*. Louisville: Baptist Book Concern, 1902.

Carroll, J. M. *A History of Texas Baptists*. Dallas: Baptist Standard Publishing Co., 1923.

Cauthen, Baker James. *Advance: A History of Southern Baptist Foreign Missions*. Nashville: Broadman Press, 1970.

Christian, John T. *History of Baptist of Louisiana*. Shreveport: Louisiana Baptist Convention, 1923.

Cole, Stewart G. *History of Fundamentalism*. New York: Richard R. Smith, Inc., 1931.

Cook, Harvey T. *A Biography of Richard Furman*. Greenville: Baptist Courier, 1915.

Cox, Norman W. (ed.). *Encyclopedia of Southern Baptists*, Vols. I and II. Nashville: Broadman Press, 1958; David C. Woolley, (ed.). Vol. III. Nashville: Broadman Press, 1971.

Cox, Mrs. W. J. *Following in His Train*. Nashville: Broadman Press, 1938.

Cox, F. A. and Hoby, J. *The Baptists in America*. New York: Leavitt, Lord and Co., 1836.

Dagg, J. L. *A Treatise on Church Order*. Charleston, S. C.: Southern Baptist Publication Society, 1858.

Davis, J. *History of the Welsh Baptists*. Pittsburgh: D. M. Hogan, 1835.

Dockery, David S. *Southern Baptist Consensus and Renewal*. Nashville: Broadman & Holman Publishers, 2008.

\_\_\_\_\_, ed. *Southern Baptist Identity: An Evangelical Denomination Faces the Future*. Wheaton: Crossway Books, 2009.

Eaton, J. *Historical Sketch of the Massachusetts Baptist Mission Society and Convention, 1802-1902*. Boston: Massachusetts Baptist Convention, 1903.

Edwards, Morgan. *Materials Toward a History of American Baptists.* Of the twelve-volume work projected, only four have been published (Philadelphia 1770-1792). Manuscript volumes are on microfilm at the Southern Baptist Historical Library and Archives, Nashville, Tennessee.

Eighmy, John Lee. *Churches in Cultural Captivity*. Knoxville: University of Tennessee Press, 1972.

Elliott, Ralph H. *The Message of Genesis: A Theological Interpretation*. St. Louis: Abbott Books. 1962.

\_\_\_\_\_. *The Genesis Controversy and Continuity in Southern Baptist Chaos—A Eulogy for a Great Tradition*. Macon: Mercer University Press. 2005

Estep, W. R. *Baptists and Christian Unity*. Nashville: Broadman Press, 1966.

Frost, J. M. *The Sunday School Board, Southern Baptist Convention, Its History and Work*. Nashville: Sunday School Board, 1914.

Fuller, B. F. *History of Texas Baptists*. Louisville: Baptist Book Concern, 1900.

Fuller, Richard and Wayland Francis. *Domestic Slavery Considered As a Scriptural Institution*. New York: Lewis Colby, 1845.

Furman, Wood. *A History of the Charleston Association of Baptist Churches in the State of South Carolina*. Charleston: J. Hoff, 1811.

Furniss, Norman F. *The Fundamentalist Controversy 1918-1931*. New Haven: Yale University Press, 1954.

Gates, Errett, *The Early Relation and Separation of Baptists and Disciples*. Chicago: R. R. Donnelly and Sons, 1904.

Gewehr, Wesley M. *The Great Awakening in Virginia, 1740-1790*. Durham: Duke University Press, 1930.

Gillette, A. D. (ed.). *Century Minutes of the Philadelphia Baptist Association, 1707-1807*. Philadelphia: American Baptist Publication Society.

Goen, C. C. *Revivalism and Separatism in New England, 1740-1800*. New Haven: Yale University Press, 1962.

Goodell, William. *The American Slave Code in Theory and Practice: Its Distinctive Features Shown by Its Statutes, Judicial Decisions, and Illustrative Facts*. New York: American and Foreign Anti-Slavery Society, 1853.

Graves, J. R. *Old Landmarkism-What Is It?* Memphis: Baptist Book House, Graves, Mahaffy and Co., 1880.

Grime, J. H. *History of Middle-Tennessee Baptists*. Nashville: Baptist and Reflector, 1902.

Guild, Reuben A. *Chaplain Smith and the Baptists*. Philadelphia: American Baptist Publication Society, 1885.

Hammett, John S. *Biblical Foundations for Baptist Churches: A Contemporary Ecclesiology*. Grand Rapids, MI: Kregel Publications, 2005.

Harrison, Paul M. *Authority and Power in the Free Church Tradition: A Social Case Study of the American Baptist Convention*. Princeton: Princeton University Press, 1959.

Harvey, Paul. *Redeeming the South: Religious Cultures and Racial Identities Among Southern Baptists, 1865-1924*. Chapel Hill: University of North Carolina Press, 1997.

Hassell, C. B. *History of the Church of God from the Creation to A. D. 1885*, rev. by Sylvester Hassell. Middletown, New York: Gilbert Beebe's Sons, 1886.

Heyrman, Christine Leigh. *Southern Cross: The Beginnings of the Bible Belt*. New York: Alfred A. Knopf, 1997.

Holcombe, Hosea. *Baptists in Alabama*. Philadelphia: King and Beard, 1840.

Hovey, Alvah. *A Memoir of the Life and Times of the Reverend Isaac Backus*. Boston: Gould and Lincoln, 1859.

Hudson, Winthrop S. (ed.). *Baptist Concepts of the Church*. Philadelphia: The Judson Press, 1959.

Huggins, M. A. *A History of North Carolina Baptists 1727-1932*. Raleigh: General Board, North Carolina Baptist State Convention, 1967.

Humphreys, Fisher. *The Way We Were: How Southern Baptist Theology has Changed and What it Means to Us All*. New York: McCracken Press, 1994.

James, Rob and Leazer, Gary. *The Fundamentalist Takeover in the Southern Baptist Convention: A Brief History*. Timisoara, Romania: Impact Media, 1999.

Jernegan, Marcus W. *The American Colonies 1492-1750*. New York: F. Unger Pub. Co., 1959.

Jeter, J. B. *The Recollections of a Long Life*. Richmond: Religious Herald Co., 1891.

Joiner, E. E. *A History of Florida Baptists*. Jacksonville: Florida Baptist Convention, 1972.

Jones, J. William. *Christ in the Camp*. Richmond: B. F. Johnson, 1887.

Kelley, Page H. *Bible Survey Series, Volume 3: A Nation in the Making*. Nashville: Convention Press. 1971.

_____. Broadman *Bible Commentary, Volume 5: Proverbs–Isaiah*. Nashville: Broadman Press. 1971.

Latourette, Kenneth Scott. *The Nineteenth Century Outside Europe*, Volume III in series, *Christianity in a Revolutionary Age*. New York: Harper & Brothers, 1961.

Little, Lewis P. *Imprisoned Preachers and Religious Liberty in Virginia*. Lynchburg: J. P Bell Co., 1938.

Looney, Floyd. *History of California Southern Baptists*. Fresno: Board of

Directors of the Southern Baptist Convention of California, 1954.

Lumpkin, William L. *Baptist Foundations in the South.* Nashville: Broadman Press, 1961.

Keen, William W. (ed.). *The Bi-Centennial Celebration of the Founding of the First Baptist Church of the City of Philadelphia, 1698-1898.* Philadelphia: American Baptist Publication Society, 1899.

King, Joe M. *History of South Carolina Baptists.* Columbia: General Board of the South Carolina Baptist Convention, 1964.

Lawless, Chuck and Greenway, Adam W. *The Great Commission Resurgence: Fulfilling God's Mandate in Our Time*, Nashville: Broadman & Holman, 2010.

McBeth, H. Leon. *The Baptist Heritage: Four Centuries of Baptist Witness.* Nashville: Broadman Press. 1987.

McGlothlin, W. J. *Baptist Confessions of Faith.* Philadelphia: American Baptist publication Society, 1911.

McLemore, R. A. *A History of Mississippi Baptists, 1780-1970.* Jackson: Mississippi Baptist Convention Board, 1971.

Manschreck, Clyde L. (ed.). *A History of Christianity* (Vol. 2, *Reformation to the Present.* Englewood Cliffs, New Jersey: Prentice-Hall, Inc., 1964.

Masters, Frank M. *A History of Baptists in Kentucky.* Louisville: Kentucky Baptist Historical Society, 1953.

May, Lynn E., Jr. *The First Baptist Church of Nashville, Tennessee 1820-1970.* Nashville: First Baptist Church, 1970.

McCall, Duke. *An Oral History.* Nashville: Fields Publishing Co., 2001.

Merriam, Edmund F. *A History of American Baptist Missions.* Philadelphia: American Baptist Publication Society, 1900.

Morehouse, Henry L. *Baptist Home Missions in America 1832-1882.* New York: American Baptist Home Mission Society, 1883.

Morgan, David T. *The New Crusades, The New Holy Land: Conflict in the Southern Baptist Convention, 1969-1991*, Tuscaloosa, The University of Alabama Press, 1996.

Mueller, William A. *A History of Southern Baptist Theological Seminary.* Nashville: Broadman Press, 1959.

Neely, H. K. Jr., *The Territorial Expansion of the Southern Baptist Convention 1894-1959*. Unpublished Th.D. dissertation, Southwestern Baptist Theological Seminary, Fort Worth, Texas, 1963.

Newman, A. H. (ed.). *A Century of Baptist Achievement*. Philadelphia: American Baptist Publication Society, 1898.

\_\_\_\_\_.*A History of Baptist Churches in the United States*. Philadelphia: American Baptist Publication Society, 1898.

Owens, Loulie Latimer. *Saints of Clay- The Shaping of South Carolina Baptists*. Columbia: The South Carolina Baptist Convention, 1971.

Paschal, George W. *History of North Carolina Baptists*. Raleigh: General Board, North Carolina Baptist State Convention, two volumes, 1930, 1955.

Patterson, Paige. *Anatomy of a Reformation: The Southern Baptist Convention, 1978-2004*. Fort Worth, Texas: Seminary Hill Press.

Patterson, W. Morgan. *Baptist Successionism- A Critical View*. Valley Forge: The Judson press, 1969.

Pressler, Paul. *A Hill on Which to Die*. Nashville: Broadman & Holman, 1999.

Reimers, David M. *White Protestantism and the Negro*. New York: Oxford University Press, 1965.

Richards, Roger C. *Actions and Attitudes of Southern Baptists Toward Blacks: 1845-1895*. Ph.D. dissertation, Florida State University, Tallahassee, 2008.

Rippon, John (ed.). *Baptist Annual Register*. London: 1790-1802.

Robertson, A. T. *Life and letters of John Albert Broadus*. Philadelphia: American Baptist Publication Society, 1901.

Rogers, J. S. *History of Arkansas Baptists*. Little Rock: Executive Board of Arkansas Baptist State Convention, 1948.

Rutledge, Arthur B. *Mission to America*. Nashville: Broadman Press, 1969.

Ryland, Garnett. *The Baptists of Virginia 1699-1926*. Richmond: The Virginia Baptist Board of Missions and Education, 1955.

Sampey, John R. *Memoirs of John R. Sampey*. Nashville: Broadman Press, 1947.

Semple, Robert B. *A History of the Rise and Progress of the Baptists in Virginia*, rev. by G. W. Beals. Philadelphia: American Baptist Publication Society, 1894.

Sheets, Henry. *Who Are Primitive Baptists?* Raleigh: Edwards and Broughton Printing Co., c1908.

Shelley, Bruce L. *Conservative Baptists: A Story of the Twentieth-Century Dissent.* Denver: Conservative Baptist Theological Seminary, 1960.

Sherman, Cecil. *By My Own Reckoning.* Macon: Smyth & Helwys, 2008.

Shurden, Walter B. *Not A Silent People: Controversies That Have Shaped Southern Baptists.* Nashville: Broadman Press, 1972.

Slatton, James H. *W. H. Whitsitt: The Man and the Controversy.* Macon: Mercer University Press. 2009.

Smith, J. A. *Memoir of Nathaniel Colver.* Boston: George A. Foxcroft, Jr., 1875.

Spain, Rufus B. *At Ease in Zion-Social History of Southern Baptists 1865-1900.* Nashville: Vanderbilt University Press, 1961, 1967.

St. Amant, C. Penrose. *Short History of Louisiana Baptists.* Nashville: Broadman Press, 1948.

Stripling, Paul W. *The Negro Excision from Baptist Churches in Texas 1861-1870.* Unpublished Th.D. dissertation, Southwestern Baptist Theological Seminary, Fort Worth, 1967.

Sutton, Jerry. *The Baptist Reformation: The Conservative Resurgence in the Southern Baptist Convention.* Nashville: Broadman & Holman Publishers, 2000.

Sweet, W. W. (ed.). *Religion on the American Frontier,* 4 vols. Vol. I, *The Baptists, 1783-1830.* New York: Henry Holt and Co., 1931.

Taylor, James B. *Memoir of Luther Rice.* Baltimore: Armstrong and Berry, 2nd ed., 1841.

Taylor, John. *A History of Ten Baptist Churches.* Frankfort, Ky.: J. H. Holeman, 1823.

Thom, William T. *The Struggle for Religious Freedom in Virginia: the Baptists.* Baltimore: The Johns Hopkins University Press, 1900.

Torbet, Robert G. *A History of the Baptists.* Valley Forge: Judson Press, 1950, 1963.

Townsend, Leah. *South Carolina Baptists, 1670-1805*. Florence, S.C.: Florence Printing Co., 1935.

Tull, James E. *A Study of Southern Baptist Landmarkism in the Light of Historical Baptist Ecclesiology*. Privately published Ph.D. dissertation, Columbia University, New York, 1960.

Turner, Frederick Jackson. *The Rise of the New West 1819-1829*. New York: Harper and Brothers, 1906.

_____. *The United States 1830-1850*. New York: P. Smith, 1950.

Vail, Albert L. *The Morning Hour of American Baptist Missions*. Philadelphia: American Baptist Publication Society, 1907.

_____. *Baptists Mobilized for Missions*. Philadelphia: American Baptist Publication Society, 1911.

Vedder, H. C. *A Short History of the Baptists*. Philadelphia: American Baptist Publication Society, 1927.

Watts, Joseph T. *The Rise and Progress of Maryland Baptists*. Baltimore: State Mission Board, c1951.

Wayland, Francis. *Noted on the Principles and Practices of Baptist Churches*. Boston: Gould and Lincoln, 1856.

White, Charles L. *A Century of Faith*. Philadelphia: Judson Press, 1932.

Whitsitt, William H. *A Question in Baptist History*. Louisville: Dearing, 1896.

Williams, Juan and Quinton Dixie. *This Far By Faith: Stories from the African American Religious Experience*. New York: HarperCollins Publishers, 2003.

Woodson, Hortense. *Giant in the Land*. Nashville: Broadman Press, 1950.

Wright, Stephen. *History of the Shaftsbury Baptist Association from 1781 to 1853*. Troy, N. Y.: A. G. Johnson, 1853.

Yeaman, W. Pope. *History of the Missouri Baptist General Association*. Columbia: E. W. Stephens Press, 1899.

# Index

## A

abolitionism  95, 98-101, 118, 133, 138
Aiken, Daniel  355
Alabama Resolutions  102, 110-111, 115
Allison, Gray  331
American Baptist Home Mission Society 69, 82-85, 94, 98, 117, 125, 142, 179, 183, 186, 205, 207
American Baptist Publications Society 81, 110, 124-127, 188, 202, 210-213, 218-220, 227, 257-258
American Baptist Seminary  286
American Bible Society  88, 145, 150-152
Armstrong, Annie W.  241-243, 281, 298-299, 362-363
Antimissionism 90-94, 134-142, 144, 150, 192
Arminian  26, 35, 66, 90, 92-93, 360
associational method 60-66, 74-76, 120,-122, 184, 251, 253-256
Crouch, Austin  289-291

## B

Drayton, B. J.  148
Baker, Larry  337, 345
Baltimore Association  92-93

Baptist Faith and Message  283, 324-325, 334-335, 351-353, 358-360, 365
Baptist General Tract Society  69, 80-81
Baptist Hundred Thousand Club  277
Baptist Student Union  244
Baptist Sunday School Board  289, 291, 323, 325, 331, 344
Baptist Young People's Union of America  218, 244, 292
Bell, T. P.  206, 218, 237, 238
Berquist, Millard  310, 323
*Bible Survey Series*  324,
Board of Domestic Missions  114
Board of Ministerial Relief and Annuities  289
Bold Mission Thrust  330, 348
Boyce, James P. 129, 130, 156, 179, 247, 248
*Broadman Bible Commentary*  325, 344
Brotherhood Commission  284, 287, 348
Bryan, Andrew  132, 364

## C

Carey, Lott  79
Carey, William  55, 61, 69, 71-72
Carroll, B. H. 91, 236, 249, 284
Cauthen, Baker James 331, 349

Calvinism  66, 90, 359-361
Campbell, Alexander  89-90, 92
Campbellism  88, 140, 150-151, 157, 257
Carnes, Clinton S.  276, 290
Crumpler, Carolyn Weatherford  339
Chapman, Morris  338-339, 361
Charleston Baptist Association  21
Christian Life Commission  288, 300, 313, 321, 336-337, 345-346
Clopton, Samuel C.  147
Comity Agreements  205
Committee of Co-operation  260
Committee on Boards  311, 313, 333-334
Committee on Business Efficiency  266
Committee on Committees  333-334
Connor, W. T.  359
Cooperative Program  2, 205, 277, 280-281, 290-291, 313-314, 318, 330, 349-350, 362-363
Coppenger, Mark  358
Cothen, Grady  331, 335, 341, 344
Cotton Grove  156, 159
Crawford, T. P.  170, 189, 222, 229
Crews, Jr., William O.  357
Criswell, W. A.  323, 338

## D

Dagg, John L.  104, 119, 128
Davies, G. Henton  325
Davis, Addie  327
Day, John  147
Dayton, A.C.  127, 156, 160, 163, 221
Department of Evangelism  236, 291
Dilday, Russell  335, 342, 355
Dockery, David  353, 359, 361
Dodd, M. E.  280
Domestic and Indian Mission Board  145, 148, 170, 180, 189
Domestic Mission Board  134, 138, 140, 145, 147, 183-185, 198
Draper, Jr, James T.  385
Drummond, Lewis  338, 354
Dunn, James  345

## E

Eaton, T. T.  205-206, 226
Education Commission  246, 273, 284-285, 313
Elder, Lloyd  331, 342, 344
Eliff, Thomas D. (Tom)  351
Elliott, Ralph  322, 357
Ethics and Religious Liberty Commission  346
Executive Committee  2-3, 244-245, 264-266, 269-270, 274, 277-281, 289, 291, 311-314, 318, 324, 330, 341-342, 344, 361-364
Ezell, Kevin  348

## F

Ferguson, Milton  356
financial representation 120, 254
First Great Awakening  25, 39, 63, 68, 83
Flake, Arthur  289-290
Foreign Mission Board  113, 136, 147, 162-163, 169, 189-191, 221-222, 227-228, 233, 274, 280-281, 286, 288-289, 295, 328-329, 334, 336, 345-348
Fortress Monroe Conference  204-206
Francisco, Clyde  324
Frost, J. M.  210, 213, 217, 235, 289-291
Fuller, Richard  84, 100-101, 110, 112, 143, 163, 179, 183
Fundamentalist Movement  281, 308, 314
Furman, Richard 35, 43, 58, 73-74, 84, 118-119

## G

Gambrell, J. B.  204, 206, 213, 225, 247, 272, 280-281
Gano, John  20-24
General Baptists  8-10, 16, 19, 23-25, 38, 56, 64, 105-106, 118, 357
General Missionary Convention of the Baptist Denomination in the United States for Foreign Missions  67-81, 106-107, 111-119, 124, 142-147, 184-185, 190
Georgia Test Case  101
Glorieta Baptist Conference Center  335, 346
Glorieta Statement  335, 354
Gospel Mission Movement 220-223
Graves, Ann J.  190
Graves, J. R. 118, 134-142, 150, 183, 191-192, 219, 221, 225, 236, 253, 260, 266
Great Commission Baptists 362, 364

## H

Hart, Oliver  19-20, 43
Helwys, Thomas  8, 55, 342
Hemphill, Ken  354
Henry, Patrick  48
Hobbs, Herschel  321-322, 332-333, 357
Holcomb, Thomas Luther  291
Holman, Russell  140, 148-149, 172
Home Mission Board  145, 181, 183, 185-189, 196-215, 229-235, 246, 248, 257, 274, 283, 288-289, 326-328, 334-336, 344-347
Home Mission Society 67-68, 80-83, 93-94, 97, 99-101, 115-117, 123-125, 139, 142, 148-149, 171, 174, 179-186, 196-200, 202-203, 205, 207, 232, 255

Honeycutt, Roy L. 334-335, 351
Howell, R. B. C. 109, 112, 126, 143, 151, 161-163
Humphreys, Fisher 355
Hunt, Alma 320

## I

nternational Mission Board 348, 360-361
Iorg, Jess 355
Ireland, James 33, 46

## J

Jackson, Richard 336
Jeter, J. B. 112, 122, 136, 142, 157, 183
Johnson, William B. 73, 107-112, 115-120, 123, 142-143, 250-251, 254, 260
Judson, Adoniram 68, 79, 114

## K

Kelley, Jr., Charles S. 350
Kelley, Page 323-324
Kerfoot, F. H. 210, 234
*Kind Words* 173, 209-211, 215

## L

Land, Richard 243-245
Landmark Movement 140, 150-151, 156, 160, 191, 196, 219
Landmarkism 138, 151-152, 155, 157, 165, 177, 191-192, 219-220, 224, 236, 256, 257
Lawrence, J. B. 274, 288-289
Leavell, Landrum 355

Lee, R. G. 329
Leland, John 50
Lewis, Larry 332, 344
LifeWay Christian Resources 343
Lolley, Randall 335-336, 352
Love, J. F. 229, 280, 288
Lunsford, William 287
Luter, Fred 350, 363

## M

Maddry, Charles E. 288-289
Madison, James 48, 50
Mallary, C. D. 112, 147
Manly, Jr., Basil 127-129, 172, 183-184, 210, 215, 357
Marshall, Daniel 21, 26-27, 30, 32, 35-36, 44, 58, 325
Mathis, Marie 323
McCall, Duke 320, 333, 339, 351
McIntosh, Martha 239
McIntosh, W. H. 197, 232
Mell, P. H. 179
Mercer, Jesse 37, 84, 141, 156
messengers 23, 92, 105, 109, 112, 121, 134, 139, 239, 252, 254, 265, 266, 267, 269, 270, 310, 312, 332, 333, 337, 360, 363
Mid-America Baptist Theological Seminary 329, 348
Midwestern Baptist Theological Seminary 321-322, 335-356

Mohler, R. Albert   350, 351, 357, 359
Moon, Lottie   189, 227-228, 240, 279, 293, 295, 297, 360-361
Moore, Winfred   334, 336
Morehouse, H. L.   184, 200, 204, 206
Mullins, E. Y.   246, 264, 267, 269-270, 280-281, 283, 314-315, 357

## N

New Hampshire Confession   156, 280-281, 357
Norris, J. Frank   281, 308, 314
North American Mission Board   285, 346, 360-361
numerical basis of representation   252, 266-267

## O

Oklahoma Decision   207-208
Old Point Comfort-Hot Springs Conference   206-207

## P

Parker, Daniel   90, 134, 150
Parks, Keith   329, 334, 336, 340, 347
Patterson, Paige   330, 349, 353, 354
Particular Baptists   5, 8-12, 16, 19, 21-24, 31, 38, 55-57, 60-61, 94, 100, 104-106, 357

Peace Committee   334-340, 351-356
Pendleton, J. M.   138, 156, 160, 219
Philadelphia Association   19-27, 36, 55-58, 62, 64, 71, 80
Philadelphia Confession   118, 280, 357
Pollard, Franklin D.   355
Pressler, Paul   330, 337, 352
Pinson, Jr., William M.   355
Powell, W. F.   290

## R

Rainer, Thom   359
Rankin, Jerry   329, 348
Ray, T. B.   288
Reccord, Robert   346
Reeve, James E.   101
Regular Baptists   28, 32, 35-38, 45
religious liberty   1, 8, 11, 15, 17, 34, 39-41, 44, 49-51, 57, 63-64, 255, 343-344
Rice, Luther   68-69, 71, 73, 75, 78-80
Ridgecrest Baptist Assembly   244
Roberts, R. Philip   356
Rogers, Adrian   329, 332-334, 350
Routh, Porter   322
Rowland, A. J.   217
Royal Ambassadors   240, 285
Rutledge, Arthur   328
Ryland, Robert   127, 132

## S

Sampey, John R. 103, 287
Sanders, G. N. 288
Sandy Creek 27, 26, 27, 29, 30, 31, 32, 34, 35, 36, 42, 56, 58-59
Scarborough, L. R. 247, 272, 280, 287
sectionalism 87, 93, 94, 116, 132, 133, 141, 188, 319
Semple, Robert 88
Separate Baptists 28, 29, 30, 31, 32, 33, 34, 35, 36, 41, 43, 45, 63, 64, 118, 255
Seventy-five Million Campaign 278, 283
Sherman, Cecil 340
Shuck, J. Lewis 77, 147, 170, 233
Stearns, Shubal 26, 27, 30, 31, 35, 42, 58, 325
slavery 15, 18, 63, 85, 87, 95, 96, 97, 98, 99, 100, 101, 114, 116, 117, 127, 128, 133, 134, 138, 185, 255, 319, 363, 364
Smith, Bailey 333
society method 59, 60, 62, 81, 120, 121, 184, 249, 250, 264
Southern Baptist Publication Society 122, 123, 125, 157, 169
Southern Baptist Theological Seminary 122, 127, 190, 214, 224, 237, 245, 282, 313, 314, 320, 323, 350

Southwestern Baptist Theological Seminary 247, 282, 283, 287, 314, 353
Spilman, Bernard W. 235, 289
Stanley, Charles 334, 347
Sullivan, James 342
Sumner, M.T. 180

## T

Tanner, William 328, 335
Taylor, George B. 189, 228, 240
Taylor, James B. 112, 168, 170, 189, 228
Teasdale, Thomas C. 188
Thomas, David 22-23, 33, 45
Thomas, John 20, 21, 23
Tichenor, I. T. 164, 199, 204, 210, 212, 230, 234, 255, 257, 288,
Toy, C. H. 282, 321
Triennial Convention 1, 72, 110, 223, 267
Truett, George W. 272, 273
Tupper, Henry A. 228
*Two Seeds in the Spirit* 90

## V

Valentine, Foy 320, 335, 343
Van Ness, I. J. 272, 289, 290, 291
Vestal, Dan 337, 339
Vines, Jerry 336, 350

## W

Washington Conference 205, 206

Wayland, Francis 61, 72, 75, 76, 100, 106, 115, 118, 146, 251
Whitefield, George 19, 25, 26, 27
Whitsitt, W. H. 155, 224
White, K. Owen 321, 323
Williams, Roger 13, 80
Williams, William 128
Willingham, R. J. 229
Winkler, E. T. 199
Woman's Missionary Training School 247
Women's Missionary Union 228, 240, 241, 246, 360, 361
Wood, Jr., James E. 343
Wright, Bryant 362

Made in the USA
Lexington, KY
09 August 2018